THE DOMAIN THEORY

Patterns for Knowledge
and Software Reuse

THE DOMAIN THEORY
Patterns for Knowledge and Software Reuse

Alistair Sutcliffe

*University of Manchester
Institute of Science and Technology*

LEA
2002

LAWRENCE ERLBAUM ASSOCIATES, PUBLISHERS
Mahwah, New Jersey   London

This book was typeset in 10/12 pt. Times, Italic, Bold, Bold Italic. The
heads were typeset in Americana and Americana Bold.

Lawrence Erlbaum Associates, Inc., Publishers
10 Industrial Avenue
Mahwah, New Jersey 07430

Library of Congress Cataloging-in-Publication Data

Sutcliffe, Alistair, 1951–
    The domain theory : patterns for knowledge and software reuse / Alistair Sutcliffe.
        p.   cm.
    Includes bibliographical references and index.
    ISBN 0-8058-3951-8 (hardcover: alk. paper)
    1. Computer-aided software engineering.   2. Computer software—Reusability.   I. Title.
    QA76.758 .S88   2002
    005.1'0285—dc21   2001040648

Books published by Lawrence Erlbaum Associates are printed on
acid-free paper, and their bindings are chosen for strength and durability.

Printed in the United States of America
10   9   8   7   6   5   4   3   2   1

Contents

Preface   xi
Foreword   xvii

1 Background and Concepts   **1**
   1.1   Reuse Approaches and History   1
   1.2   Motivations for Reuse   4
   1.3   Dimensions of the Reuse Problem   5
   1.4   Reuse of Knowledge and Designs   7
   1.5   Knowledge-Management Reuse   10
   1.6   Design Reuse   12
   1.7   Models of the System and the World   17
       1.7.1   Embedding Software in the World   17
       1.7.2   Physical World Models   20
       1.7.3   Information Models   22
       1.7.4   Models of People   23
       1.7.5   Models of Software   23
       1.7.6   Acquiring and Updating Models   24
   1.8   Outline of the Reuse Process   25
   1.9   Barriers to Success   26
   1.10 Classifying Components   28
   1.11 Classifying Knowledge   30
   1.12 Summary   31

2 Conceptual Foundations for Reuse   **33**
   2.1   Reuse Paradigms   34
   2.2   Design Criteria for Reuse   36
       2.2.1   Abstraction   38
       2.2.2   Granularity   44
   2.3   Reuse Strategies and Trade-Offs   50
       2.3.1   Design by Adaptation and Parameterization   52
       2.3.2   Black-Box Reuse by Configuration   54
       2.3.3   White-Box Reuse: Design by Composition   55
   2.4   Summary   57

3 Abstraction in the Mind   **59**
  3.1 Memory   60
    3.1.1 Working Memory and Chunking   60
    3.1.2 Long-Term Memory   61
    3.1.3 External Memory   62
    3.1.4 Organization of Memory   63
  3.2 Learning   68
  3.3 Problem Solving   69
    3.3.1 Reasoning Strategies   70
  3.4 Memory and Reasoning   72
  3.5 Cognitive Tasks and Knowledge Reuse   75
    3.5.1 Reuse in Decision Making   75
    3.5.2 Cognitive Models of Design and Reuse   78
    3.5.3 Facets of Expertise   79
    3.5.4 Task Model of Reuse   80
    3.5.5 Reuse and Creative Design   82
  3.6 Summary   83

4 Domain Theory: Foundations   **85**
  4.1 Introduction   86
  4.2 Domain Theory Framework   88
    4.2.1 Grounded Domains   92
    4.2.2 Metadomains   93
    4.2.3 Generic Tasks   94
  4.3 Representing Domain Knowledge   95
    4.3.1 Key Objects   96
    4.3.2 Agents   96
    4.3.3 Structure Objects   97
    4.3.4 State Transitions   97
    4.3.5 States   98
    4.3.6 Goals   98
    4.3.7 Tasks   99
    4.3.8 Object Properties   99
    4.3.9 Events   99
    4.3.10 Stative Conditions   100
    4.3.11 Relationships   100
  4.4 Grounded Domains: OSMs   100
    4.4.1 Object Containment (Level 1 Class)   102
    4.4.2 Object Inventory (Level 2 Class)   102
    4.4.3 Object Hiring (Level 3 Class)   103
    4.4.4 Object Allocation (Level 1 Class)   104

	4.4.5	Message Transfer (Level 2 Class)	107
	4.4.6	Object Sensing (Level 1 Class)	107
	4.4.7	Spatial Object Sensing (Level 2 Class)	108
	4.4.8	Agent Control (Level 1 Class)	109
4.5	Modeling Information Systems	111
4.6	Reusing OSMs	111
	4.6.1	Reuse Toolset Architecture	112
	4.6.2	Matching Process and Scenario of Use	117
4.7	Case Study: Describing Applications by an Aggregation of OSMs	124
	4.7.1	Decision Support Subsystem	124
	4.7.2	Information Retrieval Subsystem	125
	4.7.3	Creating a Generic System Model	126
4.8	Validation Studies	127
4.9	Formalization of the Domain Theory	128
4.10	Summary	129

5 Generic Tasks and Metadomains   **131**

5.1	Modeling Generic and Generalized Tasks	132
	5.1.1	Primitive or Generic Tasks	134
	5.1.2	Generalized Tasks	143
	5.1.3	Discovering Generic and Generalized Tasks	147
	5.1.4	Applying and Reusing Generalized Tasks	149
5.2	Generic Dialogues	152
5.3	Interaction Schemas	155
5.4	Argumentation Schemas	158
5.5	Metadomains	161
	5.5.1	Design	162
	5.5.2	Education or Training	163
	5.5.3	Management	166
	5.5.4	Research	168
5.6	Summary	170

6 Claims and Knowledge Management   **173**

6.1	Claims and the Task–Artefact Theory	175
6.2	Claims Knowledge Representation Schema	177
6.3	Documenting Claims	179
6.4	Reusing Claims	181
6.5	Linking Claims to Domain Models	184
6.6	Representing Business Knowledge in Claims	189
	6.6.1	Knowledge-Management Level	189
	6.6.2	Sociotechnical Design Level	192
6.7	Summary	194

7   The Reuse Process   **195**
  7.1   Generic Reuse Process   196
  7.2   Design for Reuse   199
        7.2.1   Cohesion Analysis   200
        7.2.2   Coupling Analysis   201
        7.2.3   Data Abstraction   202
        7.2.4   Procedural Abstraction   203
  7.3   Generalization for Knowledge Reuse   205
  7.4   Design by Reuse of Knowledge by Means of Generic Models   207
        7.4.1   Identifying Abstractions   207
        7.4.2   Composing Generic System Models   217
        7.4.3   Transferring Design Knowledge   219
  7.5   Summary   225

8   Reusing Knowledge and Claims   **227**
  8.1   Knowledge Reuse Process   227
  8.2   Generalizing Claims for Reuse   228
        8.2.1   Factoring Issues   230
        8.2.2   Factoring Contributions   231
        8.2.3   Example of Factoring   232
        8.2.4   Generalizing Claims   235
        8.2.5   Linking Claims to Domain Models   236
  8.3   Claims Networks   237
  8.4   Claims Reuse Process   240
        8.4.1   Retrieving Claims for Reuse   240
        8.4.2   Knowledge Transfer   241
  8.5   Case Study: Claims Reuse   243
  8.6   Summary   247

9   New Concepts   **249**
  9.1   Introduction   249
        9.1.1   Reuse History Revisited   250
        9.1.2   New Approaches   252
  9.2   Framework for Software Evolution   256
  9.3   Models of Evolving Software   258
        9.3.1   Component Engineering   258
        9.3.2   Programming for Adaptable Software   262
        9.3.3   Application Generation Architectures   263
        9.3.4   End-User Programming or Component Engineering?   264
  9.4   Summary   268

Appendixes

A Specification of the OSM Library   **271**
   A1   Object Containment   273
   A2   Object Allocation   283
   A3   Object Composition   286
   A4   Object Decomposition   287
   A5   Object Logistics   289
   A6   Object Construction   292
   A7   Object Sensing   294
   A8   Agent Control   298
   A9   Object Simulation   300
   A10   Information System Models   302

B Generic and Generalized Tasks Models, Dialogues,
   and Argumentation Schema   **307**
   B1   Generic Tasks   307
   B2   Generalized Tasks   315
   B3   Generic Dialogues   345
   B4   Argumentation Schemas   350

C Claims Library   **359**
   C1   Metadomain: Design   359
   C2   Metadomain: Education   361
   C3   Metadomain: Management   366
   C4   Grounded Domain: Spatial Object Sensing OSM   367
   C5   Generalized Task: Information Retrieval   368

References   371
Author Index   385
Subject Index   391

Preface

If you have picked this book up and want to know what it is about, the answer is software reuse with a difference. Software reuse is topical: the patterns movement and the commercial success of SAP and other vendors of ERPs (Enterprise Resource Plans) have seen to that. However, software reuse is still practiced in an ad hoc manner. This book is about putting reuse on a firmer footing, and it describes the Domain Theory as a solution. The difference is the multidisciplinary perspective. I am looking at reuse from the perspective of psychology and management science as well as software.

The book started as a summary of my research into abstraction and reuse over several years. The origins go back to Neil Maiden's doctoral thesis (City University) in 1993 on analogical matching, which used Gentner's structure mapping theory (Gentner, 1983) as its starting point. Analogies are a form of human problem solving, but they are also a challenging and ambitious form of reuse across domains. Research on structure matching begged the question of what were the bridging abstractions between problems commonly experienced in software engineering; thus the Domain Theory was born. From the outset the Domain Theory had an ambitious claim: that all software engineering problems could be described by a tractably small set of models that represented fundamental abstractions. The focus of the Domain Theory was requirements engineering, for two reasons: first, we wished to address abstractions in the real world, where requirements exist; second, many other computer scientists were creating abstract models of design solutions.

Problem abstractions are important because they form the entry point to solutions. Experts form abstract models of problems from their experience of developing many applications, some in similar situations in the real world, but others may occur in different contexts while at a deeper level solving the same type of problem. It is recognizing the problem that gets experts started on efficient and effective solutions. So one of the Domain Theory's motivations was to acquire, record, and systematize the knowledge held by experts when they experience the feeling of "I've come across this problem before; it's the *xxx* type problem".

Although the prime aim of this book was to explain the Domain Theory, it also has a wider purpose. The subject area that the Domain Theory fits into will probably be categorized as software reuse, assuming libraries have such a category in their classification scheme. There are plenty of books on software reuse, which mainly cover the process aspect of component-based engineering. There are even more books on software patterns, the latest manifestation of reuse. However, reuse is not limited to software engineering. We all reuse ideas and solutions every day of our lives by means of our memory. Reuse of concepts, solutions, and best practice knowledge is also a concern of management in the knowledge management and organizational learning literature. Reuse has been practiced for many years in several branches of engineering, and software engineering is a relative latecomer to this idea. Even within computer science, reuse has been addressed in knowledge engineering as well as software engineering. Hence there is a need for a book that brings together these diverse literatures so readers can see the joins and contributions from different disciplines. My background is in psychology and computer science, so although my prime emphasis in the book is on software reuse, I hope I have also introduced other areas of reuse research so the reader can explore these literatures in more depth.

Theories, ideally, should explain and predict phenomena in the world. The Domain Theory fulfills the first criterion in that it explains abstract knowledge structures that experts should acquire as a consequence of exposure to software engineering problems. It also sets out rules for abstraction in requirements engineering, so in that sense it predicts efficient mechanisms for knowledge representation. However, ultimately the Domain Theory is a contribution to design. It states a set of ideas and concepts that should have utility in designing computer systems, but also sociotechnical systems in a wider sense. Design-oriented theories have to prove their validity by the test of application, so the Domain Theory will progress or fall by two tests.

First, its rules and propositions must be shown to be consistent and manageable. If examples and tests cause the theory to be changed in an ad hoc manner to accommodate exceptions, then it will become unwieldy and inconsistent. The Domain Theory rules and propositions (a set of generic models) must stand the test of validation by example. The second test, which is the usual mode of validation of much computer science research, is the test of utility, so if the Domain Theory does not improve the process of software or systems engineering and has no demonstrable impact on product quality, then it will become nothing more than an intellectual curiosity. So far, the Domain Theory has stood the challenge of both tests; however, one motivation for writing this book is to create a stronger validation of its utility.

One way to view this book is as a long answer to the simple question "What is a domain?" The Oxford English dictionary states that a domain is "a field of thought or activity". In computer science the term *domain* is widely used but with many meanings; I hope to clarify at least one meaning of the term. Domains in mathematics are the realm of numbers over which a reasoning mechanism (i.e., equations) is applied. In computer science, domains can mean the range of values an attribute may take (to a database person); a hazy idea of an application area (to a software engineer); or a general statement of an area of interest. Many books refer to application domains, and by that they mean either sectors of industry where requirements for computer systems will be found, or classes of design problem that pose particularly interesting challenges (e.g., high-speed networks). The starting point interpretation in the Domain Theory is the concept of an application or business area. It then progresses to investigate abstractions in software engineering at a deeper level, and it proposes a set of problem-oriented abstractions for tasks and systems. The focus on problem orientation is important. Many books have been published on reuse, but they nearly all concentrate on solution-oriented models, that is, software patterns (Gamma, Helm, Johnson, & Vlissides, 1995), and software component libraries. The Domain Theory complements this work by providing problem-oriented abstractions with pointers toward appropriate solutions.

Writing books on reuse inevitably falls into the trap of completeness. Creating industrial strength reuse libraries is a collaborative project that requires many people and considerable resources, and this book makes no pretence of completeness. Instead, its claim is to provide a sound framework within which more complete libraries of reusable models could be developed. However, where the Domain Theory has been elaborated, it reflects my interests and experience. Some models and domains are therefore more detailed than others. Where this knowledge proves to be useful, so much the better; however, that is not the Domain Theory's prime purpose. Instead, it is providing a framework within which others can contribute.

The book is structured into nine chapters. Chapter 1 introduces the subject area of reuse and software engineering and explains a framework for comparing different reuse approaches. This is elaborated in chapter 2, which develops a metric-oriented framework to assess the reuse claims of three competing approaches: patterns, ERPs, and the Domain Theory Object System Models (OSMs). The latter part of chapter 2 describes the costs of different approaches to reuse in the context of a process model for design for and design by reuse. Chapter 3 explains the psychological background for reuse. The cognitive psychology of learning and memory is reviewed because reuse is a natural human practice and designers can learn much from the way people reuse knowledge. Furthermore, reuse methods, components, and tools have to be designed so people can understand them. Knowledge of user psychology can help to make reuse tools more usable. The Domain Theory makes its appearance in chapter 4. The schema for knowledge representation and fundamental tenets of the Domain Theory are introduced with its major components. The chapter then describes one of these components, grounded domains and their representation in OSMs, in more detail. This part of the theory describes generic models of transaction processes and other system problems at a high level of abstraction. The models are associated with reusable knowledge for requirements analysis. However, I stopped short of describing each model in turn; the full description of the Domain Theory models is placed in appendix A.

Chapter 5 continues with the Domain Theory and describes generic tasks and metadomains. This part of the theory deals with tasks from a human–computer interaction (HCI) viewpoint and gives requirements analysis advice on the task-support functionality that may be typically associated with abstract classes. Metadomains are the largest components of the Domain Theory that describe areas of human endeavor such as management, design, and education. Metadomains are described as architectures with subsystems, agents, and tasks. Chapter 6 introduces claims that provide a representation of design knowledge attached to Domain Theory models, and it is a schema for representing reusable knowledge in nearly any form. Claims belong to the task artefact theory created by Jack Carroll (Carroll & Campbell, 1989) and developed by him and his colleagues over a number of years. Chapter 7 reports research that resulted from the convergence of the two theories. This was mutually beneficial because claims provided the Domain Theory with a more powerful means of delivering design advice, whereas the Domain Theory gave claims a process for generalization and a library of abstract models that indexed claims for reuse. Knowledge representation and reuse of claims in design and knowledge management are described. Chapter 8 covers the reuse process in more depth. Method, techniques, and guidelines for design for reuse—the process of abstraction—are described, followed by guidance for design by reuse. Finally, chapter 9 looks to the future and elaborates the framework introduced in chapters 1 and 2 to investigate the future of reuse by different paradigms, generation of applications from requirements languages, and component-based software engineering by means of reuse libraries. The role of intelligent agents and smart components is also considered and the economics of reuse-led development revisited.

I would like to thanks colleagues at City University, notably Neil Maiden, and at UMIST, who have contributed to many of the ideas and given feedback on earlier drafts of this book and the research papers on which it is based. Discussions with colleagues on the EU basic research project CREWS—Matthias Jarke, Collette Rolland, Eric Dubois and Klaus Pohl—have shaped other ideas in this book. My thanks also to Jim Coplein for his helpful comments on draft chapters and stimulating discussion on patterns, abstraction, and many aspects of reuse. Many individuls in the HCI patterns community—Jan Borchers, Helen Sharp, John Thomas, Tom Erikson, to name but a few—have provided further insights into reuse. In particular, it is a pleasure to acknowledge the help and stimulus of Jack Carroll in advancing the Domain Theory during my sabbatical at Virginia Tech. Indeed, part of this book, the chapter on claims, belongs to Jack Carroll more than myself, so the least I can do is point readers to his books that explain claims and scenarios in more detail (Carroll, 1995, 2000). Finally, this book would never have been produced without the tireless and tolerant efforts of my partner, Gillian Martin, whose editing, document management, and personal support have been invaluable.

Alistair Sutcliffe
UMIST, June 2001

Foreword

Recently I was teaching summer school at a European university where I was listening to a fellow lecturer—a well-known rising star in the reuse area of software engineering—make claims for the success of a particular reuse approach in a large telecommunications company. He related that domain engineering had supposedly reaped benefits of 40%. In a later conversation that took place between sessions, one of the employees of that company—and someone familiar with the program in question—quietly pointed out to the speaker and me in private company that the claimed benefits were on the line of 15%, not 40%.

Certainly part of the disparity comes from different perspectives: whether one measures cost, or interval, or savings for a given project or for the long term. This difficulty in knowing what to measure is, in fact, one of the most difficult problems of reuse. But just maybe, part of the disparity comes from the fact that we *want* to believe in reuse. In fact, software engineering is so lacking in the deep foundations and formalisms that underlie any true engineering discipline that we are drawn to any glimmer of hope. We are an industry that is desparately devoid of solid things in which to believe, and reuse too often fills that vacuum of nature's storied abhorrence.

This is not an isolated incident. Ostensibly objective claims herald the exposition of most reuse techniques, perhaps to a larger degree than all other software engineering disciplines. And too many of these analyses are simplistic: they ignore startup costs, or examine only a small cross-section of a reusable asset's lifetime, or fail to examine what the cost would have been if the asset had been made *usable* instead of *reusable*. Few, if any of them, substantiate the experimental design or expose the raw data that led to these awe-inspiring numbers. Many of these claims focus on a single technique or technology, and it is too often difficult for the practitioner to separate sober deliberation and study from exuberance and marketing claims.

In this book, Alistair Sutcliffe steps back and examines reuse conceptually and soberly from a broad historic and analytical framework. He puts the reuse discipline on firm ground. He takes our hand, steps back and asks us to take a tour of the broader landscape. How has reuse evolved in other disciplines? He explores this question not by hollow or superficial analogy, but with a constant subtext that rigorously grounds the necessary arguments and concepts. What, exactly, are we trying to reuse, and where does the most payoff lie in reuse if it indeed does exist? Perhaps it isn't in the reuse of artefacts at all, but in the reuse of knowledge. Even the reuse of data and interpreted data—information—has value. We can dare talk about wisdom reuse. Knowledge reuse itself is a broad topic ranging from rules and heuristics to procedures and propositions and, yes, even to designs. And reuse is an interdisciplinary phenomenon that builds on the business considerations one finds in enterprise modeling, the economic analyses of investment, the social analyses of process, and the psychological models of conceptualization, as well as the technical models of design and technology. It is a broad and refreshing tour that reveals a landscape that surrounds all of us but which few are able to see.

To aid this exploration and these analyses, Sutcliffe develops a framework based on models of human cognition. The most difficult aspects of reuse are to know how to make something reusable and to know how to match a reuse opportunity to a foreseen solution sitting on a shelf somewhere. Even if we are not all reuse engineers, we all have struggled with coaxing a supposedly reusable component into doing our bidding. It is an issue of aligning the images in our minds with the images that were in the minds of the creators of the component. We usually try those images together at some abstract level, and abstraction is a cognitive process related to learning by generalization. But as Sutcliffe reminds us frequently, the devil is in the detail. And it is not only the devil—the blood, sweat, and tears—that live in the detail, but the deity as well—utility, firmness, and delight. The cognitive processes that bring these together are rich and intriguing. Reuse is fundamentally about learning (how do I encode stuff that is reusable and the information necessary to find and apply it?), memory (where do I find something to reuse?), and problem solving (which, if the reader will excuse me going meta here, is the reuse of previously acquired knowledge). While the goals of reuse are economic, its constructs are cognitive, and its mechanisms lie in the relative insignificance of intellect and technology. As engineers, we too often let the technical tail wag the conceptual dog.

This sobering view leads to useful insights. Reuse is hard because flexible adaptability is hard, particularly in something that is as hard as software is. Software is hard not only because the world is a complicated place but also because software is so unconstrained as to lay open the Pandora's box all of our cognitive wiles and tools. Human minds combat this complexity with classification, usually employing some kind of parameterization. However, there are limits to abstraction. To quote Sutcliffe, "As parameters increase, the dilemma of adaptability emerges. The more adaptable features an application has, the more of the programmer's job is passed on to the user. Adding more customization features becomes self-defeating as users rebel against the outsourcing of the programmer's job." The book offers many such analyses that are compelling from the perspectives of value systems, economics, and design, and which you will find resonate with your experience.

In addition, the book does not stop with these musings and models—even as useful as they are in their own right—but goes forward in a practical way, grounded in both theory and experience, with broad guidance for building reusable software. More than half the book is dedicated to this practical focus. Much of this exposition draws on Sutcliffe's excellent earlier work with Jack Carroll on *domain claims*, a broad and no-nonsense way of capturing and organizing information about real-world phenomena. It shows how to link claims to domain models, and Sutcliffe ties it all together into practical recommendations that embrace and build on software engineering practices such as domain engineering and modularity. Sutcliffe's real-world experience shows here with examples and case studies drawn from applications as diverse as life-critical applications and general-purpose middleware. He offers this guidance not in a simplistic or formulaic recipe, but as a synthesis of the insights that grow out of the deeper explorations. This leaves few stones unturned: education and training, management, knowledge acquisition techniques and the complementary techniques, and organizational structures and organizational roles that support disseminating the knowledge.

Also explored are the ideas from the more familiar territory of software engineering: domain analysis, coupling, cohesion, and all related concepts. Sutcliffe ties these back to the fundamentals, to the ever-present cognitive constructs and processes that underlie the higher level processes. Further, the exposition of each technique retains a skeptical subtext: though modularity is good, what are the limits of cohesion analysis and of de-coupling? The real world always muddies our idealistic views, and nowhere have I seen these tensions more frankly admitted, more deeply explored, and more deftly handled than in the practical offerings from this author.

More broadly, the theories and practices offered by this book are about use and reuse combined with the overall cognitive process of design. All great systems evolve piecemeal from small systems that work. That process of design always "reuses" the base and grows it by the same cognitive processes of memory, learning, and problem solving that characterize reuse. Viewed as such, the foundations in this book are a treasure trove for contemporary design. I found many gems in Sutcliffe's exposition of cognitive phenomena that relate directly to design research questions that have been dear to me for years. For example, the chunking models related to the maintenance of positive facts in working memory and the difficulty of working with negative facts, substantiated through almost two decades of cognitive psychology, casts a pall over anti-patterns. The cognitive phenomenon of confirmation bias that causes us to overlook exceptions that fit into a positive pattern raises questions about most parameterized technical domain models, because they lack the concept of negative variability. Domain theory frameworks offer a cognitive basis for separate but equally attentive models of the problem and solution domains.

These considerations drive to the foundations of design, as well as to the foundations of who we are as human beings, and as such, appeal to universal experience and experiences. I am confident that any student of design will find strong links between their research and experiences in the technical domain and the deep insights that Sutcliffe offers into who we are and how we work. It will be only through surrender to these insights that we will make great things that are more usable, perhaps more re-usable, and which will aid in the quest for that elusive quality called great design.

Jim Coplien
Naperville, Illinois
[July 2001]

1

Background and Concepts

1.1. REUSE APPROACHES
AND HISTORY

Reuse has had a long history in engineering. Designs have been reused since the Egyptians invented the pyramid and Romans discovered the arch. In civil engineering, buildings are constructed from reusable components. Many houses come as prefabricated items, for example, window frames, roof segments, floors, and walls. Building with tried and tested components reduces costs and makes the product more reliable. This message has not been lost on the software industry, but the development of component-based software engineering has been less rosy. This is not for want of trying. Reuse started with component-based reuse in programming languages; for instance, the Include statement in COBOL's file definition enabled programmers to reuse data structures. Most computer languages provide facilities and subroutines for reusable source and executable code. However, this begs the question, Just where does reuse start? Opportunistic reuse of code might be better described as salvaging or carrying code over from one application to another, whereas true reuse implies some conscious design of the module–design–code for reuse in the first place (Tracz, 1995). This distinction holds up fairly well for software-oriented reuse; however, in knowledge management, the amount of a priori design for reuse can be minimal. Generally, the more effort that is invested in making things reuseable, the better the payback.

Libraries of software components have been designed for reuse and reused for many years. Mathematical functions and algorithms have been notable examples; these include the numerical algorithms group (NAG), finite-element analysis algorithms and collections of abstract data structures (Uhl & Schmid, 1990). Component libraries have been created in aerospace and telecommunications domains (Arango, Schoen, & Pettengill, 1993; Prieto-Diaz, 1990), and reuse programs have been implemented in several industries. Savings in development costs of the order of 20–50% have been claimed in before-and-after studies of the implementation of reuse programs (Matsumoto, 1993); however, it is difficult to verify these figures, as nobody has the resource to run large-scale controlled experiments with and without reuse. Research programs in component-based software engineering and reuse have been undertaken in the United States by the Microelectronics and Computer Corporation (MCC) and in the European Esprit program, but there is little evidence for assessing the impact that these initiatives have made on industrial practice. Some European projects have reported considerable success in developing reuse processes and component libraries (Ezran, Morisio, & Tully, 1998; Morel & Faget, 1993). More significant is the U.S. military's reuse programs in the Software Technology for Adaptable, Reliable Systems (STARS) initiative (Tracz, 1995). In spite of the considerable literature reporting reuse research and practice, designing reusable components is still ad hoc, with each organization creating components that suit its own context. Unfortunately, this hinders exchange or reuse in other domains.

Although reuse has a 10- to 15-year history of research and practice, the overall impact is limited. More progress has been made in defining processes for reuse than in actually implementing them. If design for reuse has created a large number of component libraries, one might expect that a software-components market might have developed, with Internet software brokers. To an extent it has: free software components are swapped in narrow domains, but most software is still traded as packages and bespoke applications rather than components. A similar pattern exists in knowledge reuse. Collecting best practice knowledge and reusing knowledge for organizational learning has been a management science mantra for over 10 years, but the extent of practice is hard to gauge. Although there are large and growing information-provider and knowledge-vendor markets, goods and services are still traded as products: books, CD-ROMs, how-to guides, and market intelligence reports. No market in knowledge components has developed, apart from the recent interest in organizational patterns (Coplein, 1996).

Early software reuse was based on a functional modeling approach, following the concepts in structured development methods, for example, the structured systems analysis and design method (SSADM; Downs, Clare, & Coe, 1992), and structured analysis and structured design (SA/SD; De Marco, 1978). More recently, reuse has become born again in the patterns movement, even though the patterns community has had little overlap with other reuse researchers. Patterns grew out of object-oriented methods that encouraged reuse in the conception of class hierarchies. Modeling generic classes naturally encouraged reuse by specialization. Reuse of single classes in isolation evolved into groups of collaborating objects linked to responsibilities or requirements for a service (Wirfs-Brock, Wilkerson, & Wiener, 1990); then patterns were born as a development of this idea in the now-famous "gang of four" book (Gamma, Helm, Johnson, & Vlissides, 1995). The patterns movement grew out of an informal industrial meeting of minds to share development efforts. It has since grown into a society of practitioners and developers in many branches of computer science and other disciplines (e.g., HCI, management science), although its strength still lies in programming constructs and software architecture (Harrison, Foote, & Rohnert, 1999; Rising, 1998).

Architecture has provided inspiration for the patterns movement in the form of Christopher Alexander's writings. Alexander (Alexander, Ishikawa, & Silverstein, 1977) had been trying to convince colleagues in his own profession that reusable concepts and designs could be applied to problems ranging from urban planning to building design. His patterns proposed designs linked to problems or goals, with forces or arguments that justified the pattern and an example illustrating its use. Patterns are cross-referenced to relate many solutions to different parts of a problem, for example, from spatial planning of a neighborhood to design of playgrounds, meeting places, and houses. The network of related patterns forms a pattern language. The nature of Alexandrine patterns has spawned much debate. Alexander proposed using the patterns as tools for thought or as a set of ideas to influence the designers' thinking rather than reusing them verbatim. Indeed, Alexander urged his readers to invent their own patterns and pattern languages; he saw his role as only providing the framework. Others have taken his writings in a more prescriptive manner. Unfortunately for Alexander, his ideas, whatever their interpretation, have been taken up with more enthusiasm by software developers (Coplein, 1999) than architects.

Reuse has spawned an enormous literature in computer science and elsewhere; see Biggerstaff and Perlis (1989) and Tracz (1995) for surveys covering approaches to reuse and industrial experience. Most reports are experiential in nature. Industrial practitioners develop a set of components and wish to pass their ideas on to the wider world; this is a worthy motivation but one that hides a problem. Components of any origin can only be reused if they conform to a standard. Other engineering disciplines were quick to learn the merit of standards, either de facto or agreed through international consensus under the auspices of the International Standards Organisation (ISO). Standards exist for electrical components ranging from plugs to chip connections. The computer that this book was written on was designed and built from standardized reusable components: the Intel processor, RAM chips, SCSI disk drive, and so on. The software that was used was also composed of reused components but only because it came from a certain manufacturer in Seattle and the reuse was between versions of the same word processor. Software reuse, generally, is far more limited than hardware or reuse of engineering components. The lack of success in software is reflected in the industry market structure. The hardware industry is composed of component manufacturers. It might be dominated by a few major players (Intel, Motorola, and Compaq for processor chips) who set the de facto standards; however, component-based engineering is a great success. Hardware costs keep falling and power increases each year as long as the laws of physics don't catch up with Moore's law (cited in Messina et al., 1998). In contrast, software is a largely product-based industry, with a small component-based trade and limited reuse. Costs are high and show no decreasing trend. Standards in software development have made progress only in the process area (e.g., the Software Engineering Institute's Capability Maturity Model, or CMM), but few standards exist for software components and architectures beyond system software such as networking protocols (International Standards Organization Open Systems Integration, or ISO OSI; Common Object Broker Request Architecture, or CORBA; Distributed Common Object Manager, or DCOM), data-compression algorithms (Joint Pictures Expert Group, or JPEG; Moving Pictures Expert Group, or MPEG), encryption, and so on (Object Management Group, 2000). This has restricted reuse to within companies where de facto standards can be enforced.

1.2. MOTIVATIONS FOR REUSE

The basic motivation is to save time and effort. If an existing solution can be reused, this saves time and makes processes more efficient. The second motivation is to empower a flexible response in manufacture. As time to market decreases and markets demand change in response to the Internet, software has to be produced more rapidly, and bespoke development of large-scale systems becomes less tenable because it takes too long. This situation is beginning to change with the growth of the middleware market, in which component vendors are starting to emerge. Reuse-led development has also been one of the software success stories in generalized application packages and their better-known relatives, enterprise resource plans (ERPs). ERP packages have resulted in the creation of powerful new companies, notably SAP, BANN and Peoplesoft, who sell configurable suites of software to deal with industrial problems such as inventory control, handling logistics, planning materials for manufacture, and personnel payroll (Keller & Teufel, 1998). The generic application packages are a form of reuse, but it is reuse achieved by configuration. Components are selected that fit within the framework, and then they are tailored to the customer's needs by parameters and switches. However, the vendors are still selling a product. There is an allied economy of smaller companies who sell plug-ins and bolt-ons for ERP packages, but there is little true component-based engineering in software development. SAP reuses modules between versions of their R3 system but they still develop and own nearly all the code themselves. There is no market of independent ERP component providers.

All this might be about to change. One of the motivations of component-based engineering is reduced cost. The other is flexibility and response to customers' demands. Component-based engineering in the car industry enabled Henry Ford to produce very cheap cars, initially so long as they were black. Ford can now produce local variations of one design by component-based engineering, as demonstrated by the world model, aptly named Mondeo. Cars have to be produced faster, better, and cheaper, a mantra for commercial reality in a global market. Software is no different. The pace of change brought about by the Internet and e-commerce means that time to market is vital for software as well. Software design has to change and adapt rapidly to fit new requirements. It has to be produced quickly and cheaply. There is a limit on how cheap and nimble you can be with a large complex ERP. Maybe the day of the software dinosaurs is coming to an end.

If the software industry is to adapt and change, it will need a new economic model of component-based manufacture, so the market place can create new products to fulfill changing needs by integrating many smaller-scale components. Flexibility in design implies a need for smaller-scale components and wider-spread reuse. You can make many different toy objects from a generalized set of Lego building blocks. They might not be as perfect or realistic as hand crafted toy cars and buildings, but they are quicker to build and cheaper to construct. The same argument applies to software. Furthermore, as software is itself a flexible substance, and because code can be automatically written and rewritten, component-based software engineering should be able to deliver flexibility and fit users' requirements at a reasonable cost. However, this will require standards. Standardization is a slow process. It becomes slower when there are more interested parties. Standards have been successful for software architecture, but these describe how components should communicate or lay down general laws for integration, for example, CORBA and Microsoft's rival DCOM for how distributed applications can be built from services and, in the multimedia area, synchronized multimedia mark-up language (SMIL; Rutledge, Hardman, & Van Ossenbruggen, 1999; W3C, 2000) and Microsoft's rival Vital. Standards for software components for applications functionality are much more difficult to agree on.

1.3. DIMENSIONS OF THE REUSE PROBLEM

Domain-oriented functionality is both the strength of software and its Achilles' heel. A prime reason why software engineering has not made the progress it aspired to, using other engineering disciplines as a benchmark, is the adaptability of software. You can program a computer to do nearly anything, but flexibility comes with a price. Reuse is only easy at the generative level of tools that help you build more software, for example, programming language compilers, and when software-component reuse has been facilitated by de facto or de jure standards, such as widget libraries for user interfaces: dialogue boxes, sliders, and window managers (Xmotif, Microsoft Windows). For application software the devil is in the detail. Users' requirements might be similar in many cases, but individual differences in rules for business processes, calculations, data definitions, and so on make each application unique, or at least hard to generalize. Designers have always tried to overcome the flexibility problem by parameterizing programs. Unfortunately, parameterization can only partially deal with the flexibility problem. As parameters increase, the dilemma of adaptability emerges. The more adaptable features an application has, the more of the programmer's job is passed on to the user. Adding more customization features becomes self-defeating as users rebel against the outsourcing of the programmer's job. Alternatively, users become experts and demand more programming ability and the product evolves toward a general generative technology, a trend that can be seen in spreadsheets and word processors that have added macros, essentially programming languages, to satisfy the demands of expert users.

The quest for the holy grail of software is to find an economically stable compromise between the demands of flexibility on one hand and ease of use on the other. Perhaps component-based engineering can provide the answer. If only there were standards maybe this would be the solution. No doubt standards will emerge from a pragmatic process of collecting designs, comparing the similarities, and compromising over the differences. Indeed, the patterns movement may well lead to standards. However, a pragmatic process is likely to preserve a legacy of poor as well as good design, and it may weaken designs by the need for consensus. Standardization takes a long time. In this book I investigate a more theoretically principled approach to the problem and propose that there is a way to create software components that are more rationally based. If software components are engineered according to sound principles, then design quality should be improved. Components will be more reliable, usable, and easier to integrate. Sound principles exist in computer science; many have already been mentioned, such as the principles of parameterization and modularity (Meyer, 1997), and most have become embedded in programming languages, for example, guard commands (Hoare, 1969) in Occam, synchronization of processes in the Ada Rendezvous, low coupling in data hiding and parameter passing, and cohesion in design heuristics for modularity (Yourdon, 1989; Yourdon & Constantine, 1978). The problem is how to ensure that libraries of software components are designed with these principles in mind.

Some might argue that education is the answer. I partially agree, but I disagree for the following reason. Successful reuse and standards for component-based software engineering have to solve two fundamental problems. The first is the *granularity* problem: How large should reusable components be and how much functionality should any one component contain? Granularity goes to the heart of the flexibility–usability dilemma. More smaller components should be easier to compose; in contrast, fewer large components will be less flexible and require more customization. The second is the *abstraction* problem, which is related to granularity, but it raises two subquestions: the level of detail that a component should possess, and the type of functionality. The first question concerns generalization–specialization; the second is directed toward functional partitioning.

Generalization is linked to the trade-off between utility and the scope of reuse. This creates the dilemma of the utility trap. Ideally, reusable components would be applicable to many different domains yet give the designer considerable detail to reduce design effort. Unfortunately, abstract components by definition contain less detail. Less detail enables a wider range of applications to be targeted for reuse but does so at the penalty of decreased utility. A highly reusable but empty class is not much use to a programmer. Reuse requires a theory of partitioning and abstraction that predicts how components should be designed to avoid the low utility trap, while delivering sufficient flexibility to target a variety of application markets. The quest for such a theory is explored in this book.

Abstraction and generalizations lead to some interesting comparisons between hardware and software. A specialized chip can be composed from components, but most hardware comes as standardized and complex components. In microprocessor design there has been an inexorable growth in complexity, with components (i.e., microprocessor chips) becoming larger in their functional granularity even if they are physically miniature. Although microprocessors are composed of a myriad components such as gates, transistors, registers, caches, and the like these highly reusable components appear in a wide variety of computers and achieve flexibility by parameterization. Chips can be configured and microprogrammed to fulfill a range of functions within their overall designed capability. This tension between reuse by means of parameterization versus composition may have lessons for software, and this issue is revisited in chapter 2.

1.4. REUSE OF KNOWLEDGE AND DESIGNS

Reuse can be practiced at many levels. The most basic form of reuse is human memory. We all reuse problem-solving experience. Experts solve problems not because they are more gifted individuals, although this may be true for many, but primarily because they have more experience. An expert is able to retrieve the appropriate solution from memory, match it to the problem at hand, and then apply the knowledge judiciously. Novices, in contrast, have little experience to drawn on. Because the psychology of learning and memory underpins much of reuse practice, the cognitive psychology of reuse will be dealt with in chapter 3 to provide a basis for design of reuse processes and software tools to support reuse.

Human memory has a direct bearing on reuse at several levels. We reuse not only problem solutions but also facts, concepts, and explanations in several different ways. For instance, we have memories of episodes or scenes that relate to events in our lives. These can be reused as scenarios for requirements analysis. We memorize and reuse information by processing it into higher-order abstractions, called *chunks* by psychologists. Storing lower-level information would swamp even the large storage capacity of human memory, so we process low-level data and store the abstraction. This produces levels of abstraction that are commonly referred to as *data, information, knowledge,* and *wisdom.* Hard and fast definitions of each are difficult to give, but a working explanation is that, as we perceive input from the world, it initially has little meaning beyond identity. We then reason with these data and create a knowledge structure, which ends up in our memory as information. This memory has a simple structure and is often referred to as *declarative memory* in psychology (Anderson, 1990). When we reason with information in more depth we form more complex knowledge, which becomes memorized as more complex networks linking lower-level information, and finally wisdom may be considered as further complex networking between knowledge that gives deeper insight. Each of these levels is expanded below; however, the boundary between them cannot be defined in a precise manner.

Data are low-level facts and values that are often related to sensory input, such as lists of numbers, details of a picture, and sounds we have heard. We rarely reuse data, as these items have little inherent value in reasoning or problem solving. Data form the input for our reasoning that we collect at run time.

Information is data that have been processed in some way to make them more useful or comprehensible. The degree of processing to turn data into information is where the definition breaks down. One person's data is another person's information; however, the concept is best illustrated by example. Isolated facts are data, but if you form an association between facts then you have information. The association may mirror some familiar concepts in computer science such as aggregation (part-of), type (a-kind-of), or class (is-a), or organizing actions in sequences and temporal relationships. We hold information in memory, or if we cannot remember it, we look it up in books or on the Internet. This is reuse for small packets of information that can be applied to a wide variety of tasks. It is such a ubiquitous phenomenon that we don't refer to it as reuse, although reuse is manifest in memory-support tools for information retrieval, hypertext, and hypermedia systems, and in database query languages. Information is the lowest level of practical reuse.

Knowledge consists of higher-order chunks of information that have been processed further and have added value for reasoning and problem solving. Once again the boundary between information and knowledge is hard to draw. Knowledge structures are generally more complex than information structures and can be reused to solve problems directly, whereas information has to be assembled and processed before it can be used. An approximate description of knowledge is aggregations of information that describe how to solve a problem, carry out a procedure, or explain some natural phenomenon. Knowledge structures have more complex internal organization and provide explanations rather than simple associations between facts. We reuse knowledge every day of our lives as skills (how to do it) and ready-made solutions that we reapply to problems. A simple test is that knowledge is explained whereas information is simply told. Reuse at the knowledge level becomes more significant and forms the subject matter for knowledge management.

Wisdom is referred to in the knowledge-management literature in management science, so I have included it for completeness (Argyris, 1999; Davenport, 1993). Finding the boundary between knowledge and wisdom is even more difficult than that for the lower-level categories. The most productive perspective is to see the transformation from data to wisdom as a dimension of increasing aggregation and abstraction that leads to more sophisticated and complex memories that we can apply to larger-scale and more diverse problems. Wisdom has no psychological definition. It may arise from linking several knowledge structures together as a result of extensive experience enabling long-range associations to be made, and further abstraction to create general principles, heuristics, and concepts that can be applied to a large number of different problems. Wisdom is quintessentially metaknowledge, reflections on lower-level knowledge, and knowledge about how to reason. That is, it is related to the ability to think about thinking. Reuse at the wisdom level becomes more about process support and help for reusing knowledge structures.

We shall be dealing with reuse primarily at the knowledge level, because this is where the greatest payoff occurs. Fact-level reuse does merit attention, but this is supported by database technologies and information retrieval. Knowledge units that are larger tend to have sufficient utility for ready-made solutions and hence are immediately beneficial. The disadvantage is that new problems rarely match old ones exactly, so some interpretation and customization are necessary. The alternative is to make knowledge units small enough so that aggregation of many structures can create a variety of solutions to new problems. The disadvantage of smaller and more abstract knowledge units is that they deliver less immediate utility. There is no such thing as a "mental free lunch" in reuse. You have to do work either by matching and tailoring larger units to the new problem or composing smaller units to fit the problem. However, some reuse is better than none, and within the window of utility lie the questions of granularity and abstraction described earlier.

Knowledge can be subdivided into several categories, as follows: arguments, designs, semantic networks, taxonomies and classification, procedures, and rules and heuristics. Arguments are associations of facts and propositions that form memories as "frozen" lines of reasoning, conversations, and discussions. Argumentation knowledge often stores decisions and their rationales, and it has a substructure of proposals and counterproposals related to an issue with evidence for and against (Conklin & Begeman, 1988). Arguments can document design processes or be reusable objects in their own right as business strategies and tactics.

Designs are solutions to problems composed of one or more of the following categories plus the designed artefact. Designs may also be supported by arguments.

Semantic networks are networks of related facts, where the associations may fall into several subtypes: information about objects in the world, causal explanations of events or how things happen, information about people, and so on. The aggregation of information creates mental models of a problem. Mental models may describe the problem itself—a model of the requirements or problem space—or the solution: the design or solution space.

Taxonomies and classification are knowledge structures that impose structure on information as classes and categories. Taxonomic knowledge contains definitions for classes, the class hierarchy structure, and the members of each class.

Procedures consist of knowledge that describes how to do something or how something works. Procedures have a substructure of actions organized in a sequence with preconditions and postconditions. Procedures are associated with a goal that may be organized in hierarchies. Reuse of procedures includes methods, processes, and tasks.

Rules and heuristics knowledge may be formalized rules with IF-condition-THEN-action structures, or less formal rules of thumb (heuristics); and general advice stated in natural language.

Knowledge structures may be more or less formalized, depending on the precision of their internal organization. This has important consequences for reuse, because the more precise representation of components and structures enables searching on the internals of the component. If components have a less formal description then searching can only be driven by the metadata description, or index, unless free text search techniques are applicable. Support for reuse therefore depends on the level of component description, and this is reflected in the difference between knowledge management reuse and design-based reuse in software engineering, illustrated in Fig. 1.1.

1.5. KNOWLEDGE-MANAGEMENT REUSE

Components in knowledge-management systems are expressed informally as narrative text and other media such as pictures or animation. Components may be structured in class hierarchies and indexed for retrieval. Retrieval is by searching the index, although search of component contents may be possible with text-based search engines. Indexing may use faceted classification, categorization by means of a controlled vocabulary, or a strict hierarchical classification. Standardization is limited to the structure of the library because there is limited control over the contents. The degree of standardization depends on the granularity level of the taxonomy used to structure the knowledge. Detailed fine-grained taxonomies impose more control on components, and further conditions may be imposed by specifying the internal format of the component itself. An example is design rationale that can

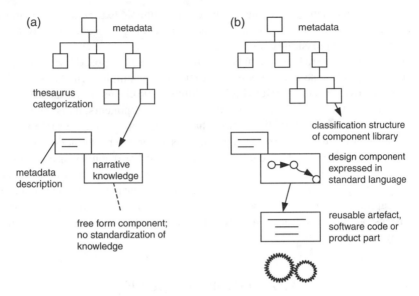

FIG. 1.1. Reuse paradigms: (a) knowledge-management reuse with free format components; (b) design component reuse that enforces a common representation of designs and artefacts.

be treated as a narrative component; but it also imposes a substructure of issues, positions, and arguments. However, the content of the components is not standardized beyond the assumption that it will be short phrases in natural language.

Examples of knowledge-management reuse are business strategies and tactics, stated as narrative. These record experiences and advice about how to approach problems, previously successful ideas, and best practice, such as "to improve customer satisfaction, praise the customers' choices and keep them informed of progress in their orders." The only formal control for this informally stated content is to attribute the source of the knowledge and provide a citation of its use. This is necessary for tracing knowledge forward during reuse and backward to its source. Slightly more control over formatting is exercised over business rules (Loucopoulos & Karakostas, 1995), which state policies and decisions in IF-condition-THEN-action format, for example,

IF customer has major account THEN give discount of 5% on all orders.

Note that this rule does not explicitly state what constitutes a major account. This could be articulated in another rule that states that all customers who purchase more than 20,000 Euros of goods in any one year are treated as major accounts. The formality with which knowledge is expressed depends on its anticipated reuse. Strategies, plans, and policies will all be interpreted by managers during the reuse process. Informal natural language is therefore a suitable expression. In contrast, rules may be reused directly either in manual procedures or in computer systems, so more formal expression is warranted.

Approaches to knowledge management have generally imposed few restrictions on formatting, because managers have criticized even simple formats like design rationale as overstructured (Buckingham Shum, 1996). This limits the ability of computer-based tools for searching and retrieval of components; it also makes the components' contents unpredictable, so that finding appropriate reusable knowledge can be difficult. In spite of these limitations, gathering best practice and other reusable knowledge is widespread. The key to success lies in gathering and reusing the knowledge in similar contexts. Either the knowledge is general-purpose management strategy and tactics, in which case it requires considerable reinterpretation when reapplied, or it is domain specific and can only be applied in the same industry or business application. Reuse in knowledge management is therefore suboptimal in many respects.

1.6. DESIGN REUSE

Design reuse uses the components' content directly, in contrast to knowledge management, in which advice contained in components has to be interpreted by people. The key difference is the degree of standardization of component description. To share designs, components have to be documented in a design language understood by both the original designer and the reuser–designer. The characteristics of reusable designs are that they are represented in a specification language and stored in a library with indexing and classification schemes. The design language in software may be formal such as VDM (Jones, 1986) or Z (Spivey, 1989), or informal diagrams such as UML (Rational Corporation, 1999). Components can be retrieved by searching on indexes or by search algorithms that use knowledge of the components' structure and semantics (Sutcliffe & Maiden, 1998). Designs may be reused either as ready-made problem solutions that are interpreted in a new problem context, or directly by an automated transformation of the design into an implementation, using application generators (Batory, 1998; Batory, Chen, Robertson, & Wang, 2000).

After designs, products themselves may be reused. This level of reuse is familiar in many branches of civil, mechanical, and electronic engineering, as new products are assembled from prefabricated components, whereas components themselves are reused to produce new variations on old designs. In software engineering the equivalent is black-box reuse of software components, in which the designer knows little of the internal code of a module but reuses it by calling functions from a public interface: application program interfaces (APIs). Examples of code reuse are user-interface components such as window managers, sliders, buttons, and dialogue boxes that are provided in many programming environments.

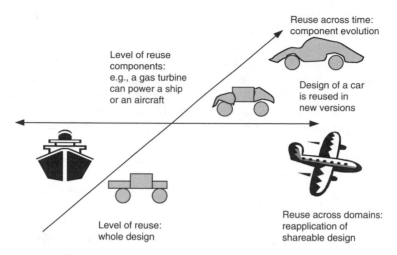

Reuse across time:
component evolution

Level of reuse
components:
e.g., a gas turbine
can power a ship
or an aircraft

Design of a car
is reused in
new versions

Level of reuse:
whole design

Reuse across domains:
reapplication of
shareable design

FIG. 1.2. Dimensions of reuse across time and domains.

Reuse may occur across domains and time (Fig. 1.2). In the temporal dimension, products and designs evolve through many versions. Temporal reuse is closer to the concept of evolution that occurs in many domains in which designers incrementally improve products. For example, civil engineers have incrementally improved the design of suspension bridges from modest beginnings by Brunel and Telford to the large spans achieved in the Brooklyn Bridge and more modern designs. Evolutionary reuse pushes the boundaries of a design concept to its limits and thereby reveals when not to reuse a design. In the suspension bridge, designers evolved longer and thinner bridges until the Tacoma Narrows Bridge demonstrated that long, thin bridges make better aircraft wings: the bridge oscillated in high winds and destroyed itself. Evolutionary reuse is widespread and a natural practice of design refinement; however, it is limited to a single domain and product line. In the software industry, products evolve through versions and releases. In knowledge management, best practice reuse is usually evolutionary because it applies within one narrow context. For example, best practice advice in treating alcoholics does not necessarily apply to drug abusers.

Across-domain reuse, in contrast, is more ambitious but can have larger payoffs. If components can be reused in many different products, then there is a larger potential market place for the component manufacturer. Standardization of smaller components has been the key to cross-domain reuse. In engineering, agreement on the shape, thread, and dimensions of nuts, bolts, and screws in the Whitworth (UK Imperial standard) and later metric systems had a mutually beneficial effect for producers and consumers. In software, many user-interface components (dialogue boxes, sliders, buttons, windows, etc.) are standardized by manufacturers such as Microsoft and Sun (Sun Microsystems, 1999). User-interface components are reused in many different application domains.

Across-domain reuse embeds two concepts. First is the product and its market; second is the function or services provided. Some products are produced for specific organizations and customers. Examples are vertical-market software products in banking applications, healthcare systems, and fly-by-wire avionics. Within vertical-market products there are components that have a wider application. For example, accounting software developed for banking systems may also prove useful for all companies who need to keep profit and loss accounts. Similarly, inventory control and personnel payroll systems have become reusable software packages that are applied to many different domains. However, some products are designed to be general purpose in the first place. These include word processors, graphics packages, spreadsheets, and presentation design systems. These horizontal-market applications have a large potential market and have to fit a wide variety of users and usages.

Within both horizontal- and vertical-market applications, reuse is possible at several layers or levels (Fig. 1.3). The first level is the functionality that is directly perceived by the user. This is the most difficult level for reuse because usage is dependent on the users, their tasks, and context. To illustrate the point, a graphics package such as Photoshop can be used by a multimedia designer to create

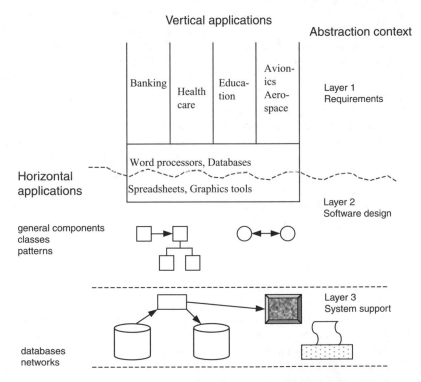

FIG. 1.3. Reuse layers and computer architecture.

advertising images, an engineer to create design illustrations, and an (expert) teenager to make fun drawings. Reuse in this case is a tribute to the flexibility of the product's functionality.

The second level of reuse is in functions that provide components to implement application services manifest at the user interface. In the graphics package, drawing object components might be designed as general classes with polymorphism so that sending a message to the "draw circle" object results in many different effects according to the parameters in the message; for example, draw a red–green circle, with a thick–thin line. This level of reuse has abstracted the problem away from the user's functionality toward a generalized design.

The third level of reuse is at the system service level. This provides operational components that the application depends on but are not directly visible to the user, such as network protocols for communication, compression algorithms for image storage in a graphics package, and database update routines.

In software reuse, layers 2 and 3 share a closer view of the solution domain. Component design is focused on the computer system rather than the outside world. Not surprisingly, software reuse has made the most progress in these layers. Object-oriented (OO) patterns provide ready-made design components for solving abstract functions, for example, monitoring and update by the Observer pattern (Gamma et al., 1995). However, the level of design reuse varies; in some cases the design comes with tailorable code, whereas other OO patterns provide a design concept that has to be interpreted and then coded. Reuse at the requirements layer 1 is more difficult because it has to deal with variation in the real world. Unfortunately, users don't always have a clear picture of their requirements; once they get a prototype they often change their minds, and, worse still, even when they are satisfied with a system, the world changes. The moving target of requirements engineering (Sutcliffe, 1996a) militates against level 1 reuse. Some argue that all software should be designed to adapt because requirements will never be complete as markets and business practices change (Lehman, 1990). The rapid growth of the Web and changes in business practice for e-commerce illustrate the point.

A summary of the components at each level of reuse follows.

1. The requirements and business level contains user-problem descriptions, domain models, vertical-sector applications, and technology-independent solutions.
2. The system design level contains algorithms, functions, data structures, objects, and solutions that solve problems in level 1 but are independent of its domains.
3. The system software contains algorithms, functions, and components necessary for computer system operation, device drivers, and network routers.

Problems at the requirements level ultimately require solutions at levels 2 and 3. Another approach to reuse is to generate applications directly from high-level

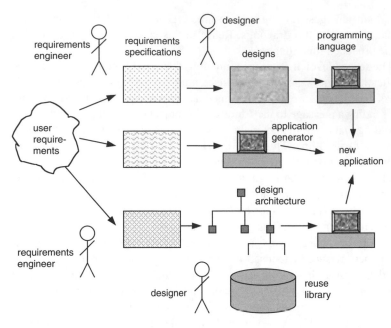

FIG. 1.4. Reuse by specification languages and generative architectures, versus reuse by composition and customization.

requirements specification languages rather than to compose them from components. Applications can thus be created by three routes: first the traditional route by means of specification, design, and programming; second by specification and generation from a high-level requirements language; and third by requirements specification and component-based engineering. This divergence in reuse philosophy is summarized in Fig. 1.4.

Reuse ultimately may be achieved by a process-generation approach, in which requirements are specified and the solution created automatically. When the requirements change, the old solution is thrown away and a new one is generated. Alternatively, reuse may take a structural approach that composes applications from libraries of components. The generative approach (Batory, 1998; Batory et al., 2000) has not met with much success so far, beyond level 3 system services. Research prototypes following this approach for levels 1 and 2 have a poor track record of commercial success (Neighbors, 1994). In a more pragmatic but limited scope, fourth-generation languages (4GLs) are a successful generative technology. The barrier to this approach has been developing requirements languages that users can understand and then designing architectures that can create detailed applications. Expressing requirements and describing components in natural language is fraught with ambiguity and potential misunderstanding. General-purpose ontologies (Sowa, 2000) can improve precision but at the expense of making requirements harder for users and designers to understand. Restricting the domain to create a subset of language that belongs to a particular application, for example, terms, phrases, and commands in air traffic control, may be a way forward, but this approach has not been applied to requirements reuse thus far. More progress to date has been made with the structural approach. Barriers to this route have been designing components that are compatible and composable across domains, and developing retrieval processes so that designers can find the components they need.

1.7. MODELS OF THE SYSTEM AND THE WORLD

A key problem in reuse is modeling how reusable components fit into the world in which they are used. Software inevitably contains assumptions and models of the application world for which it is designed. Models become embedded in system designs, and open systems—which include all software—have to interact with the real world. Unfortunately, models are general but their input–output connections have to deal with the instance-level real world. The boundary of models therefore presents a particular problem for subsequent reuse because the assumptions of the model embedded in reusable components may no longer be valid in a new context.

1.7.1. Embedding Software in the World

Software is embedded in applications. It is connected to the outer world, detects input from it, processes the input, and then provides output back to the world. Electronic systems, the precursors of software, were capable of limited interaction with the real world; for instance, early autopilots could keep an aircraft flying straight and level by interpreting signals from airspeed indicators and gyro compasses and then altering flight-control surfaces to maintain course. However, the scale of interpretation in software is different. In modern fly-by-wire control systems, software interprets events and makes decisions without the pilot even being aware of its actions. Furthermore, fly-by-wire autopilot systems actually take control away from the pilot in certain circumstances to prevent dangerous acts, for example, stalling or descending too quickly.

The connection between software and the outside world has been studied for some time by Jackson (1995), who points out that software design has to reflect known realities of the world and specify the system's response to inbound events. This has implications for systems and has to be described in models. Jackson distinguishes two types of dependency between the real world and designed systems:

- *indicative requirements*, which are implications from laws of physics and biology, such as "if the rate of climb for an aircraft is set too high then it will stall," and

- *optative requirements*, which are behaviors we want a designed system to exhibit and which emanate from the designer's interpretations of users' goals and wishes, for example, "a warning is signalled to the pilot if the rate of climb may cause a stall."

Jackson emphasizes that models have two roles: to record descriptions of the world as it works and to propose requirements about how we want the system to work in the world once it has been implemented. To take one example, if we are designing a lift-control system, we need to describe the indicative requirements such as the need to keep tension in the lift cable to prevent the car from falling down the shaft (indicative requirement) and the need to avoid closing the doors when someone is getting in (optative requirement). We therefore need to model the detectable properties of the lift, such as when it leaves and arrives at a floor, and the devices that we can use to control it, such as the electric motor, and how its response to increased power results in winding the lift cable faster or slower. The problem becomes more complex when we add detecting the open or closed state of the lift doors and the motor's response to different loads in full or empty lifts. Designing software depends heavily on our assumptions and knowledge about the world. Indicative requirements tend to be more stable over time for reuse, whereas optative requirements are prone to change by users.

Jackson has investigated how different connections between software (the *machine* in his terminology) and the world might fall into reuse patterns, which he calls *problem frames*. These are high-level abstractions of problems that specify the necessary type of connection between the system and the real world. Let's take an example. The workpieces frame (Fig. 1.5) describes a range of problems in which there is an object represented inside the computer that undergoes editing operations. Hence the design has to allow for operations to create, change, and

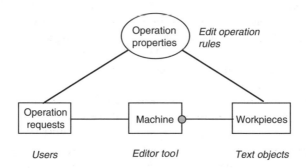

FIG. 1.5. Workpieces problem frame. The abstraction is composed of operational requests that are translated by operation rules and executed on a machine to change the state of workpieces. The instantiation of this abstraction in a word processor is given in italics.

delete the object, as well as display some representation of the object that is inspectable by the user. It doesn't matter whether the object is a word-processing text, a drawing in a graphics package, or a record in a database; the essence of the problem is the same.

Another example is the connection problem frame. In this case there is an object in the outside world that has to be monitored or detected. Events originating from the object have to be detected and then interpreted according to a model of the external world held by the machine. The machine model of the world is then updated and displayed to the user. This abstraction maps to a variety of sensing or monitoring systems such as radar detecting aircraft, sensors in the road detecting the volume of traffic, or the monitoring of a person's heart rate in a hospital intensive care system. Problem frames are a powerful abstraction that guide us into thinking about how constraints imposed by the external world should be treated in software design.

Connections fall into a continuum ranging from software systems that maintain little or no model of the outside world to ones that embed more and more complex models of the world. The connectivity issue is summarized in Fig. 1.6.

Embedded models of the world are necessary for two purposes: first, to interpret the meaning of inbound events and filter out incorrect or unwanted messages; second, to plan action in the world that is appropriate and feasible within constraints imposed by the domain. Embedded models may be either models of the physical world, models of organizations, or models of people. The computer system may

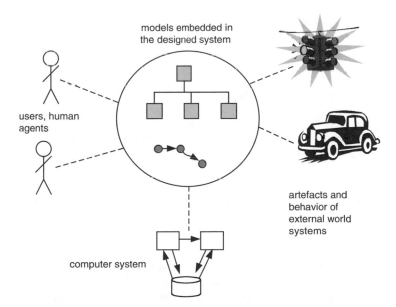

FIG. 1.6. Connections among software systems, the external world, and embedded models.

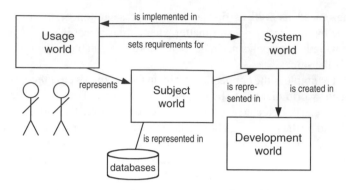

FIG. 1.7. Four worlds model.

also require a model of itself to keep track of its own history and status; furthermore, these models will interact in any one system. A useful framework for investigating the relationship between the system and the external world is the four worlds model originating in the work on NATURE by Jarke, Bubenko, Rolland, Sutcliffe, and Vassiliou (1993), illustrated in Fig. 1.7.

The framework was originally intended to describe the process of system development. It relates the system world to the usage world (where users' requirements originate, and within which the implemented system will be used) with the subject world that models objects in the real world within the system. In the following sections the worlds are elaborated into models of the physical world and data models. The final world is implementation, which contains the processes to transform a design into a working system.

1.7.2. Physical World Models

Physical world models describe physical systems that exist in the real world, and the laws of physics that govern them. One example is the model of a chemical process, which is illustrated in Fig. 1.8.

The model illustrated in Fig. 1.8 implies that the software system has to have a sophisticated view of the world. First it requires a model of the physical layout and connections between the water tanks, inlet and outlet valves, and heater. Second it requires a description of the properties of each system object such as pipes and valve flow rates, tank volume, and so on. The structure and properties of objects are represented in conceptual models of the domain, for example, entity relationship diagrams or object class models in unified modeling language (UML). However, the computer system also requires laws of physics to be embedded as constraints and differential equations that predict the effect of heating on different masses of water, the relationship between flow rates, and mixing of cold and hot water over time to create a uniform temperature. Only when the software is equipped with

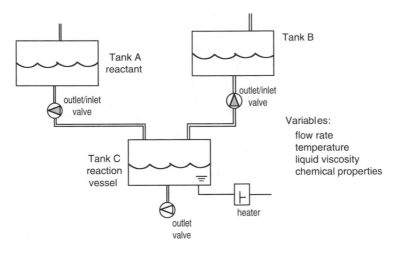

FIG. 1.8.   Model of chemical process-control system.

this mass of information can it hope to control an external system. However, the problem is not yet complete. The computer system also requires a model of its sensors, the temperature and valve status indicators, and how these devices signal changes in the world. For example, is temperature encoded as a bit pattern that can be interpreted as degrees centigrade, or as a frequency pattern that signals departure from a set reference temperature level?

Notice that the design connections to the world and the domain model can have hidden assumptions, which can derail an otherwise sound design. For instance, if the heater has a latency between being switched on and producing heat, then the time the software assumes that it will take to heat up the water will be incorrect.

Physical models may be abstract views of the real world, but that does not mean that they are simple. Many physical systems operate by complex laws, which become embedded in computer software as mathematical equations and algorithms. Take the aforementioned process as an example: modeling this simple system requires complex simultaneous equations to calculate the interaction between flow rates, heat input, and water mass just to control temperature. A less detailed and more abstract view of the system could have been modeled by just describing the controls and sensors, but that would constrain the computer system's control to trial and error. The heater and valves would have to be turned on and off by increments until the desired temperature was reached. This might be acceptable with water, but many chemical reactions have exponential runaway effects. Unless the control system has an embedded model to predict such problems, it will be unsafe. Thus some physical models might be abstract in terms of representing the world in the language of mathematics, but that does not mean they are simple abstractions. A general view of the interaction between software-control systems and external controlled processes is summarized in Fig. 1.9.

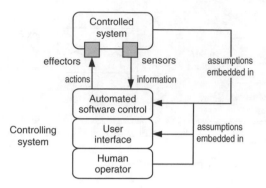

FIG. 1.9. The relationships between controlling and controlled systems.

The software system requires an embedded model of the external world to interpret input events; the model must possess knowledge of the sensory devices so it can interpret their messages and monitor that they are behaving correctly. Because this increases coupling between the software and its context of use, it makes reuse more difficult unless the abstractions can be teased out to separate the views of the system, subject, and usage worlds.

1.7.3. Information Models

Information models have structural components, which describe the organization of people into workgroups, departments, project teams, and so on. The organization of users' work is represented in objects, transactions, events, and agents that record the information about many instances in the real world. However, it is the object's instances that are more important for information processing, so when we model a customer object we are describing a person (or company's) name, address, credit rating, order history, and the like. When we reuse models we load new instances into databases, but we have to be careful that the instances in the new domain fit the types and classes in the reused model.

Computer systems embed abstractions of how people organize business processes. These abstractions are generalizations about how transactions should be carried out, but in the real world things go wrong. There are exceptions and fudges. People have adapted to the inflexibility of computer systems by workarounds and informal processes in the social system. Some exceptions and error paths will be modeled; indeed, use cases and alternative path scenarios in object-oriented design draw attention to the problem (Rational Corporation, 1999), but the dilemma for the requirements analyst is how many exceptions to model. Capturing all the possible errors and alternatives destroys abstract models by infinite detail. One consequence of designing from generalized models can be to increase control and regularity in organizations. The embedded model of work activity, procedures, and transaction processing rules all formalize manual processes that previously existed in a less formal manner. Reuse of ERP systems can illustrate the problems of abstraction and high coupling between the system and usage world. The embedded business model makes people adapt to the system rather than vice versa. Reuse may appear to promote flexibility, but when it comes to implementation, general models have to operate according to specific laws.

1.7.4. Models of People

People models belong to the usage world in two perspectives. First, models of the users are embedded in the system to tune its behavior to individual needs; second, user models attempt to track what the user is doing in the external world while the system is running. Naturally the latter is more ambitious as it entails a form of learning about the world. In both cases the system maintains knowledge about its users either as stereotypes or as individual profiles. Models of people are held by computer systems for a variety of purposes. Supermarket sales systems keep profiles of our purchases and preferences to target advertising to individual tastes. User profiles are kept in training systems so that the content and teaching style can be adapted to the student's needs and progress through the course. User models are used in human–computer interfaces to adapt the interface look and feel to the wishes of individuals.

User models may take an abstract view of humanity at design time, but the information they capture on individuals at run time will be instance-level detail. The rules and procedures for interpreting that information can become complex. Once again there is a trade-off in the detail and level of abstraction. For the computer system to adapt and change its behavior to suit the user, it requires a sophisticated model of the user. This model may be a general description of user stereotypes (e.g., profile of expert or novice); more complex but general models of user psychology, for example, cognitive models of memory are used to structure learning dialogues; or models that capture instance information on individual users, for example, models of a student's mistakes in a tutorial program, or logs of an individual's purchases on websites. The more the system knows about the user, the more able it will be to adapt its behavior to the user's need. However, unless user models can be captured at run time, reuse will be hindered by the close coupling between the system and the original designer's assumptions.

1.7.5. Models of Software

Finally, software has to keep a model of itself so that it can behave in a context-sensitive manner. These system models represent properties of software such as versions for configuration and project management, and events such as power failures that cause system crashes so that recovery procedures can be initiated.

The model in this case is an abstraction of the design itself; however, as with other models, although the schema may be general, instance information has to be kept for status records; for example, programs maintain state vectors and pointers for reentrant routines.

1.7.6. Acquiring and Updating Models

In most systems the model is created by the designer. Unfortunately, models rapidly become out of date and designers have a limited amount of time they can spend in modeling the world. Hence designers try to make their system models change by acquiring more information from the environment. Ultimately this leads to learning systems that can infer new facts about the world with induction algorithms from knowledge they already possess. The generic architecture of updateable models is illustrated in Fig. 1.10.

To update its model, the system requires some means of capturing and interpreting events from the external world. This means that the system requires data to interpret the events it detects in the external world. These metadata present another level of abstraction. In model updating, metadata are a more abstract view of the world that is used in weak or stronger forms of learning, that is, inferences made about raw data that become new knowledge. In simple cases, frequency counts of events can suffice for weak learning. For example, to update a user model the system might count the number of errors a user made with particular commands;

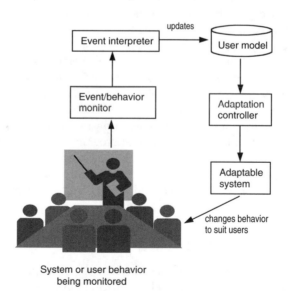

FIG. 1.10. Architecture for updateable and adaptable models, with interpreter, inference, and model update components.

if the error rate decreases, the system infers that the user has become an expert and exposes him or her to more sophisticated functions. Slightly more sophisticated systems have pattern recognizers, so regular sequences of events can be detected and then inferences drawn. An example here is to log my usage pattern in e-mail and automatically create filters for junk mail that I never read.

The problem with adaptable systems is keeping them from being too smart for their own good. System initiative and suggestions based on user profiles can often annoy rather than help users. Unfortunately, interpreting user behavior is fraught with difficulties. For example, the number of errors might be influenced by users' exploring new functions that they do not intend to use, or one user may have loaned his or her log-on ID to another, who then makes more mistakes. The software system's limited ability to monitor the real world hinders the fidelity of inferences it can make. Adaptation is impaled on the horns of a reuse dilemma. Adding more knowledge about the domain hinders reuse by increasing the coupling with the components' original design context; however, general-purpose learning mechanisms require considerable metaknowledge to be effective. Modeling metaknowledge for learning is another challenge for abstraction in knowledge acquisition and reuse.

1.8. OUTLINE OF THE REUSE PROCESS

All reuse has to start with acquisition of knowledge. Knowledge acquisition is a time-consuming process, whether it is acquisition of best practice, strategies, or specifications of design components. Indeed, the knowledge-acquisition bottleneck is one of the serious barriers to reuse. The acquisition cost of reuse may be acceptable if products and artefacts constitute the reusable objects, but documentation is usually necessary for reuser–designers to understand the functionality and structure of components. Only in narrow vertical domains where reuse is closer to product evolution does the acquisition cost diminish, primarily because the reusable knowledge resides in the head of the designer who is usually also the reuser of the artefact. Of course, this is no consolation to management when designers leave the company. One of the prime business drivers for knowledge reuse is preservation of transient knowledge held inside employees' memories. Acquisition of unstructured knowledge is much more expensive. Strategies, plans, and heuristics are often tacit knowledge that we take for granted. Eliciting unstructured (nondesign) knowledge for reuse is a time consuming, skilled process of teasing out useful ideas from experts who may be unaware that they possess them.

Acquisition of knowledge is rarely sufficient on its own. Most of our experience comes in the form or examples, scenarios, and specific designs, so the knowledge we acquire has to be transformed so it can relate to a wider view of the world. Knowledge, specifications, and designs have to be designed for reuse. This involves generalizing the knowledge so that it is easier to reapply in a new context, and then formatting it in a manner such that it can be retrieved and understood by the reuser. Once components have been acquired and designed, they have to be classified. Indexing and describing knowledge and components is also resource intensive. The designer is usually the person best placed to fulfill this role because he or she will have the most comprehensive knowledge of the component. Unfortunately, designers, especially software engineers, are notoriously bad documenters. Moreover, indexing and documentation is a skill in its own right. Some organizations assign the indexing role to information scientists and technical writers, but this runs the risk of misunderstanding across the designer–documenter gap.

Designed and indexed components are placed in a reuse library. The next step is matching requirements for the new application (or knowledge reuse context) to components in the library. This step involves information retrieval, but it can be difficult because reusers have to first articulate their needs in detail and then understand the reusable components in depth. Establishing a good match between the requirements and reusable components depends on how well they are documented in the first place. Once components have been retrieved, design by reuse can commence. This involves understanding and applying reusable knowledge either in business strategy, process improvement, or product design. When we reuse our own thoughts they are usually located in a rich network of associations, so we naturally understand them; indeed, we don't refer to reuse of our own memory. However, when we reuse other people's memories, the network of associations may not be in place, so we have to reason to understand the connections between what we already know and the concepts and components we are trying to reuse. The psychology of this process is dealt with in more depth in chapter 3. The outline of the reuse process is given in Fig. 1.11. Each stage of the process encounters barriers to reuse, both social and technical, which are described in the next section.

1.9. BARRIERS TO SUCCESS

There are several reasons why reuse can fail. First of all, we need a clear motivation for reuse. Reuse for reuse's sake achieves nothing, except possibly perpetuating some bad designs. The real motivators for reuse are to share good ideas, that is, best practice, to save time and costs by developing products from ready-made components, to improve the design process by reuse of good ideas and templates, and to improve quality by designing with certified, reliable components. Many causes of reuse program failure lie in the social domain. Even though we reuse our own knowledge every day of our lives, and education encourages us to reuse knowledge from others, in many professional domains egos get in the way of reuse. The NIH (Not Invented Here) syndrome makes people distrust other people's advice and designs. Similarly, we are reticent to share our ideas with others. The social barrier here is the lack of a reward structure. Why should we work so others

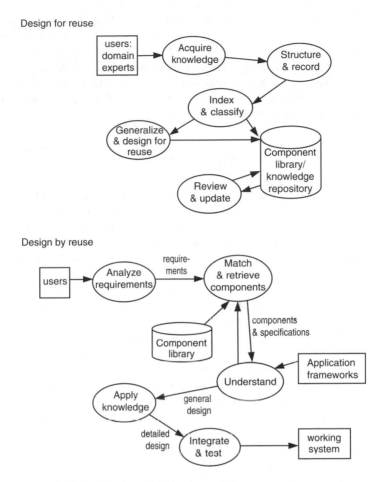

FIG. 1.11. A cognitive view of the reuse process.

can benefit for free? Management has to counteract these barriers by using the following policies.

- Process improvement incentive schemes: designers and managers have to be given rewards for designing for reuse and reusing knowledge leading to improvements in process efficiency and product quality. Rewards are particularly important during the early stages of reuse when the library is being created and early success stories are needed to motivate others.
- Counteract the NIH syndrome by giving adequate recognition for authoring reusable knowledge and rewarding application of reuse. Demonstrator projects and task groups can help to persuade others to adopt more open approaches to reuse.

- Clarify ownership, copyright, and privacy issues. Copyright on components has to be settled so that ownership is not subject to litigation. Reuse can also raise privacy and security issues if the knowledge or design components embed sensitive knowledge. Another consideration is reliability and accuracy. Reusable knowledge and designs may not always attain the quality standards claimed by their authors. Use of reference sites, pilot projects, and reliable, authenticated sources help.

An entertaining exposition on experiences and more detail on motivating reuse and managing it can be found in Tracz's book (1995). In addition to the social barriers, reuse has technical barriers to overcome. The acquisition bottleneck is difficult to address; however, techniques for knowledge elicitation can help (Maiden & Rugg, 1994) and tools (hypertext, list managers, drawing packages) can make production of documentation easier. Design for reuse has some support in software development from object-oriented methods that give guidelines for creating generalized classes from more specific components (Coad, North, & Mayfield, 1995). However, tool support is limited. Indexing and documentation may be supported by controlled vocabularies, thesauri, and methods from information science, although these still require people to describe components. Semiautomatic indexing tools can be used to classify components according to their content, but the sophistication of these tools depends on their knowledge of the domain (Cowie & Wilks, 2000). This leads back to the knowledge-acquisition bottleneck.

Tool support is easier for organization of the reuse component library and subsequent component retrieval. Database management systems can be adapted for reuse repository managers, and query languages and information retrieval tools can help searching for suitable components. Finally, application of reuse can be helped by computer-aided software engineering (CASE) tools, for validating and consistency checking of designs, although in knowledge management, reusers have to interpret the knowledge for themselves.

Tool and method support for reuse requires considerable improvement. In this chapter, one part of the process, indexing and classifying components, is reviewed in more depth because this also describes one of the dimensions of the reuse problem. The other issues are taken up in subsequent chapters.

1.10. CLASSIFYING COMPONENTS

A common problem for all reuse approaches is organizing the component library. Partitioning the world for reuse is not new. Indeed, information scientists have been categorizing the world since Linnaeus. Classification standards in information science have been agreed on for many years, for example, the Dewey Decimal Classification (DDC), Library of Congress, and Universal Decimal Classification (UDC) systems. However, these standards classify knowledge and published literature, but they do not control the content of a library book, which is still at the author's discretion. Two main methods for indexing or organizing knowledge have evolved and have been adopted by developers of reuse libraries.

The first method is hierarchical classification, in which each item belongs to one and only one class. Most library classification schemes are strict hierarchies, such as the DDC or UDC systems. The index expresses an access path through the hierarchy allowing easy retrieval; thus 004 points to computer science in the DDC schema. The disadvantage with hierarchical schemas is that when new items evolve that don't fit into the old view of the world, the schema has to be changed. DDC has undergone over 20 revisions in 100 years, and only recently computer science was changed from 001.6 (largely data processing, occupying two pages of the schedules) to the 25 pages of 004 through 006.78.

The second method is the description of items by a controlled vocabulary. Items are described by a set of terms picked from a thesaurus or controlled vocabulary. Thesauri have classification structures of their own organizing descriptive terms in hierarchies, for example, animals—mammals—primates, with synonyms and related terms at each level, for example, primates-monkeys. Descriptions may be formatted into a faceted classification schema that dictates the keywords that are permissible for each slot or facet of the schema; for instance, software components are often described with a schema with facets for function, data structures, platform, language, and application area (Prieto-Diaz, 1991). The use of several indexing terms allows a richer description of components and more flexible searching.

An alternative to classification and indexing is to rely on search of a component's contents. If the component is organized according to a specification language, then types in the language can be used to search models or source code. When components contain narrative text, searching can use algorithms that pattern match components against an example text. These search algorithms use statistical techniques to match the density and frequency distribution in one or more documents to produce goodness-of-fit metrics, for example, Latent Semantic Indexing (Landauer & Dumais, 1997), or algorithms that use a multiple strategy approach (Chi, Pirolli, & Pitkow, 2000). The use of similarity-based searching avoids one of the resource bottlenecks of knowledge reuse: the effort and skill required for indexing components.

Search and retrieval are key functions in reuse support environments. Finding appropriate design components of reusable knowledge can be supported either by query languages or by representing the indexing and classification structure explicitly as hypertext. The whole structure can be shown as a hypertext map to enable browsing. Searching ideally has to be supported by a mixture of active tools and interactive visualizations in the form of hypertext and concept maps. Representations can facilitate retrieval at the metadata and database level: concept maps of thesauri and classification structures can help the user browse metadata and form queries by pointing to terms and concepts. In contrast, hypertexts of the database contents are particularly appropriate for knowledge reuse when a rich structure of relationships can be implemented to provide users with different pathways through the knowledge, for example, novice versus expert view, links for designers or managers, and the like. Design of hypertext implies analyzing the relationships between components as well as indexing and classifying them.

Describing and classifying components is one of the most time-consuming tasks in the reuse process, and it is difficult and error prone. One person's view rarely coincides with another's because the context or interpretation of a component or piece of knowledge will differ. This can make library classification schemes frustrating to work with. The perspective of the component designer, who is usually the classifier, may well be very different from that of the reuser; consequently, access by means of description alone is insufficient. Multiple means of finding appropriate components are necessary.

1.11. CLASSIFYING KNOWLEDGE

More fundamental classifications have been researched in theories of knowledge, commonly called *ontologies*. These have proposed building blocks from which all information and knowledge can be constructed. These classifications originated in linguistics as a means of describing the components of narrative text in terms of their logical content or argument. An influential theory is Rhetorical Structure Theory (RST; Mann & Thompson, 1988), which classifies text components, or, to be exact, the relationships between components, such as

Elaboration: detail of any argument.
Enablement: procedures and how-to knowledge.
Result: effects of an event or action.
Evaluation: of an argument, quality of an object.
Motivation: persuasive argument for a proposal.
Justification: evidence or facts to back up an argument.
Solutionhood: description of a problem solution.

RST has 22 relationship types that classify text components according to their role or function in communication. This classification has been extended by several researchers to produce ontologies that categorize knowledge in any medium. A synthesis of several previous ontologies by Arens, Hovy, and Vossers (1993) gave a hierarchical schema with 33 primitive categories. The primitive components can then be used to construct larger chunks or patterns of generalized knowledge. Another leading example of this tradition is the Conceptual Structures Theory (Sowa, 1984). The theory proposes that all linguistically constructed meaning can be generated by combination of 22 conceptual relationships, such as agent, object, event, state, time, location, space, and so on, with an open-ended set of objects. The lexicon of objects is left undefined, but it could be supplied by the set of concepts in a standardized semantic lexicon. An example conceptual structure is illustrated in

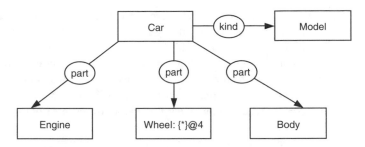

FIG. 1.12. Conceptual structure graph. The relationships (kind-of, part-of) are supplied by the modeling language; the objects (car, wheel, body, etc.) are defined in a semantic lexicon.

Fig. 1.12. This shows the relationship between a small number of concepts that are realized as a knowledge structure. Conceptual structures can be applied to models of designed phenomena, and they represent the semantics of software-engineering specification languages: states, events, actions, attributes, and so on.

Classification, indexing, and description are ultimately a continuum from data that are added to the database (or component library) to describe components, to schema that specify how components should be designed and documented in the first place. The approach adopted will depend on the reuse process. When knowledge is reused informally as advice, the contents of components are more likely to be informally documented. Reuse occurs through a process of interpreting and assimilating knowledge during problem solving. Documentation is a time-consuming process so indexing may not be elaborate, although this imposes a penalty in the future when finding appropriate knowledge to reuse is difficult, as demonstrated in many Internet searches. When the contents of components are reused more directly as specifications or software products, then specification and documentation have to be more exact. More effort can be expended in searching for appropriate components and reuse has to be standardized to enable designers to share the understanding of components. Thus reuse has many trade-offs, which will be dealt with in more depth in chapter 2.

In later chapters we inquire how people form memories of problems they have solved in the past and the commonalities between them. If people have naturally developed common patterns by learning and sharing their knowledge with colleagues, then there is a prospect that we can borrow the tenets of their approach to develop a theory of knowledge representation for software engineering.

1.12. SUMMARY

The history of reuse was reviewed. Reuse in many industries has been successful because components have been standardized. Progress in software has been hindered by the lack of standards, although collections of components such as patterns, ERPs, and user-interface widgets have been developed. To be successful, software reuse requires a sound theory that guides design of components at the appropriate level of abstraction and granularity.

A general framework for reuse was introduced that examined how the reuse of components depends on the formality or informality of the documentation. The framework separates reuse into three levels for business requirements, software design, and system software, and it indicates dimensions of reuse within and across domains.

The process of design for and design by reuse was introduced. Design for reuse involves creating generalized components and then indexing them in a reuse library. Indexing components uses methods from information science: classification, categorization, and search processes that either use the index or match text for knowledge components. The design by reuse process involves problems of understanding components, designing architectures, and then interpreting components for a new design. Barriers to reuse are social and technical.

Abstraction is not a simple matter of creating a generalized view of a domain that is used for design. The level of abstraction and scope of the modeled phenomena depend on the system requirements, and the relationship between the system and the external world. Computer systems have to maintain models of the external world to help them interpret events coming from the world and adapt their behavior. Adaptation enables a single generic system to fit the needs of individual users, variations in tasks, or different event patterns, so one abstract design can deal with the variety inherent in the world. However, adaptation poses a dilemma. The greater the power of adaptation, the more the computer has to know about the world, and that means a closer coupling with the external world. Embedding more detailed and hence less abstract models makes software less reusable.

2

Conceptual Foundations
for Reuse

Chapter 1 introduced some of the problems that successful reuse will have to solve. In this chapter these problems are explored in more depth for their implications for software and knowledge reuse. A framework for evaluating different reuse approaches is introduced with metrics that enable the merits of different approaches to be compared. Two current approaches, object-oriented patterns (Gamma et al., 1995) and ERPs (Keller & Teufel, 1998), are compared with generic models from the Domain Theory (Sutcliffe & Maiden, 1998) and design rationale (MacLean, Young, Bellotti, & Moran, 1991). The first three approaches provide software components and design for reuse; design rationale provides a more general representation for reusable knowledge. In this comparison I focus on the components or basic level of reuse in each of these approaches. Of course this is a simplified view, as each approach has a superstructure that guides the use of components, so patterns may have a pattern language, although this is not true of the gang of four patterns (Gamma et al., 1995). ERPs have resource families and modules within the families, whereas the Domain Theory and design rationale tackle higher-order structuring by a process of aggregation.

2.1. REUSE PARADIGMS

At the most general level, design knowledge is reused in methods, models, and techniques. Design methods contain process knowledge, a reusable agenda of issues and heuristics for organizing the design process. Models provide ready-made and standardized ways of representing the design problem. Techniques offer more detailed procedures to solve discrete problems such as normalizing data structures or optimizing algorithms. However, this level of reuse does not provide advice on any particular application; furthermore, the product has to be built from scratch. Guidelines do give more detailed design advice on a specific problem, but to make real savings in design time, reusable designs are necessary. Reusable designs save more time if they are ready to run code; unfortunately, executable software components frequently don't suit our purposes exactly. More flexibility comes with reusable specifications and design patterns that can be tailored before coding. Savings can be made at each stage of the life cycle, although the earlier that reuse can be achieved, the greater the saving. These savings can be summarized as follows.

- Requirements reuse, models of the domain, and generic models of require-ments specification: these save time in analyzing the problem and in providing reusable definitions of requirements.
- Design reuse, models, data structures, and algorithms that provide ready-made solutions for requirements: if designs are specified formally, tools can generate code automatically.
- Software components exist in several forms, such as editable source code, executable dynamic link libraries, and reusable software classes.

Some reuse paradigms, such as ERPs, provide support at all three stages. This is important because reuse is predicated on first understanding the new application problem. First the new system has to be analyzed and then the solution specified before it can be implemented. Reuse of requirements knowledge can accelerate the process of problem understanding, whereas specification and design reuse gives ready-made and reliable solutions, which save more development time if they are linked to reusable software code.

Reuse can only survive if libraries of reusable components have been built up. This involves design in the sense of design *for* reuse, which is the process of creating generalized and abstract components in the first place. Design *by* reuse then applies components in new designs, usually by specializing them. The ap-proach to design for reuse (generalization of components) and design by reuse has been influenced by trends in traditional software engineering. Structured system-development methods that dominated commercial systems development in the 1970s and 1980s, for example, SSADM, structured analysis and design tech-nique (SADT; Ross & Schoman, 1977), and SA/SD (De Marco, 1978), advocated functional analysis. Not surprisingly, reuse methods followed suit and functionally oriented component libraries were developed (Arango et al., 1993). More recent object-oriented methods advocated a different, more structural, modeling approach, so object-oriented reuse libraries follow that concept. Object-oriented development implied reuse within the approach of creating generalization–specialization class hierarchies and reuse by inheritance; however, reuse receives only minor attention in UML (Rational Corporation, 1999), and other object-oriented methods, for example, object-oriented analysis (Coad & Yourdon, 1991). Some advice is given about creating general classes and then subsequently reusing them by specialization, but the main thrust of UML and most methods assumes modeling new applications and development from scratch.

Traditional definitions have distinguished between *black-box* and *white-box* reuse. These definitions depend on the visibility and accessibility of a reusable component. That is, black-box modules do not make their contents visible, so the designers only have access to a set of interfaces. Black-box reuse is the common mode in hardware in which details of microcode and processor internals are not accessible to the designer. This reuse approach is true component-based engineering. White box reuse allows the designer access to the module's internal components and permits modification. Some authors also refer to *glass-box* reuse, which makes contents visible but not editable. The white-box reuse processes may involve the customization of code as well as configuration of components.

Ideally, reuse should be black box. It reduces complexity and the learning burden on the designer. Communication with the component is restricted to a few, (ideally) well-designed interfaces. Unfortunately, software reuse has not had a good track record of producing black-box components. Two factors have militated against this. First is the description problem. Software is very flexible, so this makes describing the many possible applications and behaviors a module might undertake a complex job. It is easier to let reusers have access to the code and reason about how a component works for themselves. Second is the problem of producing a set of well-designed interfaces. The interface tends to reflect the component designer's assumptions about what the module could and should do. This may limit its future potential. Furthermore, although making interfaces more complex might unlock more of a module's functionality, it also worsens the reuser's understanding of the problem. Complex interfaces also make the module less reliable because there are more interacting effects to go wrong. In spite of these limitations, black-box modules are reused by means of APIs, for example graphics libraries in programming language environments. Design by reuse may take two routes: one is to leave the code untouched and deal with intercomponent incompatibilities by bridging functions (Goguen, 1986); the other is to change the component's code to make it more compatible with the new application requirements.

Design by reuse aims to create a new application that fits the users' requirements. Inevitably, existing components do not fit the new requirements completely, so pure black-box reuse is not always possible. The fit between user requirements and design components can be achieved in three ways. The first is to compose the new application by choosing the appropriate mix of reusable components. If the component designs are sufficiently close to the user requirements then black-box reuse is possible, for example in hardware component-based design. The second is to compose the new application as aforementioned but in white-box mode, so that the code is customized to meet the requirements. The third is to make components adaptable so they can be configured to meet the requirements.

All three approaches may be used to achieve design by reuse. In a white-box reuse approach the component's code is inspectable and modifiable so reusers–designers can customize the software exactly to their requirements, albeit by expending more effort. Reuse-driven development may involve developing application-specific "glue" code to coordinate a set of reused components. Adaptation involves designing the components so that their behavior can be changed by parameters either at design time or run time. This includes setting up parameter files (e.g., user profiles) that are used to customize the software's behavior, format of output, and user-interface dialogue. Another perspective is to see adaptation as being more suitable for end-user development because it does not require technical expertise to customize software by means of parameter files; in contrast, composing applications by means of component engineering is more appropriate for software engineers because technical design skills are necessary.

Knowledge management reuse has to be white-box because the contents of knowledge components are free format or possibly semistructured. Knowledge has to be understood before it can be applied in a new reuse context. Reuse contexts are more varied than for software design, and they may vary from strategic, tactical to operational levels of management as well as provide frameworks for business requirements.

In the next section the design criteria for building a reuse library are considered, with the impact of trade-offs between these criteria on costs and the design process.

2.2. DESIGN CRITERIA FOR REUSE

The two principal criteria, *abstraction* and *granularity*, are motivated by the reuse problem posed in chapter 1. Abstraction is the selective removal or hiding of information deemed to be of diminished importance with respect to a particular perspective, concern, or focus (EASYCOMP, 2000). Hence abstraction involves reducing detail while retaining the essence from a particular viewpoint. In reuse the dilemma is deciding just what the viewpoint should be. Abstraction and granularity are not completely orthogonal. A highly abstract component will have little detail and may reflect a large application area; indeed, the generic class "system" would be highly abstract and have a large chunk size in terms of granularity. However, abstraction and granularity are separate design decisions. Granularity is the consequence of partitioning the system into larger or smaller components, whereas abstraction

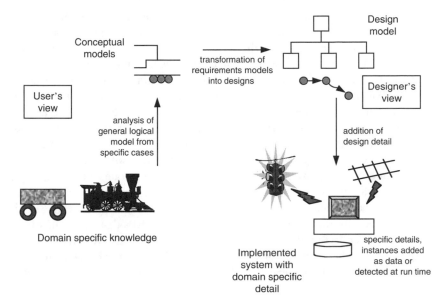

FIG. 2.1. Abstraction in the design process and transformation of views.

is a decision about detail. Abstraction is generally taken to be the generalization of components; however, it has another dimension from requirements to design. When design commences, problems are described as requirements specifications that users can understand. As design progresses, the problem is transformed from an abstract model of the external world into another abstract model of a design solution. This abstraction can be understood by designers but means little to the users. Finally, the abstract design model is specialized during implementation to create a designed system that works in the world. Abstraction therefore forms a bridge between requirements and design, but it often has two views: the user's view and the designer's view; see Fig. 2.1.

The separation of views and the starting point for abstraction depends on the layer of reuse described in chapter 1, Fig. 1.3. When middleware components are designed for reuse, the original designer and reuser can share the same specification language and hence can readily understand a common set of abstractions. This is not the case in layer 1 for requirements reuse, when users and designers do not share the same specification language. Indeed users may not understand abstractions at all, and they may prefer to think in concrete terms. This transformation from problem descriptions to design solutions will be referred to as the *abstraction context*. The abstraction context is interpreted in two senses. First, abstractions can be created to describe the problem that has to be solved or the solution to that problem. This is the process dimension from requirements to design. Second, abstractions can describe problems that users would recognize in their world, whereas other problems (e.g., network protocols) are meaningful only to software engineers (layers 2 and 3).

In software, examples of domain abstractions are sales-order processing for users, and middleware components for handling updates in distributed databases for engineers. In architecture the analogy is building design patterns (c.f. Alexander et al., 1977) and abstractions of materials used in building (joists, beams, or concrete components). The abstraction context will set the context for reuse and influence the communication barrier between different roles in the design process. The abstraction context is also related to the anticipated market for reusable components, for example, applications, middleware, or system software.

In the following discussion a framework for reuse is elaborated that accounts for abstraction, granularity, context, and other criteria. These are used to compare three different reuse approaches: object-oriented reuse in patterns (Gamma et al., 1995) as an exemplar but not representative of all patterns; ERPs that represent white-box reuse (Keller & Teufel, 1998); and Object System Models (OSMs; Sutcliffe & Maiden, 1998) that represent an object-oriented view of reuse but at the requirements rather than the design level. OSMs are described in more depth in chapter 4.

2.2.1. Abstraction

Abstraction, crudely, is the loss of detail to model a more general view of the world. It is a tricky concept, so let us start with the Oxford English Dictionary definition of *abstract*: "to separate in mental conception, to consider apart from the concrete, separated from the concrete, ideal, abstruse". In a psychological sense, which is elaborated in the next chapter, we abstract information from data by a process of chunking that establishes more general patterns from a mass of low-level detail. Abstraction lies at the heart of our reasoning and memory processes. When we learn, we analyze important facts but discard the rest. Our memory is selective, so we abstract the essential information about a problem or event and store the abstract model.

In computer science, abstraction is achieved by generalization. This derives classes from specific objects, and general data structures and algorithms from concrete examples. General models are used to represent phenomena in the real world. Conceptual models in development methods create abstract views by using the semantic constructs of entities, attributes, events, states, actions, and control structures. Formal specification languages create abstract models by defining these semantics more precisely and add more rigorous definitions for action sequences by using temporal and deontic logics (Van Lamsweerde & Letier, 2000).

The choice of how generic a pattern or class should be depends on the intended reuse target. The higher level of abstraction, the less detail a class or model possesses; hence the larger the size of the potential reuse target. This can be thought of as a reuse spotlight (Fig. 2.2): higher levels of abstraction illuminate a wider target; the penalty, however, is less detail.

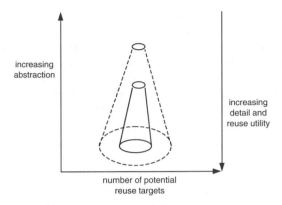

increasing
abstraction

increasing
detail and
reuse utility

number of potential
reuse targets

FIG. 2.2.   Abstraction reuse spotlight.

The level of abstraction trade-off is between the utility delivered to designers and the number of potential reusers, as expressed in the following formula:

$$N^{\mathrm{app}} f [L^{\mathrm{abs}} - (Ut^{\mathrm{des}} \times St)]$$

where

N^{app} is the estimated future number of reusable applications in a set
          reuse context–market sector,
L^{abs} is the level of abstraction,
Ut^{des} is the estimated average utility of the reusable component for the
          designer in a new application, and
St is the estimated stability of the abstracted component over time.

The formula can be used by substituting appropriate metrics, for example, utility is measured on a 0 to 1 scale, where 1 = high utility, to estimate either the level of abstraction required for a desired number of reuse targets or conversely how many targets are probable given a set level of design abstraction. Abstraction can be judged from the number of generic data structures and methods possessed by the class. Ut^{des} reflects development time savings observed for components with a similar level of abstraction, whereas N^{app} can be based on sales volume or market-share estimates in a domain. Accurate estimates of the number of application targets are not the prime purpose of applying the formula. This would require considerable case-study research to collect data to calibrate the model. The purpose is more limited. It provides a summary of the dependencies between reuse issues and a tool for thought that can be used to carry out a trade-off analysis between the design parameters in reuse.

Higher levels of abstraction increase the number of potential reusable applications within a context because the components have less detail and hence may fit a wider range of new application targets. Higher abstraction may also allow longer range reuse across domains and contexts. The disadvantage is that utility decreases as less detail is delivered to the designer. Stability affects utility because it reflects the correspondence between the reusable component and changes in the real-world requirements over time. Stability tends to be lower in layer 1 requirements reuse where it is susceptible to change in the user's external world, but it is higher in layer 2 and 3 design-level reuse where design abstractions are used by a smaller set of users. Business-oriented systems change, for instance sales-order processing over the Internet has changed the conventional model, and updates to tax laws make payroll systems unstable. Solution-oriented abstractions (layer 2) may be stable in well-known domains, for example, finite-element analysis, but less so where research and innovation are active (e.g., atmospheric modeling). If there are many changes to the source abstraction, stability will be low and the reuse value in terms of utility will decrease because many changes to the component will make it less reliable. Ideally, well-formed abstractions of problems should be stable.

Some problem domains are likely to remain more stable than others. For instance, the Domain Theory Object System Model (OSM) family that deals with object sensing describes problems (and some solutions) for detecting and monitoring changes in the world. This problem is grounded in the laws of physics, so it will probably remain constant for some time. In contrast, the OSM families and ERPs that deal with inventory and sales may be less stable as new forms of business evolve, for example, Internet trading.

Armed with these measures, the level of abstraction and reuse in generic models can be assessed. We start with ERPs that are general models of business solutions for common problems such as procurement, production, sales, and accounting. The level of abstraction is low to moderate because ERP modules possess many control variables and parameters, complex data structures, and methods. The abstraction context is layer 1 requirements across vertical-market sectors (e.g., procurement ERPs could be applied in manufacturing and banking organizations). This is achieved by some sacrifice of utility and customization. ERPs do not address more specialized applications within vertical markets (e.g., derivatives trading in the finance sector), although more specialized sector ERPs are beginning to emerge. ERPs require considerable effort to tailor implementations for any one business (see Table 2.1). For instance, ERPs for sales order processing cannot be

TABLE 2.1
Comparison of Abstraction Properties of ERPs, Patterns, and OSMs

Paradigm	Abstraction	Application Target	Stability	Utility Delivered	Abs. Context–Reuse Level
ERPs	low-medium	medium	low	high	1 requirements, business
Patterns	high	high	high	medium	3 middleware, software design
OSMs	high	high	high	low	1 software requirements

immediately implemented; instead, the appropriate modules must be selected and adapted by carrying out a business analysis to create a specialized blueprint for the organisation (Keller & Teufel, 1998). The scope of reuse for any one ERP module is low, but this limitation is overcome by having large libraries of modules that cover many different application domains. ERPs deliver considerable detail and hence utility for the designer in the form of reusable models and software components.

Patterns, in contrast, score higher on abstraction but deliver less utility as they are small-scale design solutions, as illustrated in Fig. 2.3. Patterns may be composed into higher-order solutions by means of a pattern language, but here we are considering a set of isolated patterns exemplified by Gamma et al. (1995). Object-oriented design patterns have a high level of abstraction because they contain only a few simple methods and data structures with no domain specific references. The abstraction context is layer 2 and 3 reuse. There is little reference to an application domain description in either methods or data structures. The potential reuse target is high as design-level patterns may apply in nearly any software domain that

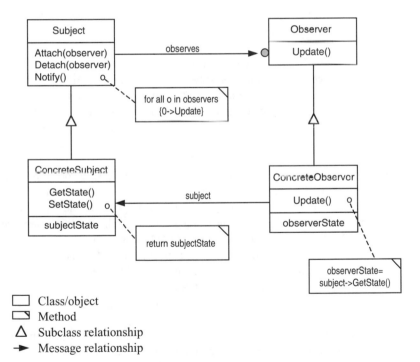

Class/object
Method
Δ   Subclass relationship
➡   Message relationship

FIG. 2.3. Observer pattern defines a one-to-many relationship between the observer object and other subject objects so that when a state change occurs in one object all its dependents are notified and updated.

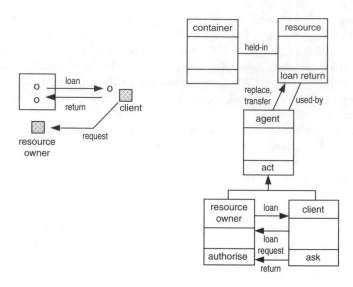

FIG. 2.4. OSM from the Domain Theory for the Object Hiring family (loans, hiring, and rental applications).

requires its services. The delivered utility is medium as each pattern only provides a high-level abstract specification, possibly accompanied by a template implementation in software, and patterns require considerable tailoring and specialization. Patterns only address software design problems, so the connection to requirements and business goals necessitates more analysis effort than OSMs or ERPs.

OSMs from the Domain Theory (Sutcliffe & Maiden, 1998), described in chapter 4, are highly abstract views of problems in reuse context layer 1. The higher level of abstraction allows the Object Hiring model (Fig. 2.4) to appear as a component in several ERPs (e.g., asset management, plant hire, or procurement) that all contain the same resource hiring problem. OSMs possess a few parameters, controls, and only simple methods and data structures. The domain reference is stronger than that for design patterns because OSMs describe generalized views of requirements rather than solutions. The application target of OSMs is also wide as they can be reused within many business sectors and apply to engineering domains not covered by ERPs. The disadvantage of OSMs lies in lower utility as each model only gives a high-level problem description with design rationale pointers toward design solutions.

Patterns are better insulated against change in the requirements world but design solutions are still prone to change in technology, for instance if object orientation is replaced by agent oriented approaches (Yu, Mylopoulos, & Lesperance, 1996). Overall they score well on stability. OSMs are closer to the external world, so they may be more prone to change and stability problems but less susceptible to technology change. Their high level of abstraction should insulate them from change in detail of business processes, albeit at the expense of utility. ERPs illustrate the converse trade-off. They are more prone to change simply because they are larger, more complex, and specialized, but they deliver more utility for the designer and can partially deal with change by parameterization. The highly abstract patterns and Domain Theory models have a higher N^{app} and stability but deliver relatively low utility; ERPs offer the converse. Note that the value of N^{app} tends to be increased by deeper layers of reuse; that is, a layer 2 pattern (e.g., Facade) can be applied as part of a solution as an interface filter in many different layer 1 applications.

Although the Domain Theory models have a high level of abstraction, their context in layer 1 reduces their utility for a designer who wants a ready-made solution. For instance, it is easier to posit a model of generic, cooperating objects for a loans–hiring application (i.e., resource, client objects, hiring agent, with events for loans, returns, etc.) than it is to specify a generic retrieval algorithm that matches users' requirements to properties of appropriate resources. Although patterns do have the merit of providing a solution, they incur a cost of mapping to requirements in the application domain, so software engineering has to know that requirements for typical monitoring applications, for example, road traffic sensors, could be implemented by using an observer pattern. There is no silver bullet in reuse. Ideally, a reuse library with mappings between requirements abstractions (OSMs) and design abstractions (patterns) could be more effective than the more monolithic, less abstract ERPs. Unfortunately no such mappings in a reuse library exist, although application frameworks (Fayad & Johnson, 2000) attempt to bridge this gap.

ERPs try to overcome their poor abstraction by adapting components through parameterization of methods, although the flexibility of their algorithms is often limited. Patterns and OSMs provide more structural and procedural abstraction, although object-oriented patterns (Gamma et al., 1995) do not provide generic methods for tasks such as scheduling, matching, searching, and the like. Task-related patterns are described in the Domain Theory library (see chapter 5) and have been proposed in the knowledge-engineering literature for problem classes such as diagnosis and planning, for example, KADS (Wilenga, Van der Velde, Schreiber, & Akkermans, 1993). Both OSMs and patterns handle complex applications by composition, whereas ERPs require more customization and adaptation to fit complex applications.

Knowledge-management reuse is represented by design rationale. Judgments of abstraction are not included in Table 2.1 because components' contents depend on the abstraction and reuse context. General reusable business knowledge will be less stable than design knowledge because trends in business practice are susceptible to management fads (Earl & Kahn, 1994). One only has to consider the glut of advice on business process reengineering, total quality management, concurrent engineering, and business evolution, to name but a few schools of thought. The knowledge created by investigations into business practice tends to be high-level strategies, heuristics, and examples. For instance, the writings on business processing reengineering (Davenport, 1993; Hammer & Champy, 1993) leave the reader to extract the generalizable knowledge from examples. The few principles and heuristics that are offered, "revolutionary restructuring not evolution, customer orientation, downsizing for flexibility, etc.", are already passé and viewed as suspect advice. In contrast, some business advice will be more stable; for instance, the principles of accountancy and sound finance have changed little over many years. The utility level of knowledge reuse is also lower than design because advice is often couched in general terms either as abstract principles or as case studies and examples that the reuser has to interpret. Case studies are very specific and leave the effort of abstracting general advice to the user.

2.2.2. Granularity

Functional points are used to judge component complexity, which feeds into assessing granularity and the level of abstraction. More abstract components tend to have fewer methods and hence fewer function points. However, if the level of abstraction is approximately equal, a larger component should have more function points. Function points are widely used to measure complexity of software and specifications. Although they are not an ideal measure, function points at least are widely used and understood (Garmus & Herron, 1996). Alternatives are to use software-complexity metrics (e.g., McCabe, 1976); more complex components will tend to be larger (higher granularity) and have lower abstraction. Object-oriented patterns are usually small, typically two to four cooperating classes, and have a small number of methods and few input–output variables; hence they have few function points. In contrast, ERPs and application frameworks are larger and composed of many objects and methods. Each ERP component within a sector framework (e.g., calculate insurance deductions within the payroll framework) usually has several methods, inputs, and outputs; consequently they have more function points. Hence granularity depends on the complexity of an application and the size of the reuse unit. Function-point complexity is also increased by customization facilities because further input parameters and methods are necessary to configure report formats, screen layouts, and algorithms.

The potential flexibility of components at a certain chunk (granularity) size will also be influenced by coupling. Coupling was defined by Yourdon and Constantine (1978) and elaborated in structured analysis (De Marco, 1978) as design principles that reduced module interdependency, such as only passing data across its interface, with no shared global variables and control links; however, there are two additional properties that we need to consider. The first is data or control dependencies in interfaces. If a component only expects to send and receive data to and from the world, then coupling is low. Coupling is further decreased if the component makes few assumptions about the type, format, and quantity of data. However, higher coupling is imposed if a component sends control parameters to another module, because this implies some knowledge of the destination component. The second property is embedded models of external components. If assumptions are made about the external world, then the component will possess some model of the world embedded within it. This increases coupling because the context of reuse is constrained by the designer. This coupling might be partially reduced by giving the component the ability to learn and update its model, but that increases complexity and hence adversely affects granularity and abstraction. There is no escape from the impact of coupling on flexibility in reuse.

Flexibility in a reuse library will be a function of granularity, level of abstraction, and coupling, expressed in the following formula:

$$F^{comp} f(Gr, L^{abs}, C_p i),$$

where

F^{comp} is the flexibility to deal with many different application problems by composing solutions from components;

Gr is the granularity of the components, estimated by using function point metrics;

L^{abs} is the level of abstraction; and

C_p is the average coupling between modules.

The ideal reuse library will contain small, highly abstract components with low coupling. Smaller-grain components are more flexible because they can be composed to fit a wide range of problems. In contrast, large-grain components will be less flexible because they have more functionality, hence increasing the probability of having to customize code and decreasing the likelihood of a good fit with a new application's requirements. The level of abstraction will decrease in higher-grain components because they are more complex and contain more methods and data structures; hence the estimate of abstraction for components is influenced by the chosen level of granularity. A reuse library of highly abstract and small granularity components with low intermodule coupling represents an ideal in terms of flexibility and composability for reuse. However, this ideal may have low utility and high costs for design. Furthermore, it depends on one's view of the payback from reuse. In software code reuse, the ideal is code that runs first time, that can also be reused in a wide variety of applications. In specification and knowledge reuse, the ideal is to transfer ideas that solve problems in a range of different contexts. In both cases, small-grain components increase the potential range of applicability, but at a penalty of more design cost in composing a solution for complex problems.

The overall success of a particular paradigm will depend not only on the level of abstraction and granularity but also on the extent of the reuse library provided for a particular context and the tool support. This adds two further variables: scope and the level of tool support. Scope is an estimate of the completeness of the component library for a particular context, that is, the level and context of reuse that the components are intended to address. This may be judged as the number

TABLE 2.2
Comparison of Acceptability Factors of the Three Paradigms

Paradigm	Granularity	Abstraction	Scope–Reuse Level	Cohesion	Coupling
ERPs	large	low-medium	high: business requirements (1)	medium	high
Patterns	small	high	medium: system design (2)	high	low
OSMs	small	high	high: business requirements (1)	high	low

of solutions provided for problems in a domain, or the number of problems that have been described in a domain. Scope may therefore be judged at the business requirements or system design levels; see Table 2.2. Tool support is the provision of retrieval, matching, customization, and design facilities with the component library that reduce the reuser–developer's effort. Hence acceptability (Acc) of a reuse paradigm is a function of

$$\text{Acc } f(F^{\text{comp}} + T^{\text{sppt}} + Sc)/Ut^{\text{des}},$$

where

F^{comp} is the flexibility measured by granularity, abstraction, and coupling;
T^{sppt} is the effectiveness of tool support for the reuse process and the library;
Sc is the scope estimated as the completeness of the library of components provided within the paradigm; and
Ut^{des} is the utility estimated as the value of the programmer in effort saved by means of reuse.

Libraries may supply not only components but also template architectures for application areas. Architecture frameworks come in different forms that offer progressively more guidance on the one hand and less flexibility on the other. *Reference architectures* provide a template to suggest how to design an application in a particular domain, but there is no constraint about how the designer actually composes and develops the application. These paper-based architectures are informative design resources rather than reusable software. *Template architectures* give an outline design with slots that can be filled with reusable components. Depending on the sophistication of the architecture, active guidance may be given to the designer by matching appropriate components to slots. Templates provide a large-scale design pattern but little actual software. In contrast, *framework architectures* consist of a design and partial software implementation of a generalized family of applications. Reusable components may be placed in slots to specialize the architecture, and some functionality (e.g., software for networking, database integrity checking) is already provided (Fayad & Johnson, 2000).

As architectures become more complex, their abstraction decreases. Large application architectures have many methods and interfaces, so their granularity increases, making them less flexible.

Assessing Acceptability. Table 2.2 summarizes the relative position of the three paradigms on this question. Cohesion measures the coherence of purpose; that is, does a component have a single goal and do all its parts contribute to that goal (high cohesion), or is it heterogeneous with many subgoals?

ERPs are large-grain reusable components. Each ERP contains several separate submodules; for instance, production logistics has six separate process modules. However, even the submodules have several interfaces and methods, so their function point scores are higher than patterns or OSMs. ERPs exist to serve a high-level business purpose, so cohesion is medium because each ERP contains subgoals within it; coupling is high because many ERP components (see Fig. 2.5) are dependent on other components. Integration between ERPs is one of their strengths; for example, coupling between manufacturing, inventory control, procurement, and accounting is part of the ERP solution. However, this makes them less flexible. These disadvantages are partially offset by the relative completeness of the ERP libraries, which cover a wide range of business requirements.

Patterns, in contrast, are small scale, highly abstract components. Scope in patterns is a moving target; although only 5 creation, 7 structural, and 11 behavior patterns were published by Gamma et al. (1995), many more have been added since in pattern languages of program (PLOP) design workshops (Harrison et al., 1999; Rising, 1998). As patterns have a large community behind their development, their design coverage and overall scope will increase. Cohesion is high as each pattern achieves one design goal or intent that is part of the definition. Object-oriented patterns also follow the law of cohesion as each pattern has a stated intent; for example, Facade presents a single interface to a subsystem (Gamma et al., 1995). Coupling between patterns is low as most have an interface definition that assumes only data parameters.

OSM families have a high degree of cohesion because each family is composed of a set of cooperating objects that fulfill a single goal. Coupling is low because each OSM assumes only data-flow exchanges with other models. Granularity is low because each model contains few function points; however, although overall flexibility is high, acceptability is reduced by the relative incompleteness of the library. Although the Domain Theory has a wide-ranging scope at a high level of abstraction, many subclasses of the families are incomplete. In addition, tool support is limited.

Knowledge-level components usually have low granularity, but as with design, granularity and abstraction interact. Reusable components may contain abstract principles, policies, and in slightly more detail, strategies couched as heuristics, for

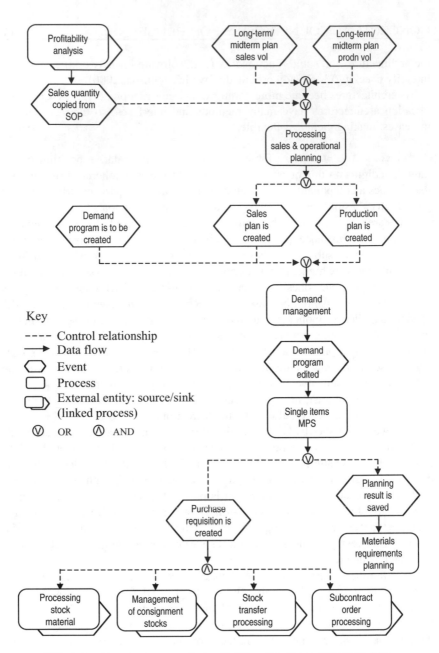

FIG. 2.5. Event process chain diagram for the subsystem "Production by lot size" within the production logistics ERP. The control flows indicate considerable coupling within the module and with other modules; also process components such as Materials Requirements Planning hide considerable procedural detail.

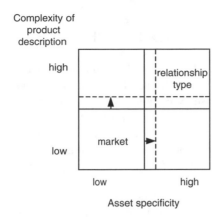

FIG. 2.6. Business theory 2 × 2 model, which predicts the type of interorganizational relationship according to the complexity of the product and asset specificity (risk of supply) in a supply chain. The dotted lines indicate that the organization types in the other two cells depend on which factor is dominant.

example, "in this situation follow advice (x)". Many business models deliver reusable knowledge as simple matrices (see, for example, Malone, Yates, & Benjamin, 1987) that show trade-offs between different variables and strategies (see Fig. 2.6).

Reuse in these matrix models approaches the highest level of general-purpose reuse delivered by methods, techniques, and models. These act as tools for thought that the reuser employs when reasoning about a new problem domain. The alternative mode of knowledge reuse is by means of specific examples of best practice that have variable granularity and very low abstraction. Best practice reports describe instances or histories for a particular organization in a certain context, the policies or strategies applied, and the outcome, possibly with some explanation justifying why the outcomes were favorable (or occasionally candid reports of failure). The reuser has to generalize the abstract knowledge by comparing several similar examples of best practice knowledge and assess whether the extracted knowledge is applicable to their problem context, for example, business process reengineering success stories (Hammer & Champy, 1993). Some reusable knowledge is designed to alleviate the reuser of this burden by pointing out commonalities between case studies, proposing general methods and strategies, or formulating general scenarios from the examples. The scope, cohesion, and coupling of reusable knowledge depend on the route taken. Examples of best practice rate low on all three measures, whereas general principles will be higher.

Having reviewed the implications of abstraction and granularity, our next issue is to investigate the costs of reuse strategies that help to inform trade-off decisions about abstraction and granularity as well as assess the implications for reuse strategies when adopting ERPs, patterns, or generic OSM models.

2.3. REUSE STRATEGIES
AND TRADE-OFFS

The following framework is intended to guide high-level design decisions about cost–benefit analysis of reuse. To facilitate discussion, we need to revisit definitions of different types of reuse. A *white-box design by reuse* takes reusable components from a library, and then it either composes an application from the components with some additional code, or the designer reuses an architecture framework and populates it with components while customizing code where necessary to create the new application. In *black-box design by configuration*, the user–designer is presented with a set of components with or without a framework architecture and given the choice about which components to choose to suit his or her needs. Configuration assumes no coding; system construction is effected by plug-in reuse. In *design by adaptation and parameterization*, the route is not strictly reuse because it involves designing an adaptable product and then tailoring it to users' needs by loading preferences and settings in parameter files to change system behavior.

From a user's point of view, the best case is a "load and go" application in which the user has to do minimal work to create a usable application. Unfortunately, this default case rarely matches the needs of individual users and cannot deal with changing requirements. Most applications incur considerable set up costs for users; furthermore, reuse also imposes design costs. These costs can be exchanged between users and designers as end-user computing and component-based engineering offer the opportunity to outsource design costs to users. This underlines the need to assess these costs so the trade-offs between designers and users can be assessed more soundly. Two levels of cost have to be taken into account. The first is design costs in creating reusable components. This includes domain analysis, component specification, design for reuse, and implementation of the reuse library. The second is costs in developing a system by reuse or adaptation. These are composed of efforts to analyze the requirements for the new application, match and retrieve components to fit those requirements, understand the components, design the application by reuse, and provide additional coding for customization, testing, and implementation.

The reuse costs can be decomposed, estimated, and controlled by following the conventional practices of project management. Of course, reuse cost–benefit models have to be long range to assess the payback over many years. First costs of setting up the design-for-reuse program have to be considered, and then each design-by-reuse project will have a separate cost–benefit analysis. The initial setup and recurrent costs of design for reuse are amortized over several designs by reuse, which should be realizing savings compared with conventional development. As with all up-front capital investments, the moot point for management is the payback period.

Design-by-reuse costs involve searching for appropriate components in a reuse library, checking their suitability for the new application, designing the new application architecture with reusable components, and customizing code if necessary. Testing is an additional cost. Black-box reuse costs are deciding which components to retrieve for a particular application context, understanding the component interfaces, and then designing the new application architecture, integrating components, and testing them. Development by adaptable systems does not escape users' costs, which result from analyzing user requirements and task needs, then loading parameter files with profiles and preferences, running the system, and testing whether the resulting behavior conforms with expectations. Design costs for adaptable systems arise from the increased software complexity. Finally, reuse and adaptation approaches both impose user costs by less than perfect adaptation, when one system version has to be tolerated by all users even though the application's functionality only matches the requirements of a subset of the users.

Some costs can be reduced by provision of tools to support or partially automate the process; for example, costs of finding components that are a good match for requirements can be reduced by intelligent search tools and constraint-based matching algorithms. Architecture also has an impact on costs and the reuse process. Application frameworks reduce costs by giving designers a ready-made outline solution, although they may impose a penalty of decreased flexibility if the user's requirements do not fit the framework. Frameworks simplify the designer's job of selecting a subset of components to fit into each slot within the architecture, but the architecture makes assumptions about design so the compatibility of components and slots will be restricted. Finally, adaptation costs can be reduced by providing stereotype user profiles and templates.

Reuse Processes.   The process model places costs in the context of reuse activities. Although software engineering for generic and reusable products shares many activities with conventional applications development, that is, requirements analysis, specification, validation, design, coding, and testing, some process specializations are necessary.

Design by reuse can incur considerable effort, depending on the goodness-of-fit between the reused components and the new application requirements. The worse the fit, the more code tailoring effort is required. In spite of these limitations, considerable cost savings can be realized by reuse. In particular, reuse may pay off when horizontal level 2 services are embedded in vertical-market products. Reuse of user-interface components is a good example of this; the reuse library of components can be applied to many different applications. Middleware components, such as network services, are also amenable to this approach to reuse.

Managers need to investigate the trade-off between the costs users might bear in relation to the potential perceived reward of the new application versus the design costs of developing component libraries and their support tools, and how these costs might be reduced by support tools and selecting the appropriate strategic approach. Strategic decisions about design for reuse and black-box or white-box customization necessitate a business analysis of the intended market, competitor analysis, and return on investment. The cost-analysis framework can contribute by making issues clear at the business level.

2.3.1. Design by Adaptation and Parameterization

Adaptation is probably the easiest case of the three. Reuse pathways are summarized in Fig. 2.7. The steps indicate the following costs:

C^{requ} is analyzing the users' requirements for personalization or adaptation;

C^{acquis} is acquiring the necessary parameters for adaptation;

C^{load} is the time taken to load the parameters into the system; and

C^{test} is the time taken to test the effect of different parameters.

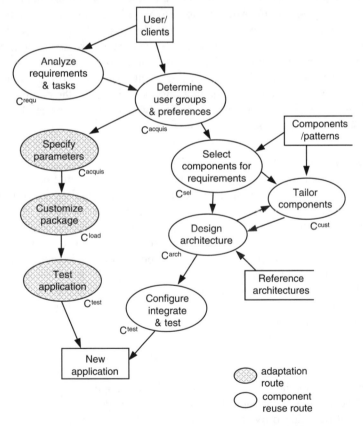

FIG. 2.7. Process model for different design-by-reuse strategies, showing process steps and costs associated with each step.

Adaptation cost is therefore

$$C^{\text{adapt}} = C^{\text{requ}} + C^{\text{acquis}} + C^{\text{load}} + C^{\text{test}}(Np \times Ug),$$

where

Np is the number of parameters (or functions) to be customized and
Ug is the number of different user groups in the target application.

The total adaptation cost is a function of the work tasks to be customized, which is reflected in the number of parameters (Np) multiplied by the number of user groups (Ug). Most costs in adaptable systems are either borne by the user or accepted by the supplier as a personalization service to the customer–user. Designer costs have to be added to these user costs. These arise from the added complexity of designing an adaptable system and the increased sophistication of testing. Designer costs will be a function of the level of ambition in adaptability, which starts with simple changes to the user-interface display, to changing user-system dialogues and functions, and finally self-adapting systems that monitor their environments and change accordingly (Browne, Totterdell, & Norman, 1990). The overall trade-off is between developers' costs, users' costs, and the satisfaction or frustration from good–poor adaptation, as follows:

$$S^{\text{accept}} f(C^{\text{user}} + 1/C^{\text{designer}}),$$

where

C^{user} are costs are taken from the previous formula,
C^{designer} are estimated costs to design the adaptable application, and
S^{accept} expresses either a positive or negative rating of the application's suitability by the user population. (If we assume the product is well designed for usability and reliability, high acceptability should reflect how well the application fits the users' characteristics and their tasks.)

Lowering designer costs will reduce system acceptability and hence increase user costs. Conversely, increased design effort should increase system acceptability by improving the user–system fit, and hence reduce user costs. It is important to note that these costs are time dependent, so preoperation adaptation costs may well influence the users' perception of system acceptability later on. However, most users do not use adaptation facilities and prefer to save effort by accepting defaults. Consequently, design for adaptation is wasted on most users apart from a minority of power users who actually take the trouble to tailor a system to their needs. The relationship among the effort users are willing to expend, their motivation, and rewards from system usage is still poorly understood.

Adaptation costs can be reduced by setting defaults, or by offering a set of profile templates that the user can choose from. These, of course, incur more developer cost and depend on knowledge of the future user population. In addition, when users accept defaults or templates, they may tolerate a less than perfect match with their requirements, so there may be hidden dissatisfaction costs.

The essence of adaptable components is that the designer builds in facilities for customizing the component ab initio, whereas other approaches imply design activity by the user to achieve customization. None of the reuse paradigms (ERPs, OSMs, or patterns) fits into the adaptation category, although ERPs come close. A better example would be the personalizing of a spreadsheet package or a graphics package. Adaptation has two aspects. The first is adaptation of the user interface for different levels of user skill and preferences, for example, verbose versus terse menus, different toolbars in a word processor; the second is functional adaptation to change the system's behavior. An example of the latter is customizing accounting packages with the codes for the users' view of cost centers, expense codes, and so on. Several ERP subsystems support this type of adaptation; however, there is a trade-off with complexity. As more adaptation is added, the cost of specifying the necessary parameters increases and further costs are incurred in understanding the implications of these parameters for system behavior and output.

2.3.2.   Black-Box Reuse by Configuration

Configuration requires a component library that covers several product families so that applications can be developed by plugging modules together. Design may start from scratch or use a framework architecture. Users may adopt a designer role if the application area is relatively simple. The problems are how many and which modules to select, understanding their interfaces, and then configuring the interaction between the modules and each slot in the architecture.

Configuration may take place in two or more reuse context layers; for instance, an application architecture may be hosted by a system services–platform archi-tecture that is also configurable. Reuse by configuration may also be mixed with white-box customization, so C^{cust} from that approach may have to be added to the development process. Developer costs are designing the configurable module library and, from the user point of view, understanding the reuse library and then carrying out the configuration.

C^{requ} is analyzing user requirements for the new application,
C^{acquis} is retrieving or understanding the configurable components,
C^{sel} is the time taken to select the modules,
C^{arch} is the effort taken for designing the system architecture, and
C^{test} is the time taken to test the configured system.

Configuration cost by black-box reuse is therefore

$$C^{\text{conf}} = C^{\text{requ}} + C^{\text{acquis}} + C^{\text{sel}} + C^{\text{arch}} + C^{\text{test}}(Np \times Ug).$$

Costs can be reduced by setting defaults for standard architecture configurations for subdomains; this may be improved by provision of methods, or more ambitiously intelligent decision support tools to guide users in module selection and installation. These, of course, incur more developer cost.

ERPs are a good example of configurable systems. The costs are higher than for adaptation because the architecture has to be assembled from predesigned components and then tailored with parameters. ERPs therefore incur costs by both routes. The costs of acquiring and selecting the appropriate modules can be considerable, and most customers require consultants to help them. Although selecting appropriate modules may seem to be relatively straightforward, the relatively low level of abstraction in ERPs means that two levels of design are necessary. The appropriate subsystems are selected from the business model blueprint to fit the organization's requirements, the selected modules are placed in the ERP application framework, and then the behavior of individual modules is adapted by parameters and customization tools, for example, report formatters and query screen builders. The procedural detail (for example, how modules calculate inventory reorder levels, match orders to customer requirements, and schedule production runs) is usually adapted by parameters, although code may have to be written for exceptional requirements. Specializing procedures and algorithms is a time-consuming part of ERP configuration.

2.3.3. White-Box Reuse: Design by Composition

In this case the reuser–designer's task is more difficult, but the payoff is a more flexible reuse of a larger number of components. The reuser's task is more difficult because components have to be retrieved from a reuse library, their functionality has to be understood, and interfaces to other modules have to be assessed. An application framework may provide the overall design and code templates for specialization. In this case the reusable components are placed in the framework slots and customized according to the user's requirements. If no architecture exists a priori, the reuser–designer has to undertake a general design to determine the high-level function subsystems before the reuse library can be searched for appropriate modules. Once these have been located, design involves defining interfaces, checking compatabilities, and customizing code to suit the new application. White-box reuse shares the same process as black-box reuse apart from the addition of the customization of code.

White-box reuse can incur considerable effort, depending on the goodness of fit between the reused components and the new application requirements. The worse the fit, the more code tailoring effort is required. The cost model for design by reuse is as follows.

C^{requ} is analyzing the new application's requirements,
C^{acquis} is the time taken to select and understand the appropriate modules,
C^{sel} is the time taken to select the modules,
C^{arch} is designing the new system architecture,
C^{cust} is the time to customize the code of reusable modules for the new application or to build new interfaces between them, and
C^{test} is the time taken to test the effect of the designed system.

The total white-box reuse cost is therefore

$$C^{\text{reuse}} = C^{\text{acquis}} + C^{\text{sel}} + C^{\text{requ}} + C^{\text{acquis}} + C^{\text{arch}} + C^{\text{cust}} + C^{\text{test}}.$$

Reuse costs are higher because of the burden of retrieving, understanding, and customizing components. Some designer–reuser costs can be reduced by providing an application framework, but this increases costs of developing the reuse library in the first place. In this approach the trade-off is between reuser and designer costs, although the overall system acceptability will still depend on the costs to the user from a less than perfect fit and any adaptation that may be necessary. Costs of customizing code and developing the system architecture are not incurred by the other development routes; but the payoff for white-box reuse is that this may be the only route if uncertain and changing requirements mean that a configurable system is hard to develop. Reuse essentially offloads more development cost from the original designer on to the reuser. This trade-off may be acceptable when the reuser–designer has no alternative, but in the face of competition from configurable architectures, the user–designers will be well advised to choose black-box reuse. Black-box reuse depends on being able to anticipate the behavior and functionality of a component in all its potential reuse contexts. This is easier in level 2 and 3 reuse where the problem space of design is less likely to change. Level 1 requirements reuse is exposed to change in the external world so totally deterministic specification of components is difficult. Reuse at this level therefore tends toward customization.

Patterns are an example of white-box reuse. They involve high analysis and design costs, as well as initial start-up costs of understanding and organizing a reusable patterns library. The payback in design-level reuse may be extensive over a long time scale if the development paradigm (i.e., object-oriented programming) remains economically practicable. OSMs save some of the requirements and selection costs in level 1 reuse because these abstractions of the problem domain are closer to the users' requirements. The disadvantage is that OSMs do not significantly alleviate design costs because they only provide design rationale as reusable knowledge rather than template designs or code. However, a combination of OSMs and patterns may reduce costs from analysis through to design, although to realize this further, research linking the two paradigms is necessary.

In knowledge management the most significant reuse costs are in acquisition. Busy managers have even less time and inclination to pass on their knowledge than software engineers. Furthermore, they are less tolerant of any format conventions for recording knowledge; hence most content is captured as free format narrative. Costs can be reduced by technology, such as facilities for voice notes and annotations. Recording knowledge by typing text takes time to compose the content as well as to physically type it. Speech is quicker, so if automatic speech recognition can be implemented, this makes recording knowledge easier. However, knowledge still has to be formatted and stored in a reuse library.

Compared with design reuse, the costs in knowledge-management reuse are perceived to be higher in acquisition, documentation, indexing, and searching. The exploitation costs are hidden because reuse becomes part of the reuser's job rather than an explicit design activity. Whatever the costs, the benefits of knowledge-level reuse can be more significant than for design reuse because several levels of process or whole organizations can be influenced rather than just improve the efficiency of a product design. That is,

- Organizational policy and strategy improve efficiency by adopting best practice from best of breed competitors and encourage self-improvement by organizational learning.
- In process management reuse, knowledge improves process efficiency, leading to reduced costs and better product quality in manufacture.
- In product development reuse, design reuse improves product quality and reduces costs.

Reuse at all three levels can be facilitated by metaprocesses to encourage the acquisition of new knowledge by organizational learning. This is described in more depth in chapter 7.

2.4. SUMMARY

This chapter has proposed an initial framework for exploring the dimensions of different reuse paradigms and investigating the cost implications for reuse-led development. The framework is a tool for thought that enables issues of abstraction and granularity to be considered more explicitly when designing for reuse. The juxtaposition of design issues and development costs raises further questions for assessing reuse approaches. For instance, the success of ERPs might be attributed to their relatively high utility in solving large-scale design problems (i.e., business application scope) even though the ERP approach to reuse incurs considerable costs, partially attributable to their relatively low level of abstraction. Commercial success may be leveraged by the high potential payback perceived by customers, whereas patterns have a less immediate connection to business applications.

Patterns have become adopted in the object-oriented developer community, who see that sharing reusable design knowledge has brought savings in development effort. In a wider context than the gang of four patterns (Gamma et al., 1995) that have been taken as the stereotype in this chapter, patterns have evolved into a variety of forms that are applicable at different levels of reuse, with different forms of representation, for example, pedagogical patterns. For patterns the attraction is that most are in the public domain, and the costs of requirements analysis are spread among an extensive designer community. Patterns are attractive because they have a large potential reuse target at the design level, where one pattern may fit many different applications. The Domain Theory OSMs, in contrast, can offer payback for analysts as well as designers. OSMs offer a high level of abstraction with a wider scope and represent the middle ground between the other two paradigms. They offer wide ranging reuse with high abstraction and lower costs than ERPs. In ERPs the costs are higher in configuration but the payback is higher than OSMs in design solutions, so the Domain Theory will have to converge with patterns to improve its utility; furthermore, the utility of patterns and their analysis costs could be reduced by links to OSMs. Application frameworks offer some of the advantages of ERPs by giving an overall solution, and they preserve flexibility by using smaller patterns to fill in slots; however, most application frameworks have been targeted to date at middleware and system software, so ERPs have the advantage of business-level or requirements-level reuse.

The reuse process imposes costs on users and designers for requirements analysis, retrieving components, designing architecture, integrating, and testing. Adaptable systems impose more costs on users in loading profiles. Reuse outsources design costs to the reuser–designer, and in white-box reuse this includes code customization.

No doubt ERPs will continue to dominate commercial reuse as they have large libraries and provide standardized solutions to business problems, thus reducing analysis effort in reuse, albeit at the expense of more customization effort. ERPs also have the advantage that they come with modeling and customization methods from vendors such as SAP (Keller & Teufel, 1998), whereas other reuse libraries give the user little help in design by reuse. However, other reuse libraries may be appropriate in middleware or real-time applications, which may require different levels of abstraction and component granularity. Furthermore, more abstract reuse libraries may have advantages in generating new applications when standardized business or reference models have yet to emerge (e.g., entertainment, virtual reality, games, or training), so the future may see a coevolution of ERPs standardizing accepted business practice with effective IT solutions while more abstract libraries help to develop new technology by reusable components.

3

Abstraction in the Mind

In this chapter I examine the problem of abstraction from the viewpoint of psychology. Abstraction is essential for problem solving generally and software engineering in particular. Our ability to discover the general and ignore irrelevant detail underpins analysis and modeling tasks, but therein lies the disadvantage of abstraction. Software design problems often have to deal with the devil in the detail, so both the abstract and the specific facts are necessary. Abstraction is closely related to the cognitive process of learning by generalization, so cognitive psychology can help us understand many aspects of software engineering and reuse, ranging from abstract models to concrete scenarios and their use in analogical reasoning.

People reuse experiences, problem-solving methods, and skills every day. Most of our actions are reused. In software reuse and knowledge management we think of reuse in terms of artefacts that can be applied many times in different situations. The motivation is fundamentally economic; we wish to save time and cost by reapplying a known solution, either directly as software code or indirectly as knowledge that guides us toward the solution, for example, best practice, templates, and patterns. Our mental life is no different. Reasoning from first principles is hard. It actually consumes more energy, which is why we feel tired after examinations. Our body's means of achieving economy of thought is by learning, committing the solution to memory, and then reusing it. We might not refer to application of skilled memory as reuse but that is just what we are doing—saving ourselves time and effort by reusing knowledge. We deal with the complexity of life by learning. This enables us to respond flexibly and adapt to our environment. Memory and the process of learning enable reuse of knowledge and the artefacts we design; for instance, reuse of everyday articles such as matchboxes as toy building blocks to make buildings. Reuse in software and knowledge implies an active process; that is, we design for reuse. In cognitive terms we design for reuse explicitly when we prepare course materials, training manuals, and other educational subject matter; however, the process applied to design for learning is really an extrapolation of what we do naturally when processing knowledge for our own use—imposing order, indexing, and structuring. Three areas of cognitive psychology have important implications for reuse: *memory*, in particular long-term memory; *learning*, which creates memory in the first place; and *problem solving* with skill and expertise when we reuse previously learned knowledge.

3.1. MEMORY

Human memory comes in two forms: long-term memory, which is our permanent filestore and is close to the everyday meaning of the word; and working memory, our cache or run-time memory that we use during reasoning. Working memory has a limited capacity and facts get overwritten by new input, so we can only hold information in our foreground consciousness by refreshing it (i.e., keeping facts in mind).

3.1.1. Working Memory and Chunking

Working memory is the human analogue of computer RAM, in other words, the cache memory of the central processor. In contrast to computers, human working memory is small and loses its contents unless it is refreshed every 200 ms. Working memory has to store information from many sources; hence it may seem strange that experimental evidence indicates that it has a very limited capacity. As working memory has a limited capacity, it is often exceeded when we lose the thread of an argument. Items are not stored as in computer memory "bytes" but in "chunks" of information. The secret of expanding the limited storage of working memory is to abstract qualities from the basic information and store the abstraction instead.

This concept is best understood by example. The string 01612363311 is difficult to assimilate and remember, but break it into smaller units, 0161-236 3311, making it recognizable as a telephone number, and memorization is easier. The more order that can be imposed on the raw data, the better the chunking. Instead of storing ten separate digits, one can store the number groups as three whole chunks, reducing the storage required. To convince yourself of the point, the following should be recalled without error once the pattern has been seen:

246
357
81012
91113

The number sequences have order within them that promotes chunking. What has been stored is some quality of the data that can be used to reconstruct it, which in the latter case is the algorithm of even–odd triplets in an ascending numeric series.

3.1.2. Long-Term Memory

Long-term memory is the main filestore of the human system. It has a nearly infinite capacity, as no one has been able to demonstrate an upper limit on what we can remember. Forgetting appears to be a problem of not retrieving what is already inside our memory. Memory retrieval is a two-phase process: *recognition* is the initial activation of a memory trace by cues; *recall* is the actual retrieval of the information itself. As a consequence, sometimes you can have a fact on the tip of your tongue (recognition) but can't quite remember it (recall). In frequently used memory, both recognition and recall are so quick that no difference is noticed. The division between working memory and long-term memory is not hard and fast. We understand most of what we see, hear, and think about by reference to memory. Our reasoning works by holding tags in working memory that link through to long-term memory by a process of spreading activation. Hence when we see a friend in the street we know it is Fred or Mary by associating their image with our memory.

Recognition then activates a network of memories about who Fred and Mary are, their likes, dislikes, recent conversations with them, and so on. Memories are found by a process of spreading activation, as remembering one fact often helps the recall of other related items. Chunking is central to working memory and long-term memory; we learn and memorize only abstractions rather than details. Thus when we are asked to recall details of our friends we can describe who they are, but giving an accurate Identikit picture is difficult. Memorization and recall are helped by recency and frequency: the more often we recall and use a piece of information, the easier it is to learn it. Retrieval of facts from memory can be remarkably fast, especially for frequently used items and procedures. Retrieval time for less frequently used information varies; it can be quick, but may be slow especially for older people.

Memorization fails because an access path either decays through lack of use or was poorly constructed in the first place. Remembering names of people you meet infrequently in conferences is a good example. Repeating the person's names just after being introduced helps memorization. If you had a long earnest conversation with the person you met, the chance is that you will remember that person years later. However, you are less likely to remember a face or the individual's name after a simple meeting without conversation. Similar facts can interfere with recall, so well-recognized access paths that are sufficiently distinct from others are helpful in preventing recall errors. Although building many cues into memory helps, the disadvantage comes when the cues can be confused. This leads to interference when the wrong item is recalled because the cues are similar. This can be a considerable problem for component versions; memory for the old version is fine but the update is slightly different. Retrieving the new version can be difficult unless interference can be avoided. Consistency helps learning by establishing a familiar pattern, but change is the enemy of consistency, so changes have to be made clear.

Memorization is usually an effortful process. Most learning is by association, in which facts are linked together to provide an access path. The greater the number of separate access paths, or the more often an access path is used, the easier a fact is to remember. Problem solving or reasoning during memorization creates more links and hence helps recall in the future. This increases the "depth of encoding," which means that when we understand something more thoroughly we tend to remember it more effectively. As reuse involves learning how design components and a future system should work, active engagement by reusers and designers in problem solving leads to better understanding and memory. More accurate memory means that less has to be recalled by looking at notes and documents, fewer errors will result, and understanding will be shared more efficiently.

3.1.3. External Memory

Because we have difficulty with processing information when we are doing several things at the same time, we rely on a variety of memory aids, such as written documents and diagrams. External representations also help memory because the act of recording descriptions of objects and classes as diagrams means we have thought about them and put some structure on the components, their functionality, and relationships. Structuring facts improves memorization and cues effective recall by providing associations between facts and categories. Reuse of specifications and designs can be helped by documentation that exhibits a natural memory structure.

Not surprisingly, documentation plays an important role in reuse. External representations are necessary for providing input to the reasoning process as well as recording the results. Diagrams and structured text notations record abstractions that form specifications of the reusable components and required system, whereas details of the domain can be represented as scenarios. Domain or problem representations help trigger memories of appropriate solutions. If we can base external representations on the structure of internal memories, then they should fit naturally and improve not only memorization but also the recall of information.

3.1.4. Organization of Memory

There are several forms of long-term memory that resemble software engineering notations. This is a good illustration of how external representations have been designed, or may have naturally evolved, to fit with human abilities.

Semantic Networks. The basic organization of long-term memory consists of linguistically based concepts linked together in a highly developed network. The organization of human memory is far from clear, although most evidence favors the view that all storage is finally of the semantic associative kind. Semantic network representations appear in "mind maps" that give informal associations between facts and concepts (see Fig. 3.1). Semantic networks may become formalized in software engineering as entity relationship diagrams, semantic data models, process dependency diagrams, and the like. The degree of abstraction depends on how the memory was created, as semantic nets may record specific associations that are closer to episodic memory or more abstract facts as found in analogical memory. Hypertext representations of reusable knowledge and designed components form semantic network models for reuse libraries.

Episodic Memory. Episodic memory, in contrast to semantic memory, is composed of more detailed facts, events, scenes, and contextual information about the world, anchored to particular episodes. This memory can store images, sounds, and physical details of an episode that is particularly salient, for instance, an eyewitness memory of an accident. However, as studies of eyewitness testimony have shown, episodic memory is highly selective and can be inaccurate. Memorization tends to be automatic and linked to the emotions: pleasure, enjoyment, or fear. In reuse, recall of episodic memory can help by providing the context for reuse; that is, remembering the circumstances in which a component was designed can help to suggest how and where it should be reused. Unfortunately, people's episodic memories are highly selective, so a sample of usage scenarios

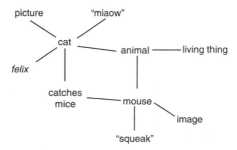

FIG. 3.1. Semantic network with type-instance nodes. This forms a reusable knowledge structure for a commonsense definition of a cat.

may represent atypical events from personal viewpoints. Scenarios combine descriptions of states, events, and behavior to give specific, contextual knowledge. This can be used either as seed corn material to create more generalized (semantic–categorial) abstractions from specific episodes, or scenarios can provide a useful reality check for the applicability of reusable knowledge.

Categorial Memory. This is memory of objects and their groupings, familiar as sets, types, or classes in object-oriented design. There is evidence that we organize the world not into discrete nonoverlapping categories but in a more fuzzy manner, with core and peripheral members (Rosch, 1985). To illustrate the idea, most people have an idealized concept of a bird. A robin fits this core or prototypical image by having the following properties: round, feathered, sings, and lays eggs. In contrast, a penguin is a more peripheral member of birds because it does not share all the attributes of the prototype image and it has additional nonstandard attributes; for example, it swims but cannot fly. The relationships between categories and members is illustrated in Fig. 3.2.

Each category is described by a property list (or type definition for computer scientists) that lists the attributes that all members should possess. The property list concept has been exploited in information science as faceted classification schemes, which have been borrowed by reuse libraries. This concept works well for concrete, physical objects, although the situation for more abstract concepts (e.g., religions) is less clear. Whereas people tend to agree about concrete facts taken from the real world, consensus on more abstract categories, such as functional requirements, is harder to achieve. Not surprisingly, when it comes to indexing and component retrieval, categories based on functional descriptions are more prone to misinterpretation. Card sorting and laddering techniques help to

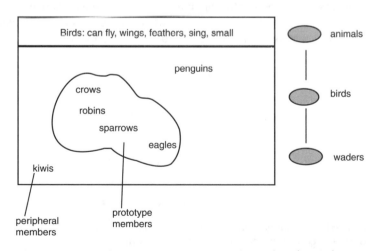

FIG. 3.2. Natural category prototype and peripheral members.

structure categories (Maiden & Rugg, 1996), whereas differences between people can be handled by viewpoints (Sommerville & Kotonya, 1998). Classification in reuse and object-oriented methods is based on categorial memory, but retrieval of components for reuse has to take on board the fuzzy nature of human natural categorization.

Procedural Memory. This is knowledge of actions and how to do things. Computer programs, macros, and scripting languages are sequences of instructions or procedures. Memory of actions is held in two different forms: declarative or rule-based knowledge and procedural knowledge (Anderson, 1985). When we start out knowing little about a subject, we acquire fragments of declarative knowledge as rules and miniprocedures. This knowledge, however, is not organized, so to carry out a task we reason with declarative knowledge fragments and compose them into a plan of action. As people become more familiar with a task, fragments of declarative knowledge become compiled into procedures that can then be run automatically. When carrying out a task, we simply call the procedure of how to perform it automatically. Scripts (Schank, 1982) are a form of procedural memory that encode a sequence of events and their context that we have learned from experience. They represent prototypical "stories" of what we expect to do in a particular context; for example, when we enter a restaurant the usual sequence of events is to receive the menu, order a meal, eat it, pay for it, and leave. The dichotomy between declarative or procedural knowledge is reflected in the choice of documenting processes as rules (declarative representation) or methods (procedures). Rules are smaller chunks of knowledge and tend to be more flexible for reuse, but they incur the penalty that several rules have to be composed into a process. This is one of the fundamental reuse trade-offs, which is also present in human problem solving.

Analogical Memory. Analogical memory links two sets of domain knowledge that on first sight are unrelated. When the knowledge has been used in reasoning, further abstract links are created in memory to store the relationships. The concept is best explained by example. Take two domains, astronomy and chemistry, with one knowledge structure representing the relationships between the sun, planets, gravity, and orbits and the other representing atoms, nuclei, electrons, electromagnetic forces, and orbits. The linking analogy is the abstraction of satellites revolving around a central node on orbits determined by forces developed from the concept outlined by Gentner and Stevens (1983), illustrated in Fig. 3.3. Analogy is a useful way of exploiting existing memory by transferring it to new situations. Abstraction is at the heart of analogy.

Analogical memory consists of two specific schema, one in the target domain and one in the source domain. Analogy is an abstract higher-order schema that explains the similarity between two or more specific instances. In design *for* reuse we are attempting by the process of generalization to create libraries of the abstract

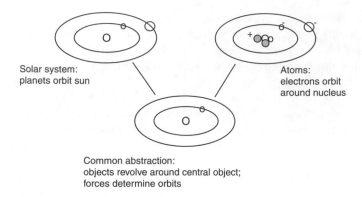

Solar system:
planets orbit sun

Atoms:
electrons orbit
around nucleus

Common abstraction:
objects revolve around central object;
forces determine orbits

FIG. 3.3. Analogical memory schema and the application of analogies in problem solving.

schema, whereas in design *by* reuse we first have to match the new domain to the appropriate abstraction and then transfer the knowledge that is common between the domains. One specific model of the problem (source) domain is linked to another specific model in the solution domain by means of an abstract bridging model that expresses the commonalities between them (the analogy). In problem solving, analogical reasoning usually involves discovering the common abstraction while reasoning about similarities between two apparently dissimilar problems. The process of reasoning by analogy has four stages.

The first stage is the formation of a mental model of the problem, which involves abstraction from the specific circumstances. The second stage is the searching of memory for an appropriate matching analogy; in the discovery of a new analogy this will involve generalization of the abstract schema from two or more specific models. The third stage is the transfer of knowledge from the source (solution) domain to the target (problem) domain, thereby solving the problem. The fourth stage is the validation of the solution by checking the abstract model against specific details in the solution domain.

Analogical memory is closely related to abstraction in computer science and has obvious implications for structuring reuse libraries and the reuse process. The Domain Theory that is elaborated in chapters 4 to 6 is based on analogical memory. The problem with analogy is setting the conceptual distance between the source and target (reuse) domain. People use a variety of short-range analogies, which we usually call *similarities* or *metaphors*; people also use longer range, more abstract matches that are true analogies. Longer-range analogies enable more flexible and inventive reuse, but at a penalty of increasing potential misunderstandings. As with many phenomena in psychology, there is no such thing as a mental free lunch. An analogy may seem to be a ready-made gift solution to a problem. It lures us into accepting the solution without thought (Sutcliffe & Maiden, 1992), only to find that transferring the analogy introduced errors through copycat reuse.

Furthermore, generating more general abstract models from specific examples and scenarios makes the models harder to understand. In spite of these dangers, analogy is a powerful problem-solving mechanism. It enables long range, cross-domain reuse, which can often lead to creative solutions to problems and forms one of the techniques in lateral thinking (De Bono, 1991).

The psychology of human memory can be applied to the modeling of knowledge for reuse in several areas that represent different types of knowledge that can be designed for reuse.

Goals and the synonyms *user aims*, *wishes*, and *intentions* are all forms of declarative memory. We frequently problem solve by top-down hierarchical decomposition, and this creates goal hierarchies in memory. Not surprisingly, goal hierarchies have been a frequent diagrammatic notation in computer science and elsewhere. However, goals may not be understood in much depth. When problem analysis is incomplete, a goal tree will end with linguistic labels. Interpretation of those labels may be ambiguous; hence reuse of goal-related knowledge is of limited value unless it is attached to something more specific. Goals have to be unpacked during the analysis process to specific requirements for the new application or more detailed models that explain how to achieve goals, that is, procedures.

Strategies, *policies*, and *heuristics* are informal knowledge structures, expressed externally as natural-language statements. They result from experience but are high-level generalizations, so interpretation suffers from the same ambiguity as goals. However, strategies usually have some direction toward action so the advice is more specific than a goal alone; for example, the goal of maximizing profit has many interpretations, whereas the strategy of maximizing profit by maintaining a loyal customer base to defend market share, or reducing costs, gives some more specific guidance. This group of knowledge structures are declarative and semantic networks in format. Linking strategies to more detailed tactics improves the reuse value.

Facts, *propositions*, and *beliefs* are areas of knowledge that may involve several different kinds of memory. First there is factual domain knowledge that could be represented as lists of entities and attributes; for instance, a red cup describes an entity (cup) that has an attribute (color = red). More complex assertions about entities are usually referred to as propositions; for example, a statement that a cup holds water is closer to a belief about the world that may or may not be directly observable. Beliefs start with commonsense assumptions about the behavior and objects but may also describe attitudes about one's self and others, for example, "I am honest but others are less trustworthy". These beliefs record our assumptions about the states and behaviors of other agents. Reuse of factual knowledge is commonplace in knowledge engineering where declarative knowledge of a domain might be reused in related expert systems. Reuse of beliefs and attitudes held by people depends on how well founded those beliefs may be.

Procedures, *processes*, and *guidelines* are created by more detailed problem solving and are expressed in declarative form as rules and guidelines or as runnable skills and procedures. Procedures are probably the most common form of reusable knowledge and are manifest in a variety of forms, such as best practice guides, operating manuals, algorithms in programs, methods, and management processes. Procedures require less interpretation than rules because the advice is specific. When rules are placed in a sequence with linked preconditions and postconditions, a procedure exists. Human memory picks out key actions in procedures (Galambos, 1986). These are essential or core components that do not vary within a family of related procedures, so analysis has to establish the core action points that are more liable to change and therefore have to be customized during reuse.

Objects and *classes* are manifestations of categorial memory. Object-oriented methods have copied the natural human process of generalizing knowledge: creating classes and then specializing them in a new context. However, object-oriented methods have discouraged the previously accepted approach of the hierarchical modeling of goals, which creates a clash with the natural approach to problem solving. This has resulted in some schizophrenia when identifying methods and operations for objects and when deciding whether objects can be concept–structure or goal oriented (i.e., exist to achieve a task). In reuse, we often start thinking of the new application in goal-oriented terms. If a reuse library is structured in a strict object classification, there may be a dissonance of views that will hinder retrieval. Analyzing interaction by means of use cases does not avoid the problem, unless goal-oriented use cases are explicitly modeled (Graham, 1996). There is no easy escape from the human tendency for top-down problem solving.

Scenarios, *examples*, and *prototypes* are related to episodic memory. Human memory for detail is not good. Although we can remember some facts in details, such as recognizing a large number of faces (Shepard, 1967), in general our episodic memory stores only a fraction of our experience. Specific knowledge structures therefore have a different role in reuse. Reusable repositories are an augmented version of human memory, with databases of scenarios and examples far exceeding the ability of human memory. The problem lies in how we understand specific examples during reuse. Scenarios and examples leverage explanation-based learning by juxtaposing specific knowledge with abstractions. This helps reasoning by challenging the applicability of generalized knowledge.

3.2.   LEARNING

Learning is the process of building new memories by reasoning with existing knowledge and facts gathered from the external world. Learning, reasoning, and problem solving are all closely related. As we reason we learn; when we problem solve our reasoning process reuses knowledge from memory, and in doing so we learn more from reapplying knowledge.

Learning is usually an effortful, conscious process. We have to concentrate and think in order to create effective memories. This can be achieved by brute force, repeating a fact over and over again, known as rote learning. The old-fashioned method of teaching children to learn multiplication tables by repetition is an example of rote learning. Memory activation is a function of the frequency and recency of memorization and reuse, so familiar and recently used memory comes back effortlessly. Less frequently used memories take longer to recall. Active reasoning creates richer memory structures (i.e., semantic nets) that represent the problem. The effort devoted to reasoning about the problem pays off in better activation of a neural net, and hence more effective memory. However, good activation has to be accompanied by distinct recall cues.

The connotation for knowledge reuse is that we tend to reuse the most recent and frequently used solutions, even when they are not optimal. This tendency becomes critical when we are under time pressure or stressed (Reason, 1990), which leads to dangerous "jumping to conclusions". Knowledge management therefore has to encourage reflective reuse. Long-range analogies and infrequently used schema may often provide better solutions. Another problem is combining fragments of knowledge. Memory schema are indexed by the context in which they were originally laid down. If we subsequently want to reuse them in new contexts, retrieval may be difficult. We will have to think laterally and explore many connections to find the knowledge we need and then reason carefully about the content of schema.

3.3.   PROBLEM SOLVING

Problem solving is something we do every day of our lives when we come up against the unexpected. It may be defined as "the combination of existing ideas to form new ideas". An alternative view focuses on the cause: problems arise when there is a discrepancy between a desired state of affairs and the current state of affairs and there is no obvious method to change the state. Simon (1973) laid the foundations of problem-solving theory by distinguishing between the problem and solution space. The former is a model of the problem before its solution (i.e., requirements and domain models), whereas the latter consists of facts describing the solution (i.e., specifications and designs). Problem solving progresses through several stages.

The first stage is preparation or formulation. The goal state is defined and necessary information for a solution is gathered. Reuse can start at this stage by retrieving memories of similar or analogous problems. The second stage is incubation or searching. Anticipated solutions are developed, tested, and possibly rejected, leading to more information gathering and development of alternative hypotheses. Many problems are solved by reusing previous solutions. Memory is searched by using cues describing the problem. The third stage is inspiration. The correct solution is identified by reasoning with the problem space. In reuse, inspiration is discovering the analogy and retrieving successful applications of knowledge. The final stage is verification. The solution is checked out to ensure it meets the goals and is consistent with the information available. This is the stage that is dangerous to omit, but finding a solution from memory tends to make us accept it at face value without going through the verification phase.

Effective problem solving requires general problem-solving strategies, and a good memory. We refer to people who are good problem solvers as experts. They usually have good general problem-solving skills but the major component of their expertise comes from long experience and memory. The desirable properties of expertise and effective reuse of knowledge break down into rich memory structures and the ability to reason effectively (Guindon, 1990; Guindon & Curtis, 1988; Visser & Hoc, 1990). Experts problem solve by several strategies that have lessons for the design of reuse libraries. First they reason about the problem domain and form a rich mental model. Experts have well-organized memories and good retrieval processes. Reuse libraries aim to mimic the structure of expert memory and retrieval processes. Knowledge elicitation from experts therefore should attend not just to acquiring the content of reusable knowledge but also to the heuristics and rules for finding it again. Once reusable memories have been retrieved, they are carefully assessed for relevance to the problem at hand. Encouraging checking and explanation facilities supports this facet of expertise (Sutcliffe & Maiden, 1994). To solve problems, experts form multiple hypotheses, reason about the outcomes, select the most appropriate solutions, and check them out. These facets are primarily a consequence of ability and experience, but validation tools for simulating solutions can help. Experts are good at reasoning with examples and counterexamples to establish boundary cases and test the applicability of reusable knowledge. Scenarios and examples can help here to check reusable solutions against a range of contexts of future use.

Finally, experts also possess many different methods and approaches to problem solving, such as using lateral thinking, using good imaginations to project how solutions might work, visualizing problems, and making long-range associations. Externalizing problem-solving models as simulations of the domain and memories as interactive hypertexts can facilitate some of these abilities. Reuse is essentially problem solving by memory. However, although some problems might have tailor-made solutions, many only have an approximate fit, so reuse has to be combined with more general problem-solving strategies. The trick is knowing what existing knowledge to reuse and how to integrate it with new knowledge to create a solution.

3.3.1.   Reasoning Strategies

People use a wide variety of problem-solving strategies. Success in problem solving often depends on using novel strategies. People are naturally conservative in their approach to problem solving and adopt the methods they are used to, so problem solving by memory is a natural preference. Problem solving is closely related to learning, so many of the mechanisms are shared.

In problem decomposition, complex problems are subdivided into smaller chunks by top-down decomposition or divide-and-conquer approaches. This results in goal-oriented decomposition to create hierarchies of functions, or subsystems. Decomposition makes problems easier to solve as each subproblem reduces complexity and the burden on working memory.

Means ends analysis or causal reasoning is reasoning about the cause of an event by using a mental model of the domain. Causal reasoning is important for understanding why things happen and then understanding how a process can be designed to effect change. More formally this abductive, or hypothesis-based, reasoning infers how a set of facts can be explained according to a causal model. It starts with an observation and reasons back to the action or event that caused it.

In the classification of objects and facts into categories, this form of reasoning creates categorial memories that underpin object-oriented approaches. For example, this includes aggregation of properties to define an object, or inheritance of properties in classes of objects; that is, lower-level objects automatically assume the characteristics of their higher-level parents. Classification uses inductive reasoning: faced with a menagerie full of cows, lions, giraffes, antelope, and tigers, one makes the observation that some animals eat other animals whereas some eat plants, leading one to the conclusion that animals can be classified as carnivores and herbivores. This case is then generalized to other situations in which it may apply.

Example-based generalization leads to the identification of classes or generalized procedures from specific examples, and it can be viewed as the process of abstraction in reasoning. Examples exert a powerful effect on our reasoning because we can identify with detail by means of our experience. Because scenarios situate examples with existing memory, they help us to understand abstractions and find generalizations from specific problems. Unfortunately, the products of the generalization process, abstractions, are not so easily understood, and reasoning with concrete examples as well as abstract models is necessary to promote understanding during reuse.

Deductive reasoning starts with assertions and discovers new facts by logically examining the relationships or properties that the assertions describe. In software engineering, we wish to specify the process that will achieve a particular state so we apply a formal method based on logic to help us deduce that the state will be reached. Formal methods use deductive logic to check the properties of specifications to ensure that undesirable states are not allowed to occur; they test for violations of invariants, deadlocks, and that desirable states are achieved (liveness conditions). Formal verification of components can give guarantees for reliability.

Case-based reasoning recognizes a triggering pattern or signature of the problem and then uses memories of solutions to similar problems. Automated and human case-based reasoning uses pattern matching to retrieve useful knowledge and then tests its applicability.

Problem solving involves holding a collection of facts in working memory as a mental model. The explanation of cognitive processes by mental models

(Johnson-Laird, 1983) has had a wide influence on cognitive psychology. Mental models may be either physical or conceptual, and they represent abstractions and more specific facts about objects and their relationships. Positive facts are held in memory without difficulty but negative facts pose problems, because representing that something does not exist does not come as naturally and consumes more chunks. This limitation has several consequences for software design. First, expression in negatives is always harder and more error prone than positives (e.g., "books should not be allowed out on loan longer than 30 days", compared with "books should be returned within 30 days of the loan date"); double negatives are even worse (e.g., "it is incorrect not to follow the appropriate security procedure"). Second, we tend to look for positive evidence to confirm our beliefs. Although we reason well in terms of positive association, when negative terms are introduced our reasoning becomes illogical. This "confirmation bias" means that we look for positive evidence that specifications are correct but we rarely look for evidence to prove they are incorrect. Worse still, we often ignore contradictory evidence when it is available. In reuse, that can lead us to jump to conclusions and accept a component as appropriate without checking it out. One remedy is to store examples with counterexamples as warnings about possible reuse mistakes.

The content and context of a problem are easier to understand than the underlying logical structure; hence reasoning in abstract terms is more difficult than with concrete examples. The important consequence is that our knowledge of the context and content of problems can obscure the underlying logical structure. This has design implications because unfortunately knowing one problem domain does not help in the learning of another domain with the same underlying logical structure, unless we make the cognitive effort to abstract a general model. Context also influences our decisions; this may result in the wrong solution being applied to a problem because superficially it appears to be similar to a previous one. Reuse therefore has to mix both the abstract, general view of problems with specific concrete detail to ensure that problems are solved correctly.

3.4.   MEMORY AND REASONING

The way we reason is critically determined by memory. The more we know about a problem, the easier it is to solve it. The influential model of problem solving proposed by Rasmussen (1986) has three modes of reasoning according to experience of the domain. If we know little about the problem, then previous knowledge and general rules of thumb or heuristics are used. In software engineering, if we have never come across the application domain before then we have to reason from first principles. Reuse at this level is in the form of general processes, methods, or models. After some experience, partial problem solutions are stored in memory as rules or declarative knowledge. Reasoning still requires effort, as rules have to be organized in the correct order to solve the problem. Rule-based reuse provides some knowledge but it still has to be compiled into a complete problem solution. The attraction in declarative, rule-based reuse is its flexibility; the disadvantage is in the design effort.

Finally, after further experience has been gained, rules become organized in memory as procedures, that is, runnable programs that automatically solve the problem. In this case we have solved the problem and it is stored in memory. Recognition of the correct calling conditions then invokes automatic procedures (or skills) that consume less effort. People tend to minimize mental effort whenever possible, so there is a natural tendency to use skills and to automate procedures with practice. Hence, if we can recognize a previous solution to the problem at hand (e.g., by means of analogical memory), we will try to reuse it (Maiden & Sutcliffe, 1992). This is the human equivalent of running precompiled knowledge.

Skill acquisition is influenced by the same factors as memorization. Frequent, regular learning sessions help skill acquisition, whereas gaps without practice increase forgetting. Skill learning is improved by the use of context-dependent learning, that is, binding activation of the skilled procedure to the correct circumstances (see also episodic memory). The reuse implication is to link examples and contextual information to the abstract procedure, method, or strategy. The skill level reuses whole procedures. This is cognitively efficient, as the whole process is run without any need for modification or even conscious thought. The disadvantage, however, is that skills have to be run in the appropriate context. This means that skill-based reuse, equivalent to complete programs in software, has larger grain size and hence less flexible reuse, which can also be prone to errors when skills are triggered in the incorrect context (Norman, 1988).

Errors may be either "slips", which are attention failures in carrying out a correct sequence of actions, or "mistakes", in which the plan of action was misconceived in the first place. Slips in reuse arise from paying insufficient attention when searching and retrieving processes as well as from sloppy checking of solutions. True mistakes, however, are either a failure in matching the correct procedure to the problem or are the result of incorrect reasoning at the rule-based level. Mistakes will occur when components and the target application problem are not understood in sufficient depth. The design implications are that functions and tasks should be structured to help users solve problems. We also need to consider how users will reason when they are using the computer system, and we need to help the user to construct a clear mental model by building on appropriate parts of the user's experience. For instance, if the users know little about the domain (novice users), then the designer should provide ways of learning procedures from rules.

Several implications can be drawn from learning, memory, and problem-solving reasoning for the process of reuse and the design of reuse libraries. First, well-structured memories of the problems and solutions in the domain, indexed by many retrieval cues, indicate that reuse libraries require clear structures and indexing–retrieval mechanisms. Design for reuse should create documentation to help the reuser understand decisions made and the original design context. We deal with the complexity of the world by ordering and classifying it. Design for reuse should support this process by imposing structure on component libraries. We understand and memorize complex information by breaking the complexity down into simpler components, using a hierarchical approach. Complex objects are remembered by storing facts that describe objects in various categories, in combination with the access path by which we analyzed and understood the object in the first place. The more structure and categorization we can put into a body of information, the easier it is to learn and remember. Abstract memories of general solutions, but grounded with examples and counterexamples (when not to apply the solution, or things that went wrong) should be reflected in reuse libraries that store not only solutions but also design experience (both good and bad), examples and scenarios linked to abstract models, and design rationale to trace the decision-making process during design.

Second, effective search skills to retrieve appropriate memories, often using external sources (documentation, literature searches, or databases) suggest requirements for information retrieval tools to support human processes of search. Intelligent tools may use metaknowledge to discover long-range associations and analogies; however, to date, less ambitious search processes that work on word density or frequency distributions have a better track record (Landauer & Dumais, 1997).

Active problem solving by reasoning and doing is reflected in constructivist learning theories (Papert, 1980), which urge active engagement: solving puzzles, interacting with simulations, trying out examples, and building artefacts to help learning. The moral here is that design by reuse must be an active process and that the designer should understand the components being reused. Another implication is to store some of the original problem-solving process as an aid to future understanding. Attaching design rationale that documents the design decisions to the reusable components helps future designers understand not only what a component does but also why it was designed in a particular manner.

Encouraging lateral thinking, long-range search, and analogical reasoning often brings the greatest rewards of creative problem solving by reusing knowledge in new ways and contexts. The disadvantage is cognitive effort. People tend toward cognitive economy in taking ready-made solutions that do not require much active, conscious thought. The siren of reuse can encourage cognitive laziness. However, this tendency can be counteracted by training and designing reuse processes that encourage lateral thinking, as well as providing active suggestion facilities, examples, and exceptions to challenge reasoning, with tools that reuse knowledge to critique solutions.

Considering multiple hypotheses and weighing the pros and cons of competing solutions can be encouraged by reuse support environments and retrieval tools that dissuade designers from jumping to simple solutions or conclusions. Goodness-of-fit tools that match solutions to problem descriptions and comparative documentation of related solutions can help. Finally, experts always check out that a solution will be effective by mentally running it in a new application context. Because testing general solutions with grounded examples and scenarios is a powerful mechanism for discovering errors (Sutcliffe, Maiden, Minocha, & Manuel, 1998), reuse methods and tools have to facilitate validation by running scenarios and examples as test data. Experts are distinguished by knowing when not to apply a solution as much as when to apply it.

3.5. COGNITIVE TASKS AND KNOWLEDGE REUSE

This section describes the cognitive or mental processes that are carried out during the reuse process. The review provides background for the more detailed description of reuse tasks in chapter 7. Knowledge may be reused in a wide variety of tasks; however, they all contain some element of judgment and decision making, so that is one reuse context that is investigated. The second context is the design task and cognitive implications for component-based software engineering.

3.5.1. Reuse in Decision Making

Reuse of knowledge in management and organizational learning involves decision making. There are many theories of human judgment and decision making. The following model is based on an amalgam of image theory models (Payne, Bettman, & Johnson, 1993), adaptive decision-making models (Payne et al., 1993), and dual-processing models (Cacioppo, Petty, & Kao, 1984). The course of decision making depends on the nature of the decision and the effort spent on reasoning.

Fast-path decisions are based on previous memory of the problem. Judgment is made by comparing one or more attributes describing each object and then selecting the most favorable fit with the decision criteria. A fast path judgment may be systematic when all the attributes are considered in turn, but more often decisions are irrational and based on a person's "gut feeling"; for example, a purchase may be made on brand or aesthetic feel rather than cost, convenience, or utility.

Slow-path decisions use a mental model of the problem space as networks of information relating to each choice, linked to decision criteria and trade-offs. The decision-making process is systematic and rational. Methods such as decision trees, tables, and weighted options may be used.

In the fast-path case, knowledge reuse is minimal. Lists of salient attributes can help to summarize the key features of each option; however, ideally decisions should be rational and slow path, so one role of knowledge reuse is to encourage slower path reasoning. In slow-path decisions, knowledge can be reused in several forms. Models of the decision space can be reused if the context of decision making is similar. Representation of mental models as interactive simulations enables users to ask "what if" questions when exploring different trade-offs. For instance, simulations of physical systems can help decision making in process control (Alty, 1991). Interactive simulations have the advantage that a wide range of decisions can be made by reusing the simulated world with parameters to model different contexts. However, reuse is limited by assumptions made by the original designer. For instance, a simulated engineering system such as a nuclear power plant can be used to make decisions about normal operating procedures and handling emergencies during training only for plants with the same design. A simulation with a wider remit is marketing simulations in business. General-purpose models predict market success of products according to algorithms that combine price, product, unique selling points (USPs), place, and promotion (Singh & Yang, 1994). For accurate predictions, general-purpose algorithms have to be tuned with historical data from similar situations, so general-purpose models have a wider range but incur more customization cost.

Models of previous decisions can be represented as hypertexts to show the advantages and disadvantages of each option or object. Design rationale and argumentation structures, that is, issues, positions, and arguments, help to lay out the decision space in a systematic way. Tracing links between decisions and their underlying assumptions helps subsequent decision makers share the experience of their predecessors and reduces the frequency of reinventing the wheel. Decision making is influenced by experience; unfortunately, in organizations this is lost as staff retire and move on, so there is a considerable incentive to create some form of corporate memory. Recording and reusing previous decisions is a step in this direction.

Systematic decision making may use quantitative techniques, that is, *criteria*, *measures*, and *metrics*, to reduce the subjective element of judging the relative importance of attributes. In a simple case, decision tables can be used to score each choice on a set of criteria and then total the scores. Criteria should be stated to make the decision more objective. Measures and metrics provide reusable procedures for assessing whether criteria have been met in a design. Metrics and measures knowledge may be either general methods following measurement theory approaches (Fenton, 1995), more specific but general techniques such as goals quality measure (GQM; Basili & Rombach, 1988; Basili & Weiss, 1984), or specific metrics for assessing nonfunctional requirements such as usability (Shackel, 1986) or reliability (McCabe, 1976).

Human decision making is prone to several cognitive pathologies that knowledge reuse can partially cure. Some of the more common errors are as follows.

Models of the problem domain are often incomplete, may be biased in scope, and contain inconsistent facts. Only a small number of facts can be held in the foreground working memory at any one time, so we tend to form incomplete and partial models of problem domains. This tendency leads to many reasoning errors because facts are not available or are incorrect. Knowledge reuse counteracts this problem by supplying more complete models as external representations, but they have to be appropriate to the new problem.

Errors may exist in the problem-solving process, such as thematic vagabonding (a butterfly mind that does not concentrate on any one topic long enough to solve the problem) and encysting (getting bogged down in detail and not being able to see the forest for the trees). Reuse can help by setting the correct level of detail and providing agendas for the problem-solving process (i.e., methods).

There may be a confirmation bias. We tend to overlook exceptions and accept facts that fit into a positive pattern (Johnson-Laird, 1983). This leads to confirmation biases (looking only for positive evidence), halo effects (ignoring exceptions), and poor causal reasoning.

Exponential effects may exist. Working memory limitations make it difficult for us to forecast future system behavior, particularly when there are covert exponential effects. Instead we tend to assume that causes and effects are linear, whereas in many systems they are not. Some examples are chemical reactions in which there is a runaway effect, or the spread of forest fires in which the area of fire raises temperatures that then help the fire to spread more quickly and increase the area, and so on. Positive-feedback loops are often underestimated. Reuse knowledge of similar systems with exponential effects can warn about such errors.

A more specialized set of biases, which affect human judgment with numerical estimation problems, has been described by Kahnemann and Tversky (1982) among others. For example, one set is the availability of data. The frequency of an event is judged by the ease of recall. Recall is effected by frequency and recency of memory use (Reason, 1990), so a biased data set is the norm rather than an exception. Memory of a recent aircraft accident may bias our estimate of how safe flying is. Reuse provides more realistic data samples. Another set is the belief in small numbers. Small samples are judged to represent the variation faithfully in a larger population. In adjustment or anchoring, once an estimate has been made, we tend to be conservative in revising it; this is a consequence of "sticking to the known hypotheses". Reuse of history data and large data sets counters this tendency. In representativeness, the probability of an object or event belonging to a particular class depends on how prototypical it is or how well it represents the overall class. Reuse of knowledge structured in natural categories that contain typical and atypical members can help judgment.

Finally, knowledge reuse depends on the type of task. Decisions to adopt a particular proposal, policy, or strategy assume a plan or course of action exists; the problem is whether or not to follow it in the current circumstances. Reuse in this case is similar to skill knowledge, but the decision to follow a procedure is at a more conscious level of whether to match the procedure to the circumstances. Unfortunately, many reusable policies and procedures do not fit the new domain, so we need to tailor them in light of experience. However, people tend to be cognitively conservative and run with what they are used to. Reuse can hinder decision making by giving people ready-made choices, so we need to be on our guard against copycat reuse.

3.5.2. Cognitive Models of Design and Reuse

Design is the cognitive context for software reuse and knowledge reuse in engineering domains. It is an opportunistic and creative task, so on the surface it would seem that reuse could be a hindrance rather than a help. Reuse provides ready-made design solutions that can encourage people to take the easy way out rather than to come up with a novel solution. In some cases this may be true, so design reuse is about targeting solutions on appropriate problems. There is little point is being creative in solving mundane problems. Here reuse is the answer; however, in more novel problems, creativity should be encouraged, although reuse has a role to play.

Models of the Design Task.   Design is closely related to models of general problem solving. It is generally held to be an opportunistic activity (Hayes-Roth & Hayes-Roth, 1979), although it varies considerably between disciplines. In some it will be an open-ended process of creative imagination (e.g., visual design), whereas in others it is a more constrained engineering process. A model based partially on software engineering design (Guindon & Curtis, 1988) and architecture (Akin, 1986) has the following steps.

A first step is the collation of information and facts pertinent to the design problem. This creates the initial problem space (Simon, 1973). At this stage knowledge is specific to the problem domain, so reuse is limited to examples, scenarios, and case studies.

Another early step is the choice of analytic and synthetic methods, or ways of reasoning to solve the design problem. This step is usually an unconscious activity, but it can be supported by hints about analytic approaches, and general method-level reuse, for example, top-down decomposition, object-oriented analysis, and the like.

The analysis and modeling step creates a model of the design problem, the goals to be achieved, and constraints within which it will have to be achieved. Requirements reuse at level 1 can help here by providing abstractions of similar classes of problems with reusable guides toward their solution.

Another step is the synthesis of the design solution, either by generating hypotheses and testing them, or by constraints-based reasoning to eliminate treatments that will not work. In software engineering this stage frequently proceeds by refining a high-level architecture to low-level design. Design and component reuse come into play at this level.

Finally, validation and testing occur to check that the design actually meets the initial objectives and users' requirements. In software engineering this stage involves system integration testing, requirements validation, and usability testing. Scenarios and examples can be reused to provide test data for assessing that the system can achieve its goals or can deal with problems described in requirements.

As the design process proceeds, reuse progresses from specific examples to general components and then back to specific scenarios and examples. Specific knowledge helps reasoning by anchoring arguments in knowledge structures familiar to users, that is, details of the domain that they know. Specific knowledge is also a necessary precursor for generalization. Analysis and modeling both involve example-based generalization to create higher-order abstractions. These are then transformed into designs by application of technical knowledge where reuse of design components can play a part. Once a candidate design has been selected, then specific knowledge is necessary to carry out testing. A common pathology at this stage is "hovercraft" reasoning, in which people don't reason in detail whether a design will work in a real-world context; instead they make weak assumptions and hope for the best. In most design the devil is in the detail. Scenarios and examples help to ground arguments and encourage sound testing.

Design is also a reflective process (Schon, 1983), so part of the process is trying to improve design in the future. This leads to process reuse in which the organization of the design task is critiqued and documented with improvements for future reuse. Reflection may also improve products. Solutions are investigated to see where lessons can be learned for creating new components for the reuse library or improving the design of existing ones.

3.5.3. Facets of Expertise

The human exemplar of good reuse practice is the expert. Experts are usually intelligent people who are good problem solvers; however, being an expert is not just the possessing of innate intelligence. The most important aspect that marks experts apart from novices is their knowledge. Experts reuse knowledge with care. A good expert does not just pick a possible solution from memory, but reasons carefully about its applicability and then tailors the previous solution to the new problem. Reuse support tools have to mimic the properties of human experts; however, this is often a hard task. The main facets of expert problem-solving performance can be summarized as follows.

First, one must construct a sound mental model of the problem space and gather all the necessary facts pertinent to the problem. This suggests support for representing the problem, fact gathering, and reuse of similar abstractions of the domain knowledge at the requirements level. Second, one must match the current problem to memories of related problems. Experts have rich memories of abstract descriptions of problems, so they can easily understand the deeper structure. Reuse support is necessary for matching problem descriptions to abstract models of the domain. Third, one must retrieve candidate solutions for the current problem. Expert memory is probably a rich structure of interconnected problem and solution models, so the processes of recognizing and understanding the problem automatically suggests the solution. Reuse libraries have to implement similar links as hypertext structures or provide search processes that match problem models with appropriate solution classes. Fourth, one must reason about boundary cases when reusing solutions. Experts reason carefully about differences between domains, and they use counterexamples to critique favored hypotheses. This helps to increase the richness of the mental model schema. Reuse tools could support reasoning with comparative pattern matching tools. Fifth, one must consider candidate solutions. Novices tend to jump the gun, whereas experts avoid premature commitment and consider several solutions before arriving at an optimal one. Reasoning with multiple hypotheses imposes an excessive load on working memory, so design support tools have to provide notepads and aide-memoires for comparison, with functions for ranking, sorting, and prioritizing solutions according to different criteria. Finally, one must use thorough validation and testing. Experts test a design solution against fitness criteria and run scenarios or test data against the design to make sure it will achieve its objectives. Any problems encountered lead to design improvements and further testing in a prototype-and-evaluate cycle. This also has to be borne in mind when reuse support tools are designed.

Models of human expertise can inform design of reuse support environments in several ways. First the structural aspects of expert memory can be used as a basis for design of component libraries, metadata for component description, and schema for reusable knowledge. Second, aspects of the problems of retrieval and matching knowledge as well as reasoning about several candidate solutions suggest how the task of design-led reuse might be structured.

3.5.4. Task Model of Reuse

Reuse of designs and knowledge more generally consists of *design for reuse*, which involves knowledge acquisition, structuring, and formatting, and then indexing and storage for subsequent reuse; and *design by reuse*, which commences with retrieval and matching of the new problem context to the appropriate reuse structure, customizing the component where necessary, applying knowledge in problem solving, and testing the solution.

A more elaborate breakdown of the reuse process is described in chapter 7, so this section deals with the cognitive issues inherent in reuse. The stages in the cognitive task are illustrated in Fig. 3.4. In design for reuse, the first problem is knowledge acquisition. This is a time-consuming task. People are prone to omit key facts and may be economical with the truth for a variety of social and political reasons, such as fear of losing their jobs if their knowledge is captured for reuse by others. Furthermore, much knowledge is tacit because it is compiled skill that we are not aware of; consequently experts often omit mundane details that they assume the analyst knows. These details are often key assumptions and details about a design or process. Knowledge-acquisition problems can be counteracted by getting experts to explain tasks to each other, or better still to novices. Another approach is for the analyst to perform the task under expert guidance. This elicits not only baseline knowledge of the design, process, or strategy but also the additional explanatory knowledge the expert has built up during explanation-based

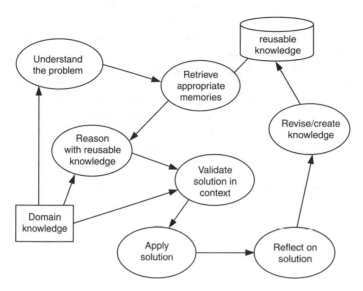

FIG. 3.4. Cognitive tasks and resources involved in reuse.

learning (how to teach the process–design to a novice). Apart from the volume of knowledge that may have to be acquired, there are further problems of terminology and understanding that gradually unfold as the analyst acquires more domain knowledge (Sutcliffe, 1997).

Once knowledge has been acquired, it has to be structured, formatted, and indexed. Formatting and structuring is a trade-off. More effort put into this task will result in a deeper understanding of the knowledge by the knowledge acquirer, because one has to reason about knowledge to structure it, and this increases the depth of encoding. The disadvantage is that the structure reflects the analyst's viewpoint, so it is advisable to document the formatting and structuring principles. The reuser can then appreciate the viewpoint of the original analyst. Indexing involves language, so the designer's description of a component may not match the reuser's. No easy solution has been found to this problem in several decades of information science research. The conventional solution is to adopt a controlled vocabulary that is shared by the indexer and the population of reusers. Unfortunately, arriving at such agreed vocabularies is a difficult task, especially in diverse and fast-moving areas such as computer and management science.

Design by reuse starts with the retrieval–matching problem. In human memory this works by spreading activation in network schemas, so retrieval of one knowledge component tends to activate its nearest neighbors. This concept can be applied to retrieval processes to suggest similar and related knowledge structures. Creating a comprehensive library is a necessary precondition for successful reuse; unfortunately, problems arise in the different levels of abstraction adopted by individuals when problem solving. It is unlikely that a reuser–designer will think about a problem at exactly the same level of abstraction and chunk size as the original analyst. For instance, the original analyst may see a library in terms of a transaction-based abstraction of loaning and returning resources (books), whereas the reuser–designer may conceptualize the same domain with a task viewpoint of the librarian authorizing loans, receiving returns, processing renewals and over-dues, and so on. Matching this clash of viewpoints in reuse is one of the most difficult problems to solve. There is no silver bullet; however, the Domain Theory, which is described in chapters 4 and 5, is one step on the path toward a solution. Ulti-mately, developing shared viewpoints on knowledge is a process of standardization.

3.5.5. Reuse and Creative Design

Reuse has a strange relationship with creative design. On one hand, any relationship appears to be a tautology. To reuse knowledge or designs is to avoid creation. On the other hand, reuse may involve long-range analogical reasoning and reuse across domains. Here solutions can be creatively applied in different contexts. At the extreme, reuse of knowledge is a prosthesis for creative thought. Techniques for lateral thinking reuse ideas and artefacts to deliberately provoke a long-range analogy as part of the creative process. One approach is relabeling (Djajadiningrat, Gaver, & Frens, 2000), in which a familiar everyday object is taken as a seed and then applied to a new domain to stimulate analogical reasoning. The well-known Swiss army knife is a good exemplar design to try. It has components that fulfill specialized functions (e.g., the corkscrew) as well as more general-purpose knives, scissors, saws, and so on. Relabeling a proposed application by drawing analogies with the Swiss army knife can stimulate lateral thinking. To illustrate the process, if a diary management product were being designed, then functions would be needed to map to specific requirements (arranging meetings) and more general-purpose requirements (managing a to-do agenda list). Next, how do the knife's functions suggest new requirements? Taking the knife, can we design a function to cut through the bureaucracy of arranging a meeting, or with the saw can we cut off constraints on time and place? Even the corkscrew might suggest that social and recreational aspects of meetings are important.

Another idea is reuse in role-playing. Role-playing is common in requirements engineering and brainstorming methods. Reuse of stereotypes and extreme char-acters stimulates our imagination and encourages creative thinking. The concept is best explained by example. Take a well-known stereotype character, such as the Pope, or former president Clinton. What requirements would these individ-uals have for a diary manager product? One can assume the Pope would need a product with filters for different priorities of meetings, many of them personal with annotations to remind him of the many personalities he is about to meet, purpose of the meeting, and so on. President Clinton may have similar needs, but he is a less formal person, although he leads a more pressured and less predictable life, so rapid change and update could be important, as may secrecy and clandestine meetings. Reuse in both of the techniques is using knowledge for creative thinking by stimulating long-range analogy and shifting the context for reasoning. As we are cognitively conservative by nature, reuse of knowledge that challenges our assumptions and habits has an important role to play in creativity.

Reuse in the cognitive context of ideas is universal. Indeed, it merges into social learning and culture. One only has to consider patterns in Roman mosaics reused in art deco decoration, Arabic geometric motifs reused in Spanish ceramics, and Gaudi's architecture to see how regularities in form and style reappear through the ages (see Gombrich, 1984). In architectural form, reuse was practiced for many years before Christopher Alexander proposed his patterns. The Greeks invented the theater as a structure to facilitate the sharing of a performed drama; the Romans borrowed the concept and reused it directly, and then they extended it to a 360 degree experience in the amphitheatre. Good ideas are naturally adopted, even though their reuse can sometimes hinder new more creative solutions; for instance, the Roman rounded arch was a standard solution to spanning spaces for windows and roof supports for a millennium until the Gothic rounded V-shape evolved in 11th century Europe to enable higher roofed churches and other buildings. Reuse in some cases provides the pattern that is reapplied simply off the peg to save effort; in other cases it forms the springboard to something new. The debate about the relative merits of reuse as off-the-peg economy or a prosthesis for creation is ongoing. Alexander saw his pattern languages from the latter viewpoint, but his readers have often adopted them verbatim.

Creative design is still a poorly understood process. We need to encourage creativity to advance design while leveraging reuse for the economic benefit of development where the design problem is at least reasonably well understood. Unfortunately, most of us have a tendency to be cognitively conservative and lazy; hence we adopt the known solution if given half a chance. Reuse therefore can be the enemy of invention. However, this need not be so. Creative design is encouraged by experience, motivation (both individual and peer group inspiration), and ability. The experience component is cognitive reuse. In creative design it will be used more adventurously in the longer-range reworking of ideas through analogies and lateral thinking. In more prosaic development, reuse will be the reapplication of generalized experience, through the expert's realization: "Aha! I have come across this problem before". In the following chapters the Domain Theory is proposed to describe my view on what those expert experiences should be.

3.6. SUMMARY

Cognitive psychology can help in understanding important human requirements for the design process. Software design commences with analysis that involves comprehending facts, models, and other representations. When we analyze requirements, we engage in problem solving. Our ability to comprehend and solve problems depends on well-formed memories and the ability to reason effectively when reusing memories. Information has to be structured in reuse libraries to reduce loads on working memory and make comprehension easier. Reuse has to promote active problem solving to avoid shallow, copycat reuse. Partial mental models omit key facts, so the description of the problem domain may be incomplete. Inaccurate or incomplete models may increase errors in reuse; also, poor ability to hold negative facts in mental models increases confirmation bias and leads to validation failures.

Reasoning is heuristic in situations when little is known about the problem. Heuristic reasoning requires considerable effort. The early stages, in which we know little about the problem, are the most difficult. Experience leads to the results of reasoning being stored, first as declarative, rule-based knowledge and then as automatic procedures. Domain knowledge and reuse of previous solutions play key roles in solving software engineering problems. Mismatch between memory of a previous solution and the current problem can lead to inappropriate reuse. Failures can lie in analogical memory, poor cues for retrieving previous solutions, and inadequate reasoning in copycat reuse.

Reuse libraries need to be organized and structured to support learning and memory by use of clear categories, multiple, nonambiguous retrieval cues, and search tools to help retrieval. Reuse support tools should help users retrieve components and consider alternatives while discouraging copycat reuse. The structure of reuse libraries and the process of reuse should be based on models of memory and problem solving, in particular analogical memory and case-based reasoning. Reuse aims to emulate the properties of experts. Hence reuse support requires rich models (memory schema); mechanisms for retrieving and matching problems with appropriate solutions; and validation techniques to check that reused solutions are appropriate for a new context. Explicit representation of models, critiquing, and aide-memoire tools help. Reuse of knowledge is important in decision support tasks as rationale or simulations that represent domains. In design, reuse involves solutions, components and arguments as well as process knowledge. A clear mental model of the problems and solution space is necessary. Mental models of reusable solution components and problem descriptions can be promoted by using animated diagrams or interactive simulation to engage the user in active problem solving. This encourages better depth of encoding in memorization. Reuse of long-range analogies can help creativity in problem solving.

4

Domain Theory: Foundations

This chapter introduces the Domain Theory that describes a knowledge representation ontology for generic reusable models of application classes, and a library of models that cover a wide range of software system-development problems. The Domain Theory is based on a cognitive model of analogy, in particular structure-matching theory (Gentner, 1983). The theory has been developed over the years in collaboration with Neil Maiden (Maiden & Sutcliffe, 1994, 1996; Sutcliffe & Maiden, 1998) and Jack Carroll (Sutcliffe & Carroll, 1998). It has also stood the test of validation and application (Maiden, Mistry, & Sutcliffe, 1995; Sutcliffe, 2000a). The motivation for the theory was to capture and formalize reusable knowledge at the requirements specification level, essentially translating the memory that expert consultants retrieve when they recognize "I have come across this before and it is the *xxx* problem". The theory explores long-range analogies to push forward the boundaries of reuse across domains, and it proposes an answer to the abstraction and granularity problems that were introduced in chapter 1.

4.1. INTRODUCTION

The Domain Theory is a hybrid theory that bridges cognitive science and software engineering. As a consequence, its foundations in different perspectives require some explanation. Essentially the theory is motivated by cognitive science and belongs to theories of knowledge representation and memory in the categorial tradition. However, it also functions as a theory of expertize that is applied in computer science to predict and explain concepts of abstraction that should have demonstrable utility in requirements engineering and software reuse. To elaborate these points a little further, the Domain Theory draws on three precursor theories in cognitive science.

The first theory is Rosch's theory of natural categories, in its various forms (Rosch, Mervis, Gray, Johnson, & Boyes-Braem, 1976). This describes human memory for objects in terms of approximate memberships of categories, with exemplars (called prototypes; e.g., a robin is a prototypical bird) being better members than atypical examples (a penguin is a rather atypical bird). Natural categories theory proposes that knowledge is organized in three-level hierarchies in which the basic level is the middle (e.g., birds), with more detailed subordinates (species of bird) and superordinates (birds being members of the category "animals").

Although natural categories seem to work well with physical concrete objects, the theory is less predictive for abstract and functional categories, for example, classes of events and tasks (Hampton, 1988). The notion of simple categories has evolved into radial categories that extend the categorial concept of Rosch toward networklike schema (see Lakoff, 1987, for a review). A further problem is whether natural categories are a representational theory of knowledge structures in the mind, or a generative theory whereby categories are simply manifestations of processes mediated by language. This debate is ongoing in psychology.

The connection from natural categories to the Domain Theory is indirect. The notion of classes and prototype examples has its origins in Rosch's work; however, the Domain Theory models are motivated by teleological, functional, and structural properties.

The second precursor theory is Gentner's structure-matching theory of analogy (Gentner, 1983). This is a process and representational theory. Analogical knowledge follows schema theory origins (Quillan, 1966; Rumelhart, 1975), which propose that memory is organized in semantic networks of connected facts, or schema. Structure-matching theory proposes that abstract schema are learned when people recognize and solve problems. The abstract schema is built from the concrete source domain and has mappings from the source to the analogue schema and to a new target domain. An example is the analogy between electrical circuits and water pipes. Both share an abstract structure of connections that determine flows, with particles (water molecules, electrons) flowing along connections (pipes, wires). The abstraction of electrical resistance can be conceptualized as being similar to a volume constraint in the water pipe. Both impede flow and increase pressure;

however, in detail the analogy begins to break down. The relationship among current, voltage resistors, and impedances in electric circuits is governed by Ohm's law, which does not translate into the world of fluid dynamics. Establishing common abstractions that maximize shared knowledge and minimize erroneous interdomain transfer is a key concern of the Domain Theory.

Gentner's theory forms the most important baseline for the Domain Theory, which proposes a set of analogical abstract schema as Object System Models (OSMs). Rather than describing analogies in everyday life, the Domain Theory proposes a set of analogies built up by repeated exposure to similar problems that come from different applications. Hence the Domain Theory is indeed a theory of analogy, as the concrete examples that form the analogy belong to dissimilar contexts (e.g., library loans and car hire), yet they share a common abstraction (loaning resources).

The third precursor theory is Schank's theory of ecological memory. Schank's (1982) work on dynamic memory schema as scripts and memory-organized packets has been another important influence. Script–memory theories propose that we remember patterns of experience associated with specific constructs and purposes, for example, satisfying hunger by eating a meal. Scripts encapsulate objects, actions, and events in an expected sequence that achieves a desired goal. Memory is developed by generalization from many specific instances of similar episodes, so we apply a generic script to situations by recognizing their entry conditions. The concordance between the script and events in the real world determines how typical we judge a situation to be and our prediction of the appropriate responses to make.

The Domain Theory task models are equivalent to scripts for achieving system goals. They represent a collection of objects, events, and procedures that achieve a purpose. Unlike everyday scripts, the Domain Theory models are deeper abstractions of problems; hence they are unlikely to be so easily recognized as scripts for everyday problems, for example, going to the supermarket or on a car journey.

A further influence from computer science is theories of modularity, based on the principle of cohesion (Meyer, 1985; Yourdon & Constantine, 1978), which asserts that systems exist to achieve a goal. Goal-oriented modeling is a common abstraction in representations of knowledge (Johnson, 1992), so reusable libraries of goal-oriented models should concord with people's naturally occurring memories. However, the Domain Theory also applies principles of abstraction to defining cohesive models. One of the problems with goal-oriented approaches is the recursive nature of cohesion. A module that appears to be cohesive at one level will, when examined in more detail, contain several subgoals. So a definition of a cohesive, nondecomposable goal is required. First, goals must be decomposed to a level where they can be expressed as a state that the system should achieve or maintain, following the concept of goal refinement in software engineering (Van Lamsweerde, 2000; Van Lamsweerde & Letier, 2000). Second, the system goal must represent the endpoint in a life history of transformations on an object, adopting Jackson's (1983) idea of entity life histories as "slow running processes" that reach an end state even though they may halt at intermediate states. The notion of life history endpoints works reasonably well for object-oriented domain models but, as we shall see, more functionally oriented abstractions present some problems for defining end points in task decomposition.

In summary, the Domain Theory has two viewpoints. First it is a *theory of abstraction* in that it defines a schema for generic domain knowledge, and second it is a *theory of naturally occurring expertise*. The latter view asserts that generic models of domain knowledge are naturally occurring phenomena held by expert software engineers and, to a less precise degree, by users. The theory proposes that these models exist as a result of reasoning about related classes of problems, leading to the formation of generic abstractions by human cognitive processes of analogical reasoning (Gentner, 1983). It facilitates reuse of knowledge over a wide range of applications that share a common abstract model, for example, loans applications in car hire, library loans, video rentals, and the like. Domain models are structured in a class hierarchy drawing on cognitive theories of memory (Anderson, 1990; Cheng & Holyoak, 1985; Chi, Glaser, & Rees, 1982), memory schemata (Anderson, 1990; Riesbeck & Schank, 1989), and natural categories (Rosch, 1985; Rosch et al., 1976), which assert that human memory is organized as an informal hierarchy. There is good evidence that memory for several different types of knowledge (e.g., objects, procedures and plans) is organized hierarchically (Johnson, Johnson, Waddington, & Shouls, 1988). Furthermore, generalization, specialization, and inheritance of objects are familiar concepts in software engineering.

4.2. DOMAIN THEORY FRAMEWORK

The Domain Theory posits an ontology of knowledge for representing generalized views of problems commonly encountered in the design of computer-based systems. First, the meaning of problem models should be clarified. Newell and Simon (1972) made the distinction between models in the problem domain in contrast to those in the solution domain. Problem models help the designer understand the domain so that it can be reasoned about to arrive at a solution. The Domain Theory rests on the conjecture that people experience similar problems many times and, in the process of solving such problems, build up abstractions in long-term memory.

People may experience problems in different situations, but the key to requirements reuse is recognizing the abstract problem, which is not tied to any one context. The theory is based on empirical findings that experienced designers tend to recall and reuse knowledge structures or abstraction models when specifying new systems (Guindon, 1990; Guindon & Curtis, 1988). The focus of the Domain Theory is abstraction of the problem space rather than design models of computational functions, algorithms, and abstract data types. Models at this level of abstraction have been proposed by Shaw (1991), Harandi and Lee (1991), and in more detail by Smith (1992) and Gamma et al. (1995). The Domain Theory follows an object-oriented approach but proposes reuse at a higher level of granularity than a single class. In object-oriented parlance, the Domain Theory posits generic models of object collaborations; that is, it is a collection of objects that transform initial states into a single desired goal state.

The fundamental tenets of the Domain Theory are as follows.

1. Problems in software engineering and many other design-related activities can be modeled by a small number of abstract models. These models will be stable over time and are independent of any implementation technology. They therefore represent abstractions of commonly experienced problems.

2. Problems are described by a minimal set of objects and actions that achieve a goal that solves the problem. Goals are expressed as states that must be achieved or maintained. The definition of a goal in the Domain Theory is, "A goal represents a state that the system must maintain or achieve at the end of its life history." It follows from this assertion that the Domain Theory must specify how a goal state is achieved by actions.

3. Domain Theory models are coherent because they contain only the minimal set of actions and objects to achieve the goal. Actions are organized in life histories that must run to completion to achieve the system goal. The coherence of Domain Theory models is governed by the closure principle. This states that only necessary actions are present to achieve the system goal state that terminates the life history. Intermediate states may be present, but these are not goals because they will always be changed eventually within the domain model life history.

4. The level of granularity is determined by system goals that cannot be decomposed. Models at the primitive level of the theory, OSMs and generic tasks, are unique and contain no embedded subgoals or life histories.

5. The level of abstraction is determined by impact principle: all system goals must result in a state change in the external world. This principle firmly targets the Domain Theory in the realm of requirements analysis (layer 1 reuse).

6. Applications in the real world are modeled by aggregation of Domain Theory models, and the Domain Theory models are the smallest units of abstraction that can be meaningfully used for the modeling of generic classes of problems.

These tenets require further explanation to situate the Domain Theory within other abstractions. At higher levels of abstraction than the Domain Theory are general ontologies in knowledge engineering, such as Sowa's (2000) conceptual structures, which are closer to a modeling language. Similarly, highly abstract database schema are modeling languages (entity relationships; Chen, 1976), as are semantic data models and CRUD (create, replace, update, and delete) actions. Closer to the

Domain Theory are object-oriented patterns, but these belong to the design world (Gamma et al., 1995) because they do not obey the impact principle. They may change states inside a computer program but have little or no bearing on the external world. The closest relative is the conceptual modeling patterns of Fowler (1997), which describe organizational structures of hierarchies and networks with some transaction patterns for accounting applications (sales, money transfer). The Domain Theory is both a modeling language and a library of reusable generic models.

The goal concept in the Domain Theory is linked to life history by the closure principle. However, there is room for tautology here. Goals can be self-defining according to any person's view of when a life history is deemed to be complete. Take a library book as an example. We might expect that the normal life history of a book is to be loaned, possibly renewed, and then returned. Return of the book creates the axiom of closure that "all books must eventually be returned to the library." Indeed, this is the very axiom of the Object Hiring abstraction that models library lending. However, a book may be modeled with a longer life span from being purchased, to having a class mark assigned to it, being entered into stock, and then going through a cycle of loans and returns until it is finally sold, archived, or destroyed (Fig. 4.1).

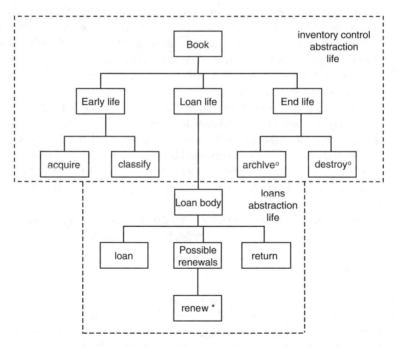

FIG. 4.1.   Book object life cycle. The notation used is Jackson's (1983): the asterisk denotes iteration, and the degree symbol represents selection.

The Domain Theory solves the problem by the exclusive contribution principle. This states that an action life history belongs to a goal only if it cannot contribute to any other system goal. Goals must have a unique impact in the external world and the temporal organization of their life. Hence in the model shown in Fig. 4.1 the book object participates in two domains. First there is the life of loans and returns, which affects the user and the choice of books available. The second abstraction describes inventory control; the early life and end life of the book is a specialization of a generic life describing objects in any stock control system (purchase, place in stock, sell, discard). Refutation of any Domain Theory model is therefore by testing with counterexamples. If any other domain model can be found that the action sequence belongs to (whether recorded in the Domain Theory or not), then the life cycle of the model being tested is incoherent. In the case of the book, the actions of being acquired, being assigned a class mark (registration), and being sold or archived also belong to the inventory control abstraction. The Domain Theory principles cause two abstractions to be discovered in this life history and create minimal models at the smallest level of granularity.

To summarize, there are three fundamental principles that govern the composition and structure of Domain Theory models. The first is the closure principle: in any domain model, only the necessary actions are present to achieve the system goal state that results from the termination of the life history. The second is the impact principle: all system goals must result in a state change that is observable or detectable in the real world. The third is the exclusive contribution principle: for each domain model, actions in a life history result in a system (goal) state defined by unique observable or detectable changes on structures and agents in the real world.

Closely related research is the work on problem frames by Michael Jackson (Jackson, 2001), who also posits a set of generic models that describe recurring problems. However, problem frames model reusable knowledge at a higher level of abstraction. Jackson draws our attention to the connection between the design system and the real world in which it is–will be embedded. He sees requirements engineering as the process of precise specification of the dependencies between designed systems and the external world they sense and respond to. Domains are divided into three types: *lexical*, which are symbol systems such as text, diagrams, and models with physical manifestations; *causal domains*, which model laws and predictable behaviors in the real world; and *biddable domains*, which exhibit behavior but have no guarantee of reliability; for example, human users are biddable in the sense that they may or may not respond.

Generic problems are described in a total of five frames. Each frame encapsulates objects in the real world, objects in the required system, and connections between them that formally model the assumptions made about the system scope. The first requirements frame asserts that a design machine must respond in a predictable manner to a set of requirements defined within the bounds of assumptions recorded in a set of domain properties. The second information display frame concerns the faithful representation of information about a set of entities in the real world. The third workpieces frame describes the interaction between events and their effect on a model held in the machine, which shares many aspects with the Domain Theory object-manipulation generic model. The fourth command frame is similar to the agent-control generic model and concerns how events cause behavior in the world. The fifth frame describes problems involving transformation of one representation into another. Jackson's problem frames and domains are more abstract than the Domain Theory, which models generic knowledge closer to the real world and with more detail; however, the Domain Theory does share Jackson's concern about defining the focus between the designed system and the external world.

The Domain Theory consists of three major components. The first is a meta-schema or modeling language, which defines the semantics for generic models of application classes. The second is a set of generic models organized in a class hierarchy. The third is a computational matching process, developed from analogy theory (Holyoak & Thagard, 1989) for retrieving generic models appropriate to a set of facts describing a new application.

The generic models state problems as they exist in the world. Attached to these models are generic requirements that indicate typical problems that should be attended to when specifying the software system that will interact with the domain. Generic requirements also indicate high-level solutions to the problems. The Domain Theory models were constructed from knowledge-acquisition interviews with expert designers, by investigations and abstraction from specific problems published in the literature, and by refining the models by means of empirical testing (Maiden et al., 1995). To deal with a wider range of applications, the theory proposes a component-based ontology composed of three families of generic models: *grounded domains*, *metadomains*, and *generic tasks*.

4.2.1. Grounded Domains

Grounded domains form the original core of the Domain Theory (Sutcliffe & Maiden, 1998). These domains achieve a purpose and may be associated with one or more tasks (described in chapter 5). Grounded domains can be located in the real world and have a distant association with physical structure, in that a work task takes place at some location and involves physical, as well as possibly abstract, objects. Some examples of grounded domains are hiring applications that characterize libraries, car hire, and video rental, or monitoring applications that sense the behavior of objects and their movement in air traffic control, road traffic monitoring, shipborne radar systems, and so on. This leads to the following definition.

- Grounded domains are abstractions of real-world problems that have a physical existence with observable objects, actions, and tasks that achieve the system goal. Grounded-domain models are a set of collaborating objects that achieve a goal or provide a service, hence following object-oriented concepts of responsibility modeling (Wirfs-Brock et al., 1990).

Grounded domains are expressed as abstract models that are instantiated in any one application. Domain models are a consequence of shared problem solving rooted in a real-world context, in other words, observable, purposeful activity that appears in many different business and engineering applications.

Grounded domains fall into two subclasses: Object and Information Systems Models.

- OSMs describe the essential transaction of the application in terms of a set of cooperating objects and their behavior, such as use cases (Jacobson, 1992). We introduce the concept of "structure objects" as a bridging abstraction that preserves some manifestation of the physical structure found in the real world. This enables OSMs to express facts about the real-world domain that would not normally be included in conceptual models such as entity relationship diagrams, for example, environmental phenomena such as buildings, rooms, and warehouses.
- Information System Models (ISMs) contain processes that report on and provide information about an OSM. Object systems define the essential model of the problem (McMenamin & Palmer, 1984), that is, the application's objects or entities and behavior related to achieving the system's purpose, whereas ISMs describe processes that provide reports, ad hoc queries, and other information requirements. This distinction is a development of Jackson's (1983) ideas on separating the fundamental entity model of a system from the functional processes that acquire information from that model.

4.2.2. Metadomains

However, much human activity is not characterized by physical, observable action. To deal with such phenomena we propose metadomains. These are composed of generalized tasks (see section 4.2.3) that can be applied to grounded domains. In some sense metadomains are empty unless they are applied to a grounded domain. The definition of metadomains emphasizes human activity in problem solving, analysis, and creative design that still achieves a purpose but has indirect reference to the world of physical objects.

- Metadomains are characterized by the cognitive tasks that achieve a complex goal to transform knowledge, artefacts, or organizations within a domain, and operate on grounded domains and tasks.

Examples of metadomains are Education, Management (including governance), Research, and Design. These models describe high-level abstractions of organizations and societies with a common thread of purposeful activity to achieve goals of control, mutual benefit, or increased knowledge. Metadomains, in contrast to grounded domains, are not concerned with transactions and interaction with the real world; instead they constitute human activity that is applied to the grounded domains in the real world. For instance, one can teach people how to operate a stock control system or design a new one. Metadomains are composed of functional components that deliver high-level services, tasks, and agents. Tasks are either defined in the generic task component of the Domain Theory or refer to general cognitive activities such as decision making, reasoning, and problem solving. Metadomains describe more complex phenomena than grounded domains and generic tasks, so they are modeled as subsystems with architectural components that achieve particular functions.

4.2.3. Generic Tasks

The final component, generic tasks, is carried out by agents to change the state of some object and thereby achieve a goal. Generic tasks cause state changes that may not be immediately observable but are often precursors of change that becomes observable in a grounded domain; for example, reserving a book is a generic task that causes a state change of a book to be reserved as a precursor to a possible loan. The definition is as follows.

- Generic tasks are self-contained procedures that run from initiation to completion without halting, to achieve a goal that is described in a postcondition state.

Generic tasks are small units of activity that are larger than the concept of "unit tasks" described in the HCI literature (Card, Moran, & Newell, 1983) and have a functional interpretation that is closer to language-based ontologies such as Rhetorical Structure Theory (Mann & Thompson, 1988). Examples of generic tasks are Comparing, Evaluating, Identifying, and Classifying objects. Similar but not so extensive taxonomies have been described by Zhou and Feiner (1998), who focus on tasks involved with visualization of information, and by Wehrend and Lewis (1990), whose taxonomy covers generic information-processing tasks with mapping to suitable visualizations of information. In contrast, generic tasks in the Domain Theory are intended to cover all human mental activity, including the cognitive precursors of action. However, physical tasks are specific manifestations of activity; hence they are excluded. Furthermore, the Domain Theory assumes the existence of basic cognitive functions for human reasoning, problem solving, and action. Generic tasks are composed into composite structures, called *generalized tasks*, which are defined as follows.

- Generalized tasks are composed of two or more generic tasks to achieve or maintain a system state. Generalized tasks may run to execution without halting or go through several intermediate states.

Generic tasks have been described in the knowledge engineering literature (Breuker & Van der Velde, 1994); however, these tasks record problem-solving processes as templates for building expert systems. In contrast, the Domain Theory's generic–generalized tasks are descriptions of human mental activity, which indicate functional requirements for supporting and collaborating with users. Generalized tasks may have a *deterministic* structure, in which case the composition and execution order of generic tasks can be specified; or they may be *nondeterministic*, so that only their probable subcomponents can be specified with no particular execution order. Generalized tasks are closer to the everyday meaning of a task and have a wide application in many grounded and metadomains. Some familiar examples are as follows.

* Diagnosis: determining the cause of some malfunction in a system, locating its cause, and proposing remedial treatment. Examples may vary from medical diagnosis of a patient's illness to a technical diagnosis of a fault in a photocopier.
* Information retrieval: finding information to satisfy either a task or curiosity-driven need, locating the appropriate information resources, searching for the necessary items, assessing their usefulness, and extracting the required information.

Generalized tasks may occur in many different grounded and metadomains. In a similar manner to grounded domains, generalized tasks represent families that are specialized into more specific tasks; for example, diagnosis is specialized into fault finding for machinery, diagnosis of pathologies in living entities, and diagnosis of problems in organized systems. Generic tasks and metadomains are dealt with in more depth in chapter 5.

4.3. REPRESENTING DOMAIN KNOWLEDGE

The metaschema defines eleven knowledge types that form the primitive components of OSMs. The structure of the metaschema is shown in Fig. 4.2, using the format of an entity–relationship diagram.

The semantics of each component were defined more formally in the Telos knowledge representation language (Mylopoulos, Borgida, Jarke, & Koubarakis, 1990; Sutcliffe & Maiden, 1998). Telos itself has object–oriented semantics with inheritance, and its semantic primitives are mapped to first-order logic definitions, thus providing a formal knowledge representation language for the Domain Theory. The Telos models have been implemented in ConceptBase, a deductive database system (Jarke, 1992). First-order predicate logic provides a formal basis

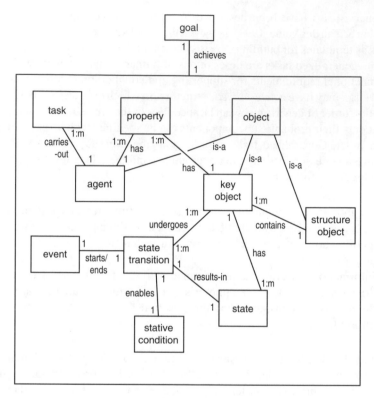

FIG. 4.2. Schema of knowledge types for Object System modelling, expressed as an entity–relationship diagram. The schema itself is a composite entity that achieves the system goal.

for reasoning to assist the understanding of linguistic expressions of states, goal states, and behavior during requirements definition.

4.3.1. Key Objects

Objects are specialized into key objects, agents, or structure objects. Key objects are the subject matter of the essential system transaction and therefore undergo state change. Key objects may be physical and subject to laws such as gravity and momentum, or they may be conceptual objects without physical instantiation.

4.3.2. Agents

Agents are specializations of objects and carry out tasks that may create events initiating state transitions. Agents can be subtyped as human or automated agents to describe a required computer system or a manual operator in a paper-based system.

4.3.3. Structure Objects

Structure objects are abstractions of physical aspects of the real-world domain. They bridge the gap between domain-specific models (Arango et al., 1993; Fischer, Girensohn, Nakakoji, & Redmiles, 1992) and modeling languages (Dardenne, Van Lamsweerde, & Fickas, 1993; Meyer, 1985) that provide a general set of semantics. There are two motivations for introducing this concept. The first is to bridge between linguistically based knowledge representation (Sowa, 1984) and more formal semantics. The second is that structure as a semantic primitive helps analogical computational matching. Structure objects represent passive objects and environmental facts that would not normally appear in data models, for example, warehouse, library, or air corridors in air traffic control. Specializations in OSM families may add further structure objects; for instance, a distributed warehouse application is modeled by several container structure objects representing branch warehouses.

Structure objects model real-world entities that must be persistent, have spatial properties, and express containment or possession of key objects; for example, a library contains books. The relationship between key and structure objects is equivalent to a state. Objects change state with reference to a structure; for example, an object is sold and physically moved out of the warehouse structure to a customer structure. This is logically equivalent to a state transition from in-stock to issued-from-stock.

Structure objects can model physical entities and states in two ways. The first is by creating an internal structure within a structure object. This is used in Object Allocation and Object Sensing OSM families in which the structure object is conceptually divided into an arbitrary number of parts. These parts are then used to record the state of a key object; for example, in Object Sensing, aircraft (x) is in structure object subpart (a^1) air lane sector. The second way is by creating additional structure objects when an OSM family is specialized; for instance, in Object Inventory, further structure objects may be added in a subclass to model a central warehouse and branch warehouses. This would be advisable if there are significant state transitions between the two structures, for example, if stock is taken from the central warehouse and distributed to branches before being issued. If, however, the purpose of the system is to record where stock is located without controlling its distribution, a single structure would suffice.

4.3.4. State Transitions

State transitions are central to the Domain Theory for two reasons. First, they provide the structural association necessary for analogical retrieval, and second they model behavior that achieves the system's goal. A state transition changes the state of one object by transferring its membership between structure objects to achieve desired goal states.

FIG. 4.3. Key components of OSMs.

The power of state transitions to discriminate between models is best illustrated by example in Fig. 4.3. In the first OSM, stock is dispatched from the warehouse to the customer, whereas in the second OSM, books are lent from the library to the borrower. Both systems have structures representing objects held in and leaving a container, but the library is distinguished by an additional state transition returning the outgoing object to the container.

Actions do not form a primitive component of grounded domains; however, they are equivalent to state transitions and are modeled explicitly in the schema of generic tasks (see Fig. 5.1 in chapter 5).

4.3.5. States

States are described in two ways. Primary states record the containment or possession of objects in structures. Secondary states describe the outcome of generic or generalized tasks acting on objects and agents, such as books-are-reserved or journey-scheduled. The distinction between primary and secondary states is a consequence of structure objects. The combination of structure objects and state transitions provides good discrimination between domains, whereas secondary states are less powerful. For instance, object hiring (library lending) is distinguished from a stock control class by a return state transition; however, object reservation (a secondary state) does not distinguish between classes because reservation (Associate generic task) occurs in many domains, including stock control and library lending.

4.3.6. Goals

Goal states describe a future required state that the system should achieve, maintain, or avoid. Goals are operationalized as states that should be satisfied at the termination of the life history of state transitions contained within the OSM model. Requirements are usually expressed linguistically as intentions for goals, aims, and objectives. These statements can be refined into more formal expressions of a future state that the system should (or should not) attain. Such state expressions link linguistic statements of goals to OSMs. Goals are specified in three ways. First, goals describe states that the object system must achieve or maintain (Anton & Potts, 1998; Potts, Takahashi, & Anton, 1994). These requirements are satisfied by state transitions on key objects. Second, functional requirements describe tasks and processes that must be carried out to satisfy the goal state. The completion of the task causes a state transition to attain the goal state. Generic tasks are described in chapter 5. Third, functional requirements may necessitate the production of information, satisfied by tasks associated with the ISM. Each OSM has a goal state definition that is part of the essential model of the system's purpose.

4.3.7. Tasks

Generic tasks (*activities* in earlier versions of the theory) are carried out by agents and are processes that run to completion, resulting in a state change within an OSM. Tasks model human activities or automated procedures, and hence in software engineering they are equivalent to methods in UML, or algorithm-level detail in other specification languages. Tasks are composed of event or actions that are nondecomposable primitives that result in a state transition following Jackson's (1983) definition. Actions are ordered with control constructs of sequence, selection, and iteration. Tasks change primary or secondary states; for example, the generic Associate (resource) task can become the transition of a library book from available to reserved, whereas Diagnose will change the status of a key object from damaged to repaired in the Object Servicing–Repair OSM. A single generic task may occur in many different types of application; for example, comparing, interpreting, and classifying occur in many different systems.

4.3.8. Object Properties

Properties define characteristics of key objects that constrain their behavior. Three subtypes are distinguished. Physical objects are subject to physical laws such as gravity or momentum. Examples of physical objects include library books in the lending library domain and aircraft in the air traffic control domain. These objects can undergo transitions resulting in physical change. Conceptual objects model information or abstract concepts. Examples of conceptual objects include transaction-related documents, for example, purchase orders, tickets, and vehicle licences. Financial objects are a subtype of conceptual objects that have an agreed value in a society and represent currency or some token worth. Examples of financial objects include cash in an automatic telling machine, chips in a casino, and the currency in a foreign-exchange transaction.

4.3.9. Events

Events are defined in two subtypes: domain events and time events. An event is a single point in time when something happens, following Allen's (1987) conception of temporal semantics. Events are treated as semaphores that initiate a state transition. Temporal semantics are also expressed in stative conditions (see the next subsection). Events are implicit in state transitions. As a way to avoid redundancy, only initiating "triggers," that is, those events that start state transitions, are modeled. For instance, the dispatch of goods from warehouse to customer is triggered by a customer order (a request event). Triggering events are not needed to start behavior in all object systems as autonomous behaviour can be a normal property; for example, aircraft move between sectors in an air space without any initiating event. Domain events model the result of some external activity in the real world, whereas time events emanate from a clock.

4.3.10. Stative Conditions

Stative preconditions and postconditions are tests on primary and secondary states. Several types of conditional tests are used for discriminating between lower-order OSMs. There are tests on primary states that must be successful for the state transition to be initiated; for example, a book must be in the library before it is loaned. There are tests on the number of key objects contained in an object structure; for example, stock is replenished when the number of stock objects in the warehouse reaches a minimum level. Finally, there are tests that enable transitions to secondary states; for example, a theatergoer's request must match the attributes of an available seat before the place can be reserved.

4.3.11. Relationships

Relationships add further structural information to OSMs that is used to discriminate between lower-level classes. Relationships are subtyped as follows. Cardinality relations express the expected membership of key objects within an object structure; for example, many aircraft can be in one airspace. Temporal relations indicate that an object A should persist in structure A^1 for a significantly longer time than object B does in structure B^1. These are defined as A is longer than B. Scale relations indicate that an object structure A should have a larger set of key objects than another object structure B. These are defined as A is greater than B. Relationships provide additional structure to enable analogical matching and to discriminate between OSMs. The schema defines the reusable knowledge held in OSMs that express problem domains, and generic tasks that describe activity in abstract terms.

4.4. GROUNDED DOMAINS: OSMs

OSMs represent aggregations of objects that cooperate to achieve a particular system goal. Their heritage draws upon responsibility modeling in object-oriented design (Wirfs-Brock et al., 1990) that argued for collections of objects that cooperate to discharge a responsibility. OSMs model a general view of responsibilities for a variety of information systems and other software engineering problems. Any

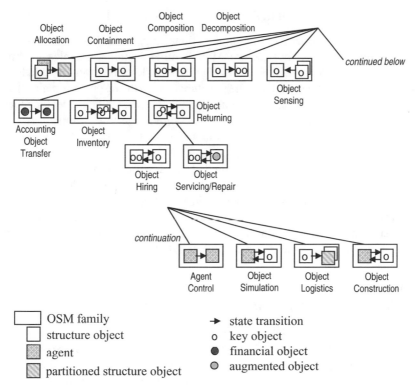

FIG. 4.4. OSM hierarchy showing subclasses of the Object Containment model.

one application is composed of an aggregation of object systems, generic tasks, and information system models.

The overall OSM hierarchy is illustrated in Fig. 4.4. The top levels of the tree have been pruned, because models at such high levels of abstraction do not contain sufficient knowledge for structure matching and are not informative. The hierarchy therefore starts with nine separate trees, which are called OSM families. A brief description of each top-level class is given with lower-level detail of the Object Containment family. OSMs are annotated with requirements problems that indicate typical issues that arise with applications of that class. Generic requirements are provided as partial answers to the problems and can be specialized into functional requirements in the new application. The OSMs and their attached reusable knowledge help requirements analysis, first by providing models of the essential abstraction and second by acting as a checklist of issues that require in-depth analysis. In a subset of the models, further solution knowledge is provided in one form of design rationale, claims and pointers to reusable design models (see chapter 6). Further details of the OSM library are given in appendix A.

4.4.1. Object Containment (Level 1 Class)

This class is characterized by the unidirectional transfer of key objects from an owning structure to a client structure. More familiar examples are sales order processing systems; specializations in this family also describe inventory and loans-type applications. The model has one structure object (the resource container), one key object (resource), one agent (client), and two events, which model the request for the transaction and its fulfillment. The common purpose of this class is the orderly transfer of resource objects from an owner to a client who requires the resource. The goal state asserts that all requests for key objects to be transferred to the requesting client must be satisfied. This class only models the transfer of objects; a subclass is used for the monetary aspects of sales. The Object Containment family models a wide variety of inventory-type applications and may be specialized to many nonsales systems where resources are transferred, for example, internal supply or donations of resources. The requirements problems inherent in this family are controlling transactions and determining the state of objects in the container.

4.4.2. Object Inventory (Level 2 Class)

This specialization of the Object Containment object system adds another object structure to model the source of new objects, an agent for the resource owner, and a further state transition to represent the transfer of objects from a source to the owning object structure (see Fig. 4.5). This specialization corresponds to a variety

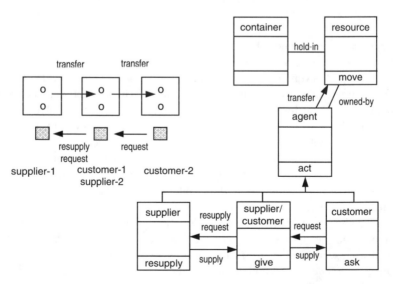

FIG. 4.5. Object Inventory OSM in a supply chain to illustrate supplier–customer views: a level 2 class.

of inventory management systems with outbound and inbound transfer of objects. The purpose in this case is not only orderly transfer of objects to a client but also replenishment of resources from suppliers; so the goal state is that all outbound requests by clients and requests initiated by the system for inbound transfer of key objects must be satisfied. Object inventory concatenates two or more models to represent supply chains, whereas the minimal model is an aggregation of two Object Containment Models: one represents supply of stock, and the other is supply of stock to the customer.

The software system requirements for Object Inventory concern the orderly management of transactions. This implies tracing dependencies between individuals objects; that is, an order for product a^1 is followed by delivery of product a^1 and notification to Accounting Object Transfer to invoice for product a^1. Another concern is ensuring the integrity of stock records; this involves the Object Sensing OSM family to check that physical objects in the store tally with the information system's tally. Generic requirements include those listed here and algorithms for monitoring stock levels and triggering reordering.

Accounting Object Transfer (Level 2 Class). This class is a special case in which structure has not been used to differentiate classes at the top level. Financial and accounting systems share many structural properties with object classes. Furthermore, in many domains, accounting systems are aggregated with purchase-order inventory transaction processing. Given that finance is a salient descriptor of business information systems, this class is discriminated by possessing a financial key object. The top-level structure is the same as Object Containment, and this class shares many of the same structural specializations. Loans, for instance, have the same object structure as the Object Hiring abstraction, as the loan is augmented by being repaid with interest. The goal states are similar to the Object Containment family, with the addition that a monetary value must have been exchanged between agents and structure objects.

Object Returning (Level 2 Class). This model is the third subclass from the Object Containment model. In this case the specialization adds a single state transition inbound from the client to the owning object structure. The purpose of this object system is the orderly transfer of resources to a client and the return of those resources to the owner. This class specializes in hiring, servicing, and repair-type applications. The goal state asserts that all loaned key objects must be returned to the container at some specified time in the future.

4.4.3. Object Hiring (Level 3 Class)

The purpose of these systems is to control the loan, hire, or temporary transfer of ownership of some resource from an organization and a client who requests possession of the resource. This object system is characterized by two structure

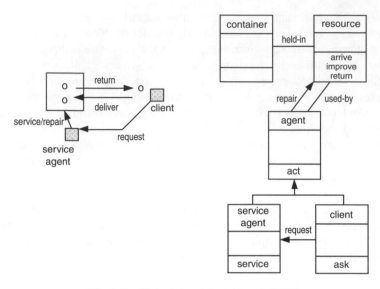

FIG. 4.6. Object Servicing–Repair OSM.

objects, the owning organization and the client; one key object (the resource); a request; and two transitions representing outbound transfer of the resource to the client and a subsequent return. The goal state is the same as for the Object Returning model, as is the key object.

   Object Servicing–Repair (Level 3 Class).   The purpose in this object system is to control the exchange of objects between a client and a servicing organization (see Fig. 4.6). In service and repair applications, the key object is in some way improved or has value added to it by the servicing object structure. This subclass has the same object structure as in the Object Hiring model, but it is differentiated by the concept of augmentation of the key object and the role of the agent that is responsible for improving the key object. This concept is represented by a relationship bet-ween the inbound and outbound state transitions and is specified in the goal state. The requirements problems in the Object Hiring and Servicing–Repair OSMs are matching events on individual objects to ensure that book x^1 is returned as book x^1 and that the object is returned without damage or is serviced to a satisfactory standard.

4.4.4. Object Allocation (Level 1 Class)

This family models applications that create an object state change that is a pre-cursor to some other transaction, for example, booking types of applications. The purpose of such systems is to establish an association between a key object and a client so that a further transaction is enabled. The second transaction is consummatory in nature when the allocated resources are used by the client; however, this is modeled in a separate OSM family, for example, inventory control in the Object Containment family. This class is modeled by two structures—the source of unallocated objects and the destination of allocated objects—and an agent that is responsible for the activity that determines the link. The destination structure is conceptually partitioned to model the structure of slots with which key objects may be associated, examples being theater seats after booking, timetable slots allocated to lectures, and the like. This OSM is often aggregated with Containment and Hiring models, and it is associated with matching generalized tasks.

Requirements problems in this family are how to satisfy the demands of customers when there is insufficient resource. Solutions to Object Allocation problems lie in constraint-based matching and nonlinear programming algorithms that try to optimize the distribution of resources between clients according to the match of client requirements and resource properties. When resources are limited, algorithms have to be selected for prioritization, democratic sharing, first come first served, and so on.

Object Composition (Level 1 Class).   In this class the purpose is to aggregate key objects and thereby synthesize new ones, so the goal state is that all input objects should be composed into one or more new composite key objects. Concrete instantiations are a wide variety of manufacturing systems that take in raw materials and compose them by some process into a product such as packaging applications that assemble and wrap goods, or conceptual assembly of components for a holiday (flight, hotel, car hire, etc.). This object system is characterized by two structure objects: the source of objects to be composed and the destination of composed objects; two sets of key objects components and composite objects; and one transition for merging component objects into composites. A controlling agent is also present in this model to organize the process. Robotic manufacturing systems are matched to this family, aggregated with the Object Construction OSMs.

Requirements problems in the Object Composition family concern the identification of parts for assembly and the control of the composition sequence. Parts have to arrive in a set order for assembly, and this problem is found in Bills of Materials Planning in ERP systems.

Object Decomposition (Level 1 Class).   This is the opposite of Composition; it maps to concrete examples of systems that disaggregate objects, for example, disassembly, unpacking, or breaking up. In this case the goal state at the end of system activity is that no composite key object should exist. This system is characterized by source and destination structure objects; two sets of key objects, composites and components; and one transition representing decomposition. As with Object Composition, a controlling agent is present. In Object Decomposition the problems are identifying the parts for decomposition and how they are to be removed. Ordering of the operations is also a concern.

Object Construction (Level 1 Class). In this class the key object does not change state with respect to structure; instead it may undergo many incremental changes that alter its secondary state. The state transitions model a change emanating from an agent that alters a key object and feedback from observed change to the manipulated key object. The goal state specifies that any change requests from the agent are acted upon by the key object. No key object movement is involved in this abstraction; instead an agent and one object structure model the device that facilitates or carries out the manipulation, for example, a machine or a computer. This family is differentiated from Object Composition by goal state and impact. Object Construction adds, deletes, or modifies key objects, whereas Object Composition only assembles them. Object Construction is the Domain Theory equivalent of Jackson's workpieces problem frame. The class represents a large family of applications including computer-based tools for word processing, graphics packages, decision support, design support, CAD systems, and the like. From the design viewpoint this class also contains all computer programs. However, the focus of the Domain Theory is on requirements, so the essence of this class is applications that require manipulation of an artefact in its own right. These systems are characterized by an agent, who carries out actions on the key object mediated by a machine or computer support tool. In previous versions of the Domain Theory this family was called Object Manipulation, which has been relegated to a subclass that acts on symbolic information, that is, computer-based representations of artefacts.

Object Construction shares the ordering problem with the Composition family; however, it has a further problem in controlling the type of operation that is carried out in a sequence. As Object Construction models manufacture, the problems are how to organize a set of operations (a, b, c) carried out by machines (x, y, z) on different objects, possibly in distributed locations (p, q, r) all within a set order. Object Construction therefore involves complex control systems and hence is associated with the Agent Control family. Other problems are flexible manufacture and being able to change actions and machines to produce product variants, the need to reconfigure in case of breakdown, and for intelligent flexible manufacturing systems to be able to dynamically compose a set of manufacturing operations in response to a product specification. Requirements issues also involve observability of state changes and predictability of action, that is, that the user can predict the effect that system controls will have on the artefact, and the consequential changes to the artefact will be faithfully reflected, as described in the gulfs of execution and evaluation (Norman, 1988).

Object Logistics (Level 1 Class). The purpose of this class is to move key objects within a partitioned structure object from a starting location to a destination set by the controlling agents. The OSM is composed of key objects that must be translocated, structure objects that represent the topology or geography over which movement will occur, agents that are purposeful originators and receivers of key objects and, optionally, an agent that mediates transport. The goal state of this family asserts that all key objects must arrive at their destination; however, within subclasses the key object may be conceptual or physical. Physical or conceptual key objects create subclasses for logistics; that is, the key objects to be distributed are physical goods or conceptual messages. The goal state for this family simply asserts that all key objects must be delivered from the sender to the receiver. Computer-supported cooperative work (CSCW) applications are usually aggregations of Message Transfer, Communicate generic task, and Object Construction.

4.4.5. Messenger Transfer (Level 2 Class)

The purpose of this class is to communicate key objects that have some information value between structure objects representing the communication network. The class is characterized by one or more conceptual key objects, which are messages; two or more structure objects representing the network topology through which communication takes place; and state transitions for exchange of messages. Specializations in this class add more structure objects for communication topologies (e.g., star, network, bus, etc.) and more transitions with relationships to represent different communication protocols (e.g., simplex, half-duplex, full-duplex communication, reply–acknowledge, etc.).

Requirements problems in the Logistics and Message Transfer classes are ensuring the integrity of arrival by tracking the transfer of objects or messages; problems with security and safety in transit, so encryption and protective barriers are often necessary; and problems with network congestion when traffic flows impair performance. These classes are associated with Object Sensing, Monitoring, and Forecasting tasks.

4.4.6. Object Sensing (Level 1 Class)

The purpose of this class is to monitor the physical conditions or movement of objects in the real world and record their relative state with respect to a spatial or physical object structure; see Fig. 4.7. For this family, the goal state is that changes in key objects must be detected and signalled to the agent. Key objects change with respect to this structure, and these changes are reported to the sensing agent as an event. This class includes a sensing agent that reports on this behavior. Specializations are spatial sensing (e.g., radar detection of air traffic), monitoring behavior, and property sensing applications (e.g., monitoring temperature or pressure in process control applications). In a subclass of this family, structure objects model significant spatial components of the real world and can be partitioned, such as sectors within an air corridor. Object Sensing Models are often

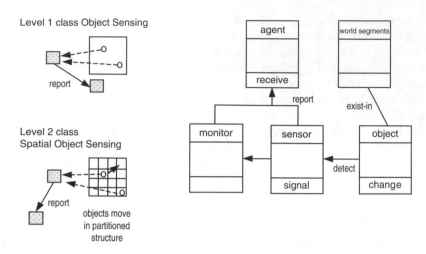

FIG. 4.7.   Object Sensing OSM family.

aggregated with the Agent Control class, and Monitoring and Interpreting generic tasks.

4.4.7.   Spatial Object Sensing (Level 2 Class)

In subclasses of this family, structure objects model significant spatial components of the real world and can be partitioned, such as sectors within an air corridor. Key objects change within this structure, and these changes are reported to the sensing agent as events. Further subclasses specialize the problem in either three-dimensional spaces (e.g., air traffic sensing) or two-dimensional sensing (road vehicle traffic and shipping), and at the next level according to movement constraints placed on key objects, that is, constrained space (traffic on roads) versus unconstrained space (ships at sea).

Agent Behavior Sensing (Level 2 Class).   In these subclasses, actions of an agent are monitored; hence an agent becomes the key object. Behavioral change by the agent within a physical world or a conceptual task structure are detected and reported to the sensing agent as events. This class monitors action detail of an agent in contrast to gross movement of the agent as a whole unit (Spatial Object Sensing), as well as change in an agent's state (Object Property Sensing).

Object Property Sensing (Level 2 Class).   This subclass detects properties of a key object such as temperature, size, density, or weight, that is, any information about an object except spatial semantics of movement, position, and direction. Typical applications are sensors in process control, chemical plants, and equipment monitors.

Active Sensing (Level 2 Class). This subclass models sensors that emit a signal in order to detect change, such as radar, and another transition is added to model the echo returned by the sensed object. Further specializations of this subclass differentiate between agents that emit sensing signals and domains in which the key object activity emits a detectable signal as part of its design, such as an aircraft transponder.

Passive Sensing (Level 2 Class). Applications in which the device detects chemical or physical change in the environment but the sensed object does not emit a signal are modeled as passive sensors. Requirements problems in the Object Sensing family concern the fidelity of detection. Detecting events depends on the sensing devices, which may be prone to several errors. For example, they may detect false events, miss real events, or signal events of the wrong type, events too late, or in the wrong order. A complete taxonomy of event-level errors is given by Hollnagel (1998). Generic requirements are to calibrate the sensing device, to periodically check and monitor its performance, and to run screening algorithms to eliminate false positives.

4.4.8. Agent Control (Level 1 Class)

This OSM family models command and control applications. The class is characterized by a controlling agent and one or more controlled agents contained in one object structure (their environment); see Fig. 4.8. In this class, agents are contained within a structure that models a controlled part of the real-world environment, for example, airspace in air traffic control. The transitions represent messages passed from the commander agent to the subordinate agent to change its behavior in some way. Agents respond to commands and change state within the structure, and specializations of this class refine how that change occurs (e.g., deterministic or nondeterministic response change in behavior, change in property, number, etc.). The goal state asserts that the controlled subordinate must respond to the commander in a satisfactory manner and that all commands should be obeyed.

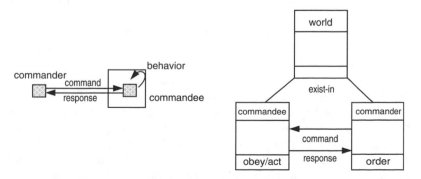

FIG. 4.8. Agent Control OSM.

Specializations of this class are command systems that add further agents for military command and control applications, controllers and pilots in air traffic control systems, and so on. This class is often aggregated with Object Sensing and Messaging abstractions, and it is associated with Planning, Analyzing, and Modeling generalized tasks.

Agent control poses feedback and compliance problems. The commander needs to know that the order has been carried out; however, this may be difficult when communication is poor, there is a delay between command and execution, or when the effects of the subordinate action are hard to detect. Further problems arise when subordinates cannot be assumed to be honest and employ subterfuges to fool the commander that they have complied. Another set of problems arises in the controllability of the subordinate agent; for example, in many systems with highly inert objects, the time delay between command and effect can be considerable.

Object Simulation (Level 1 Class). The purpose of this class is to represent a model and its behavior to an external agent. The class is composed of a structure object, the modeled world that contains one or more key objects that represent components in a real-world domain or a design. This family represents a wide range of simulation and display applications, including multimedia presentations, simulations, interactive microworlds, and virtual reality. The architecture follows the Model View Controller abstraction (Krasner & Pope, 1988). The model represents phenomena in the real world (e.g., model of a pond ecosystem) or designed artefacts. A mediating agent may be present to handle the external representation of the model's output. This family models simulation systems in which a model is run or interacted with by the user. No change is caused to the model itself by the state transitions; however, the user agent may input parameters that change parts of the model. This may result in different behavior, depending on the model's sophistication. When objects in the simulated world are changed, this family is aggregated with Object Construction. Substitution of intelligent agents for objects in the model extends the range of behavior. The external agent may also have a simulated presence in the modeled world, such as avatars in virtual reality applications. Simulations for decision support and design environment fall into this class, as do most computer games.

The requirements problems in this class are providing a faithful representation of the modeled world. Compromises may have to be agreed to when the modeled world's behavior is too rapid or too complex for normal human perception. Similarly, very slow changes may have to be accelerated.

This is the breadth of the Object System Model space as it currently stands. Further analysis of applications may lead to the discovery of new OSM families; however, the set described herein has remained stable over several years and survived the challenges of successive analyses of real-life applications and case-study descriptions taken from the software engineering literature. It is important to emphasize that, in any one application, there is usually an aggregation of OSMs.

For instance, a typical library domain will have an Object Hiring system to handle book loans, an Object Inventory system for book stock control and new book stock acquisitions, and possibly Accounting Object Transfer for book purchase with Object Servicing–Repair to return damaged books to a satisfactory condition.

4.5. MODELING INFORMATION SYSTEMS

ISMs differ from OSMs. They represent processes that feed off, report on, and provide external representations of information contained within OSMs. OSMs contain information in primary and secondary states, but they have no means of producing reports or external representations of that information. Producing information for users, who may be human agents, is the responsibility of ISMs. Thus in an inventory application, the key objects in stock maintain information about their state. Accessing that information is carried out by an ISM process that may produce an inventory report as its output. ISMs provide information to agents for their decision making and action, so this definition is narrower than the concept of information systems, which also encompass transaction processing.

ISMs have actions (modeled as state transitions) that produce reports, queries, and other information outputs. These can belong to agents, are triggered by events, and are controlled by using preconditions as in OSMs. As a way to illustrate the roles of OSMs and ISMs, a package express delivery business matches a subclass of Object Logistics. The essential model of the business is getting packages and the like from one customer to another by means of a series of depots. This would be modeled in an OSM with key objects (packages) being moved between structure objects (sender, receiver customers, depots). The number of structure objects and their topology depends on the level of specialization. The information system that then tracks the progress of packages from source to destination is handled by a Progress Reporting ISM, which samples each structure and reports where each key object instance is. The library of ISMs is given after the OSMs in appendix A.

4.6. REUSING OSMs

OSMs are reused by identifying one or more generic models that represent abstractions of a new application problem. A preliminary model of the new application is therefore necessary to start the matching process; however, this model is minimal and the process of requirements discovery and domain analysis proceeds hand in hand with cycles of fact gathering and retrieval of OSMs. The OSM library is supported by a matching tool that automates the retrieval of appropriate reusable components. For the system to be illustrated in action, the system architecture and a typical session with the toolset are described. More details on the architecture and the matching process can be found in Maiden (1996), and Sutcliffe and Maiden (1998).

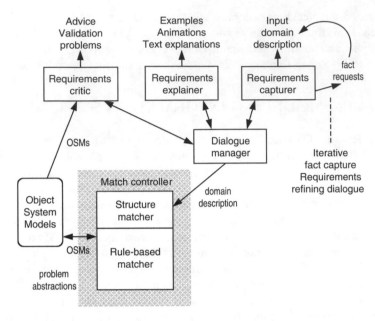

FIG. 4.9.   Architecture of the AIR toolset.

4.6.1.   Reuse Toolset Architecture

This section reports the reuse support tools that we developed to support OSM reuse. Details have been published elsewhere (Sutcliffe & Maiden, 1994, 1998); however, a summary is included here because the tools have some interesting lessons for the design of software architecture and algorithms to support reuse libraries more generally. The architecture of the Advisor for Intelligent Reuse (AIR) consists of six major components, illustrated in Fig. 4.9. The input model represents the new application that the software engineer wishes to design. This model is built up incrementally by a system-directed dialogue with the tool in which the user enters a few facts about the new domain. The system assigns types to the facts by directing data entry to specific fields in a form and by asking questions for clarification. The system then retrieves candidate OSMs that match the input model, thus building up the conceptual model of the new application, explaining the reusable abstractions implicit in the model, and then offering requirements analysis and design advice associated with the OSM models.

The constraint-based matching algorithm uses different search heuristics as it narrows the search space. Thus the algorithm starts by matching objects, transitions, and structures, looking for triplet graph structures in the input model that are shared with one or more OSM models in the library. The process is illustrated in Fig. 4.10.

The algorithm computes a goodness-of-fit matching score for any two (node-arc-node) graph triplets. The maximum score is achieved if the two objects have

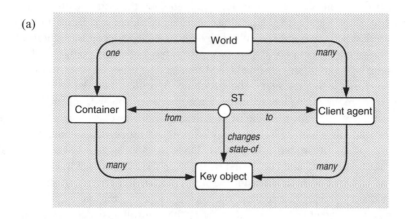

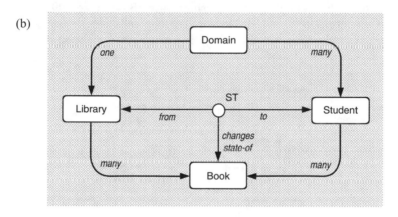

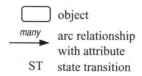 object

many ──▶ arc relationship
with attribute

ST state transition

FIG. 4.10. Structure matching between the input model of a new domain and OSM model. The matcher algorithm compares the types of nodes and arcs in network topologies to identify similar structures. Semantic networks describe (a) the Object Containment system model and (b) the input model.

the same type and are connected by a relationship of the same type; thus "library contains book" fits well with the OSM structure Container-holds-Resource. As the algorithm controls the user system dialogue, so it acquires facts in the order needed to refine the match. Hence the input facts Student and Book are typed as (client) agent and (resource) key object by entry into the appropriate slot in a form-filling dialogue. Once a basic structure match has been achieved, the algorithm selects the best candidate top-level OSM family. The user can confirm the system choice or force it to backtrack. The matching algorithm then descends the OSM family tree, requesting facts to discriminate between lower-level models in the class hierarchy. It swaps the type of facts it uses in lower-class levels to mix pure structure matching with search heuristics for object properties, agents, tasks, and relationships, as illustrated in Fig. 4.11. Once the appropriate lower-level OSM model has been found and confirmed by the user, the system backtracks to the top level and asks the user to augment the input model if necessary to find the next OSM that may exist in the application.

The domain matcher, composed of the match controller, structure matcher, and rule-based matcher, is implemented by using ConceptBase (Jarke, 1992) with Telos (Mylopoulos et al., 1990) and BIM Prolog. The tools and dialogue manager and the three tools (requirements capturer, critic, and explainer) are also implemented in

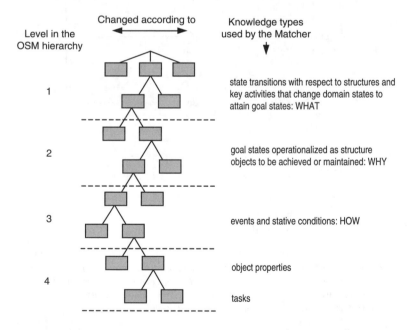

FIG. 4.11. Matcher algorithm hierarchical search and adaptive change of heuristics.

BIM Prolog by using the X Windows user-interface environment. Each component is described in more detail, as follows.

The Match Controller. The match controller controls two mechanisms for retrieving OSM classes. At the beginning of the matching process, facts are acquired from the user in a system-directed dialogue. These create the input model of the new application. The structure matcher uses a breadth-first strategy for matching input facts to high-level OSMs, and then the rule-based matcher follows a depth-first search down the closest matching OSM tree in an iterative cycle of fact acquisition and matching until one or more leaf nodes in the OSM family tree is reached. Facts to build the input model are requested in the order of the OSM specialization, so the system asks for the fact types it requires according to the depth of search in the hierarchy.

The Structure Matcher. Previous analogical matching mechanisms (Falkenhainer, Forbus, & Gentner, 1989) were computationally complex and had excessive run time (Holyoak & Thagard, 1989), so the structure matcher attempts to overcome these problems by identifying structural patterns by using a small number of related fact types. The structure matcher uses a sophisticated yet pragmatic search strategy to reduce the search space and avoid the exponential explosion of combinatorial search. Structure matching occurs in two phases.

In the first phase, local mapping acts as a filter to select the best candidate OSM for structure matching. Local mappings are controlled through a semantic lexicon, and they detect instances of the same knowledge type; for example, the input fact book can be mapped to a *resources*-object because both are typed as *objects*. All pairwise combinations of the input model and each candidate OSM are locally mapped by type to calculate a local match value that must exceed a preset threshold.

In the second phase, structure matching takes the input model and one or more OSMs, depending on the local mapping filter, and determines a quantitative score of similarity between the input model and each OSM. The nearest-neighbor mapping algorithm carries out an exhaustive search of pairwise combinations of knowledge types, constrained by the current locus of search. The topography and type of nodes and arcs are mapped between input models and candidate OSMs to determine a goodness-of-fit score. Structure matching is refined by weighting the importance of certain mappings. State transitions with respect to structure objects are central to discriminating between domains; therefore, these mappings are assigned a higher score.

The Rule-Based Matcher. Full structure matching at lower subclass levels would be redundant because the structural similarity already detected is shared by the subclasses. The rule-based matcher therefore maps isolated facts within the context of an existing structure match. The process dynamically swaps knowledge types according to the level of search within an OSM tree; moreover, the fact-acquisition dialogue requests facts from the user appropriate for search strategy. Rule-based matching has two roles: to infer knowledge-type mappings needed to distinguish between candidate OSM subclasses, and to match an entire domain model once the specialization has been selected. Output from the rule-based matcher is a quantitative score of matching with a leaf node OSM.

Rule-based mapping uses 110 rules to test permissible neighboring mappings for each knowledge type. This ruleset constrains the expected connectivity for any one primitive according to the OSM schema, so component pairs can only be mapped if they conform to schema relationships (see section 4.3). The local mapping rule fires if and only if a fact describing the target domain and an OSM fact are instances of the same knowledge type and have the same attributes.

The Requirements Capturer.   The requirements capturer acquires facts that discriminate between OSM classes. A mixed initiative dialogue enables iterative fact capture, retrieval of domain abstractions, and guided development of a requirements specification. The capturer has two approaches for acquiring new facts from the software engineer. First, the dialogue requests fact types that are powerful discriminators, thereby enabling matching and selection of appropriate OSMs. Second, free format input by means of a form-filling dialogue has a limited error-repair capacity for facts that do not match the system's lexicon. In this mode, the user has to configure a semantic lexicon that matches an input fact first to its own type and then to the Domain Theory schema (e.g., conference proceedings is a book is a key object). In both approaches, the aim of the requirements capturer is to acquire facts about the target application that permit retrieval and explanation of domain abstractions.

The Requirements Critic.   The requirements critic aids domain understanding and requirements validation by comparing the input model and retrieved OSMs, detecting inconsistencies, and reporting these to the software engineer. The critic has three major features. The first is a *problem classifier,* which reasons about mappings inferred by the domain matcher to detect and classify problems in the input model representing the user's requirements. The classifier can detect incompleteness, inconsistencies, and overspecification in requirements and explains its rationale for detecting these problems. The second is *critiquing strategies* for requirements validation determined by the detected problem. The third is a *controller* for intelligent selection of strategies. Strategies are selected to encourage specification of complete requirements for an application class and to assist detection of inconsistencies, ambiguities, and wishful thinking in the specification. The requirements critic combines guidance and critiquing strategies in a mixed initiative dialogue (see Fischer, 1996).

The Requirements Explainer.   Critiquing is aided by explanation of retrieved OSMs by using guided exposure to prototypical examples, visual animation of retrieved models, and descriptions of analogical mappings. Diagrams representing

OSM structures and state transitions are annotated and supported by text descriptions to aid recognition and understanding of domain abstractions (Maiden et al., 1995), because people learn analogies more effectively if they are presented with informal diagrams illustrating critical determinants of the problem (Gentner, 1983). Prototypical examples are also used to aid understanding of the OSM abstractions, as people often understand new concepts by using concrete examples (Rosch, 1985; Rosch et al., 1976). Finally, OSMs can be animated to illustrate domain behavior. Animations are interactive and permit playback with pause facilities to facilitate exploration.

Dialog Management. The dialogue controller selects explanation–critiquing strategies based on properties of the requirements specification and simple states of user–system dialogue. Guidance is controlled by a set of heuristics derived from a task model of requirements analysis and validation. Active guidance in explaining–critiquing input by using OSM abstractions is interleaved with user-driven browsing of the OSM hierarchy. The requirements critic intervenes when serious omissions or inconsistencies are detected, to explain retrieved OSMs and detected problems. Passive critiquing is used when the problem classifier detects less critical problems, which are posted on a notepad as issues to be resolved when the software engineer chooses.

4.6.2. Matching Process and Scenario of Use

A scenario is used to demonstrate active guidance and critiquing during a matching–model retrieval session. The critic explains retrieved domain abstractions to the software engineer to assist development of a specification for computerized stock control facilities in a library. The dialogue controller manages a mixed initiative dialogue to provide effective intervention and guidance (Maiden & Sutcliffe, 1993). The dialogue controller has configurable rules to trigger system initiative so system explanation and critiquing can be customized to users' preferences. The system maintains a lexicon of fact types that is extensible. This is used in combination with the knowledge representation schema, described in section 4.3, to classify facts by type as they are entered. If the system cannot find a suitable classification, it prompts the user to assign the new fact within the structure of its lexicon displayed as a menu hierarchy. Alternatively, the lexical checking may be turned off so that the system will accept any identifier the user enters for a specific fact type. This enables the system to be independent of domain-specific detail.

The Requirements Problem. The software engineer has conducted an initial interview that revealed the need for a stock control system. The system must identify missing or damaged books that are no longer in the library. It must also permit a stock-take of books within the library and ensure that books cannot be purchased without the librarian's authorization. The scenario has three capture, retrieval, and critique cycles that use three OSMs, Object Containment, Object Returning, and Object Inventory, in descending order of specialization.

Fact Capture and Matching in Cycle 1. First the requirements capturer acquires facts to enable retrieval of a high-level OSM. Active guidance in the fact-capture dialogue ensures that fact types necessary for the system's matching strategy are entered. The system prompts the user to enter facts in fields labeled with the fact types it expects, such as object, state transitions, and events, as illustrated in Fig. 4.12. The dialogue illustrated shows the lexical checking options turned off so that users may enter any identifier they choose in the fact-type input field. Text explanation helps the user decide where facts should be entered. Once the system has acquired a minimal fact set, in this case the objects Library, Book, and Borrower with the transition Deliver, the first round of matching is initiated. The system captures state transitions by reference to the objects; for example, Deliver is communicated to the system by the user linking the transition from Library to Borrower. In this manner the system does not need to maintain a lexicon of the state transitions. The system searches the top-level families of models in its library and retrieves the closest match, the Object Containment OSM. In the example the user has entered facts that are incomplete and inconsistent; however, the power of the domain matcher ensures that it retrieves the Object Containment model as the best fit for stock control or loans.

Explanation in Cycle 1. The requirements critic explains the retrieved model to improve the user's understanding. The retrieved Object Containment model is explained by using visualization and text-based descriptions of the abstraction and its mappings to the current application, as illustrated in Fig. 4.13(a). The mappings show the user-entered terms for the objects (book, library, and borrower) with the types the system has used to classify these objects (key object, resource, container, and agent, respectively). The problem classifier has detected one problem, illustrated on the notepad, shown in Fig. 4.13(b). This is caused by entry of the agent, a borrower of books, which does not fit the OSMs available at this level of abstraction. The matcher flags this fact as an inconsistent categorization, but it allows the dialogue to continue and stores the extra fact for future matches. The requirements engineer is prompted to confirm or reject the current match. In the scenario, the user confirms the match and the system then prompts the user to enter further facts.

Model Selection and Explanation in Cycle 2. The user enters further facts describing a supplier agent, object structure, and a state transition representing book delivery from the supplier. This allows the matcher to search further down the Object Containment family and retrieve the Object Inventory subclass. The dialogue controller selects active guidance to present a set of windows in an ordered sequence, illustrated in Fig. 4.14. The critic explains the retrieved model by using informal graphics supported by text-based descriptions to draw attention to

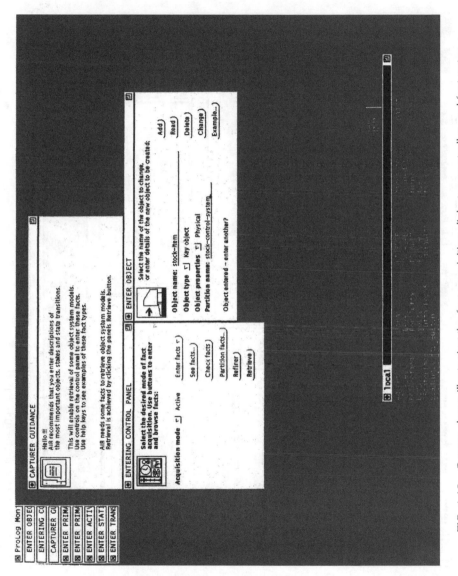

FIG. 4.12. Screen dump illustrating the fact-acquisition dialogue controller and fact entry.

119

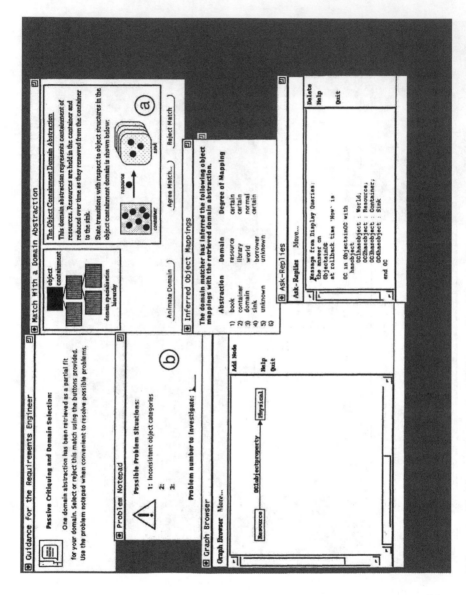

FIG. 4.13. The first cycle matcher dialogue showing windows for: (a) explaining the retrieved generic model, and (b) the problem notepad.

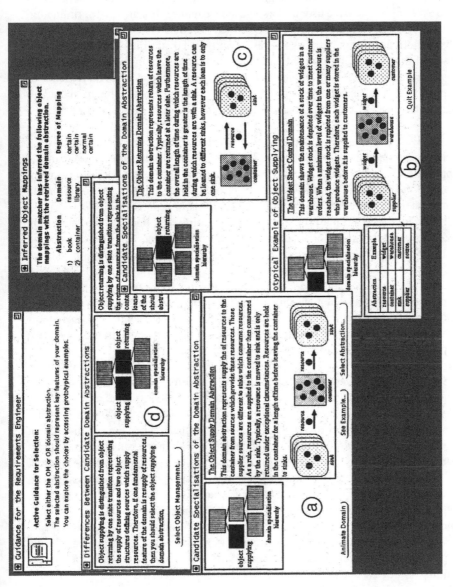

FIG. 4.14. Explanation dialogue showing (a) and (d) retrieved OSMs, (b) an example of one of them, and (c) the differences between them.

121

fundamental differences between the input model and the OSM structure and behavior, shown in Fig. 4.14(a), with an example as shown in Fig. 4.14(b). The other OSM (Object Returning) that was not selected in the Object Containment family is also explained to help the user understand the system's rationale for discriminating between models; see Figs. 4.14(c) and 4.14(d). Gradual exposure to the candidate abstractions and prototypical examples is controlled by the dialogue manager. The result of this bout is an extended, but still incomplete, requirements specification. The user can request prototypical examples of the Object Inventory model to supplement earlier explanations and browse the list of detected problems, including incompleteness, inconsistencies, and ambiguities, from the problem notepad.

Critiquing in Cycle 3. The user enters further facts describing a relationship between the supplier and the customer but has not identified that the customer in this application is in fact the library. The dialogue controller selects active critiquing because the problem classifier detects an inconsistent fact that it cannot reconcile with either the current OSM or with any subclass models; see Figs. 4.15(a) and 4.15(b). Reconciling this problem is achieved either by deleting the fact or by indicating that the customer and library objects are the same. The user chooses the latter option. This completes modeling of the stock purchase part of the application, so the user initiates a second matching. Further explanation of associated ISMs, such as inventory control reports, is provided for functional requirements. Guided explanation of information systems with prototypical examples is given by using text descriptions, diagrams, and animation. The software engineer can request critiquing at any time by rematching the requirement specification, so iterative explanation and critiquing continue until the user is satisfied.

The user requested a second pass to match facts, so far unused, for example, the role of the borrower. An object property is entered to subtype the key object as augmented when the dialogue is at the early stage of identifying the Object Containment family of models. This causes the matcher to retrieve the Object Returning model rather than Object Inventory, which was retrieved when the supplier object structure was entered. If circulation control for book stock were required and a return transition delivering a book from the borrower to the library were entered, this would lead to retrieval of the Object Hiring OSM to describe borrowing types of applications. In this case the matching is among an owning object structure, the library, a client (the borrower), a resource (a book), and two state transitions, one for the outbound loan (from owner to borrower) and the return in the opposite direction. In this manner the matcher can help refine requirements for large-scale applicationsthat are composed of several OSMs. For further detail of the heuristics, guiding strategies, and the critiquing–validation dialogue, the reader is referred to Maiden and Sutcliffe (1993).

The lessons learned from developing and testing the AIR toolkit were that the support tools for explaining and critiquing were very necessary to promote understanding of OSMs (Maiden & Sutcliffe, 1994). The retrieval algorithm worked

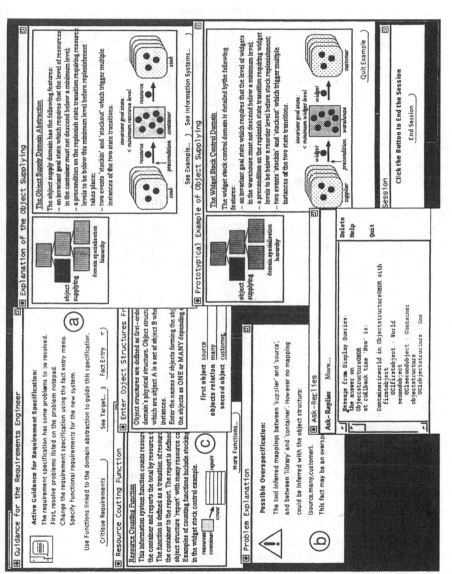

FIG. 4.15. Critiquer dialogue with active guidance for explaining inconsistent facts (a) and (b), and an ISM (c).

123

well, but its effectiveness was only as good as the initial model. In early stages a sparse initial model could lead to matches with several OSM families, and that confused users. A better strategy was to create a more detailed initial model of the new application and then invoke the matching process.

4.7. CASE STUDY: DESCRIBING APPLICATIONS BY AN AGGREGATION OF OSMs

The case study describes an application of the Domain Theory to the INTUITIVE Project. INTUITIVE started life as a single product in two versions: first a database front end for querying multiple distributed databases, and second an exemplar application that used this technology. In the middle phase of the project the decision was taken to reengineer INTUITIVE as a set of reusable services to enable better exploitation.

INTUITIVE is composed of two subsystems: first the common reusable functionality that supports information retrieval, and second the application in which information retrieval is embedded, in this case a decision support system for shipboard emergency management.

4.7.1. Decision Support Subsystem

The emergency management system is safety critical, which points to Object Sensing and Agent Control OSMs. The prime goals are to detect emergencies, analyze their cause, and then plan an appropriate response first to contain the emergency and then to take action to deal with it. In the case of fire, the hazard has to be contained and then extinguished. The captain has to locate the hazard, determine the type of fire (chemical, electrical, etc.), and decide on appropriate countermeasures. This is followed by giving instructions to fire-fighting crews. Finally the captain has to discover the extent of the damage and undertake repair actions if possible. The agents involved are the captain, other officers, the crew and fire-fighting teams. Objects include the ship's compartments, fire-fighting appliances, other equipment in compartments, cargo, and the fire itself.

Detection indicates sensing the status of objects, in this case the fire, and the status of nearby objects such as inflammable cargo. Information is passed to the captain who has to diagnose the problem and plan a response. This suggests that two generic tasks are necessary to diagnose the type of hazard and plan the appropriate response. Once the response is determined, the captain has to give instructions to fire-fighting teams. Questions indicate Agent Control and Object Messaging models. The fire-fighting teams then take action to deal with the fire; however, they should report back to the captain so he or she can assess the situation.

This implies Object Messaging; furthermore, the crew have to act as an Object Sensing system for the captain by detecting and reporting changes as fire fighting progresses.

The information requirements are for status reports on the fire, details of the type of fire and nearby equipment or cargo, and the location of the problem, emergency teams, and proximal compartments. The status reports describe the history of the emergency, so Progress Tracking as well as Reporting ISMs are necessary.

The main structure object is the ship itself, which is subdivided into compartments. Question subsets refine the choice of abstract models down the hierarchy for each family. In the Object Sensing model, questions about the sensed object and the space in which it is located help to identify the appropriate class 2 model as Spatial Object Sensing in a three-dimensional space. The questions about active or passive sensors are left open; sometimes the captain may ask the emergency team for a status update, and otherwise the crews report by radio on their own initiative. However, there are active sensors for heat and smoke detection in most compartments. These signal the location of fires on a panel display on the bridge.

In summary, the emergency system is composed of three OSMs, Agent Control, Object Sensing, and Object Messaging; two ISMs, Reporting and Progress Tracking; and five generalized tasks (described in chapter 5), Diagnosis, Analysis–Modeling, Planning–Scheduling, Explanation–Advising, and Progress Tracking. Analysis–Modeling is unlikely to be a separate task unless the problem is complex; in most cases analysis will be subsumed in Diagnosis.

4.7.2. Information Retrieval Subsystem

There are two views of this subsystem, depending on whether it is analyzed for the specific requirements of the task or for general information searching. Clearly the generalized task of Information Retrieval is implicated. The requirements for the external decision support system are for information in response to specific requests that can be predetermined, that is, preformed but customizable questions about different types of fire hazard, hazardous cargo, location of emergency teams, fire-fighting equipment, and so on. Spatial information is important as are status reports and progress tracking. The search component of the task requires support but articulating queries, browsing, and evaluating feedback are less important. This suggests that only a subset of the information retrieval functionality is required.

If there are more general requirements for information searching, such as nonemergency shipboard information management and decision support, then different subgoals in the generic task will require support from system services, such as browsing facilities, help with query articulation, that is, a thesaurus, and a query language. The information subsystem contains one ISM, and two tasks: Information Retrieval and Classify. Information Retrieval is interactive in nature, so it has an interaction pattern as well as an algorithmic, automated component implemented in a database search engine.

4.7.3. Creating a Generic System Model

The next step is to integrate the OSMs and the tasks to create a generic system model. This is achieved by unifying the models according to shared agents, objects, and structures. Tasks are often paired with models, such as the Information Search ISM that represents the problem and system structure and the task that models the necessary activity. Further state transitions may be added to complete the system description. The model covering both subsystems is illustrated in Fig. 4.16.

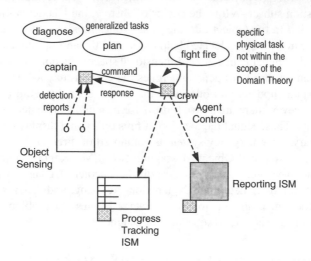

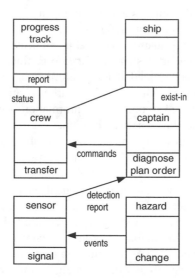

FIG. 4.16.   Generic system model for shipboard emergency management.

The emergency decision support system is composed of an Agent Control model, with the captain being the controller agent and the crew being the controlled agents. The Object Messaging system models the radio link connection between the crew and the officers, who are represented as receivers of messages and as command agents within the Control model; hence instruction messages are conveyed to the crew as commands for action. The Object Sensing model has two sets of objects to detect—first the fire itself and second the fire-fighting crew. These are merged into one model. The captain needs to locate the fire, appliances, and the crew, whereas the crew also need information on fire and location of appliances. The Reporting and Progress Tracking ISMs serve the captain's goals. The crew are information providers, whereas the captain is the information user.

Application of the Domain Theory to the redesign of INTUITIVE for reuse produced a family of flexible classes for information retrieval services that has since been reused in several systems. It also promoted reuse-oriented development of messaging and monitoring functions motivated by the Domain Theory models.

4.8. VALIDATION STUDIES

The OSM library structure and semantics were validated by experiments that elicited the memories of problem abstractions from experienced software engineers and users. Protocols and knowledge-acquisition techniques following established practices were used to elicit experts' mental knowledge structures and domain categories (Chi et al., 1982). Experimental studies used card-sorting exercises to test whether expert software engineers naturally sorted descriptions of specific applications into generic categories predicted by the Domain Theory. Each card had a scenario narrative that described a real-world application that mapped to a Domain Theory OSM family. The experts were asked to sort the cards into similar problems by using their own judgment and criteria. Independent judges then assessed whether the resulting categories produced by the experts could be justifiably labeled according to the Domain Theory abstractions. Further details of the methods and results can be found in Maiden et al. (1995). Three OSM families and three Object Containment subclasses were tested with 20 experienced software engineers, who were also asked to judge the utility of the intermodel discrimination criteria proposed by the Domain Theory.

The experts' categorization agreed with theory predictions apart from the Accounting Object Transfer family, where ironically experts categorized according to the underlying structure of the exchange and placed these applications with the Object Containment family. Accounting Object Transfer was originally a separate top-level family. It has since been relegated to its correct structure position in the Object Containment family. In retrospect, the theory confirmed its own assertion that structure and transaction behavior, not properties, determine generic classes. However, some experts did create a new category based on safety critical properties, so categorization by attribute rather than structure requires further investigation.

The experts agreed with the Domain Theory discrimination criteria, so, overall, there is good evidence that the theory has cognitive validity in predicting memory of problem abstractions. Further details of this study are described by Maiden et al. (1995). The theory has also been applied to reuse of requirements knowledge and conceptual models in two major European projects, INTUITIVE (Sutcliffe, Bennett, Doubleday, & Ryan, 1995) and Multimedia Broker (Sutcliffe, Ryan, Hu, & Griffyth, 1998), in which OSM models and design advice were identified in the first project and then reused in the second. This demonstrates that the theory has practical utility as it saved development time and simplified requirements capture. This case study is described further in chapters 6 and 8.

4.9. FORMALIZATION OF THE DOMAIN THEORY

Computer science readers of this book will have noticed that formal specification languages have not been used to define the Domain Theory models. This omission is deliberate. Formal descriptions can be made perfectly well in English. Translating them into set theory or logic would merely make the text inaccessible to noncomputer scientists and, I suspect, add little to the understanding of most computer science readers. The absence of formal description of the Domain Theory does not mean that I see no role for its formalization. Quite the opposite: formal representation of the models enables them to be used by reasoning mechanisms in knowledge acquisition and reuse. Indeed, considerable formalization of the Domain Theory has taken place by coding the OSMs in Telos, a formal knowledge representation language. This enabled the reasoning mechanisms of the Domain Theory matcher to operate on the models and provided consistency checking and query facilities so the OSM knowledge base could be applied in other reuse applications.

However, Telos is a semantic data-modeling language that formally inclined software engineers might not prefer. Accordingly, a subset of the Domain Theory was represented in order-sorted first-order logic (Taylor, Sutcliffe, Maiden, & Till, 1995). Order-sorted first-order logic was an appropriate yet rigorous formalism that was well suited to the Domain Theory because its type and class structure mapped to sorts or objects while first-order logic predicates described the behavioral aspects. I expected that formal expression of the Domain Theory models would expose inconsistencies in the schema and models, because a set of informally derived models may contain overlaps and incomplete behavior. However, expression in order-sorted first-order logic and validation of the behavior of the models did not expose any such problems. The OSM models appear to be well formed and isomorphic. One might interpret this in one of two ways. First, it is a credit to the Domain Theory that its models and schema are well formed, even without the assistance of formal languages and reasoning. Second, it is a critique of the investigative power of formal methods. I suspect there may be some truth in both points. I don't think all the Domain Theory models are completely isomorphic and consistent; any astute reader can spot a few of the fudges without any mathematical knowledge. Also a stronger formalism such as the KAOS specification language (Dardenne et al., 1993) that enables reasoning about the dependencies between goals expressed as states and the behavior specified to attain those states may well demonstrate more insights. If any formal methods person feels underemployed, here is a ready-made project.

4.10. SUMMARY

This chapter introduced the Domain Theory and explained its background as a hybrid theory of knowledge representation in computer and cognitive science. The main components of the theory, grounded domains, generic tasks, and metadomains, were reviewed. A schema for representing domain knowledge was described, followed by an overview of the library of grounded domain models. Domain Theory models are described for inventory control, loans, servicing, and allocation transactions. Other OSMs cover assembly, decomposition, and construction in manufacture. Object Sensing and Agent Control describe monitoring and command and control with simulation and decision support applications. Applications are modeled by an aggregation of OSMs and ISMs that report information on system status. Further details of lower-level classes are given in appendix A. The architecture of software tools to support reuse of grounded domains was explained with the structure matching algorithm that takes an input model describing the new application and retrieves one or more OSM generic models that map to the application class. OSMs are then used to explain requirements and the conceptual model of the domain to the user by critiquing tools. The process of reuse during requirements analysis is illustrated with a scenario of a library application. Finally, validation studies on the Domain Theory models were summarized.

5

Generic Tasks
and Metadomains

In chapter 4 the models describing generalized transactions and problem domains were introduced. The generic models and context of reuse were primarily intended for software engineering. We now turn to reuse in human-computer interaction (HCI). This alters the context for reuse. The OSMs in chapter 4 were generic models of application problems, which could be used as starting points for conceptual modeling. They were also linked to requirements issues and generic requirements (explained in more detail in appendix A), so the context for reuse was ideas, concepts, and suggestions for requirements engineering. In HCI these motivations still apply, but we also have to consider how the user's activity or task is supported by computer system design. This is usually referred to as the *functional allocation problem*. The starting point is to analyze human activity without prejudice to automation and then decide what activities, processes, and the like are suitable for people or computers. Such issues are covered in depth in the HCI literature (see Sutcliffe, 1995; Sutcliffe, in press; Wright, Dearden, & Fields, 1999). In the Domain Theory the questions we have to answer are "Are there generic models of human activity?" and, if so, "Can we specify requirements for task support for such models?"

Consequently, this chapter investigates abstractions in human problem-solving activity (*generic tasks*) and then looks at how generic tasks form part of larger-scale general models of human activity and organization. The Domain Theory has an ambitious scope to model phenomena that occur as problems amenable to computerized solutions. In the process of investigating the range of human activity that has been subject to computerization to some degree, problem areas emerged that did not fit neatly into small-scale models. As a way to deal with these composite problems, the concept of metadomains evolved to describe endeavors such as learning systems and management and decision support systems. Metadomains model the systems that humans have created in order to control, analyze, and understand the world.

Hence this chapter deals with generic models of human activity on two scales: in the narrow, as tasks carried out usually by individuals; and in the wide, as metadomains involving groups or people who collaborate to achieve a shared objective. This chapter and chapter 4 both take an ontological view of entities in the world, but they ignore generic knowledge in the form of discussion, arguments, and strategies. The final component of the Domain Theory, claims, is described in chapter 6. Claims provide a representation of design-related knowledge that is attached to generic models and knowledge for strategic planning and business best practice.

5.1. MODELING GENERIC AND GENERALIZED TASKS

Generic tasks describe abstractions of human activity. Tasks are functional, goal-oriented abstractions that achieve or maintain a state and act on objects in the world. The schema of task knowledge follows definitions in the HCI literature, for example, Task Knowledge Structures (Johnson, 1992), which are similar to those found in knowledge engineering (Chandrasekaran, Keuneke, & Tanner, 1992; Wilenga et al., 1993). Tasks are composed of the following primitive components: *actions* that change the state of objects; *control constructs* that compose actions into procedures (selection, sequence, iteration, and parallel); *objects* and their attributes that are acted on by actions; *states* of objects changed by task actions; *preconditions and postconditions*, which are the states before and after a task has been completed and that define the goal; and *goals* expressed as postconditions that the task should achieve or maintain.

The task knowledge schema is summarized in Fig. 5.1. Tasks have a goal hierarchy structure that describes the overall organization of activity. In some task modeling languages, the upper levels of the goal hierarchy are referred to as plans (Johnson, 1992). Upper-level goals are decomposed into subgoals that are expressed as procedures, which are composed of actions organized in a sequence by control constructs. Actions act on and change the state of objects. Actions are the primitive components of tasks that take place in short periods of time. The definition of action is related to state transitions in the grounded domain OSM schema.

Generic tasks are organized in a class hierarchy so that generic models can be specialized to specific tasks. Generic tasks are composable so aggregations of

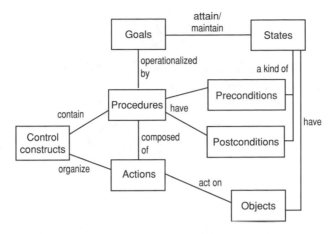

FIG. 5.1. Schema of task knowledge.

more primitive tasks can be reused as composites. This creates a one-to-many relationship between generic tasks and more complex goals. Taking the task of diagnosis as an example, we see that the commonsense definition of diagnosis is to discover the cause of some malfunction so that it can be remedied. Generalized models of diagnosis may be specialized to domains such as medicine or the servicing of electronic machinery. The goal state for diagnosis might be defined as finding the cause of a fault or problem and returning a defective system to a correctly functioning state.

However, diagnosis can be decomposed into several subtasks, each of which can have an independent existence and hence reuse potential (Fig. 5.2). First the cause of the problem has to be observed and located, such as the stage that might examine symptoms in medical diagnosis. The causal hypotheses have to be created, more evidence gathered to discriminate between the hypotheses, and the best candidate explanation selected for the cause of the problem. The end state of this part of the task is understanding the cause.

The next part of diagnosis is deciding what to do to fix the problem; this is the treatment and repair side of diagnosis. This might be another person's responsibility, so tasks have to be reusable as primitive, nondecomposable components as well as composite tasks. Once a repair has been planned, it has to be carried out and then tested to make sure the cure was effective.

Unfortunately, even this description may not account for all the activities that could go on during diagnosis. For instance, the operator may need to search for signs and symptoms to understand the problem; furthermore, an information search may be necessary to find the appropriate treatment. When a repair is carried out it may be necessary to disassemble the artefact to change a component. In a medical application, a surgical procedure would be the equivalent specialization. Tasks therefore become interleaved in real-world contexts. The question is how to

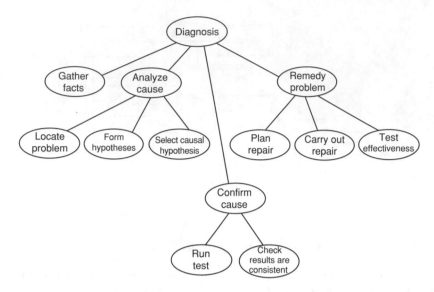

FIG. 5.2. Task model for diagnosis, showing the subgoal structure and intermediate end states.

separate the components of tasks so that they are composable and useful without being too abstract for comprehension. The answer is to specify a layered structure of primitive, abstract tasks and composite tasks that accord with our everyday perceptions of activity. Primitive, generic tasks preserve flexibility for reuse but are less immediately comprehensible by users, whereas composite, generalized tasks are more easily recognized as the vernacular interpretation of a task, although the large chunk size of composites reduces their flexibility in reuse. The subclasses of the diagnosis generalized task and its relationship to more primitive generic tasks is illustrated in Fig. 5.3. The Domain Theory therefore distinguishes between primitive, generic and composite, generalized tasks as follows.

- *Generic tasks* are the primitive activity components composed of a single procedure that runs to completion to achieve a goal. If the activity of a generic task is decomposed, the goal cannot be achieved.
- *Generalized tasks* are composite components composed of two or more generic tasks. Generalized tasks have subgoal structures and several procedures that contribute to the top-level task goal. The pattern of execution is variable.

5.1.1. Primitive or Generic Tasks

Primitive or generic tasks have simple procedures and achieve single goals. Such a task cannot be decomposed further without impairing the goal attainment; also, primitive tasks run to completion in finite time. To stop a generic task is to abandon

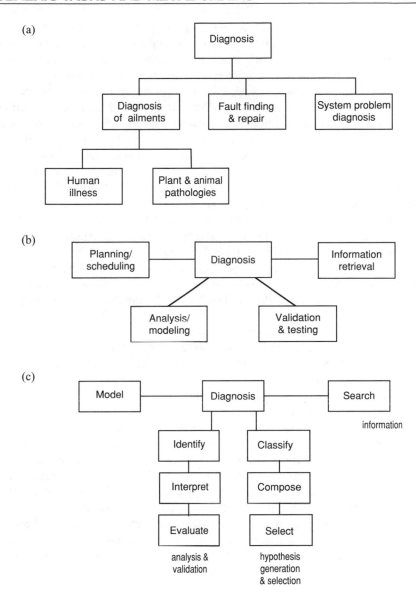

FIG. 5.3. Diagnosis generalized task showing (a) subclasses in the family, (b) its relationship to other generalized tasks, and (c) generic tasks that form its components.

it. Generic task actions are fully cohesive with respect to their goals; that is, all the task actions and only those actions contribute to the goal. Generic tasks may be interleaved in the sense of one task calling another as a subroutine; however, the execution of the task will be uninterrupted unless an error occurs. The sources of generic tasks come from several different levels of abstraction. First there is the general view of action espoused by Norman (1988) in his model of action, which is composed of the primitive steps of action specification, action execution, and recognition, interpretation, and evaluation of change. Generic tasks elaborate Norman's model of action by proposing models of goal-oriented cognitive activity at approximately the same level of granularity. More general still are primitive functions of cognition such as perceiving input, memory retrieval, and action execution. This level of primitive actions forms the components of the GOMS (Goals Operators Methods Selection rules) language for expressing any task (Card et al., 1983; John & Kieras, 1995). These primitive perceptual, cognitive, and motor operators describe action at a more general and lower level than generic tasks, such as recognize cursor, move mouse, decide menu option, and press key. In HCI, task primitives are defined as "unit" tasks that are nondecomposable actions. Cognitive complexity theory (Kieras & Polson, 1985) adds operators for manipulating goals in working memory (e.g., load–pop goal).

Taxonomies of generic tasks have been described to motivate the choice of visualizations (Wehrend & Lewis, 1990; Zhou & Feiner, 1998). These taxonomies describe generalized information processing needs such as comparison, classification, and associations; however, they do not consider human activity in other domains. The Domain Theory has been informed by this research but goes further to propose a comprehensive taxonomy of human mental activity.

Generic tasks primarily describe cognitive activity, although some involve physical action. The Domain Theory does not describe generic models for physical tasks because the motivation is to define task-support requirements primarily for problem solving and decision making; however, the library of generic tasks could be extended to cover manipulations and physical actions. This research may prove useful in defining support requirements for virtual-reality applications.

The population of primitive generic tasks is illustrated in Fig. 5.4 and briefly described as follows. Each generic task has a schema definition in structured text format; some are illustrated in this chapter, and the remainder are described in appendix B. Generic tasks fall into four families:

- *action*: Plan, Interpret, Evaluate, Assemble, Disassemble, and Transform;
- *information processing*: Model, Sort, Associate, Classify, Select, Identify, Compare and Decide;
- *communication*: Record, Communicate, and Explain; and
- *exploring–sensing* the world: Monitor, Search, Orient, and Locate.

Representatives from each group are discussed with their implications for task-support requirements and potential automation.

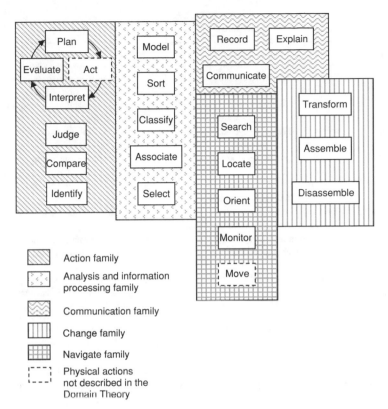

FIG. 5.4. Relationships between families of primitive generic tasks.

Action Family. These tasks owe their origins to Norman's model of action (1988), which has been used extensively in the HCI literature. Norman's model has six stages: form intention, specify action, execute action, recognize, interpret, and evaluate change. It is a generic model of action in the world that applies to physical tasks. In the Domain Theory the six stages are coalesced into three generic tasks (Plan, Interpret, and Evaluate), with action being implicit. The Domain Theory does not model physical action explicitly. Given the wide variety of possible human action, it would not be helpful to do so; moreover, such generic models already exist in robotics and for faithful representations of human action in software simulations of people (e.g., Carroll, 2000). However, the Domain Theory does have placeholders for physical action, in three families, and it makes the distinction between physical action, acts that control another system (i.e., machinery), and acts that move oneself: locomotion and movement. The tasks in this family are summarized in Table 5.1. The potential automation in this and all generic task families depends on the knowledge-acquisition bottleneck. Plan, Interpret, and Evaluate are all knowledge-intensive tasks. They can be automated

TABLE 5.1
Generic Tasks in the Action Family

Generic Task	Automation[a]	Task-Support Requirements[b]
Plan	knowledge-intensive expert system	display of options, constraints, possible actions, simulations
Act	robotics; complexity depends on planning	tools, devices, machines to empower human action
Interpret	meaning assigned to events; look-up tables, reference files	information displays, encyclopedias, databases
Evaluate	knowledge-intensive expert system: context, domain	histories, explanations, complex displays, maps, charts, visualizations
Assemble	robotic procedures; complexity depends on planning & flexibility	instructions, diagrams of parts
Disassemble	robotic procedures; complexity depends on planning & flexibility	illustrations of sequence for disaggregation
Transform	information transformation or material change related to act–control	preprocess information, options, techniques & tools to help human-mediated change
Control	direct action of another machine–agent; depends on planning	control devices, feedback on effects, warnings, alerts, system model, & states

[a]Automation assumes the computer takes complete responsibility for the task.
[b]These requirements assume people are in control and carry out some or all of the task.

with increasing sophistication, but only at the penalty of acquiring more complete domain knowledge and developing more sophisticated reasoning processes. Task-support requirements, in contrast, are easier to implement. The computer provides the human user with information to carry out the task. The pertinent design issues are preprocessing and visualizing information to help users.

The Action family tasks fall into two categories: first the action cycle of Plan-Act-Interpret and Evaluate; and more specific actions that change objects in the world: Assemble, Disassemble (Destroy), and Transform. A subset of the tasks is discussed in more detail, and a complete listing can be found in appendix B.

Plan is forming an intention to act, organizing actions in a sequence for execution. Postconditions are actions that are planned to arrive at the task goal. The planning generic task describes human activity of mental planning for action, whereas the high-level view, for instance, the generalized task of planning a holiday, embeds several generic tasks and subgoals.

Generic task: Plan
Precondition: Problem space model is present
Action sequence:
      Load actions into working memory
      Locate external affordances (objects) for action
      Interpret affordances
      Order actions into sequence for execution
Postcondition: Procedure present in working memory

This generic task describes planning for acting in the world and hence elaborates the intention formation and action specification stages of Norman's model. Planning may also be interpreted in the mental problem-solving sense; however, general models of problem solving (Simon, 1973) are not described by the Domain Theory. The task schema only specifies an idealized sequence; for example, if the affordances were ambiguous or inappropriate for action then the task would not be completed, leading to a search for new affordances or replanning.

Interpret is making sense or comprehending a state or state change in the environment. It is ascribing meaning to a state change.

Generic task: Interpret
Precondition: A state change is perceived
Action sequence:
    Recognize change
    Map change to objects in memory
    Create working memory schema of change stimulus with associated memory
    components
Postcondition: A state change is understood or the change is incomprehensible
                  (error condition)

Evaluate assesses the implications of a state change with respect to progress through a task or a perceived state of the world. Evaluation has two specializations, one covering state change evaluation, the other evaluating properties or qualities of an object. Support for this task either involves automation so a machine can arrive at a judgment (e.g., in air traffic control, evaluate if two aircraft radar tracks have a safe separation), or the computer provides information for human decision support (e.g., a ranked list of suppliers to evaluate which one is best on price and delivery). Functional allocation depends on the sophistication of knowledge placed in the machine, an expert system requirement.

Information Processing Family.   This group of generic tasks all involve reasoning and processing information. Hence they form an intermediate layer between generalized models of human problem solving that were described in chapter 3, and generalized tasks. The information processing family shares three generic tasks with the action family: Plan, Interpret, and Evaluate. If the subject matter of Norman's model is changed from action in the world to reasoning about facts and knowledge, it becomes a general model of problem solving with a cycle of Model-Interpret-Evaluate-Plan-Decide-Test. The information processing family of generic tasks is summarized in Table 5.2, omitting duplication of Plan-Interpret-Evaluate.

Model constructs a mental model of the problem at hand, the environment, or other phenomena (agent's beliefs, roles) implicated in reasoning. Modeling in the software engineering sense will involve analyzing (interpretation and evaluation) to understand the facts, and then building the internal mental model as well as recording the model externally as a diagram or specification. Computer support for

TABLE 5.2
Information Processing Family of Generic Tasks

Generic Task	Automation	Task-Support Requirements
Model	learning systems; build model of external world	model representation, editors, consistency checking, simulation
Sort	sort algorithms; automation common	task usually automated; information visualization shows order, rank
Classify	automation depends on class criteria & detecting attributes	visualization to show common items, similar objects
Associate	depends on criteria, rules, & inference to discover links	display of network diagrams, tables, or visual coding for relationships
Select	depends on Search and Identify generic tasks, selection–matching algorithms	visual coding–display to show selectable items, filters
Identify	image and audio processing; depends on recognition criteria	visual coding of candidate items, additional information, filters
Compare	algorithms to calculate similarity or difference	visual display of similarity, variable comparison tools
Decide	depends on criteria; related to Compare and Evaluate; filters, matching, goodness-of-fit algorithms	summary of options, prioritized sorted lists, decision tables, trees, what-if simulations
Test	checking or testing can be automated, given known rules and test criteria; test generators, formal verification tools	validation of potential solutions by providing test scenarios, information, simulations, what-if tools

modeling raises two issues. First is representation where reuse comes in the form of notation to express the model (i.e., the many diagram forms in UML); second there are requirements for checking the consistency of modeling syntax. The latter need can be described as patterns of consistency-type checking for objects, relationships, and dependencies between them. A necessary part of modeling is to *Associate* objects or form a relationship between two or more items. This task differs from categorization because the relationship or the type of association is important rather than group membership. Association may link individuals to each other, allocate resources to agents, and the like, and it is strongly related to modeling. Association is supported in modeling tools by node-link representations and automated by rules and reasoning processes that identify links between objects in a data set.

   Sort is closely coupled with classification that groups instances into sets. *Classify* is defined as organizing items into categories according to rules that explain their commonalities; sorting, ranking, and prioritizing are treated as one generic task because they all reflect ordering and subgrouping with increasing constraints. Sorting has a dimension or metric that allows ordering but the end state is an ordered list expressing priority, preference, or importance. Sorting is a classic automated task that gave rise to solution patterns before the concept of reuse was even invented; the bubble and heap sort algorithms have been part of the computer science curriculum for several decades.

Compare is a specialization of the evaluation task in which judgment is made between two or more phenomena (events, agents, objects), either relative to one another or against an external benchmark standard. Comparison can be automated whenever the criteria are known. Quantitative comparison (e.g., rainfall in locations, populations of cities) lends itself to visualization support by charts and graphics. *Decide* is choosing between options or accepting a course of action, based on judgment about the qualities of an object or action as good–bad or gradations in between. This generic task is referred to as *valence assessment* in psychology and is closely related to the Evaluate-Properties–Qualities task. Judgment is a quintessential human task because it usually involves multivariate comparison and tacit knowledge. Automation is possible, but the domain and judgment criteria must be well known.

Communication Family. This family contains only three tasks: Record that creates a permanent record of information, Communicate itself, and Explain that models the goal of imparting understanding and knowledge rather than just messages. The potential automation and task-support requirements are summarized in Table 5.3. Automation in this family poses considerable problems because human abilities for communication are so well developed and rely on complex knowledge-based processing.

Communicate is the act of sending messages to another party either by speech or another medium. This task is elaborated by dialogue patterns that describe turn taking between agents in conversations that achieve particular goals (see appendix B3). Communication poses interesting problems for design at two levels. First is the communication channel, a problem related to the Object Message OSM, in which issues of the modality (video, voice, synchronous, asynchronous) have

TABLE 5.3
Communication Family

Generic Task	Automation	Task-Support Requirements
Record	media capture, audio–speech, image data, event logs	editing tools, text & word processing, diagram drawing, forms, list processors
Communicate	simple event semantics & message protocols; more complex language requires AI processing & planning	computer-mediated communications, audio–video channels, structured messaging, dialogue patterns
Explain	interagent exchange of knowledge; most systems imply human recipient & require complex KBS for explanation delivery	explanation patterns, visualization, animation, simulation, intelligent question answering

to be addressed; second, there are content issues. Communication is rarely auto-mated because people have the advantage of built-in natural-language processing; however, computerized speaking agents are becoming more common, and generic models of conversations can be reused in their design (Winograd & Flores, 1986).

Explain provides facts and information with reasons and supplementary infor-mation; this is answering problem-related questions in follow-up explanations. This task is associated with Communicate. The type of explanation and its con-tent structure are elaborated in argumentation schemas described in appendix B4. Explanation depends heavily on human qualities of natural language, so it is not an easy task to automate. Nevertheless, many prototype explanation systems have been developed (see Maybury, 1993; Moore & Swartout, 1990 for a selection). Explanations can be described as set types so patterns of explanation types can be proposed as potential solutions (Sutcliffe & Dimitrova, 1999).

Exploring–Sensing Family.   The Action family also interacts with the world, so in this family interaction is viewed from the egocentered point of view of sensing, moving, and exploring the world. In many domains the action and exploring fami-lies will be integrated in cycles of action. The Exploration family also has a cycle of action that involves tasks from the Action family, for example, Monitor-Interpret-Evaluate-Plan-Decide (direction), Orient-Act (move). The potential automation in this family is considerable, as software sensing devices for locating positions and detecting signals in the world have become increasingly sophisticated. However, the extent of automation is still limited by the knowledge-acquisition bottleneck that limits the intelligence in automating Interpret, Evaluate, and Plan. Task support and automation implications are summarized in Table 5.4.

TABLE 5.4
Exploring–Sensing Family

Generic Task	Automation	Task-Support Requirements
Monitor	sensing devices; extent of automation depends on Interpret and Evaluate	event postprocessing depends on Interpret, Detect, & Transform signal
Search	in logical structured search algorithms in DBMS, KBS; in physical world depends on intelligent sensing	maps, diagrams, & models of the searchable world; waymarks, paths, bookmarks
Locate	related to Search and Identify; implies coordinates in physical world, e.g., GPS, radio, audio, etc. tracking	highlights for salient objects, landmarks, filters, pathways
Orient	requires directional sense and world model (map), implicit in Act–Move for navigation, autopilots	compass, maps, models of world topology, pathways

Monitor involves observing the environment for state changes of interest. Monitoring is related to the generic tasks for interpreting and evaluating change but is itself the act of observing and detecting events. This task is interesting because it poses difficult human functional allocation and computer system-design problems. People are poor monitors. We rapidly become bored by repetitive tasks, so monitoring is a good candidate for automation. Unfortunately, this raises the computer science problems of detectability and tuning, which may lead to signaling false alarms or missing significant events. False alarms and monitoring omissions feed back on to the human problem of attending to events signaled by automated systems. Too many false alarms mean we tend not to take system warnings seriously; omissions reduce our trust in the reliability of the monitoring system.

Search tasks have to find items of interest in the environment, either visually or by using other senses (audio, olfaction). Searching is related to monitoring, but it describes an active goal-oriented process for locating an entity, whereas monitoring concerns detecting state change. Support for human searching lies with image and text-processing systems that can automatically find items of interest given some search criteria. Search illustrates the different perspective of human tasks from software procedures. Automated search tasks are algorithms that locate items in data structures, for example, tree search process and heuristics. These may become part of the solution for supporting a human task, but they also exist as patterns for system software reuse. *Orient* finds the direction for travel or location of an object in an environment, including finding orientation cues. This task is related to searching but differs because the orientation is a prerequisite for movement and identifies a reference point of one's self. *Locate* is a prerequisite for Orient that identifies the spatial position of an object in a space. Locate is composed of perceptual actions not described in the Domain Theory (e.g., scan, recognize) and is associated with the Identify and Search generic tasks. Automation of these tasks implies sensing devices to detect the world (see Monitor generic task and Object Sensing OSM). Complete automation is possible as demonstrated in autopilot systems; task support can be provided by maps with location and direction indicators.

5.1.2. Generalized Tasks

Generalized tasks are larger units of abstract activity that map to tasks that people readily identify in the real world, such as analyzing, diagnosing, scheduling, and the like. Generalized tasks are composed of generic tasks, but their structure is less predictable, so a generalized task should be seen as a prototype or typical example of an activity pattern. The following list of generalized tasks is not exhaustive; these models are therefore a sample of the abstract models that describe familiar everyday activities. Appendix B2 contains a full listing of generalized tasks with template structures, requirements problems, and generic requirements for computer support that are frequently associated with each task.

Information Acquisition is eliciting and gathering facts and data from people or other sources. This task involves Communicate, Interpret, and Classify generic tasks with several specialized techniques (e.g., interviews, observation, repertory grids) and dialogue strategies.

The *Analysis–Modeling* task involves organizing facts in a coherent representation (i.e., modeling) and then inferring interesting properties of the modeled phenomena. Although some may separate analysis from modeling, in most cases the two tasks are inseparable. Note that analysis often forms part of diagnosis; however, analysis can be performed without diagnosis, for instance analyzing the structure of a symphony.

Validation–Testing is checking that a design or a problem solution satisfies a set of sufficiency criteria. Validation uses the Compare, Test, and Evaluate generic tasks to assess whether a model is acceptable according to a set of criteria.

Progress Tracking is analyzing how a process is operating or how an object–agent has progressed through states in a life history. This composite task is an aggregate of Monitor, Evaluate, and Model, with ordering of the output.

Planning–Scheduling is the act of organizing future activities or events so that they happen at a certain time, or some resource occurs in a specific place. The essence of planning is ordering the future. In the Domain Theory, planning is interpreted in the cognitive sense of creating a knowledge structure of intentions, that is, a task goal structure that describes a high-level approach to solving a problem or carrying out an activity (see Task Knowledge Structures; Johnson, 1992). Scheduling involves planning, but it can have spatial as well as temporal constraints. The time dimension implies Sorting–Ranking generic tasks.

The *Navigation* task has several variations. Agents may navigate by following a bearing, taking a pathway between two known points, or following cues in the environment that suggest possible routes. Navigation involves planning where to go, executing movement and monitoring the environment to assess progress, and deciding when the destination has been reached. Navigation also uses orientation to locate cues and elect a direction for travel. Similar task models of Navigation have been proposed for virtual environments (Darken & Sibert, 1996; Hix et al., 1999).

Diagnosis is a more complex task that has two major substructures, causal analysis and repair. Diagnosis uses several primitive tasks, such as Interpret, Evaluate, Compare, Sort, and Model. Diagnosis has subclasses for diagnosis of ailments in living things, rectifying faults in designed artefacts, and curing problems in systems; see Fig. 5.3(a). A generalized model of diagnosis as a fault-finding task is described by Rasmussen (1986).

Information Retrieval (IR) involves searching for information items but also deciding the strategy for searching (browsing, use of query language), selecting search terms, and evaluating the relevance of search results. IR has subclasses for goal-directed search and exploratory information browsing. A detailed model of (IR) tasks is described in Sutcliffe and Ennis (1998) and in Marchionini (1995).

In *Judgment–Decision Making*, decisions may concern a course of action (policy adoption), accept or reject one option (unitary decisions), or select one or more objects from a set of possible options (multiple decisions). This task has two main variants: fast-path attitude or memory-bound decision making, which is composed of the judgment generic task; and slow-path reasoned decision making, in which a mental model of the decision space is made and a systematic process is followed to establish the best decision in the circumstances (Evaluate, Compare, Sort, Select generic tasks).

The *Explanation and Advising* generalized task is closely associated with the Education metadomain but it also occurs in tandem with many other tasks. Explanation has a process component that is described in appendix B1, and a content component that is specified as argumentation patterns in appendix B4. Explanations can either be preplanned, scripted, or composed dynamically. It has three main phases: planning the explanation, delivery, and follow-up summary.

Matching is the process of finding the goodness of fit between a set of requirements and properties of objects that might satisfy those requirements. In computation terms this problem is solved by constraint-based problem solvers and linear programming algorithms. This generalized task is closely related to the Object Allocation OSM and employs the Associate generic task.

Forecasting predicts a future state by extrapolating from current data and history and is related to Analysis and Planning–Scheduling. It depends on a model of the represented world and algorithms or inferential processes that extrapolate from current data to the future. Forecasting algorithms usually have a mathematical basis that deals with complex multivariate interactions over a time series to predict future states. The accuracy of the forecast is a function of the sophistication and validity of the model, the algorithms, and the reliability of available data.

If generalized tasks have a deterministic structure, their composition from primitive generic tasks can be specified with some confidence; however, generalized tasks frequently have a less predictable structure so that only a typical sequence can be described with a composition from a collection of generic tasks, and many different execution sequences are possible. Template models of generalized tasks as goal hierarchies illustrate the normal course of the task with alternatives. An example goal structure for the Navigation task is illustrated in Fig. 5.5.

The library of generalized tasks is described in more detail in appendix B2. Each task has a goal hierarchy schema that describes its typical pattern with variations. The variation points are marked to indicate areas where the generalized model will need to be specialized during reuse, following the practice of analyzing points of variation in application frameworks (Fayad & Johnson, 2000). The relationship between families of generalized tasks is illustrated in Fig. 5.6. Analysis–modeling, Diagnosis, and Validation–Testing are all involved in problem solving, which is in turn a precursor of Decision Making. Navigation is not closely connected with other tasks, although navigation in its conceptual sense is necessary for Information Retrieval when wayfinding through large information spaces.

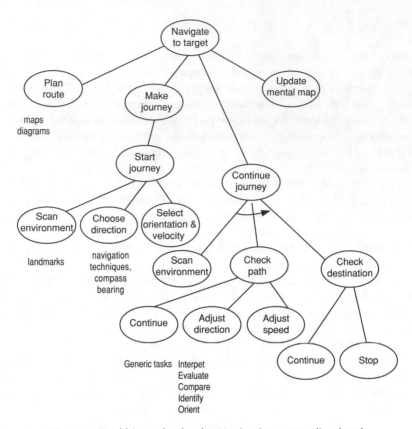

FIG. 5.5. Goal hierarchy for the Navigation generalized task.

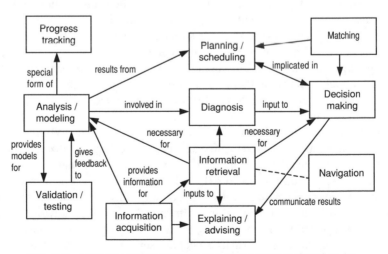

FIG. 5.6. Relationship between families of generalized tasks.

One group of tasks is associated with various forms of problem solving ranging from discovering the reasons for observed problems to designing new objects. Another group involves planning and ordering future activity in a system, scheduling, and planning; a third group concerns processing or finding information. Physical tasks are not described because their structures and procedures are closely associated with details of machines and objects in the environment. For instance, driving a car or riding a bicycle depends on details of the artefact's controls, so abstracting generalized physical tasks does not promise much reuse payoff. The reuser would have to add considerable detail to specialize the abstraction to the new machine context and operation. However, the cognitive activity associated with physical tasks can be generalized. For instance, driving a car involves Navigation and Planning generalized tasks.

A library of generalized tasks at approximately the same level of granularity and abstraction was described in the KADS project (Breuker & Van der Velde, 1994). This library was narrower and deeper than the Domain Theory and concentrated on diagnosis synthesis (design), analysis, and composition tasks. However, KADS generalized tasks are closer to the solution domain for level 2 reuse and do not model human activity.

5.1.3. Discovering Generic and Generalized Tasks

As a way to illustrate the process of discovering generic tasks, specific activity within an application is analyzed and then mapped to the generic task library. The example domain is familiar to most readers: a library that contains subsystems for controlling book loans, managing the book stock, and facilities for searching for items. First there are specific tasks that deal with the transaction processing, stock control, indexing, document management, circulation control, and information searching. The second group involves communication with the public, information searching, question answering, information provision, and explanation. The final group is composed of less structured and more complex tasks found in Management, Education, and Research metadomains, covered in section 5.5. Space precludes an exhaustive listing of all the tasks in the library, so a sample is presented to illustrate the diversity of generic tasks.

Circulation Control (Generic Tasks: Communicate, Associate, Evaluate). This specific task controls the loans of books and other items from the library. In transaction terms it maps to the Object Hiring OSM. The goal of this task is to control the loan of resources and their return to a resource holder. The cognitive generic tasks are evaluating requests from a reader, communicating authorization for the loan (or possible refusal), and then associating the reader with the loan to record the loan. An outline script, with the specific instantiation in parentheses, is as follows.

Record resource requester (reader ID: Record)
Ascertain reader details (call up reader ID on computer system: Select,
   Communicate)
Receive resource (receive book from reader: physical action)
Record and authorize loan (date stamp book, enter loan into system: Identify,
   Evaluate, Associate, Record)
{renew loan}
Receive returned resource (receive returned book: physical action)
Check resource OK (check that book hasn't been damaged, make sure it is not
   overdue: Interpret, Evaluate, Compare)
{request penalty for damage or late return: Evaluate, Communicate}
Sign off loan (update system to Record returned book: Disassociate).

In practice, this task can be more complex. Possible actions are denoted in braces.
Other actions that are not shown in the outline script involve communication with
the reader, such as requesting the reader's identification. These are modeled as
dialogue patterns. More general problem-solving actions are possible at several
steps, such as questioning a reader's identification, or fining readers for overdue
books. The deeper abstraction of this task, shared with many transaction processing
domains, is evaluating or checking that an action is permissible and then creating
an association to record the transaction, as a database relationship between book
<id> and reader <id>. The generic task Associate (loan items to readers) is linked to
the Object Hiring OSM that describes the requirements for this type of transaction,
with generic tasks such as establishing identity and evaluating validity of the
reader.

*Document–Book Classification (Generic Tasks: Identify, Interpret, Evaluate,
Classify, Associate, Record).*   This task covers describing and indexing all new
items, assigning class marks, and entering a record of the item into the library stock
and circulation control databases. The task may also involve determining the shelf
location of an item and its loan status (short loans, general release, etc.). In more
abstract terms it involves describing and recording the presence of an inventory
item so that it may be efficiently retrieved. The outline script is as follows.

Categorize the object (e.g., book, periodical, document: Identify, Classify)
Describe object properties (categorize book's subject matter: Interpret, Evalu-
   ate, Classify)
Determine its storage location (Associate, Search)
Enter the resource description in the inventory database (Record).

Assigning a unique shelfmark or a class mark so that the book or document can
be identified is followed by describing it with keywords for the catalogue. This
specific task fits closely with the generic tasks Evaluate and Classify, but notice

that there are two instances in the example. First the item is classified as a type of resource, and then its subject matter is catalogued.

Information Retrieval (Generic Tasks: Identify, Search, Interpret, Evaluate, Sort, Select). This task characterizes the expert intermediary role, a librarian who advises on information searches and helps users carry them out (Ingwersen, 1996). This task requires knowledge of automated IR systems, query languages, information location in different databases, and skill in search strategies. Communication with the end user is a further skill, necessary to acquire the users' needs, clarify them, and translate them, into search terms. An abstract view of the retrieval task is as follows.

Ascertaining the information need (Communicate, Identify)
Clarifying the search request (Explain, Identify, Scarch)
Translating the search request into a query (Model, Evaluate, Transform)
Submitting the query to a search engine to find the document (physical action)
Evaluating the relevance of retrieved items (Interpret, Evaluate, Sort, Select)
Delivering the result to the requester (Communicate, physical action).

IR is a complex generalized task that is composed of many primitive tasks. The early phase is similar to analysis and modeling when a picture of the user's information need is built up. This is followed by translating the need into a language suitable for an automated search engine. Finally, once results are retrieved, they have to be interpreted, evaluated, and sorted before the relevant subset can be passed on to the user. The instantiation in this case depends on the type of search system being used, such as keyword search, hypertext, or structured query language (SQL); for instance, hypertext will involve the search task to find link cues on an interface. Further details of tasks and examples are given in appendix B2.

5.1.4. Applying and Reusing Generalized Tasks

Generalized tasks provide a starting point for conceptual modeling in a similar manner to OSMs, so task analysis can be guided by the generalized task library. Requirements issues and generic requirements are reusable knowledge attached to the generic models that help to shape the agenda of creating the solution to the problem. The best way to explain how the Domain Theory generalized task can be used in design is by example. Ideally, each generic task should be extended into the solution domain to create a model of the problem and solution components. In the case of Information Retrieval I have created such a model in collaboration with Mark Ennis (Sutcliffe & Ennis, 1998, 2000; Sutcliffe, Ennis, & Hu, 2000). The basic task structure is illustrated in Fig. 5.7.

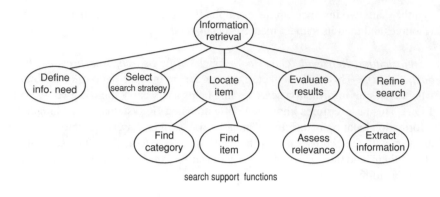

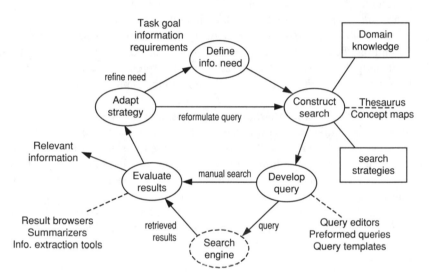

FIG. 5.7. Models of the Information Retrieval generalized task.

The task model is decomposed into goals and subtasks for defining the search problem, articulating the search request, formulating and carrying out the search, and evaluating the results. Each subtask is associated with a set of human resources and system requirements that are necessary to achieve the goal. These resources and requirements (called *task-support facilities*) frame the trade-off decision for potential automation, as illustrated in Table 5.5.

The initial stage, define information need, has a low automation potential because it is knowledge intensive and depends on the user's external task that creates the need. The next stage is potentially more automatable, but it depends on the required information belonging to a well-known domain with a sophisticated semantic lexicon. Expert systems to infer an articulation of users' needs from

TABLE 5.5
Information Retrieval Task

Task Step	Human Resources and Knowledge	Task Support Requirements
Define information need	Domain knowledge search concepts	Problem lists, information categories
Select search strategy	IR task knowledge information sources	Expert advisors' search strategies, browsing tools, reusable queries, information maps
Define search terms and query	Knowledge of retrieval systems, query keywords, domain	Search tools: natural language, menu lists, query languages, Boolean operators, hypertext, thesauri
Execute search	Knowledge of location of documents, sources and access paths thereto	Search algorithms, similarity pattern matching, statistical techniques, information extraction tools
Evaluate results	Domain knowledge evaluation strategies	Browsers, summarization and presentation tools. Relevance feedback function. Relevance ranking, evaluation advisors

high-level concepts have not been very successful (Sutcliffe, Ennis, & Watkinson, 2000). Formulate and execute query is where automation has had more success, in the form of search algorithms and engines. The final stage, evaluate results, is more knowledge intensive so complete automation is not possible; however, considerable task support can be provided by sorting and ranking results by relevance to the query.

The generic task model was then used to create an expert system advisor that provided search-strategy guidelines at appropriate stages of the task while also invoking appropriate tools that implemented the task-support requirements. We created and evaluated the expert Information Retrieval Advisor in the Multimedia Broker project, which searched the Internet for media resources and then matched a user's requirements (Sutcliffe & Ennis, 2000). However, the theoretical work went further, proposing a set of correspondence rules that linked users' profiles (e.g., novices or experts with different levels of domain, lexical, and device knowledge) with the appropriate and available task-support facilities. Thus if a user had little domain knowledge at the articulate search stage, the system invoked thesaurus tools and provided search-strategy advice appropriate to novices, such as sample queries, browse the thesaurus, or a classification map, and suggested iterative drill-down queries. If similarity matching tools were available, for example, Latent Semantic Indexing (LSI; Landauer & Dumais, 1997), then the system suggested entering a real or fictitious example of the expected result. The rules embodied trade-offs between users' resources and system task-support facilities that implemented the requirements in Table 5.5. This created an adaptable IR environment that could provide advice and software services that were appropriate for the user's capabilities. Further work extended the generic task to account for different search types to improve the effectiveness of adaptation, for example, strategies and facilities for information searches with a general or specific level of detail, well or poorly known needs, or single or multiple search targets. This research is still in progress; however, what it has demonstrated to date is that it is possible to create minitheories for generic tasks that build on the Domain Theory framework to create intelligent adaptable systems for users with different levels of expertize and needs.

5.2.   GENERIC DIALOGUES

Dialogue models are generic conversations that elaborate the Communicate and Explain generic tasks. Six dialogues are described: Questioning, Clarification, Propose Action, Propose Idea, Command, and Negotiate Position. In linguistics, conversations are composed of speech acts that are structured into moves and exchanges (Searle, 1969). Conversations are built up of pairs of *dialogue acts*, the most basic of which is the question and answer. Adjacency pairs are composed into *generic dialogues* between two agents that are motivated by a shared goal. Exchanges are typically composed of three acts, but longer chains are possible. Some examples are

- Question–answer–acknowledge
- Check (test question)–answer–confirm or correct
- Propose–agree or disagree–act

Conversations have goals that are set by the task, so dialogues are structured to provide the means to achieve these ends. Primitive conversation structures were originally described in conversation analysis by Sacks, Schegloff, and Jefferson (1974), whereas larger-scale dialogue models associated with tasks were specified in the conversation for action research by Winograd and Flores (1986). The Winograd and Flores models represented conversations linked to tasks such as purchasing and requesting information, which are dealt with in the Domain Theory by interaction schema in section 5.3. Although natural human discourse is very variable even when associated with specific goals such as buying and selling goods, the dialogue models have utility in planning structured conversations and provide models for natural-language processing systems to interpret users' speech.

Dialogues are composed of *discourse acts*, which are segments of natural language dialogue that achieve a particular purpose in communication. The surface form of the language may be different but the intent of the speaker will be the same. Some acts are obvious, such as questions, whereas others are more variable in their surface form. For example, to test your understanding (Check) of the concept of a discourse act, I could ask you a question, "So you have understood the concept, haven't you ?" or I could make a statement and wait for you to deny it: "So you see discourse acts are utterances that can be classified as sharing a common communicative intent." Dialogue patterns are specified by acts drawn from the following set (Sutcliffe & Maiden, 1991).

- Request: the speaker requests information from another. This category includes explicit and implicit questions seeking information on a topic, for example, a user's goal, how an event occurs, or an example of an object, event, or problem.
- Inform: the speaker provides information, either prompted or unprompted, and answers questions, elaborates details, and gives examples. Also included are giving background information, causes, results, and examples that demonstrate rationale.
- Check: the speaker requests clarification of a current topic, for example, "So is it delivered before or after the dispatch note?" This act tests one agent's understanding after information has been received. It can be manifest by either explicit questions or noninterrogative statements: "So first you go through the pre-flight check list then you get OK to start engines."
- Confirm: the speaker confirms his or her own or someone else's understanding of a current topic, usually in response to a check; for example, "Yes, it's the goods that are delivered after. . . ."
- Summarize: the speaker gives a synopsis of a preceding conversation, that is, an overview of topics that have been discussed.
- Acknowledge: the speaker gives a signal that the other party's utterance has been received and understood.
- Command: the speaker directs the other agent to carry out an action or adopt a belief. Commands have more force than proposals and do not invite the other agent, for example, "Shut down the computer immediately."
- Propose: the speaker proposes an action or topic to be discussed or makes statements about planning action or conducting a meeting, for example "Let's write these requirements on the whiteboard." Proposals may be a solution to a problem, state a requirement, or suggest how a problem may be solved.
- Augment: the speaker adds new facts and propositions to develop a proposed solution, develop a course of action, or refine a requirement.
- Agree: the speaker confirms that he or she shares the same belief in a proposition or course of action and signals support for a proposal.
- Disagree: the speaker signals that he or she does not share the same belief as a previous speaker and would not support a proposal.
- Correct: the speaker states that a previous assertion was wrong and explains why, giving an alternative proposal or assertion.

These acts are integrated with cognitive and physical actions to describe communication associated with generalized tasks.

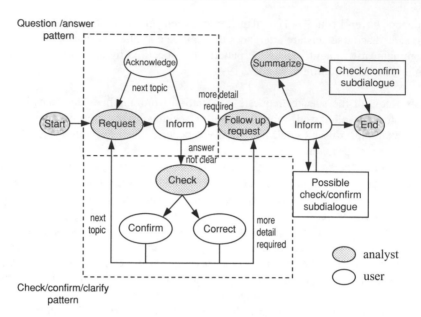

FIG. 5.8. Typical questioning dialogue with an associated clarification dialogue that handles follow-up questions.

A model of the question pattern associated with the check–confirm dialogue is shown in Fig. 5.8. Dialogues can be embedded within each other or chained together to model interactions for generalized tasks. Thus dialogues provide the same composability for reuse as generic tasks.

Other families of generic dialogues are command structures associated with the Agent Control OSM; making proposals and idea building associated with the Analysis–Modeling generalized task; and reporting facts, explanations, and negotiations associated with Validation–Testing. In the command family the dialogues are specialized according to the coupling between the agents and the constraints imposed by the command on the subordinate's action. In strict hierarchies the command should be followed to the letter of the law, and the only response expected is acknowledging the command and reporting back on completion. In less hierarchical organizations, the subordinate has the choice to clarify the command first, possibly refine the course of action, and then execute the action and report back. As the power balance between the parties becomes more equal, the command evolves into the proposal and liaison dialogue in which one party makes a suggestion, both parties discuss it, and both agree on a plan of action. The strict command dialogue and proposal are illustrated in Fig. 5.9.

Commands not only have different forces but also impose constraints on action. The recipients may either be told to carry out an action in some detail or may be given a higher-level goal with considerable freedom to interpret the plan of action.

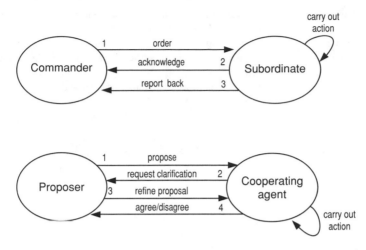

FIG. 5.9. Command dialogue contrasted with proposal. These dialogues are associated with deterministic and nondeterministic Agent Control OSMs.

A middle ground is giving the subordinate the goal and some guidance about how to plan the action. Other variations depend on the group structure. A command might involve a single agent, or it might require one agent to coordinate the work of others. The degree of autonomy influences the dialogue structure. Commands that instruct one agent but give detailed instruction for how a whole group should act become complex and prone to misinterpretation, but in some circumstances, for example, subordinates with little training of domain knowledge, they may be necessary. The dialogue family is described in appendix B3.

5.3. INTERACTION SCHEMAS

Interaction schemas are larger scale dialogues that specify task-related conversations. These describe interaction between agents that are associated with grounded domains and generalized tasks. An interaction schema is a template describing the conversation between agents that achieves a system goal within the domain. The purpose of these templates is to provide a profile of the agents involved and the conversation exchange, which will become an outline specification for the human–computer dialogue. Interaction schemas are composed of the agent descriptions and an interaction diagram that illustrates the exchange between the agents. First the participating agent's properties are specified.

Agent Properties

Expectations: Beliefs held about the purpose of the dialogue in the domain of interest

Knowledge structures: Relevant information or memory held by the participating
                         agents
Competencies: Skills, abilities to discharge the obligations in the domain
Responsibilities: Obligations placed upon the agent to achieve the purpose
                         in the domain
Role: Tasks and actions the agents carry out and their roles as
                         initiators or responders in a conversation

Because communication and action frequently proceed in parallel, interaction
schemas and generalized task models form two interlinked threads of activity. Two
example schemas, one for a grounded domain and the other for a generalized task,
are illustrated in Figs. 5.10 and 5.11.

Library Loan: OSM Class Object Hiring
Client Agent:
   Expectations: To gain a resource (book)
   Knowledge structures: Identity of required resource
   Competencies: Communication skills
   Responsibilities: To return resource
   Role: Request, initiator; depends on Holder Agent

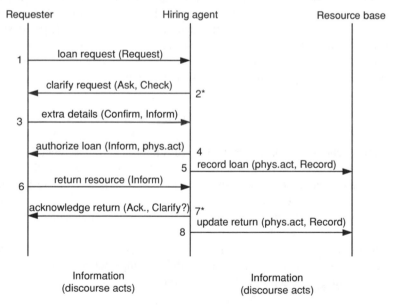

FIG. 5.10. Interaction schema for the loan transaction Object Hiring OSM. Numbers indicate turns; possible clarification subdia-
logues may occur at turns marked with an asterisk.

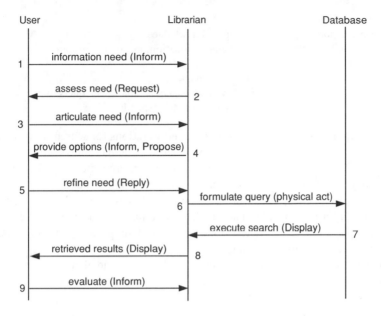

FIG. 5.11. Interaction schema for the IR generalized task.

Resource Holder Agent:
    Expectations: To loan a resource
    Knowledge structures: Available resource
    Competencies: Loan procedures, assessing client's needs
    Responsibilities: To service client requests
    Role: Loan, responder

In this case the conversation is closely anchored to the transaction. The resource requester has to ask for the item; this may be followed by a clarification subdialogue, and then the conversation progresses to authorizing and recording the loan. A separate schema handles loan renewal. Interaction schemas, in common with generalized tasks, have points where variations can occur. These are marked as calls to dialogue subroutines.

Information Searching–Retrieval
Knowledge Requester Agent
    Expectations: To gain knowledge
    Knowledge structures: Domain of interest (may be partial knowledge of)
    Competencies: Articulate request
    Responsibilities: To be accurate, honest in articulating request
                     (Grice maxims)
    Role: Articulate request, formulate query, evaluate
                     results, initiator, depends on responder

Requestee Agent
    Expectations: To supply knowledge
    Knowledge structures: Available information, location of resources
    Competencies: Search procedures
    Responsibilities: To service requests
    Role: Retrieve and display results, check query and
                       information needs, responder

This schema has a structure of two nested iterations for search refinement and clarifications within each search. The interaction schema follows the procedure in the generalized task and indicates how task-support processes should be designed and ordered within a dialogue. For instance, the assess need subgoal may be partially automated by providing a thesaurus; likewise, formulating a query can be helped by a form-filling dialogue. The schema helps design when combined with design rationale to suggest possible ways of supporting the users' task and specifying the dialogue structure.

Generic tasks are carried out by a single agent and therefore do not have associated interaction schemas.

5.4. ARGUMENTATION SCHEMAS

Conversations have both a dialogue structure and content. The information contained within a conversation will depend on a variety of factors, such as the task, user motivation, knowledge of the other party, location, culture, and so on. Given this list of contextual influencing factors, proposing regularities in content may seem to be a lost cause. However, this is not the case. Researchers in linguistics have long since recognized that regularities occur in how we express ideas, especially in written texts. One view of the higher-order schemas is prose styles and poetic forms, sonnets, and the like. In contrast, argumentation schemas are lower-level components that owe their heritage to functional theories of language, notably Rhetorical Structure Theory (RST; Mann & Thompson, 1988). RST specifies a schema of relations that express the nature of the argument linking two information components; the first subject is referred to as the *nucleus* whereas the second supporting component is called the *satellite*. RST describes 22 relations all told, of which the more useful are as follows.

- Enablement: procedural or how-to explanation
- Elaboration: adds detail to describe an object, agent, or event
- Solutionhood: proposes a means of solving a problem
- Summary: précis of a preceding argument or conversation
- Result: describes the postconditions of an event or causal sequence
- Cause: explains the reasons why an observed event (the result) happened

- Motivation: encourages the reader or listener to accept an argument or proposal
- Justification: provides evidence for an argument or proposal
- Background: adds general description of the subject matter
- Circumstance: provides contextual information relating to an event, action, or location
- Comparison: compares two objects, events, or agents

RST relations can be applied just as well to define the content of each node in an argument, and this has been used in artificial intelligence planning systems that automatically construct explanations from a library of components (Andre & Rist, 1993; Maybury, 1993; Zhou & Feiner, 1998). The Domain Theory uses RST components to describe content schemas to explain the generic task. These are based on observations of human–human explanations (Sutcliffe & Maiden, 1992) and an analysis of rules embedded in computer-based explanation systems.

Following the usual tenets of the Domain Theory, explanation schemas consist of a set of components that achieve a single goal. Explanation schemas are a sequence of arguments that convey understanding about a body of facts to the reader or listener, so they are larger units than simple factual statements. Explanations have a hierarchical structure of subarguments that contribute to the overall theme, and a sequence that represents the presentation script. These schemas are illustrated as hierarchy diagrams to show the composition of arguments. Reading along the base of the diagram gives the sequence of components in a presentation order (Fig. 5.12).

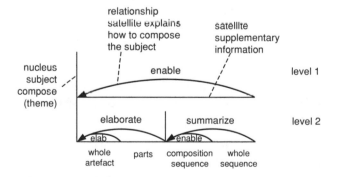

FIG. 5.12. Argumentation schema for composing an artefact, showing composition of content and RST relations. The schema is composed of two subcomponents. The first introduces the artefact and its parts, with an elaboration. The second explains the order of composition with a summary and shows how to compose information; hence the enablement relation.

In some cases, explanation schemas are closely associated with generalized and generic tasks; for example, causal explanations are frequent in diagnosis and analysis tasks and may explain the generic tasks with which they are associated, such as Classify.

A sample of the explanation schema library is given as follows, with more details in appendix B4.

Classification explains how instances of objects, agents, events, and the like belong to categories. First the category is introduced, and then examples of well-formed members are given, followed by poor examples and members of related categories. The schema concludes by summarizing the classification rules. This schema is associated with the Classify generic task.

- Elaboration introduces the category, its attributes, and its position in a taxonomy (circumstance).
- Comparison describes a good member by pointing out the member's features that agree with the category's attributes.
- Comparison explains a related category member or counterexample.
- Summary summarizes the classification rules, supplemented with Elaborate for a large taxonomy.

In a *composition* (whole–parts) explanation, the schema explains the composition of objects in terms of its components and how they fit together. The schema can be specialized to illustrate *decomposition* rather than composition. This schema is linked to the Composition–Decomposition grounded domain OSMs.

- Elaboration introduces the whole object and describes its role or function.
- Elaboration then describes or shows its parts.
- Enablement is used to illustrate the composition–aggregation sequence from part to substructures to the whole.
- Summary is used to recap facts about the object and its parts and to point out major subcomponents.

In a *task-based* (how to do it) explanation, the physical task sequence given here is specialized for abstract cognitive tasks. The sequence first provides the task goal (purpose), and then details of the procedure. It is followed by a summary.

- Enablement introduces the overall plan and explains the task goal. This may be accompanied by a diagram of the plan.
- Circumstance gives the preconditions for the task to commence.
- Enablement describes the task steps.
- Summary integrates the explanation and describes the postconditions for task completion.

A *causal* (why or how it works) explanation starts by introducing the domain, important objects, and concepts. Then the causal model is explained, followed by background knowledge to back up why the events happen. A summary concludes with key events and their causation. This task is closely associated with analysis and diagnosis.

- Elaboration introduces the domain and important objects.
- Cause followed by Result describes the sequence of cause and effect, possibly supplemented by Background to explain key facts and background knowledge.
- Summary is used for key events and causal explanation if the explanation concerns natural phenomena or Solutionhood for a how-something-works explanation.

Explanation schemas form canonical scripts that are specialized to construct arguments, and they may also be transformed into multimedia presentation schemas by applying rules to select appropriate media to convey the content (Sutcliffe & Dimitrova, 1999). Transformation rules take the explanation schema and change it into a multimedia presentation schema, taking into account the RST relations and information types that describe abstract or physical properties of the content.

5.5. METADOMAINS

Metadomains are the largest components of the Domain Theory. Accordingly, they are not modeled at the same level of detail as grounded domains and generic tasks. Metadomains share the same basic tenet of goal-oriented cohesion with other Domain Theory models, although higher-level goals tend to be more diffuse. Metadomains characterize complex areas of human endeavor that may or may not be supported by technology. Hence they are models of sociotechnical systems consisting of agents, groups, organizational units, and technology. Tasks implement activity, as do grounded domain models; however, both may form subject matter that is acted on by the metadomain. The schema for describing metadomains is as follows.

Goals are high-level aims and objectives of the metadomain. Goals at this level cannot be realized as state expressions; instead, they are a set of constraints that the system has to satisfy. *Functional components* are architectural components of metadomains that achieve high-level goals. Architectural components can be decomposed into models of agents who carry out tasks with objects and resources. *Resources* are databases and other resources used by functional components. *Communication flows* are channels for information exchange among functional components, agents, and resources. A metadomain is a set of components connected by communication flows that act on resources to achieve a common purpose. Thus far, four metadomain classes have been described: Design; Education or Training; Management; and Research.

5.5.1. Design

Design is a complex, ill-structured activity that involves several generic tasks; for instance, analyzing, modeling, planning, and validating all take place in design. Design is a creative activity that can be described at a high level with a regular structure; for instance, in architecture, design progresses through phases of gathering requirements, constructing a first-cut model, and then evaluating layers of constraints to refine the solution so it meets social, human, aesthetic, and structural criteria (Akin, 1986). However, design varies radically between domains (Candy & Edmonds, 2000), and attempts to specify a generic task model have not proven useful; hence design is a good candidate for description as a metadomain. Design takes a grounded domain or a generalized task in an initial operational state and improves its operation by design of tasks, artefacts, or application of technology. The goal of design is the creation of new artefacts, which may involve the analysis or modeling and validation of generalized tasks, and frequently creative problem solving. In the family of metadomains, design is closer to a generalized task than others; however, it is typically an unstructured, reflective process (Schon, 1983). Models of the design process have been proposed for specific domains, for example, architecture (Akin, 1986), that describe a sequence of fact gathering, problem modeling, developing solutions, and constraint-based reasoning, leading to the selection of a solution that meets all the requirements. However, in other domains, design does not follow such a predictable process (Visser & Hoc, 1990).

The subsystem architecture model of the Design metadomain is illustrated in Fig. 5.13. Design rarely innovates completely de novo. Instead, designers reuse and adapt ideas. Designs have to be proposed and critiqued. This leads to a set of resources and functional components that describe the metadomain.

The more task-oriented components of design environments are tools to support analysis and modeling of the problem domain. Models are resources that are worked on to create new solutions, which have to be validated to check that they meet with requirements and quality criteria. However, this is just one view of design. New products or processes can be designed by adapting existing solutions or composing solutions from ready-made components, following the reuse theme in this book. Hence design environments have to provide well-designed components for reuse, good and bad examples to learn from, and critics (human or automated) that use good examples to assess the current design. Other support components are notepads, tractability tools, and hypermedia for information services and recording ideas. Designs have to be checked out, usually the earlier the better, indicating components for visualization, simulation, and prototyping tools. A close realization of this architecture can be found in Fischer's (1996) Domain Oriented Design Environments (DODEs), which are a generic software architecture that can be tailored to a variety of problem domains, such as kitchen design or design of windows in graphic user interfaces (Fischer et al., 1995). DODEs are a good example of a metadomain model instantiation in practice with a grounded domain as subject

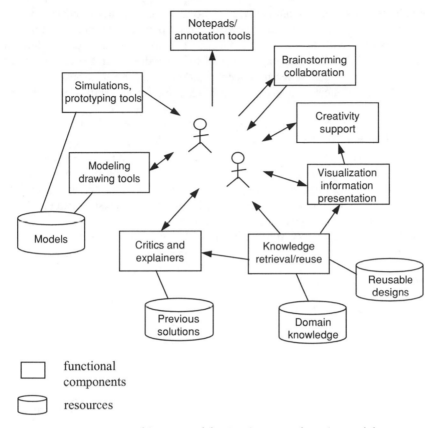

FIG. 5.13. Architecture of the Design metadomain model.

matter; in the case of kitchen design, this is a spatial planning generalized task in the Object Composition (assembly) grounded domain.

In summary, a design metadomain exists to create new artefacts and processes from existing materials, and it involves human cognitive processes of analysis, modeling, creative inspiration, and validation, with resources of previous designs, components, and ways of recording and simulating designs. Design occasionally creates new instances of grounded domains; for example, the World Wide Web is a new grounded domain instantiating the generic domain class of distributing and communicating information (Message Transfer OSM).

5.5.2. Education or Training

This includes training, teaching, and explanation, and it has a purpose to help someone acquire a body of knowledge that he or she did not initially possess. The goal in this domain is to transfer a new body of knowledge to one or more individuals. This metadomain is divided into training and education. Training is the delivery of specific skills and knowledge for a particular purpose. In training, the goal is to provide task-related knowledge to improve some aspect of human performance. Education has a broader goal to instill deeper understanding about a subject so that students learn concepts, theories, and abstractions as well as practical skills. Education also aims to provide metalearning skills (learning how to learn).

As with most metadomains, description of the complete architecture could consume a whole book because these domains form intellectual disciplines in their own right (i.e., educational psychology). The Domain Theory's purpose is not to repeat such knowledge but simply to summarize it in an architectural form so that the detail of methods, strategies, techniques, and claims can be located in appropriate areas for reuse. The architecture of an Education metadomain is shown in Fig. 5.14. The Education domain consists of the generalized task of explaining and critiquing with the more complex task of Explanation–Advising that is specialized into roles of teaching by the expert, while the student contributes learning, experimenting, and analyzing. Tutorial architectures have a long history in intelligent tutoring

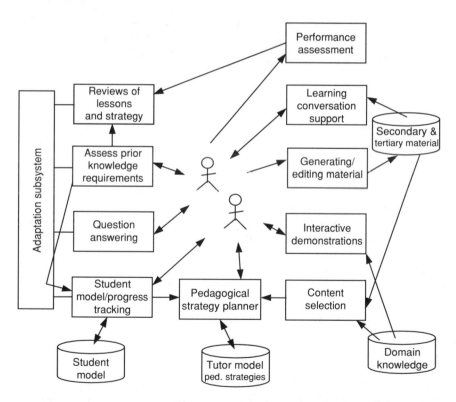

FIG. 5.14.   Architecture of the Education metadomain model.

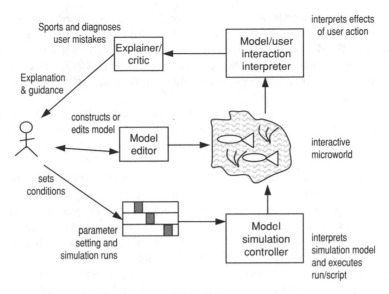

FIG. 5.15. Tutorial interactive microworld architecture.

systems, which were traditionally composed of three major components: the domain knowledge base, tutor models that deliver instruction, and student models to monitor progress (Wenger, 1987). More recent architectures have moved toward interactive tutoring by simulation and microworlds (Elsom-Cook, 1988, 2000), following the move from instructionist to constructivist learning (Laurillard, 1993; Papert, 1980). This is reflected in components that display the world and control user interaction within it, an assessment component that tracks the user's progress and analyzes mistakes, and a critiquer–explainer that provides feedback to the user (see Fig. 5.15). More complex architectures might incorporate question answering for student-initiated dialogues, but this is rare in commercial products. Limited querying facilities are usually provided.

Education-support architectures tend to be more complex than training systems because their ambition is higher, to instill deeper learning rather than skill. However, most computer-aided learning (CAL) architectures share the interactive microworlds with tutoring environments. The metadomain architecture reflects three major educational traditions: constructivist learning by active engagement and doing (Papert, 1980); social conversational learning, which emphasizes collaborative and communication aspects of learning in groups (Laurillard, 1993); and minimalism, which takes a gradual approach to learning (Carroll, 1995). For constructivist learning, the architecture has additional pedagogical control components and editors for building and experimenting with interactive worlds. Customization facilities and adaptive components add more sophistication in the pedagogical response so that teaching styles, initiative, and tactics can be adapted to individual learners' needs. A user-acquisition dialogue component asks users for their needs while a student model tries to track the student's progress to drive adaptation. The degree of intelligence and adaptation differs between designers who believe in a less interventionist approach (e.g., Lewis, 1993) and those who follow the intelligent tutoring systems tradition (Anderson, Corbett, Koedinger, & Pelletier, 1995).

For minimalist learning to be supported, components are added for controlling the exposure of domain knowledge in layers, and hence adapting the sophistication of the simulation, as well as providing more feedback to students on their progress. The adaptation mechanism interacts with the student model and pedagogical strategies components to control teaching style according to the students' needs and progress. Conversational learning adds components to support group-level interaction as chat or e-mail exchanges and changes interactive microworlds into shared facilities; hence access control and dialogue management components become necessary. Conversational learning also places more emphasis on secondary supporting learning material (examples, critiques, etc.) and tertiary learning material that students generate themselves (e.g., comments, annotations, or discussion on problems). Components to manage and access databases of education materials are necessary, as are editors to moderate, synthesize, and collate tertiary material. More details can be found in the pedagogical patterns website or in the vicarious learner project (Cox, McKendree, Tobin, Lee, & Mayes, 1999; Stenning et al., 2000).

5.5.3. Management

One view of the Management metadomain is to characterize the organizational concerns of companies, that is, accounting, inventory control, marketing, sales-order processing, logistics, and personnel. Enterprise resource plans can be seen as a specification of the Management metadomain because they provide sector models for the preceding activities plus those concerned with controlling manufacture, such as bill of materials or production planning (Keller & Teufel, 1998). Some of these abstractions are specified in grounded domains, for instance inventory management, sales, and accounting, so the metadomain description focuses on the prime objective of management: to set the strategic direction and control the activity of an organization. Following traditional frameworks, this domain distinguishes tactical and operational management carried out by junior and middle managers from strategic management as carried out by senior executives (Argyris, 1999; Davis, 1995). Another influence on the domain architecture is Porter's conception of value chains that represent the main economic process of generating goods and services, and the administrative services (accounting, personnel, communication) necessary to support the value chain (Porter, 1980).

The purpose of the Management metadomain here is to control and improve the performance of a system by reorganizing work patterns, motivating people, investing in technology, and so on. Management at the tactical and strategic levels motivates operational teams, controlling their tasks, setting objectives, and deciding strategic issues such as establishing standards and setting policy. Management also involves duties of budget preparation and expenditure control, personnel management, workflow monitoring and control, reporting, and policy execution in operational procedures. The generalized tasks of analysis and diagnosis are important for problem solving in management as well as forecasting and planning for the future. Note that management is similar to design and, indeed, contains some design-related tasks; however, the purpose is subtly different. Management's prime aim is performance improvement of an existing system, whereas the purpose of design is to create new artefacts and systems. Managers, of course, undertake design activity when they create new organizations, and this illustrates how one person can occupy roles in more than one metadomain.

The architecture of management information systems, as with all metadomains, varies among organizations, industries, and approaches to management. The style of management is also reflected in the architecture. More hierarchical management structures are closely related to the Agent Control grounded domain and rely on clear lines of command and feedback. Less hierarchical models, with autonomous teams in flexible matrix management structures, require better monitoring processes because high-level managers set the goals and then monitor performance without planning activity in detail. Information systems are at the core of management support (see Fig. 5.16). Databases and IR services form the first layer, which feeds from transaction systems (which will be implementations of OSMs, ISMs, and generic tasks) and external information sources. Internal and external information may be integrated in corporate Intranets. Information-analysis tools such as the ubiquitous spreadsheet, financial-analysis packages, planning tools, and decision-support systems form the next layer of components. These tools utilize models of the business and its environment to forecast effects, and they share many characteristics with interactive microworlds in the Education metadomain.

Another set of components in the Management metadomain supports organization, coordination, and communication. Management is concerned not only with the internal control of an organization but also with coordination of relationships between organizations. Some relationships will be collaborative whereas others, between competitors, will be adversarial. The nature of these relationships can be determined by analyzing the transactions between organizations (Williamson, 1981) as well as by looking at policy objectives for mergers and outsourcing. Market style relationships require subsystems for searching for products, advertising, broking, and matching of customer requirements and then handling purchase. In contrast, when transactions involve more expensive goods with few competitors, relationships tend to be more contractual. In this case management subsystems have to support contract negotiation, workflow coordination, and quality assurance (Sutcliffe, 2000b; Sutcliffe & Li, 2000). Interorganizational views of the Management metadomain are illustrated in Fig. 5.17.

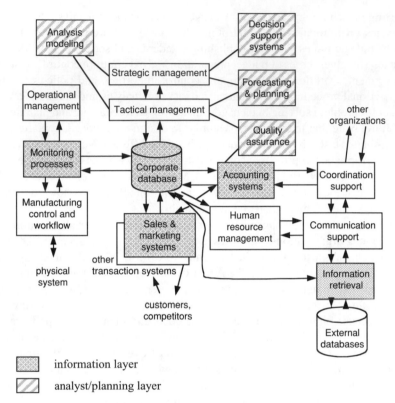

information layer

analyst/planning layer

FIG. 5.16. Management information system and executive support system architectures.

Coordination tools include groupware systems for coordination of meetings and documentation, video conferencing, brainstorming support tools, and the like. Coordination is supported by workflow management tools that form a controlling layer above transaction systems. Visualization and modeling tools feed from decision-support tools for presentation support in meetings and marketing presentations.

5.5.4. Research

This is the most abstract and general metadomain. The purpose is the generation of understanding and new knowledge. Research requires subject matter of grounded domains or generalized tasks, but it may also encompass another metadomain, such as educational research. The architecture of this domain supports the generalized tasks that compose it, namely analysis, modeling, diagnosis, testing or validation, and information retrieval. Because research shares many attributes with design, the

Hierarchical control

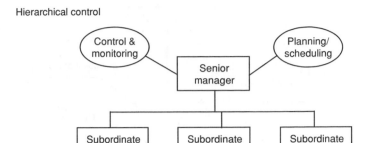

Network (peer) relationships

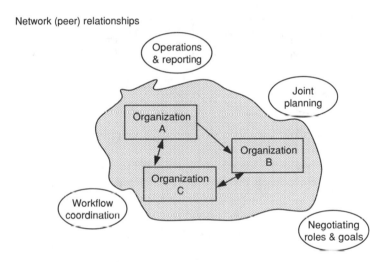

FIG. 5.17. Management metadomain architectures for different styles of interorganizational relationships.

architectures share many components. Both metadomains involve creative activity; the main difference is that research has a longer time scale and produces new knowledge, whereas design tends to produce new products and processes. Of course, research into engineering and areas of artistic design blurs the boundary. Research requires database components for literature searches, documentation and idea-management components such as hypertext, brainstorming tools, and simulations to test ideas. The research domain architecture is the most difficult one to produce even a generalized view of, because the technology support and activity differ radically between subject areas; for instance, documentation analysis tools in history and archives research, surveying and document management tools in archaeology, or scientific visualization and simulation tools in organic chemistry.

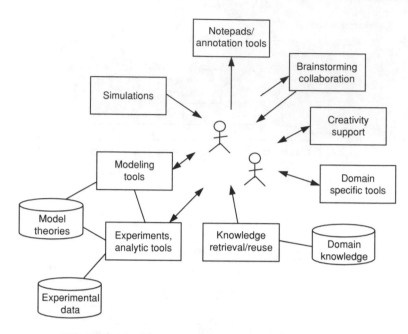

FIG. 5.18. Architecture of the Research metadomain.

The architecture in Fig. 5.18 is therefore restricted to general support tools, with placeholders for components that specific research areas might require.

5.6. SUMMARY

A schema for generic tasks is composed of actions organized in a sequence that changes object states to achieve a task goal. Generic tasks are coherent units of activity that run to completion. Generalized tasks are large components composed of generic tasks. Generic tasks fall into five groups. First are tasks that extend Norman's (1988) model of action, Plan, Interpret, and Evaluate. The Analysis and Modeling group includes classifying, sorting, and selecting. The Communication group contains explanation and recording, and the Navigation group covers monitoring, orientation, search, and location. The last group covers transformation and construction.

Generalized tasks describe human activity with requirements for computer support. Examples are diagnosis, analysis, validation, navigation, and information retrieval. Generalized tasks have a template goal structure with variation points where different techniques and procedures may be used. Generic dialogues elaborate conversations for the Communicate generic task. Dialogues are composed of discourse acts such as question, inform, propose, and command. Dialogue patterns are described for questioning, clarification, commands, proposals, and so on. Interaction patterns are large-scale dialogue patterns associated with generalized tasks and OSMs that describe goal-oriented conversations.

Argumentation schemas describe the content of Communicate and Explain generic tasks. These patterns are composed of rhetorical acts and describe explanations for procedures, causation, composition, and the like.

Metadomains are large-scale models of human activity acting on grounded domains. Metadomains are composed of subsystems, generalized tasks, agents, and resources. Four metadomains are described: Design, Education, Management, and Research.

6

Claims and Knowledge Management

So far we have considered the reuse of application classes or problem domain models. These models describe either phenomena that exist in the world (grounded domains), generalized models of human problem solving activity (generic or generalized tasks), or high-level architectures of systems that control, construct, or understand the world (metadomains). What is missing are models of designed components and design advice that can be used to solve problems expressed in the Domain Theory. The range of design models, even generic ones, is vast and has already been recorded in several books. I therefore give some pointers to where libraries of solution models can be found, but I do not go into any detail of design solutions. Instead I explain a knowledge representation theory that provides a modus operandi for establishing the link between requirements and design as well as for delivering design knowledge in its own right. The relationships between different parts of the Domain Theory are summarized in Fig. 6.1. The families of grounded domains, tasks, and metadomains all specify abstractions of problems inherent in the real world. The subject matter of this section, claims and design rationale, provides solution-related knowledge that augments the reuse utility of domain models.

One way in which design knowledge is recruited to the Domain Theory is by design rationale. Design rationale is an informal representation of arguments or the decisions that were made during the design process, rather than a design

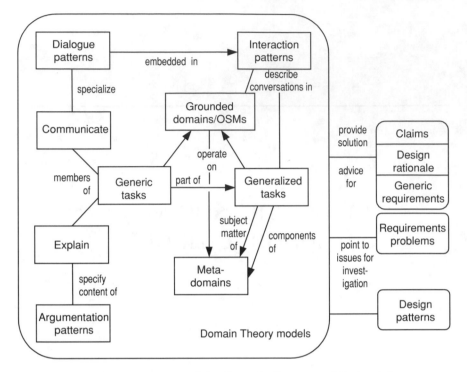

FIG. 6.1. Components of the Domain Theory and their relationship to solution knowledge.

component per se. The origins of design rationale go back to the argumentation theory of Toulmin (1958), who proposed a schema for text-based arguments that consisted of statements, justification, and warrants (evidence or guarantees) that the argument is valid. Argumentation theory was extended in issue-based information systems (IBIS) to record decisions as a structure of design issues, positions, or solutions to the issues and arguments to justify one or more positions. An example of the graphical representation gIBIS (Conklin & Begeman, 1988) is illustrated in Fig. 6.2.

Design rationale in the gIBIS format has been applied to documentation in software engineering and as a proactive design tool. The HCI variant is questions options criteria (QOC; MacLean et al., 1991), which poses a usability–requirements issue as a question; options map to positions or design guidelines, whereas criteria become arguments or nonfunctional requirements, essentially quality or performance criteria against which options can be judged. The design rationale tradition was extended into psychologically motivated rationale by Carroll (Carroll & Campbell, 1989) as claims, and it is this representation as well as design rationale that has been integrated with the Domain Theory.

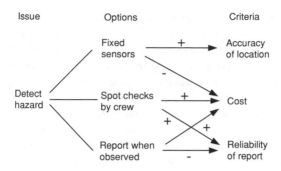

FIG. 6.2. Design rationale graph. The design issue is linked to positions or decision alternatives that are supported by arguments or criteria.

6.1. CLAIMS AND THE TASK–ARTEFACT THEORY

Claims are not original components of the Domain Theory. They are a complementary theory of knowledge that has had an even longer heritage than the Domain Theory, with an origin in the task–artefact theory of Jack Carroll (Carroll, Kellogg, & Rosson, 1991). Collaboration between Jack Carroll and me integrated claims with the Domain Theory to provide a more complete theory of design-related knowledge. The marriage was mutually beneficial for two reasons. First, one criticism of the Domain Theory is that it provided models at a high level of abstraction, which was fine for flexible, compositional reuse but provided the designers with insufficient detail. The second motivation was the specific nature of claims. Claims deliver specific advice in the form of psychologically motivated design rationale. The advice is anchored in context with a scenario of use and a product that exemplifies application of the claim. Claims suffered from the opposite problem of domain models: they delivered high utility but at a penalty of low flexibility and a narrow scope for reuse. The weakness of claims was their very situatedness in a specific context provided by the artefact and usage scenario. If the two theories could be integrated, perhaps we could have the best of both worlds: general models for flexible reuse with detailed design advice and contextual examples. The rest of the chapter describes our progress thus far toward this ideal.

Claims express a design treatment with upside and downside trade-offs that may be expected from implementing the claim; for instance, in a tutoring application that gives feedback on the learner's progress by means of a goal tree, a claim is that "providing a dynamic fish-eye view of a goal hierarchy" will help learners monitor their progress and thereby improve performance. This has the advantage of "reducing the complexity of the display and focusing the learner's attention on the part of the hierarchy pertinent to current learning context" but also the downside that "it could conceal parts of the hierarchy of interest to the learner." Claims are psychologically motivated design rationale that encourage designers to reason about trade-offs rather than accept a single guideline or principle.

One advantage of claims is that they associate theoretically motivated and empirically justified knowledge with a designed artefact and context of use, expressed as a scenario. This makes knowledge available to designers who can recognize the applicability of a claim to a new design context by means of similarities in user tasks, scenarios, or artefacts. Claims have been developed in a variety of design projects, drawn chiefly from the domains of tutoring systems and programming and software design tools, and they have demonstrated that scenario-based design rationale can effectively guide design decision making (e.g., Bellamy & Carroll, 1990; Carroll & Rosson, 1991, 1995; Rosson & Carroll, 1995; Singley & Carroll, 1996). Claims and the task–artefact theory follow in the empiricist tradition of HCI (Landauer, 1995), which sees usability develop through incremental improvement of artefacts by evaluation and redesign.

The validity of claims rests on the evolution of an artefact that has usability demonstrated by means of evaluation or with their grounding in theory. Theoretically based knowledge may be recruited to design, which is also informed by task analysis (see Fig. 6.3, after Carroll & Rosson, 1992); hence the artefact should embody not only features that enhance usability from a theoretical viewpoint but also the results of a thorough user-centered analysis of requirements.

Artefacts are usually complex and consequently pose a problem in attributing the contribution that different claims and features make toward the usability of the whole product. To illustrate the point, the GoalPoster claim (Carroll, Singley, & Rosson, 1992) describes functionality to support learning; however, the usability of the artefact depends not only on effective functionality but also on a well-designed visual user interface and dialogue.

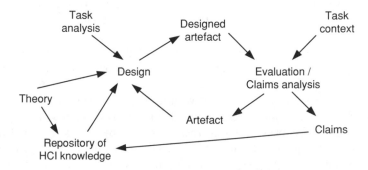

FIG. 6.3. Task–artefact cycle.

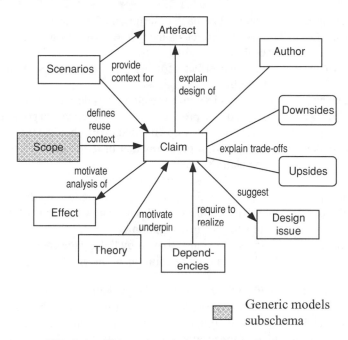

FIG. 6.4.   Claims description extended schema.

6.2.   CLAIMS KNOWLEDGE REPRESENTATION SCHEMA

The original claims schema was composed of the claim expressing a design principle, with upsides and downsides describing the usability effects of applying the claims with a scenario of use illustrating the problem and an example artefact motivated by the claim. This schema was extended (see Fig. 6.4, after Sutcliffe & Carroll, 1998) to make the assumptions, usability effect, and dependencies in the claim explicit, and to explicitly link claims to theory and a more generic reuse scope in Domain Theory models. The theory slot points the designers toward the designer's motivation for the claim in more basic cognitive theory or HCI principles based on psychology. Downsides and design issues point toward disadvantages that can lead to subclaims or design guidelines. Dependencies indicate architecture components or steps in the development process.

The schema components are as follows.

1. Claim ID: unique identifier for the claim
2. Title: given by claim's author
3. Author: researcher(s) or practitioners who developed the original claim
4. Artefact: brief description of the product or application in which the claim originated

5. Description:	natural-language description of the claim
6. Upside(s):	positive effect of using the claim on a system goal or usability
7. Downside(s):	negative effect of using the claim on a system goal or usability
8. Scenario:	scenario in which the claim was derived or is now used
9. Effect:	desired, and preferably measurable, system goal–usability effect that the implemented claim should achieve
10. Dependencies:	other design problems that have to be solved to achieve the claim's effect
11. Issues:	design issues influenced by the claim
12. Theory:	underlying theory explicitly referenced by the author
13. Relationships:	interclaim links that describe how claims evolved during a history of investigation
14. Scope:	scopes the reuse context by linking the claim to a Domain Theory model or component thereof.

All slots are filled with informal, natural-language text, the extent of which depends on the depth of analysis provided by the claim's author. The classification schema is extended by hypertext links to contextual material in a variety of media (e.g., screen dumps, video of the artefact), to the product itself, to relevant design documents, and to related claims. Slots 6 and 7 are typically iterated, as two or three upsides and downsides are usually stated. Slot 12 may either be filled by a reference to the underlying theory or may act as a link to a claims map that describes a series of claims that share a common theoretical base and problem initiation. The relationship slot, slot 13, contains a pointer to other claims that are associated with the current claim in terms of their subject matter or the history of investigation; slot 14 links the claim to a more abstract context for reuse in one or more Domain Theory models.

An example of a claim formatted with the schema is illustrated as follows. It describes a claim that was created by research on tutoring tools for teaching Smalltalk programming, a specific domain; however, the claim has a much wider application in many tutorial environments.

Claim ID:	CCTD
Title:	Color-Coded Telegraphic Display.
Author:	Singley, M. K.; Carroll, J. M.
Artefact:	MoleHill tutor–GoalPoster tool.
Description:	The presentation of individual goals in the window is telegraphic, consisting of several words at most. However, the learner can expand any of the telegraphic goals (through a menu selection) to display a fuller explanation of whether the goal is worthwhile to pursue or not. Thus the system provides both shorthand feedback on correctness and access to further help.

Upside: Provides persistent feedback on the correctness of actions as well as access to further information.

Downside: Learners must learn the display's feature language and controls.

Scenario: The learner is trying to create an UpperCaseTextPane; the system infers that the learner is "searching for relevant classes and methods" and posts this phase in the GoalPoster; the learner selects the posted goal to display an expansion of why the goal should be pursued and how it can be advanced; the learner resumes work navigating to the Window class and causing this subgoal to be posted in the GoalPoster.

Effect: Improved learning by provision of appropriate feedback.

Dependencies: Tracking the user's progress in learning tasks, known goal structure.

Issues: What sorts of feedback displays are effective and under what circumstances? Is hue coding effective for indicating the three-way distinction among achieved subgoals, apparently correct subgoals, and apparently incorrect subgoals?

Theory: Feedback in discovery-based learning (Lewis & Anderson, 1985).

Scope: Education metadomain, feedback for learning assessment, and progress-tracking components in tutorial systems.

6.3. DOCUMENTING CLAIMS

The process of creating claims takes results from usability testing or validation of designs and records the reusable knowledge as follows. Assuming claims are input in their minimal form of a description, scenario of use, upsides, and downsides; the process starts with initial documentation followed by a description of the artefact's features and the claim's effect by stating the usability goals or expected outcome on improved task performance. Claims are documented and classified by the following steps.

The first step is initial documentation. Record the claim's author. Access to the claim's author is vital to get a satisfactory understanding of its origin and motivation. Assign a unique identifier and fill in the slots for author, artefact, claim description, scenario, upsides, and downsides. Trace the artefact and scenario to provide links to an example artefact or recordings of its use. Similarly, links to evaluation data and scenario of use should be added.

The second step is to scope the effect. Describe the intended effect of implementing the claim. This should be implicit in the upsides of the claim, usage scenario, and possibly the background theory. The intended effect is stated at a high level of satisfying user goals, reducing errors, or improving task performance.

The third step is to explore dependencies and issues. Trace dependencies implicit in the claim by asking "What features–knowledge–assumptions does implementation of this claim depend on?" For example, implementing a strategy may depend on availability of certain actions, knowledge, or system functions. Identify assumptions about the user and implementation environment necessary for the claim to be effective, for example by asking "What knowledge should the user possess for the interaction (with the design) to be successful?" Describe design issues that are not directly addressed by the claim but are important usability features for delivering the claim's effect. Issues posed as questions often point to new claims that have to be investigated.

The fourth step is to assign theoretical derivation. Specify the theory that motivated the investigation leading to the claim or underpinning its origins. Generally, theory relates to a whole claim, although the upside and downside slots in a claim schema may have different relationships to backing theory. For instance, a feature displaying current learning goals provides feedback and a model to a user pursuing these goals. This benefits learning by promoting self-awareness as described by the theory of Lewis and Anderson (1985).

The link of claims to theory is particularly important, and it is classified by one or more of six different kinds of relationship. In *theory prediction*, the claim is a direct consequence of some theory's prediction in a design context. For example, pedagogical theory predicts that active engagement in constructive learning environments should be more effective (Fischer, Nakakoji, Otswald, Stahl, & Summer, 1993). A *grounded theory* is an indirect consequence or interpretation of a theory by the designer. For example, memory schema theory suggests that reuse of design templates should improve developer efficiency and problem solving (Maiden & Sutcliffe, 1994). *Experimentally derived* claims are based on results of a controlled experiment, such as the explicit task-related labeling of commands that reduces user errors (Franzke, 1995). *Empirically grounded* claims rest on an analysis of observations (quantified or qualitative) with a scoped context; this covers case studies, ecological studies, and usability evaluation. Most published studies of claims fall into this category. *Proof of concept* claims rest on the fact that they can be interpreted and constructed as an artefact that works effectively. Claims for software algorithms would fall into this category. *Operationally grounded* claims have been demonstrated to work in practice by market success, process improvement, or quality improvement. The claim may have been derived from intuition or by theoretical inspiration; see theory prediction and grounded theory.

This classification allows us to integrate and differentiate a variety of approaches in HCI and software engineering. For instance, industrial practitioners might create claims based on their experience and product success in the market (i.e., operationally grounded), whereas software engineers may embody a claim for a novel algorithm in an implementation that is demonstrated to run efficiently or reliably (proof of concept). One claim may have more than one theoretical justification. Theory is important because it allows authority of the claim to be checked and if necessary questioned. Another benefit of this classification is that claims can be related to certain theoretical assumptions, which may be useful in their interpretation. For instance, a claim for grouping related items in lists may be justified by recourse to a memory theory of natural categories (Rosch, 1985); alternatively, a slightly different claim for the same design issue could be linked to script schema theory (Schank, 1982). One orders claims and artefacts by classes, the other in sequential or procedural order. Knowledge of the backing theories helps one to gain understanding of the claim author's motivation. Although the theory may be of more interest to academic users and validators of claims libraries and less interesting for practical designers who reuse claims, more knowledge is better than less. The designer can always choose to ignore the link.

6.4. REUSING CLAIMS

To enable effective reuse, claims have to be classified and organized in a library so that designers can locate the appropriate claims for their current application problem. The Domain Theory provides the generalized context of use to situate design knowledge encapsulated in claims. This extends the reusability of claims to a range of contexts beyond their origin while improving the utility of the Domain Theory by augmenting its design advice. Claims are associated with OSMs, generalized tasks, or metadomain components that classify the claim in terms of associated functions and a general context of use. However, claims initially express specific design knowledge anchored by a scenario of use and example artefact. The act of classifying and relating claims exposes different levels of granularity and abstraction within claims and the artefacts they belong to; furthermore, decomposing their contributions may lead to the design of new artefacts with associated claims.

Specific claims are partitioned by a walkthrough method (Sutcliffe & Carroll, 1999) that questions the usability contributions made by different user-interface components. For example, the contribution of different components of the GoalPoster artefact can be factored and expressed as new "child" claims. The telegraphic display claim evolved from its original motivating example into a more general and widely applicable claim for progress tracking user interfaces in any system with hierarchical, deterministic tasks. However, the usability of this claim still rested on several design issues. For instance, linear representations (see Ahlberg & Shneiderman, 1994) rather than trees might be more suitable for temporal or sequential information, whereas lower-level design issues (e.g., choice of color) depend on guidelines.

Classification exposed problems for both theories. Claims had to be generalized so that they could be related to a Domain Theory model at an equivalent level of abstraction, whereas the Domain Theory models had to be extended to account for all the contexts of use that were applicable in existing claims. Describing abstractions of designed artefacts was not within the original remit of the Domain Theory, which concentrated on problem abstractions rather than the solution space. The theory was extended to include abstractions for human–computer interface artefacts, as these were pertinent to many existing claims. The extended framework for classifying claims using the Domain Theory's models is illustrated in

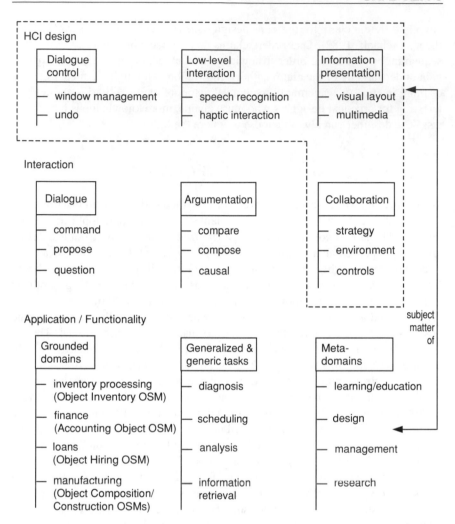

FIG. 6.5. Framework for claims reuse, showing claims organized into groups that share the same high-level design goal, with Domain Theory or design models.

Fig. 6.5. Three "superfamilies" contain the major components of the Domain Theory: grounded domains, generic and generalized tasks, and metadomains. Four new abstract HCI design model families have been added. These can be viewed as the outputs from the Design metadomain. One represents abstractions of higher-level dialogue components of user interfaces, a second describes lower-level interactive components, a third represents designs for information presentations, and the fourth contains designs for multiuser interaction and groupware. All of these new families belong to the realm of design abstractions, and some are more constrained by technology than others. In other words, the lower-level interaction family depends on designs of communication technologies and input–output devices. The dialogue control family describes functions that support user interaction with computers independent of any application domain, for example, undo facilities, window managers, menu palettes, pan–zoom controls, and so on. Components in this family will be used to compose user interfaces that implement interaction patterns described for generalized tasks and grounded domains. Information presentation patterns contain claims for the design of visualizations, multimedia, virtual environments, and realizations in multimedia of generic argumentation patterns. Finally, low-level interaction patterns provide implementation of dialogue patterns by means of different modalities and devices, and they provide basic building blocks for dialogue control models.

The motivation for developing the framework was to classify claims with a context for reuse that designers will recognize. Three user-interface families are related to interactive components in agent-based architecture, for example, PAC (Coutaz, 1993; Nigay & Coutaz, 1995), that separates presentation, control (dialogue), and application (grounded domain, generalized task) components. The dialogue control family could be populated by claims associated with specifications for agents, or interactors (Duke & Harrison, 1994) for design of features such as undo (Dix & Mancini, 1998), window managers, or cascading style sheets. The presentation family may contain visualization design advice for complex information structures such as Cam cones (Card, Robertson, & Mackinlay, 1991) or multimedia scripts to represent generic explanations, for example, multimedia explanations of procedures (Sutcliffe & Dimitrova, 1999). In the application layer, claims advise on supporting generic tasks; transaction processing in grounded domains such as inventory control; and cognitive activities in metadomains such as learning and decision making in management. The GoalPoster and many of Carroll's claims belong in the third family. Claims that articulate support for generalized tasks describe novel designs with demonstrated usability and functionality to support the user's working practice or to empower users to achieve their goals in new ways.

However, claims are not limited to the families illustrated in Fig. 6.5; indeed, one of their appeals is that claims are a general knowledge representation formalism, that can apply to any domain. The extension of the Domain Theory framework also illustrates its flexibility. For instance, new families could be added to describe abstractions in other classes of design phenomena, such as electronic circuits or power engineering. In this manner the framework of the Domain Theory and claims could be expanded to cover civil, mechanical, and electronic engineering, and beyond to any area of design. However, design was never the prime intent of the Domain Theory; instead, requirements and problem description are its main focus. These abstractions are more enduring than designs; for instance, the Domain Theory describes the requirements for navigation and logistics that may have solutions in several areas of engineering, ranging from aircraft design to automotive engineering and space flight.

Representing knowledge in a federation of claims (Carroll, 2000) helps designers by providing a rich network of knowledge to draw on, but this approach still recruits design knowledge from theory by an indirect route. Claims contain scenarios and artefacts that can frame questions for theory development. For instance, an active window scenario (dialogue control family) posed a realistic design issue for theoretical modelers in the AMODEUS project (Bellotti, Buckingham Shum, MacLean, & Hammond, 1995; Bellotti et al., 1996). This problem and its solution, a visible status indicator on the active window, is recorded as a claim connected to a generalized model of the designed artefact, in this case a window manager component, within the family of dialogue control models. Hence claims can be used as a bridge from theoretical models to real-world design issues, but the range of issues that can be addressed by current theory is an open question.

6.5. LINKING CLAIMS
TO DOMAIN MODELS

Claims are attached to domain model components that serve as an indexing mechanism. The generic model acts as a context for reuse by indicating the task, requirements problems, or architectural component that can be addressed by the claim, as well as by providing a retrieval mechanism.

As a way to illustrate the process, claims derived from our previous research into safety critical user-interface design (Sutcliffe, 1996b, 1996c) are associated with the Object Sensing generic model illustrated in Fig. 6.6. This describes sensing the behavior or movement of objects or agents in a physical space and maps to specific monitoring applications in air traffic control, road traffic monitoring, shipborne radar systems, and the like. The claims originated in an instrument-monitoring application and advise how displays should be designed to improve the reliability of human monitoring and interpreting events. For instance, claim 1 in Fig. 6.6 relates to trade-offs in displaying a model of the monitored world, whereas claim 2 describes trade-offs in filtering detected events; claim 3, automatic highlighting rare events, has the upside of making events more noticeable, but the downside of decreasing user awareness if it detects too many false alarms. Details of these claims can be found in appendix C. Claims are linked to the components in the model that provides the closest match to their properties.

The description for claim 3 in Fig. 6.6 is as follows.

Claim ID:	SF3.
Title:	Rare event monitor.
Author:	Sutcliffe, A. G.
Artefact:	User interface for a chemical analysis instrument control system.
Description:	Infrequent, dangerous events (in this case, operational failures in a laser gas chromatograph) are detected by the system and a warning is issued to the user.

Level-2 class Spatial Object Sensing

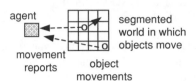

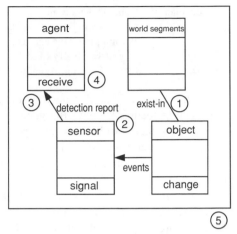

Generic requirements	Claims
Reliable event detector and interpreter	1. System model
Sampling rate control	2. Event filters
Tuning sensing mechanism to eliminate false alarms	3. Rare event monitor
Interpreters/filters to eliminate false alarms	4. Event interpretation
Log file for history analysis of events	5. Trace history

Problems

Fidelity of detecting events to avoid false alarms
Sampling rate and frequency of state change in
the world, to avoid missing rapid changes
Interpretation of events and the context of change
False events caused by oversensitive detecting devices

FIG. 6.6. Spatial Object Sensing model illustrated as an informal diagram and in UML notation. Claims are attached to either the whole model (as in 5) or specific components, depending on their intended usability effect on the associated artefact.

Upsides:	Automatic detection of dangerous events relieves the user of constant monitoring; automatic detection and warning gives the user time to analyze the problem.
Downsides:	Issuing too many warnings may lead the user to ignore critical events; automated monitoring may lead to user overconfidence in the automated system and decrease his or her situation awareness.
Scenario:	When an abnormal event is detected by the laser emission, power supply, or sample container sensors, the system gives an audio warning to the user and visually signals the location of the problem on a diagram of the instrument.
Effect:	The user is aware of the dangerous event and its location; error monitoring is more dependable.

Dependencies: Reliable detection of dangerous events: multiple evidence, filtering
                false warnings, detecting locus of events.
Issues: Warning message and feedback given to the user.
Theory: Cognitive Theory Models of human error (Reason, 1990).
Scope: Object Sensing, Agent Control models.

The above claim shared properties of <detecting events, issuing warnings, and providing feedback> with the generic model; in addition the claim and its originating artefact both have agents <power supply, etc., sensors> for detecting and reporting events <voltage and emission fluctuations> to users <laboratory technicians>. The claim and model are matched by inquiring which class the specific agents, objects, and tasks belong to and investigating the match between specific design issues and generic design properties. In a similar manner, claims can be associated with generic tasks and interaction patterns. Scenarios in original claims are instances of interaction that can be generalized to use cases. An interaction pattern for the generalized task of information retrieval is illustrated in Fig. 6.7 with associated claims based on research into information-seeking behavior (Sutcliffe & Ennis, 1998) and information visualization (Sutcliffe & Patel, 1996). Claims may also be associated with interaction diagrams for generalized tasks and grounded domains. Claims that advise on either design of the user-system dialogue or implementation thereof are classified in the dialogue and presentation families.

The first three claims describe trade-offs for design features that help query formulation by either providing libraries of preformed queries, conceptual maps of the database, or an active thesaurus which suggests alternative query terms. The second claim, conceptual maps, was derived from research on information display artefacts (Sutcliffe & Patel, 1996) and is described in more detail as follows.

Claim ID: IR-VIS2.
Title: Visual conceptual maps.
Author: Patel, U.; Sutcliffe, A. G.
Artefact: Camerawise information display system.
Description: A graphical map displays a model of the database contents so the
                user can query by pointing to concept keywords on the map.
Upsides: Visualizing the database helps the user browse and explore the
                available information; query by pointing to categories is simple.
Downsides: Finding specific items in large maps is difficult; maps can become
                cluttered as databases scale up; expressing complex queries by
                pointing is not possible.
Scenario: The user wishes to find information on camera aperture settings.
                The user scans the map to find the category camera settings and
                follow links to apertures. The user double clicks on this category
                node to retrieve information from the database.
Effect: The user can scan the map display to locate required information
                quickly.

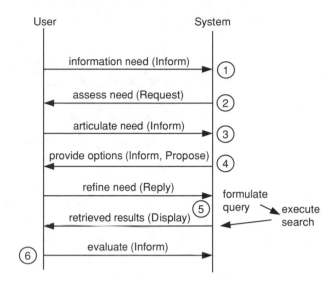

Claims

1. Preformed queries
2. Conceptual maps
3. Active thesaurus
4. Intelligent strategy planner
5. Feedback/browser presenter
6. Relevance feedback

FIG. 6.7. Interaction pattern for the IR generalized task. Claims are attached to either the whole task or specific components, depending on the original task–artefact context.

Dependencies:	Well-structured information space that can be modeled.
Issues:	Design of map layouts and information categories that match the user's conceptual model, event interpreter for query by pointing.
Theory:	Spatial memory and landmarks (Kosslyn, 1980).
Scope:	Information retrieval task, subclass browsing.

A glossary of design issues and synonym tables aids identification of generalized tasks and OSMs when classifying claims; for instance, functional requirements of an artefact expressed as searching, seeking, retrieval, information access, or browsing all point to the information retrieval generalized task.

Figure 6.8 illustrates an architecture model for the Education–Training metadomain and its associated claims. Some of these claims have been reported in previous research on tutorial support environments (Singley & Carroll, 1996); for instance,

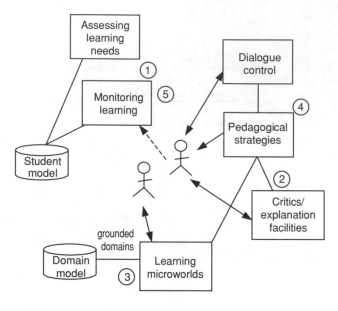

Claims
1. Color-coded telegraphic displays
2. Active critics
3. Reactive simulations
4. System generated goals
5. Plan-based error messages

FIG. 6.8. Simplified view of the Education–Training metadomain for the minimalist learning approach, showing major system components and associated claims.

system-generated goals describe trade-offs in providing the learner with an explicit representation of learning goals, while plan-based error messages and color-coded telegraphic displays are related to design of feedback to help users monitor their own learning. Other claims are extracted from the other research, for instance, the trade-off between active and passive critiquing styles. Passive styles let learners make mistakes and then suggest corrections, whereas active tutors try to prevent learners from making the mistake in the first place. Passive styles have the upside of allowing the user more initiative, but the downside is insufficient guidance for novices. Another example is the trade-off between constructive simulations that you have to build yourself compared with ready-made simulations; the former encourages better learning by doing, whereas the latter saves the user effort (Fischer et al., 1993).

   As with grounded domains, metadomains are indexed with a set of keywords and contain descriptions of design issues and dependencies that have to be addressed for implementation of the conceptual architecture. Matching claims to metadomain models uses these properties and investigates the fit between user agents and their tasks. To illustrate one claim in more detail, the color-coded telegraphic display (see section 6.2; Singley & Carroll, 1996) applies to artefacts that provide feedback on the student's progress in learning systems.

The desired effect of the design is to improve learning by provision of appropriate feedback, although this depends on tracking the user's progress in learning tasks with a known goal structure. Matching between the claim and model components was driven by the issues of providing feedback in the learning process and encouraging active learning by problem solving.

6.6. REPRESENTING BUSINESS KNOWLEDGE IN CLAIMS

Although claims evolved to describe HCI knowledge for designing user interfaces, they are more widely applicable as a knowledge representation schema. Three levels of claims have emerged from research into knowledge reuse, ranging from design advice to management strategies and tactics (Sutcliffe & Li, 2000). Claims exist at the knowledge-management level; these describe trade-offs in strategies and tactics for organization design, human resource management, and other aspects of policy making. Claims exist at the sociotechnical design level; these advise on alternative configurations of people and technologies for classes of application domains or goals. Claims also exist at the artefact design level; these describe trade-offs in the design of human computer interfaces, but they also apply to software engineering and any designed artefact. As claims at the artefact design level have been covered in some detail in preceding sections, only the sociotechnical and knowledge-management level claims will be explained in more depth.

6.6.1. Knowledge-Management Level

Reusable business knowledge comes in a variety of forms, ranging from general statements of policy and heuristics for dealing with management problems to best practice guidelines. The essence of claims is to describe a strategy, policy, or principle while drawing attention to trade-offs in the impact of applying the knowledge. Reuse of knowledge is rarely productive if it is applied blind in an unthinking manner. Instead, knowledge reuse must be accompanied by reasoning to ensure that it really does apply in a new context. Hence claims highlight the tensions associated with a piece of advice.

This makes claims-based knowledge management different from most other approaches that simply state the advice, occasionally with some health warning about its application (Harvard Business Review, 1998). The claims schema is adapted for knowledge management by eliminating the reference to the designed artefact, which no longer applies. Other components of the schema are interpreted as follows.

1. Claim ID: unique identifier for the claim
2. Title: description given by claim's author
3. Author: researcher(s) or practitioners who developed the original claim
4. Description: natural-language description of the claim as a principle, heuristic, or best practice procedure
5. Upside(s):   positive effect of using claim on a management objective or system effectiveness
6. Downside(s):   negative effect of using claim on a management objective or system effectiveness
7. Scenario: two scenarios are documented: (a) an originating scenario in which the claim was derived, and (b) a more generic scenario illustrating how the claim may be used in the future
8. Effect: desired, and preferably measurable, effect that the implemented claim should achieve
9. Dependencies: other problems that have to be solved to achieve the claim's effect, for example, resources or motivation
10. Issues: management issues possibly influenced by the claim, such as changes in authority or responsibility
11. Theory: underlying theory explicitly referenced by the author
12. Relationships: interclaim links that describe how the claim evolved during a history of investigation
13. Scope: links the claim to Domain Theory models, Management metadomain, sector models of industry (e.g., ERPs), or management frameworks (e.g., market classifications).

To illustrate the use of a claim to document management best practice, the following claim describes advice on planning interorganizational relationships (IORs).

Claim ID: TC-IOR/Contract.
Title: Closely coupled interorganizational relationships.
Author: Sutcliffe, A. G.
Description: Closely coupled IORs with long-term contracts are advisable if the unit value of goods or services being supplied is high, the volume is low, and there are few competitors.
Upside: Closely coupled relationship reduces the risk of supply for the customer and gives the supplier a guarantee for production.
Downsides: Close coupling reduces flexibility of the customer to take advantage of new market developments; choice of a suboptimal supplier may be hard to reverse.

Scenario: (a) A manufacturer of aircraft is seeking a source of high-quality
                 software for avionics systems. Few suppliers exist; the product is
                 high value and very specific to the aircraft; and only one purchase is
                 likely. The aircraft manufacturer and the software house enter into
                 a long-term contractual relationship. (b) An e-commerce company
                 wants to find a reliable billing system for processing online sales.
                 Few competitors exist and the system represents high value for the
                 customer. The credit-card clearing organization supplied the
                 software to the e-commerce company under a long-term contract
                 for shared profits.

Effect: The long-term contract should improve the security of supply,
                 thus reducing disruption of the customer's business and insurance
                 costs.

Dependencies: A trustworthy supplier has to be found, and an appropriate contract
                 negotiated.

Issues: The contract will create a power relationship between the
                 organizations that may be asymmetric. Exit conditions from the
                 contract have to be carefully considered.

Theory: Transaction cost theory (Williamson, 1981, 1992).

Relationships: Market and hierarchy IORs.

Scope: Management metadomain, component for controlling IORs.

Business management claims express principles and trade-offs that are inherent
in many management science theories that propose strategies according to the
intersection of two or more variables.

Other forms of advice may be contained in best practice guidance; however,
this is frequently expressed as a script or scenario of what to do in a particular
circumstance. In this case the best practice guidance fits into the generalized scenario slot of the claim, and the principle with trade-offs may have to be derived.
For example, in the domain of social policy for treating repeat offenders, a best
practice policy is

> to target individuals who are high-risk repeat offenders and provide additional support
> as soon as they can be identified. The support provided depends on the nature of the
> offense. For drug offenses, rehabilitation programs should be offered; for violence
> and burglary, counseling is appropriate. Where possible, employment or occupation
> diversion programs should be given and change in housing considered.

This best practice policy gives a series of recommendations that can be split into
several claims for targeting repeat offenders and the type of treatment offered for
particular types of crime. A claim to illustrate the repeat offenders best practice
policy is as follows.

Claim ID: Social Policy RepOff.
Title: Repeat offenders.
Author: Home Office, Crime & Disorder Act of 1999.

Explanation:	Repeat offenders are identified as soon as their pattern of crime can be detected. The individuals are given treatment and support to reduce the probability of further offenses.
Upside:	Targeting resources at individuals who have a disproportionate influence on crime statistics ensures that resources get to the most needy while being efficient in reducing crime.
Downsides:	Individual care is expensive; targeting individuals can result in mis-identification problems; individuals may reject the support offered.
Scenario:	John, a long-term drug user with a heroin problem, finances his habit by shop lifting and occasional muggings. His name appears on several crime reports and hospital records for overdoses and emergency admissions. He is visited by Social Services, who offer new housing away from other addicts and persuade him to attend a voluntary drug detoxification program as part of the conditions for his probation order given by the Magistrates' Court.
Effect:	The additional support reduces the crime rate by removing the offender's motivation to commit crime.
Dependencies:	Information sharing between agencies to identify at-risk individuals, additional support resource available.
Issues:	Privacy of individuals, data protection.
Theory:	None cited.
Relationships:	Social motivation claims.
Scope:	Management metadomain, social systems subclass, human resource management component.

Generation of this claim illustrates how the claim schema acts as a framework for structuring knowledge. The original best practice advice was refined into several claims, each of which made the implications and context of the advice clear. The process of generating claims is discussed in more detail in the following chapter.

6.6.2.   Sociotechnical Design Level

At this level, artefacts are considered, so the original claims schema is used. The purpose of these claims is to record generic requirements for technology to support group-level processes and principles for the design of sociotechnical systems. Reusable design advice for computer-supported cooperative work (CSCW) and computer-mediated communication fits into this category, such as claims for the design of shared artefacts in a design environment where the problem of turn taking has to be resolved.

Claim ID:	CSCW-SharedArtefacts1.
Title:	Shared artefacts in design environments.
Author:	Rodden, T.
Artefact	Groupware design environment (Rodden, 1991).

Description: In same time–different place CSCW, two or more designers want to manipulate an object. Turn taking is controlled by a request–allocate–release protocol while the current owner and the status of the shared artefact are communicated to all participants.

Upsides: Controlling access reduces confusion from several users attempting concurrent manipulations; signaling status allows each participant to be aware of his or her turn and promotes sharing.

Downsides: Some individuals might get locked out if others take very long turns; cooperative, concurrent action may be inhibited.

Scenario: Dave takes control of the ship design in the shared CAD tool and makes changes to the layout of the cargo holds. Carol and Hamed in separate offices follow his changes and make requests to take over. Carol's request arrives first so the system gives her editorial control. She adds extra strengthening braces to Dave's design and adds a note explaining why. Hamed takes over control.

Effect: The resource is shared efficiently among several individuals.

Dependencies: Timing in the communication protocol, number of people interacting, queues of access requests.

Issues: Access contention, interrupts.

Theory: Usability evaluation of artefact.

Relationships: Groupware, same time, same place claims.

Scope: Design metadomain, HCI design family, collaboration subclass.

Whereas this claim describes a design principle, other claims in this class offer advice on how to design interaction in sociotechnical systems. For example, in many command and control systems, the operators face a dilemma that the events happen very quickly (e.g., aircraft emergencies), so human intervention is not possible or is restricted. Designers therefore automate most of the control functions as well as responses to errors, failures, or unexpected events. However, it is rare that designers can anticipate every possible future circumstance so requirements for an override are usually specified. The nature of that override can have important consequences for the relationship between people and the machine. For example, a common model assumes automated response but the system tells the operator what it plans to do and gives an opportunity for an override. Unfortunately, when an emergency happens, most operators will not have sufficient time to reason about whether to respond and their low level of interaction will bias them toward accepting the system's advice and against invoking the override. Even if they did override the system, they would have a woefully inadequate mental model of the situation that they were dealing with. Expressing these principles as trade-offs in a claims format exposes the weaknesses and should encourage the designer to think twice about how overrides are constructed.

The final level of claims involves specific design advice, related to users' tasks or other aspects of product design rather than sociotechnical systems. These claims have already been described in depth, so this layer is not described further.

6.7. SUMMARY

Claims and design rationale provide solutions and design advice that can be attached to Domain Theory models. Claims are part of the task–artefact theory of design knowledge that views well-designed artefacts as theories represented by psychological design rationale (the claim), a scenario, and the artefact. Claims are documented in an extended schema composed of issues, dependencies, assumptions, motivating theory, and scope. Scope specifies the reuse context by attaching the claim to a Domain Theory model or component thereof. Claims are generalized and attached to Domain Theory models that provide a context for reuse. Links to theory justify the claims origin as well as evaluation of its effectiveness in application. Claims may also be related to design models that were introduced into the Domain Theory. Four families cover HCI design: dialogue, presentation, devices, and collaboration; however, claims and design models can be described for any area of human activity, so the theory is general. Claims are a general knowledge representation format that can describe business knowledge for strategy, policy, and best practice as well as design advice.

7

The Reuse Process

This chapter describes processes for creating abstract models and reusing them to design new applications. The Domain Theory posits a set of abstractions that cover a wide range of problems. No doubt this is a considerable challenge; however, the high level of abstraction and small grain size allow the Domain Theory models to be composed into reusable specifications for a wide variety of applications. Furthermore, extension of the Domain Theory library by means of specialization of families of models allows more detail to be included in the future. This will proceed by further case studies that test the set of abstractions proposed so far. The design process for grounded domains and generalized tasks is focused on design by reuse and involves domain analysis, component retrieval, and design by composition and customization.

The Domain Theory assumes a compositional approach to reuse; however, reuse can be achieved by reshaping and customizing components rather than by plugging them together in a Legolike fashion. Furthermore, many programming languages include elements that may be termed *generative architectures*. These allow systems to be developed with reusable components and flexible adaptations at run time (e.g., aspect-oriented programming). We shall suspend the debate on different reuse paradigms until chapter 9. This chapter illustrates the Domain Theory approach, which is one contribution to the wider problem of flexible, economic software development by means of reusable software architectures.

The method is intended to be used by software engineers who, in a dialogue with users (the domain experts), identify the appropriate abstractions in a new application and thereby access the library of reusable domain models and, more importantly, their associated design rationale and claims. The method starts by identifying requirements for a new application and then progresses to match these to an appropriate abstraction. The next stage is to investigate the interfaces between the generic models and create an integrated abstract description of the new application. This uncovers system design problems and creates hints for the software engineer to follow up in subsequent analysis. Once the integrated abstraction has been created, the claim or design rationale attached to the generic models is used to guide further analysis activity and to provide pointers to solution patterns and designs. Two process models for reuse are described—first a generic process that does not rely on the Domain Theory, and then a specialization thereof that does assume Domain Theory models.

7.1.   GENERIC REUSE PROCESS

The starting point for design for reuse is a domain analysis. This involves a wide-ranging requirements analysis, possibly by market surveys, to create a high-level scope of the product area. Domain analysis methods for this purpose (Griss, Favaro, & d'Alessandro, 1998; Prieto-Diaz, 1990) follow systems analysis approaches but are more exhaustive, although there is only rudimentary guidance about what and how much should be analyzed. First the target domain for reuse library is selected and then a domain analysis of requirements, user activities, and existing automated functions is carried out.

Fact gathering, eliciting users' goals and validating requirements, can be difficult as users may not be accessible; even if they are, their future needs may be hard to articulate. Analysis for reusable software has to consider not only the functionality of the product components but also requirements for supporting software that will help users or designers to customize components. For reuse library products, the pathway for requirements discovery starts with the problem of defining the market place for the component library. The designer then creates generic components and the support tools for reuse. Domain analysis specifies the functions of the reuse library components and interfaces to other modules; then their functionality has to be indexed and documented. If no architecture exists a priori, the reuser–designer also has to undertake a general design to determine the subsystem framework and high-level functionality of components before the reuse library can be searched for appropriate modules. Once these have been located, design involves defining interface compatibilities and possibly customizing code to suit the new application.

Designers are a different stakeholder group who need powerful yet easy-to-use customization and development support tools. Requirements for support tools for configuring the target system have to be investigated, with the necessary user–system models, parameter files, and their editing–testing interfaces. Requirements for reuse libraries also concern nonfunctional criteria such as ease of construction, portability, interoperability, and maintainability. These in turn become further functional requirements for developing support tools and software frameworks for promoting ease of reuse. Reuse can encourage a copycat approach, leading to errors, so it should be treated with care. Explanation facilities and design advisers are necessary to encourage a systematic approach to reuse (Sutcliffe & Maiden, 1990).

The steps in the design for reuse process are summarized in Fig. 7.1. The design for reuse process generalizes the components or objects produced by the domain analysis and then documents them to produce the reuse library. Documentation involves adding metadata descriptions and indexing terms so components can be retrieved. The content of the reuse library is integrated with the support tools that assist designers of future reusable components and, more importantly, reuser–designers who need to retrieve components and build applications from components. Requirements and task analysis for design support forms a separate branch of the process.

In the design by reuse, the process depends on assumptions about the approach. If reuse has a limited ambition, and adaptation of an existing system is anticipated, then the analysis questions are as follows.

1. How many different user groups need tailored user interfaces and functionality; alternatively, if no groups are apparent, then is adaptation necessary at the individual level? This entails analysis of the user population to gather information on their goals, tasks, and abilities.

2. What aspects of the system or user interface require tailoring? The first distinction is between adapting static features, such as displays of prompts, choice of color, screen backgrounds, and dynamic features that change system behavior; for instance, setting system initiative for a help wizard. Adapting dynamic features, such as dialogues and system functionality, is usually more complex.

3. How well do the users' requirements fit with the available application packages; that is, is customer-off-the-shelf (COTS) procurement an option? Do users want to add their own customized features? If the system cannot provide an acceptable range of options, then the design problem implies a need for further adaptation or design by reuse.

In reuse by adaptation the process becomes one of matching requirements against the properties of packages and components and then adapting them by parameters and user profiles. Once adaptation has been completed, the system is integrated and tested.

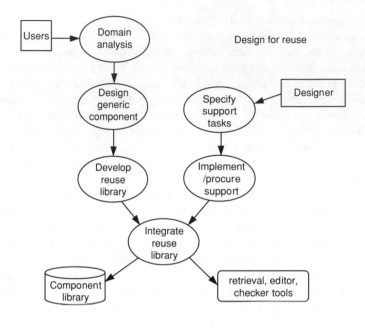

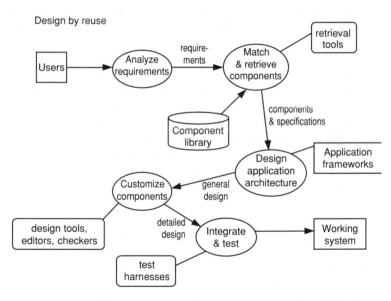

FIG. 7.1. Process model of reuse with component libraries.

For more ambitious reuse with component-based engineering, the analysis questions are as follows.

1. What user groups are present and how can their requirements be satisfied by different module configurations?
2. What is the range of functionality that should be selected from the available product families? The function requirements become input to the matching process that retrieves appropriate reusable components.

This leads to process steps for

- selecting appropriate components from the reuse library, and understanding their behavior and interfaces so the design can be planned;
- designing the product architecture and tailoring the component functionality to fit the results of the requirements analysis, or refining the application framework by adding components into customization slots;
- coding bridge modules and specializing component code where necessary; and
- testing the reused modules and application architecture to ensure integrity between components and functionality.

Component retrieval uses standard information science approaches of keyword searching and use of query languages. Faceted classification schema allow search on a combination of attributes to locate components, such as functions, data structures, platform, original domain, and so on (Prieto-Diaz, 1991). The design tasks depend on the support provided by the reuse library. If application frameworks are present then the designer–reuser has to choose appropriate components to specialize variation points or hotspots in the framework (Fayad & Johnson, 2000). If no application framework is present then the application architecture has to be designed, followed by specialization of components. The final steps are integration and testing. The design by reuse process is essentially similar to standard software engineering, apart from retrieving and matching components' properties to requirements followed by the need to understand abstract components before reusing them.

The next section returns to the design for reuse part of the process, which is very different from standard software engineering, and it covers the process of creating generalized components in more depth.

7.2. DESIGN FOR REUSE

The following process describes an approach to design for reuse based on the premise of creating a set of generic models and then reapplying them in different applications. Other reuse models are discussed later in chapters 8 and 9. The heuristics and techniques in this section can be applied independently of the

Domain Theory to create abstract reusable components according to the designer's wish. Design for reuse, or the process of abstraction, consists of four analyses that are carried out on specific components to convert them into more general reusable models: cohesion and coupling analyses, and data and procedural abstractions. The level of abstraction is not easy to judge. Where classification hierarchies exist for attributes and objects in natural categories such as taxonomies of animals, the level of abstraction can be taken from the hierarchy level (animals–mammals–primates–man). However, functional abstraction for methods is more difficult, as few external standards exist. To achieve the abstraction of components at a certain chunk (granularity) size, we revisit the axioms of structured analysis and design (De Marco, 1978) and apply cohesion and coupling as design criteria for well-formed generic models.

7.2.1. Cohesion Analysis

With the assumption that a detailed specification of the components exists, abstraction has to discover the goal components and then generalize the data structures and procedures. The process may involve splitting or factoring the component if it appears too complex or does not possess a single well-defined purpose. Cohesion is tested simply by asking the following questions.

1. Do all the procedures in the component contribute to a single common goal?
2. Can that goal be specified as a simple expression of a state that can be achieved or maintained? If not, decomposition is indicated.
3. Are all the data structures in the component required by the procedures?

However, achieving cohesion is not so simple. A component may be cohesive for a design purpose; alternatively, it may achieve a requirements goal. Thus a sorting algorithm will be a cohesive component for the design goal of ranking a set of numbers, but this is very different from a cohesive function for validating a customer's order. Cohesion therefore has to be judged along a dimension from requirements to design. It also depends on the application domain and the target of the reuse library. Cohesive functions for a middleware library may be a set of network protocol control algorithms, whereas for an application-oriented library, accountancy goals might determine cohesiveness, such as amortization calculations for loans and debts. The baseline definition of cohesion from Yourdon (Yourdon & Constantine, 1978) has to be extended as follows.

- Functional cohesion exists if all the actions in a component achieve a single end state or maintain an existing state by taking corrective action.

Functional cohesion is the most desirable degree of cohesion according to Yourdon; the definition here extends it to account for goals as states, either to be achieved or maintained by the process, following the relationship between intentional goal statements and the states implicit within them (Van Lamsweerde & Leiter, 2000). The second extension places the contribution of the model's goal in either the problem or solution space.

- Functional cohesion exists if all the actions in a component achieve a single goal according to the user's viewpoint of the problem or solution space.

Cohesion will be high if the reusable component has only one goal and all the methods and actions therein contribute to achieving that goal. If subgoals are present then the component will have lower cohesion and hence will be less abstract. The cohesion principle was proposed when functional decomposition was the favored means of partitioning systems, so some reinterpretation is necessary for object-oriented design. Active objects (i.e., agents) will be cohesive if they contain a small number of methods that all contribute to one goal. Passive (i.e., data structure) objects will be cohesive only if they contain methods that contribute to their life history update and maintenance. Collections of objects (i.e., patterns) will be cohesive if all the objects and their methods contribute to the stated responsibility, that is, the service or goal of the pattern.

As users may be end users or designers, the goal definition may be expressed in viewpoints (Sommerville & Kotonya, 1998). For example, a customer–user may want a component to rank suppliers in order of preference and reliability; in contrast, a software engineer wants an algorithm to sort a data structure according to two or more parameters. The abstract solution for both users is the same, a sorting algorithm, but the expression of the problem and actions contained in the component may vary. The customer is closer to the problem domain, whereas the software engineer is interested primarily in the solution space. Cohesion therefore has to be judged by reference to layers of reuse in the abstraction context (see chapter 1).

7.2.2. Coupling Analysis

Reusable components should exhibit low coupling. Following Yourdon's definition (Yourdon & Constantine, 1978), this means components should only pass data between their interfaces and that the data should not embed values that control the behavior of another component. Any direct control reference between components increases coupling. Low coupling indicates little or no dependency; hence each component can be reused in a separate context. When components are composed into an application, they only have to share a common definition of data passed across their interfaces. Coupling will be low only if the component makes no assumptions about the presence or absence of other components and only exchanges data. As more data parameters that have processing implications (e.g., switches) are passed, coupling will increase; furthermore, any dependencies (both implicit or explicit) between components will increase coupling. High coupling is also caused by shared global variables and control links.

Coupling is decreased by encapsulating local variables and making sure components only pass data across well-defined interfaces. However, coupling is linked to cohesion, as higher-level goals often require several components (objects) to collaborate to achieve a purpose. In OSMs a set of objects cooperate to achieve a generalized goal. For instance, in the Object Hiring OSM, data coupling is present among the hiring agent, the client who borrows the resource, and the resource that is loaned. There is only data flow coupling among these three objects so each could be reused independently of the Object Hiring application class; for instance, the client object could appear in sales order processing, as could the resource. The hirer agent is more closely coupled to the Object Hiring goal, but it could be specialized to become a general authorization agent with minor changes to its method. Some coupling and dependencies between objects have to be preserved in generic models to make goals attainable. Higher coupling will decrease abstraction, but this has to be judged in relation to the component's cohesion.

7.2.3. Data Abstraction

Data abstraction can be achieved by eliminating specific attributes and making other attributes more general; for example, a book in a library loans application becomes a resource in an abstract hiring model. The following heuristics encourage development of more general data structures.

Substitute domain-specific references for more general objects and attributes. This should be a natural outcome of creating class models in object-oriented design. Domain-specific references can be tested by questioning the range of application that an object applies to. For instance, a loan transaction in car hire will have an attribute 〈car〉. This can be generalised to 〈vehicle〉 to cover loans of bikes and cars, and ultimately to 〈resource〉 for many different types of loan applications. Cross-referencing the appropriate domain model, in this case the Object Hiring OSM, helps to suggest generalized attributes.

Decrease the number of attributes per object. Many attributes indicate domain-specific detail. Attributes that deal with exceptions and variants can be reduced by generalizing objects; also decomposing larger components reduces the complexity and hence number of attributes.

Investigate higher-level classes for objects and eliminate lower-level classes if possible. Complex components may be aggregations of simpler objects, so generalization and decomposing components are often interrelated.

Reduce or eliminate constraints on attributes such as ranges on values, set membership in attribute values, update integrity constraints. Constraints indicate dependencies on other components. Ideally data structures should be stand-alone reusable components free from functional dependencies; however, if data components are aggregated with functionality (i.e., they are objects), check that the constraints are absolutely necessary for achieving the object's goal.

Reduce or eliminate calculated values for the same reasons as constraints. Derived or calculated values indicate functional dependencies.

Decompose complex data structures (multidimensional arrays, lattices, or large trees). Smaller data structures will be more flexible for reuse. Split complex structures according to any possible functional subgroups, common subtrees, and the like.

Many of the data structure constraints are removed by data modeling and normalization, so traditional specification techniques should create abstract data structures (influencing the last three properties), whereas the process of creating generic classes reduces domain-specific references. Although OSMs follow most of the properties listed here, they do preserve dependencies between data structures to facilitate goal-oriented reuse; hence there is a tension between data abstraction and how the subsequent reuse context will be defined. Highly abstract data structures become programming language constructs (e.g., types, arrays, or sets) and lose their application context for potential reuse.

A summary of data abstraction is as follows. A component should *not* possess high values for the following properties (i.e., higher values decrease abstraction):

- many attributes per object/module;
- many low-level attributes assessed by reference to an externally accepted class hierarchy;
- many domain-specific references;
- value range constraints on variables;
- set membership constraints;
- many calculated values;
- many update dependencies; and
- many complex data structures (*n*-dimensional arrays, lattices, or trees).

7.2.4. Procedural Abstraction

Procedural abstraction is more difficult to achieve. Two strategies may be followed. In *parameterization*, algorithms can be made more flexible by adding control variables that change their behavior. For example, in a booking–reservation application (airline flight booking), the algorithm involves constraint-based matching of client requirements against properties of available resources. The algorithm can be made more flexible by parameters that control preferences (e.g., weighting for important customers) and behavior (e.g., switches that cause the system to output near matches to customer requirements rather than only perfect matches; Lam, McDermid, & Vickers, 1997). In *modular decomposition*, subprocesses are segmented so complex behavior can be composed into several smaller components; for example, in flight booking, a filter to eliminate routes that the customer doesn't want, based on past preferences, is separated from the constraint-based matching method.

The following heuristics can be applied to create procedural abstraction.

Reduce the number of methods per agent–object. More complex agents will be less flexible for reuse and are likely to have poor cohesion. Highly abstract objects should have only one main method. The Domain Theory generic tasks can be used to test the level of abstraction in methods.

Reduce or eliminate domain–specific reference in methods by generalizing actions. Generic tasks contain highly abstract actions that set the level to be attained.

Substitute parameters for hard-coded variables. Eliminating hard-coded values makes procedures more flexible. This allows the method to respond more flexibly to different reuse contexts. For example, a matching algorithm could have parameters that set the number of variables to be tested, indicate the priority order of those variables, and even determine the behavior of the matching process (allow only perfect match versus best fit). The penalty of increased parameterization is complexity. As the number of parameters increases, the cohesion of the method decreases because it can fulfill many slightly different goals; in addition, the algorithm becomes more complex with many selections.

Reduce the number of selections and iterations. More conditions mean more state variables, which have to be tested, and this increases complexity.

Reduce the number of operations per method. This can be achieved by looking for possible breakpoints in a procedure and asking whether processing could halt at any stage. If processing can halt, this indicates a temporary data store with two procedures that could be run independently. Splitting the method at the breakpoint will factor it into two smaller units and increase the cohesion of each unit.

Reduce the number of variables and constants per method. More variables indicates less data abstraction, whereas constants embed domain references and designers' assumptions.

Eliminate subroutine calls and external files–library inclusions. Ideally, reusable components should make no reference to external components. For reuse primitives such as generic tasks this may be possible; however, larger reusable components (e.g., generalized tasks) may necessitate references to smaller-scale components.

Eliminate control structures. This encourages decomposition of procedures to declarative (rule-based) forms. All procedures can ultimately be decomposed to a set of IF-condition-THEN-action rules. Control structures may not be necessary if each rule is specified with a unique condition. In practice this leads to loading the condition clauses with more attributes to make sure the rule has a unique set of triggering conditions. This also leads to pathological hidden control coupling through variables; that is, rule 1 fires and sets variable $A =$ true, which is a necessary condition for rule 2 to fire. Conversion of procedures to declarative specifications can be helped by encapsulating rules in objects to reduce the interrule dependency problem.

Allow specialization by multiple inheritance. Generalizing methods allows polymorphic inheritance, in which methods can have multiple effects when they are sent different messages. As illustration of the concept, a generalized draw object method is specialized into methods for drawing circles, squares, and lines. Parameters allow the color and thickness of the line to be specified; hence sending the message draw, object ⟨color, 12 point⟩ will have a very different effect in the circle, square, and line method.

Procedural abstraction is produced by standard techniques of specification refinement and program design, which split complex procedures into smaller declarative components. Judgment on the desirable level of abstraction and granularity will be influenced by views on the subsequent reuse process. Design-level components will be smaller and show high procedural and data abstraction, such as object-oriented patterns (Gamma et al., 1995). However, this incurs a penalty of increasing the distance between requirements and design. The reuser–designer will have to spend more effort selecting appropriate design abstractions to match to the user's requirements.

A summary of procedural abstraction is as follows. Components should *not* exhibit the following properties, and high values decrease abstraction: a large number of specific methods, many domain-specific references, a large number of parameters, many selections and iterations and operations per method, a large number of variables and constants per method, many subroutine calls and external files–library inclusions, or many control instructions. Heuristics for generalizing methods address the second and third properties by making methods more flexible with parameterization to substitute specific values with types, and switches to control methods behavior.

7.3. GENERALIZATION FOR KNOWLEDGE REUSE

Abstraction in knowledge-level reuse is more difficult to assess because the knowledge components can vary widely in their contents and scope of application. One sense of abstraction is the span of potential impact of the reusable knowledge. Abstraction therefore has two senses: one is closely related to the reuse target, whereas the other describes the content, following a subset of the properties for design components. The reuse target dimension is summarized in Fig. 7.2.

At the strategic level, knowledge reuse may influence company policies and the direction of whole organizations. Knowledge reuse here is abstract in the sense that policies, aims, and mission statements are necessarily high-level statements of ambition. These higher-level goals are decomposed into objectives for tactical management and more detailed goals at the operational level. The level of abstraction decreases as more detail is added to specify goals in terms of outcomes, measures by which outcomes can be assessed, and possibly directions about how goals should be achieved, with constraints on interpretation. As abstraction decreases so does the formality of representation, enabling goals expressed in natural language to be transformed and described as attainable states, benchmark

increasing
abstraction

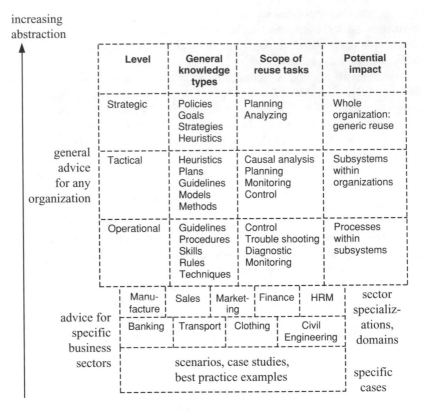

Level	General knowledge types	Scope of reuse tasks	Potential impact
Strategic	Policies Goals Strategies Heuristics	Planning Analyzing	Whole organization: generic reuse
Tactical	Heuristics Plans Guidelines Models Methods	Causal analysis Planning Monitoring Control	Subsystems within organizations
Operational	Guidelines Procedures Skills Rules Techniques	Control Trouble shooting Diagnostic Monitoring	Processes within subsystems

general
advice
for any
organization

advice for
specific
business
sectors

Manufacture | Sales | Marketing | Finance | HRM

Banking | Transport | Clothing | Civil Engineering

scenarios, case studies,
best practice examples

sector
specializations,
domains

specific
cases

FIG. 7.2. Reuse target dimension, showing levels of knowledge reuse.

measures, and metrics (Sutcliffe & Maiden, 1993). However, abstraction can also be interpreted in terms of the area of application. For this purpose we situate knowledge in Porter's (1980) value chain to describe proximity to the application area. Reusable knowledge may be applied directly to value chains in a business (manufacturing, service provision); to processes within value chains (acquisition of material, preproduction processing, manufacture, quality assurance, product delivery); or to the support activities possessed by most organizations (personnel management, accounting, workflow coordination). This knowledge may apply to vertical or horizontal domains in business–requirements layer 1 of the reuse framework. Within these categories, abstraction will be judged by the domain-specific references in the content that restrict applicability of the knowledge to any one company, industry, country, or culture. The ideal abstraction for reusable knowledge is advice that is independent of location, nationality, and culture, but of course this ideal is rarely attained. Unfortunately, the cultural and national assumptions in business knowledge are rarely stated explicitly.

In the next section we turn to the process of design by reuse, which assumes that a library of generic components exists. Although the method is based on the Domain Theory models, the process will be similar for any abstract component library.

7.4. DESIGN BY REUSE OF KNOWLEDGE BY MEANS OF GENERIC MODELS

The method assumes that a library of domain models exists and that design starts with requirements analysis. The Domain Theory models can be reused in several ways. The method identifies the abstract domain models that are present in a new application, and then it reuses the knowledge indexed on those models (as design rationale or claims) for designing the new application. However, domain models can also be used to harvest reusable components by setting levels of abstraction. Design by reuse starts by identifying high-level components in the new target application. The role of domain models is to guide the discovery of appropriate abstractions in the new application while not biasing the requirements specification. The process of analysis provokes thought about the nature of abstraction and hence a deeper understanding of the problem; furthermore, design rationale and claims knowledge suggest many questions to guide subsequent analysis. However, the software engineer does not want to spend too much time specifying the domain in detail, only to find that design advice attached to the domain models is no longer appropriate or necessary. The method to guide identification of appropriate abstractions and careful analysis should avoid any bias.

7.4.1. Identifying Abstractions

The method is organized in six stages (Fig. 7.3). First, requirements for the new application are analyzed and an initial model of the system produced to identify subsystems and major components. In object-oriented approaches, top-level use cases would be produced. Use-case and interaction diagrams help map out groups of cooperating objects that can be matched to their corresponding abstractions in the Domain Theory library. This enables the process of matching subsystems to abstract models to start. This proceeds in iterative cycles of refinement: as more models are discovered, these suggest new areas of requirements investigation and vice versa; as the requirements specification develops, further abstract models are found. The domain models can then be applied as templates to develop conceptual models as class collaboration diagrams, use cases, and the like. The next stage transfers design knowledge as rationale, claims, and generic requirements to the requirements specification. This in turn provokes further investigation of design issues, requirements refinement, and validation. The final stage is reuse of designed components that are associated with claims or design rationale.

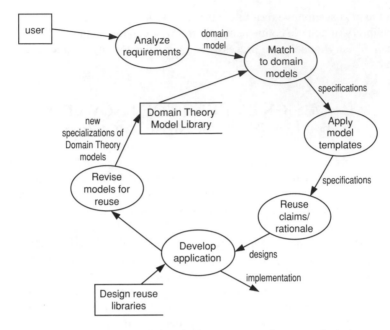

FIG. 7.3. Overview of the design process for reuse-led development by means of domain models.

Most of the process will follow standard development approaches of incrementally refining models and specifications from requirements to designs (e.g., following the unified process and modeling language; Rational Corporation, 1999). The part of the method that requires further explanation is the process of identifying domain abstractions within the emerging model of the new application.

This is the most difficult part of the method because abstractions are rarely explicit in any domain. A set of heuristics guides the software engineer in identifying subsystems in the application and then matching subsystems to OSMs in the reusable pattern library. Alternatively, the matcher tool may be used for finding grounded domain models (Sutcliffe & Maiden, 1998). The first need is to partition the application and then to establish its goals. This is followed by an analysis of the objects, structures, agents, and state transitions in each subsystem to match one or more OSMs by a unique signature. The process follows a walkthrough-style analysis in the following steps.

Step 1 is to identify subsystems in the application. These may be suggested by geographical distribution, ownership by different parts of the organization, or by locating agents who operate the system.

Step 2 is to establish the purpose of the subsystems. Here heuristics from the Inquiry Cycle (Potts et al., 1994) are used to point toward certain OSM families.

- Is the goal of the subsystem to change an existing state of affairs, that is, an attainment goal? This applies to most abstractions except Object Sensing, in which the only sense of attainment is signaling any departure for a state in the real world.
- Is the subsystem goal to maintain an existing state of affairs, that is, keep the current system state stable? This indicates that Object Sensing and Agent Control models should be consulted. Maintenance applications invariably have to detect deviations in system states and then correct them.
- Is the subsystem goal to correct an undesirable state of affairs, that is, repair an object or correct an error? Correction and repair goals indicate Object Sensing, Agent Control, and Object Servicing–Repair models.

A lexical analysis points to OSMs by using keywords that indicate system goals and activities. As keywords alone are unreliable indicators of functionality and purpose, synonym tables are used to improve the precision; however, identification relies on several other facets, so it is not dependent on lexical analysis. The following questions indicate the presence of specific OSMs in the domain.

Does the subsystem involve purchase or supply of goods? This points to the Object Inventory and Accounting Object Transfer families. Does the goal involve hiring, renting, or loaning objects? This points to the Object Hiring family. Is the goal to repair damaged goods or service an object to maintain it? This points to the Object Servicing–Repair family, and possibly Object Decomposition. Is the goal to match a customer's request against a set of available resources, as in brokering, allocation, and matching applications? This indicates Object Allocation, and Matching generalized tasks. Is the purpose to transport goods or move objects from one location to another? Models in the Object Logistics family are indicated. Is manufacturing involved? This points to Object Composition–Construction, with Agent Control and Object Sensing. Does the subsystem involve command and control? This suggests Agent Control, usually aggregated with the Object Sensing behavior subclass. Does the subsystem involve monitoring the world or detecting changes? This indicates models in the Object Sensing family. Does the subsystem have real-time or safety critical properties? These nonfunctional requirements are good indicators of Object Sensing and Agent Control families. Is the goal to generate information for decision making and management? This points to Information System Models, and Judgment–Decision Making generalized tasks. If the subsystem involves decision support, Object Simulation and Judgment–Decision Making generalized tasks are indicated.

Some examples of synonym tables for OSM families are as follows; others are given with the OSMs they apply to in appendix A.

Object Inventory
    Main terms ⟨supply, purchase⟩
    Alternative terms ⟨donor, inventory, goods-supply, purveyor⟩
    Related terms ⟨producer, manufacturer (cross-reference Object Composition),
    source, resource-holder, stock control, inventory control⟩

Object Hiring
  Main terms ⟨hire, rent, loan⟩
  Alternative terms ⟨borrow, lease, temporary ownership, allow use of⟩
  Related terms ⟨hire purchase, rental⟩

Synonyms are taken from standard sources (e.g., Roget's *Thesaurus*). Cross-references indicate where a term might have connotations for more than one OSM family. The next steps are as follows.

Step 3 is to describe the end state that the system goal should achieve. This helps to refine understanding of attainment, maintenance, and repair goals.

Step 4 is to describe the agents, physical structures, and objects in the subsystem. First the objects that are involved in, or changed by, activity in the application should be noted. These are candidates for key objects. Agents may be traced by asking who or what is responsible for each system activity or by tracing system input and output. Human and automated agents are separated and analysis focuses on people first. This step encourages identification of the essential transactions with the following questions.

Are the objects involved in the domain contained in a building or designed structure, or are they part of the natural world? Objects contained in designed structures indicate transactional OSMs in the Object Inventory, Hiring, Composition, Decomposition, and Construction families. Objects in the natural world are indicative of Sensing type problems. Are the objects altered in any way by the system activity in a permanent manner? If they are, this suggests Composition or Construction OSMs, although if "altered" is interpreted as a change in ownership then this points to an Object Inventory abstraction. Are objects physically moved by system activity? Movement indicates Object Logistics models; however, many people associate inventory transactions with movement, so this question has to be qualified by a constraint of change in ownership. Is the agent performing activity in the system in response to commands? This indicates an Agent Control abstraction. Is the agent a client or customer of the system? If so, then Object Inventory and Object Hiring models are indicated. Does the agent exhibit behavior and is it embedded within the system? This points to Object Simulation applications.

Step 5 is to identify and describe the events and state transitions in the subsystem. Events are traced from their external source through state transitions to system output by identifying the agents that are the source of input, activities that process events, and agents or objects that are the recipients of output. At this stage the set of candidate OSMs can be refined to give a more precise match, with the following heuristics.

Does the system have a clear input event that triggers activity? If it does then transactional OSMs are indicated (Object Inventory, Object Hiring); otherwise, Agent Control. Does the system have state transitions that result in the key object changing ownership or location? This suggests Object Inventory or Object

Logistics families. Does the system have state transitions that result in the key object being returned to its original location or owner? This points to Object Hiring OSMs. Does the system involve sorting, allocating, or prioritizing objects? This suggests an Object Allocation OSM, with matching, sorting tasks. Do system events partition or aggregate objects? These events point to Object Decomposition–Composition OSMs.

Step 6 is to describe the tasks that the agents carry out. Keywords given with the description of tasks in appendix B2 help to link the specific activity to the appropriate generic, or more usually generalized, task. Some examples of specific tasks that map to the diagnosis generalized tasks are trouble shooting, debugging, fault finding, error correcting, and problem analyzing. Generic or generalized tasks cause state transitions in OSMs once they are complete, so the analysis of tasks and state transitions in object models is usually interleaved. Once specific tasks have been listed, the following questions help to identify the corresponding abstractions.

Does the activity involve processing information? This indicates Classify, Identify, Compare, and Evaluate generic tasks with the Analysis–Modeling and Progress Tracking generalized tasks. Is ordering objects in the world or in time involved? This indicates the Planning–Scheduling generalized task. Is the activity cognitive, that is, does it involve reasoning and problem solving? These questions will indicate the more cognitive generic tasks such as Interpret, Evaluate, Model, and Compare, and the generalized tasks for Diagnosis and Analysis–Modeling. Are judgment and decision making involved? If so Select, Judgment, and Compare generic tasks are possible abstractions. Does the activity require navigation or wayfinding? This indicates the Navigation generalized task, and the Orient generic task.

A further set of questions draw attention to possible Information System Model abstractions.

Do any of the activities depend on information being provided? If so, what is the source of the information and does it require a subsystem to generate it? This points to the need for ISM models. Do any of the activities depend on information about any of the OSMs identified so far? If so, this points to a Reporting ISM for each OSM. Does the user require historical or time-sequence data on objects? If so, this suggests a Progress Tracking ISM. Are reports on spatial distribution or properties of objects in the real world required? This suggests Object Sensing models, with a Reporting ISM.

A subset of these questions is illustrated in a decision table format in Table 7.1 to identify the OSMs that may fit within the new application. Once a set of candidate OSMs has been selected from the library, the next stage is to integrate it into a generic system model for the new application.

The next section introduces a case study of discovering Domain Theory abstractions in an application; transferring reusable knowledge is then described. The case study is the computerized call dispatch system of the London Ambulance Service,

TABLE 7.1
Summary of Model Identification Heuristics*

	Hiring–Renting	Repair & Maintenance	Broking & Matching	Supplying Goods	Manufacture	Command & Control	Monitor World	Real-Time & Safety Critical	Models & Games	Information & Decision Support
Object Inventory				●						
Object Hiring	●									
Object Service–Repair		●								
Object Allocation	○		●	○						
Object Composition					●					
Object Decomposition		○								
Object Sensing					○	○	●	●		
Agent Control					○	●		●		
Object Logistics					●					
Object Construction					●					
Object Simulation									●	
ISMs	○	○		○	○		○			●

*Darker shapes indicate a strong association between the subsystem property and an OSM family; the lighter shapes indicate a secondary association.

212

which was a notorious requirements failure, and application of the Domain Theory shows where reuse of knowledge might have averted some of the more critical mistakes.

Case Study: Description.   The London Ambulance Service (LAS) computer-aided dispatch system was initiated in 1991. The intention was to replace a resource-intensive manual system with a computerized one that would, in essence, enable one human controller to manage an entire incident from call taking to the arrival of the ambulance at the incident scene. The implementation in October 1992 encountered many problems, and operations reverted to the manual system 1 month later after a series of well-publicized catastrophic failures.

The LAS operations are real time and mission critical, in that people can die if an ambulance does not arrive in time. They require information about patients, emergencies, hospitals, road conditions, and ambulance locations to function effectively. The system is also both distributed and embedded, in that it relies on hardware to define the location of ambulances and communicate with ambulance crews. Indeed, the mobile nature of its operations in London made the system very complex and prone to problems. The original manual system had evolved over a considerable period of time. Ambulance crews had considerable knowledge of London as well as emergency conditions, and the control room staff worked as closely knit teams in constant communication with each other to dispatch the most appropriate ambulance to the accident. The system relied on skilled individuals with extensive domain knowledge, including the geography of London.

The manual ambulance dispatching system had four main functions: call taking from the public; resource (ambulance) identification; resource mobilization; and resource management. Call taking involved telephone operators and control assistants who used local knowledge and a map book to complete an incident form. These incident forms were passed to resource controllers and allocators, who allocated resources to calls. The incident report was amended and passed to the dispatcher, who made radio contact with ambulance crews. The ambulance was then dispatched. The new computer-aided dispatch (CAD) system was intended to automate as much of this process as possible, thus reducing the workload and reliance on control room staff. It included a computer-based gazetteer of London, and a resource-allocation system linked to an Automatic Vehicle Location System (AVLS). An overview of this is shown in Fig. 7.4.

Immediately following the system cutover, the call traffic load increased (but not to exceptional levels). The AVLS could not keep track of the status and location of ambulances. This led to an inconsistent database so that ambulances were not being dispatched optimally. Frequently, more than one ambulance was being assigned to one call. The public were repeating their calls because of the delay in response. As a consequence, there were a large number of exception messages and the system slowed down as the message queue grew. Unresponded exception messages generated repeat messages and the message lists scrolled off the top of

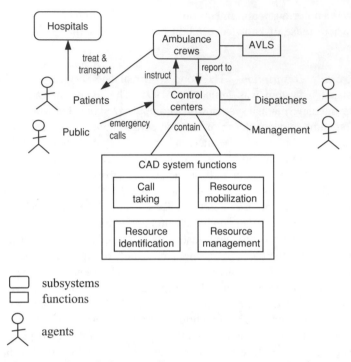

FIG. 7.4. Informal diagram illustrating components in the LAS CAD system.

the screens so that important messages were lost from view. Ambulance crews were frustrated and, under pressure, were slow in notifying their status to central control. They could not, or would not, use their mobile data terminals and used incorrect sequences to enter the status information. The AVLS no longer knew which units were available and the resource allocation software was taking a long time to perform its searches. As a result, the entire system ground to a halt. It was taken offline and the LAS reverted to the manual dispatching system.

Case Study: Analysis of Domain Models. The LAS can be divided into two subsystems: central control and the ambulance crews. Taking the central control subsystem, one sees that the attainment-type goals are to answer emergency calls and dispatch ambulances. Input events (emergency calls) trigger actions in the system to process them. The system involves command and control, which suggests an Agent Control model. It also has some safety critical implications, as patients may die if responses to emergency calls are too long, suggesting that Object Sensing abstractions may be involved. The end state of the system is that all emergency calls should be answered within a tolerably short time period and instructions given to crews to answer the call.

The next set of analysis questions focuses on objects, agents, and structures. These are the control center, ambulance crews, patients, phones from which the call is made, and the emergency call itself. From the controller's viewpoint the emergency call is the key object that is processed; however, it is not altered by the processing. This assertion is open to interpretation, as updating the emergency call record does in some sense update the key object. In this case it points to an information system abstraction (Progress Tracking ISM). The telephone calls are an indirect manifestation of change in the environment (i.e., accidents and incidents), and the calls themselves contain information about changes that have to be responded to. This indicates an Object Sensing abstraction that functions at two levels: first the member of the public who detects the emergency and makes the call (Message Transfer), and second the controller who monitors the telephones and responds to the call. The only apparent structures are the control center building itself and the geography in which the system operates (streets, roads and buildings, etc.). The agents are the call taker, controller–dispatcher, ambulance crews, and the patients. Ambulance crews respond to dispatchers' commands, corroborating earlier indications of an Agent Control model. The generalized task is matching that maps to the Object Allocation OSM; however, the controller also carries out planning, scheduling, and prioritizing tasks, with considerable communication to the crews.

A use-case interaction diagram that summarizes the ambulance crew and dispatcher subsystems is illustrated in Fig. 7.5. The emergency call triggers system activity. Subsequent transitions are either commands to the ambulance crews, providing further evidence of an Agent Control abstraction, or reporting events from the crews to the dispatcher, indicating a Message Transfer. So far the questions have identified Agent Control as the prime abstraction for the control subsystem, with an ISM for Progress Tracking the emergency call. Questions on activity suggest that planning responses to emergency calls and instructing the crews are the main activities of the dispatcher agent. This maps to an Object Allocation model, as calls have to be matched to available resources (ambulances). Another duty is to eliminate duplicate calls. These activities depend on knowledge of the crews, the emergency, and ambulance location, so this suggests a need for detecting the location of these objects in the world. This uncovers a hidden Object Sensing model that is not apparent from the previous analysis.

Taking the ambulance crews' subsystem, one sees that the goals are to respond to emergency calls, navigate (generalized task) to the scene of the accident, treat patients at the accident site (physical task not within the Domain Theory), and take them to hospital. Goal-related questions indicate that transport is important, pointing to an Object Logistics model. The crews respond to commands, so they share an Agent Control model with the dispatchers; navigation to the accident implies movement and corroborates the Logistics model. Commands and reports are messages communicated by radio, either by voice or by means of the mobile data terminals. This indicates a Message Transfer model shared between the crews and dispatchers. The objects, agents, and structures are the crews, patients, members of

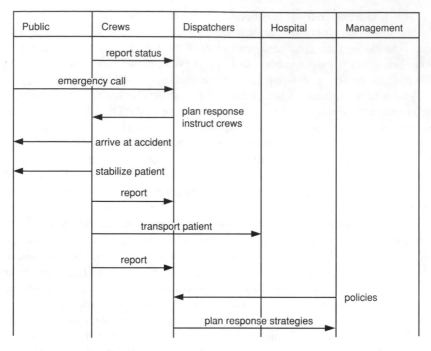

FIG. 7.5. Use-case diagram for call dispatch. The sequence of events reads approximately from top to bottom. The behavior of hospital agents (i.e., doctors) is not shown, as this was beyond the remit of the LAS.

the public who placed the call, and hospitals. Treating the patient can be regarded as a form of repair, so a Servicing abstraction might be suggested, although this is not the main goal of the subsystem. State transitions for instructing crews provide further evidence for an Agent Control model and indicate the presence of a Reporting ISM. Task analysis uncovers the need for decision making and planning to navigate to the scene of the accident, making judgments on how to stabilize the patient and then planning the best route to the nearest hospital. Spatial knowledge of locations of the accidents, hospitals, and the layout of streets are prerequisites for route planning, so this also points to a hidden Object Sensing model.

Question subsets refine the choice of abstract models down the hierarchy for each family. In the Object Sensing model, questions about the sensed object and the space in which it is located indicate that the appropriate class 2 model is Physical Object Sensing in a two-dimensional space. The questions about active or passive sensors are left open, as both approaches are used in the manual system. Sometimes the controllers ask the crews for their location; otherwise the crews report their location via radio. The AVLS assumes active sensing of ambulance location by radio signals.

In summary, the whole system is composed of five OSMs, which are Agent Control, Object Sensing (two instances), Allocation, Message Transfer and Object Logistics; three generalized tasks, which are Matching, Planning–Scheduling, and Navigation; several generic tasks, Identify, Interpret, Evaluate, Plan, and Communicate; and one ISM, Progress Tracking. Other ISMs may be present for creating management reports, but these did not feature in the LAS report.

7.4.2. Composing Generic System Models

The composition process depends on the complexity of the new application domain. If metadomains are present, composition will start with the one or more metadomains that have been identified and then progress to map OSM and generalized tasks to components in the metadomain architecture. The Domain Theory only gives an outline architecture for metadomains, so these templates have to be specialized by further analysis.

If the application is composed of grounded domain and generic tasks then composition proceeds by looking for the interfaces between the retrieved models. Interfaces between OSMs can be found by looking for shared agents, transitions, or key objects. Shared agents include agents with similar responsibilities; for instance, the customer in Object Inventory will probably be the same as the debtor agent in Accounting Object Transfer. Shared transitions, events, or processing dependencies are between models; for example, events output from one OSM may be necessary input for another. A typical coupling is signals from Object Sensing models needed by Agent Control models to determine what to do next. Shared key objects, for example, a resource in Object Hiring, may be shared with the Object Inventory system that creates the stock of loanable objects.

The OSM library contains many cross-references that indicate common aggregations of grounded domain models, so following these links also helps to compose a systemwide generic model. The next step is to aggregate generic and generalized tasks. This is more difficult because tasks do not have such a strong association with each other or components of grounded domains. The following heuristics point toward some associations, whereas cross-references in the Domain Theory library suggest other links.

Identify the agent responsible for the task. The generic task library does not nominate agents who may be responsible for each task because the set of potential agents for each task is too large; however, agents' roles are more readily identified from OSMs and interaction patterns. Asking the question about "which agent is responsible for, or executed, the task?" will point to a role, and if this also occurs in a grounded domain then the association with a task can be made.

Investigate the causes of state transitions in grounded domains. These are usually caused by generic tasks, so the endpoint of a task can be traced to a state change in an OSM.

Investigate the objects changed, used, or manipulated by generalized tasks. If the objects involved in the task are also shared with the OSM key objects, then an association can be made.

Examine the overlap between the task goal or postconditions and the OSM goal. Sometimes the goals are similar, for instance in the Monitor task and Object Sensing models.

Interfaces among OSMs, generalized tasks, and generic tasks can be discovered by event tracing from system input through to output by inquiring which model or task responds to the first input event, what output it produces, and then where this output becomes input to the next model or task. This event tracing analysis links the generic models in a data flow sequence. Alternatively, interfaces can be determined by pairwise comparison of OSM and generic tasks and listing the information flows between them, with shared objects and agents. The resulting model describes an abstract application composed of several OSMs and task models. A library system example is illustrated in Fig. 7.6.

Interfaces between the external world and the system, as well as between modules within the system, are frequent sources of design errors. Hence is it advisable to trace the flow of events between models to ascertain that changes are detected and updated correctly. For instance, an Accounting Object OSM may be updating bank balances at regular intervals rather than in real time, so a Reporting ISM could show a balance in credit when in fact debit events haven't been processed.

Case Study: Composing the Generic System Model. Integrating the OSM models to create a generic system model for the LAS application is achieved by unifying the models by shared agents (dispatcher, ambulance crews), objects (calls, ambulances), and structures (control rooms, city road plans). The model covering both subsystems is illustrated in Fig. 7.7. Both subsystems share an Agent Control and Messaging model, with dispatchers being the controller agents and crews the controlled agents. The Object Logistics model belongs to the crew subsystem, but this shares the crew agents with the Agent Control model; hence instruction state transitions trigger movement in the Logistics model. Both subsystems share the Reporting and Progress Tracking ISMs, although the role of the agents differs. The crews are information providers, whereas the dispatchers are information users. Finally, the two Object Sensing models are merged. The dispatcher needs to locate the ambulances, accidents, and hospitals, whereas the crews also need information on street layout and traffic conditions. The agents' requirements for sensing differ. Dispatchers need to locate ambulances, accidents, and calls that may not be made from the accident scene; crews need to know about any obstacles on a prospective route.

The controllers carry out most of the tasks because they are responsible for matching the call to the available ambulance, planning the dispatch, prioritizing emergencies, and communicating instructions to the crews. The ambulance crews have a generalized task of navigating to the location of the incident and performing

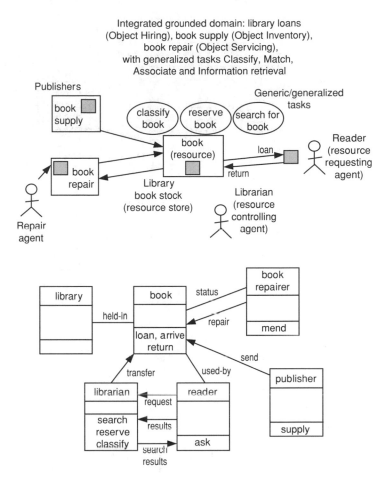

FIG. 7.6. Generic system model of a library composed of OSMs and generalized tasks.

several tasks that are outside the remit of the case study, such as providing paramedical care to the casualty, moving the casuality to the ambulance, and gathering facts about the incident, as well as communicating with all the concerned parties (police, relatives, witnesses, etc.). Then the ambulance crew have to navigate to the nearest hospital while reporting their progress to the controller. The navigation tasks are linked to the Object Logistics OSM.

7.4.3. Transferring Design Knowledge

Design knowledge in the Domain Theory refers to an aggregation of four types of knowledge that point the software engineer to further analysis issues or high-level design trade-offs.

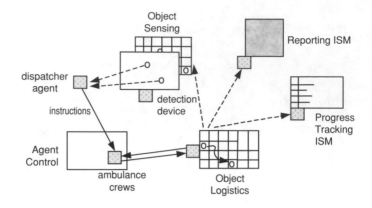

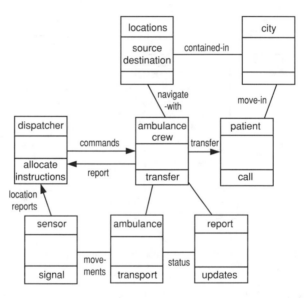

FIG. 7.7. Generic system model for the CAD system created from retrieved OSMs and ISMs, and the equivalent model represented in UML notation. The Message Transfer model has been omitted for brevity. It fits between the dispatcher and crews to ensure arrival of messages.

Requirements problems are brief informal statements of typical problems encountered in a particular application class. An example is pointing out the detectability problem in Object Sensing applications. This knowledge is attached to all OSMs and acts as an alert for the analyst.

Generic requirements are high-level descriptions of functional requirements that are associated with OSM components or generalized task stages. Generic

requirements help the requirements engineer to complete the requirements specification; they also provide reusable knowledge for design and act as pointers for
further analysis.

Design rationale and claims are knowledge structures that provide design knowledge in the form of requirements issues, possible solutions, and trade-offs. Design
rationale is the less comprehensive of the two and only states a requirements
issue, two or more possible solutions, and arguments for and against. Claims, in
contrast, recommend a solution as a principle or treatment, then draw attention to
the advantages or disadvantages of the solution with a large amount of contextual
information as scenarios, example artefact, and dependencies to help the designer
interpret the claim. A sample of design rationale and claims is provided for many
OSMs and tasks but the library is incomplete (see appendix C).

Design components, patterns, artefacts, and reusable software code are not part
of the Domain Theory itself, but the Domain Theory models do contain pointers
to reusable designs from other sources.

Knowledge transfer starts by inspecting the problems, generic requirements,
claims, and pointers associated with each component in the generic system model.
A sample of the issues and reusable knowledge associated with one OSM is shown
in Fig. 7.8.

The design advice is located where possible with the component to which it is directly relevant. Requirements problems and generic requirements influence the process of requirements analysis by pointing the analyst to further issues that may have
been missed or require further investigation. Generic requirements may be transferred into the requirement specification for the new application; however, they
have to be specialized into more specific functional requirements. Claims transfer
design experience and examples of best practice designs. The trade-offs in claims
and alternative solutions have to be evaluated to determine if they are suitable for
the new application. Advantages and disadvantages are weighed in the light of the
new application's context. Claims encourage the designer to refine the requirements and prospective design by promoting active reasoning about application of
the knowledge by drawing attention to advantages and disadvantages; giving a
scenario of use for interpreting how the function or design principle will apply;
providing an example process or designed artefact to illustrate how the general
knowledge may be specialized for reuse; pointing out the dependencies that the
design process has to account for when implementing the claim; giving a statement
of effects that indicate possible metrics that may be used for quality assurance;
and linking to other claims and background theory so that the knowledge is not
applied piecemeal.

Claims reuse is the most powerful form of knowledge transfer that is directly contained in the Domain Theory; however, the Domain Theory is an open
framework so authors and reusers can index their own component to different parts
of the library. Transfer of design solutions offers the highest utility payback for
designers, but it comes with a sting in the tail. Copycat reuse of solutions may

Level-2 class Spatial Object Sensing

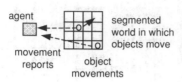

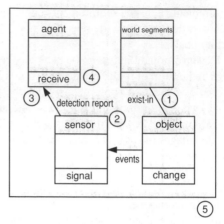

Generic requirements
Reliable event detector and interpreter
Sampling rate control
Tuning sensing mechanism to eliminate false alarms
Interpreters/filters to eliminate false alarms
Log file for history analysis of events

Claims
1. System model
2. Event filters
3. Rare event monitor
4. Event interpretation
5. Trace history

Problems
Fidelity of detecting events to avoid false alarms
Sampling rate and frequency of state change in
the world, to avoid missing rapid changes
Interpretation of events and the context of change
False events caused by oversensitive detecting devices

FIG. 7.8. Spatial Object Sensing level 2 OSM annotated with claims, generic requirements, and problems.

overlook key aspects of the problem, so a solution that looks ideal may, in fact, be a poor fit for the problem (Sutcliffe & Maiden, 1992). Furthermore, hasty reuse may fail to assess the component's design quality. Unreliable designs or inappropriate advice can be more of a danger than a help. Reuse of artefacts and designed solutions therefore has to be accompanied by carefully considering the appropriateness of the solution's fit with the problem, identifying any mismatches, and then planning alterations to change the component to fit its new purpose.

Transfer of claims and generic requirements into the final design will have to be validated with users and tested for reliability and performance. Finally, the process of design by reuse has to be evaluated to discover what worked and what did not. The process has to be reflective, in Schon's (1983) sense, so that it improves. More knowledge is added to the library as a result of experience, with notes and annotations to pass further reusable knowledge forward to future generations of designers.

Case Study: Knowledge Transfer and Reuse. The first level of reuse uses the requirement issues associated with each OSM and generalized task. Object Sensing models are associated with issues of detectability and interpretation of changes, and with the fidelity and accuracy of reporting change in the environment. The analysts who carried out the original specification would have been well advised to pay more attention to these issues. Poor detection of the ambulance's location because of radio blackspots was one of the key factors in system failure. Agent control is also a key feature of the system—subclass Nondeterministic agents because the crews are not under military discipline. The OSM draws attention to the problem of failure to obey commands with 100% accuracy and the problem of giving incentives to agents to encourage the desired responses. Again these pointers to requirements issues could have provided timely warning to the requirements analysts. The failure of the ambulance crews to accurately report their positions was a combination of poor motivation and poor user-interface design. The generalized task of matching depends on accurate information, which unfortunately was never received. Other problems such as accuracy of maps for navigation are indicated by issues associated with the generic models.

Generic requirements for the Object Sensing OSM point out the need for reliable detectors, or, if reliability cannot be guaranteed, then a second (metalevel) Object Sensing system is required to monitor the detector. For the matching generalized task, the task-support requirements advise on providing lists of prioritized matches but leaving the user in final control. In the LAS system, matching and ambulance allocation was automated, which depended on very accurate information. The requirements issue associated with this task warns about just such a danger. Generic requirements provide further advice for the Agent Control abstraction such as providing clear feedback instructions, and automating feedback where possible to avoid intrusion into the agent primary task.

The second level of design knowledge is expressed in claims or design rationale that describe requirements issues and design solutions that are frequently associated with the generic model. Design rationale is recorded in an adaptation of the QOC format (MacLean et al., 1991; Fig. 7.9). Each graph contains one issue related to the OSM or generalized task. Two or more design options are given for solutions to the issue, with criteria (or nonfunctional requirements) associated with options by positive or negative relationships. A positive relationship means that the design option will help to satisfy the nonfunctional requirement; a negative relationship implies the opposite. Several rationale diagrams are associated with each OSM to describe all the problems inherent in the model. Design options also have links to reusable solution components that are either specifications, designs, or actual software code. This enables the software engineer to trace from the problem states in the OSM and its rationale to a potential solution of their choice. Links may be included to several different reuse component libraries to facilitate cost reliability and performance trade-offs.

The rationale associated with the Object Sensing OSM is shown in Fig. 7.9. Sensing applications pose several problems of event detectability, how events are

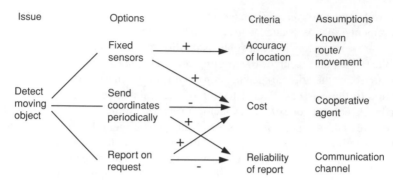

FIG. 7.9. Design rationale with the Object Sensing OSM two-dimensional spatial detection subclass, showing assumptions that the options depend on and criteria that influence trade-offs between options.

encoded, and timing of change and delays in signaling the same. Further problems are implicated in the subclass for active sensors in spatial domains, the Spatial Object Sensing OSM appropriate for the case study application. The relationship between the timing of event detection and change in the environment is important, as is the choice between an active report from the object or a passive response to a sensing signal.

Design options for the problem of detecting a moving spatial object in a two-dimensional world are shown in Fig. 7.9. The first option is to detect the object by fixed sensors in the world; the second relies on the object to signal its presence and coordinates to the sensor; and the third sends a polling message that the object responds to. The relationships to the criteria also indicate the assumptions that the options depend on, that is, presence of a fixed topography in the world or the ability to transmit polling messages, as well as the nonfunctional requirements, such as response timing, accuracy of sampling, and reliability.

The first option, detection by fixed sensors, is not feasible because it incurs a high cost for deploying a sensor network and rests on the assumption that the objects will only move on a small set of fixed routes. This is not true for ambulances, but note that this option is applicable to Object Sensing of vehicles at traffic lights and on railway tracks. The rationale diagram also points to further OSM abstractions, in this case a third-level class for Object Sensing in two-dimensional worlds with a restricted set of pathways and active sensors. In this manner, problem understanding and the search for solutions is helped by cross-references between the rationale diagrams and OSM models. The second and third options are potential solutions. In the LAS development the second option was chosen to replace the manual system. This used radio to implement a mixture of options two and three in the manual system, as the crews used to report their locations and sometimes the dispatcher would call for crews close to a location. Selecting option two allows

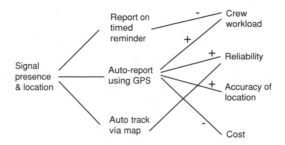

FIG. 7.10. Lower-level design rationale diagram: communication requirements.

the solution to be traced to a lower-level diagram, which poses a further requirements question to be resolved: how to signal presence and coordinates. This lower-level rationale diagram (Fig. 7.10) shows potential solutions by radio, using a set time reminder for crew reporting, automatic emission of location messages using Global Positioning System (GPS) technology, or detection using location input into a coordinate map system. The nonfunctional requirements point to trade-offs that influenced the real-world system, such as warning about the fidelity of updating state changes detected in the environment. Failure to update the gazetteer map system was one of the reasons for failure of the AVLS.

Further rationale diagrams provide design advice on Agent Control protocols, with coordination and reporting logistics systems for the Physical Object Transfer models. Rationale can advise on the extent of automation that may be desirable and design of human computer cooperation (Bailey, 1982; Sutcliffe, 1995) with pointers to sources of appropriate algorithms and reusable software components.

OSMs and rationale diagrams provide software engineers with a rich source of reusable knowledge to explore potential solutions, and they warn about possible pitfalls to avoid. The Domain Theory, through its class structure of models with claims and design rationale, provides an extensible library that can be scaled up as many authors contribute their experiences with applications that share the same generic model. This case study has only analyzed a small fragment of the LAS to illustrate the method.

So far reuse has been illustrated by design rationale. In the next chapter, knowledge reuse is elaborated to include the claims component of the Domain Theory.

7.5. SUMMARY

The process of reuse is described first in general terms and second for reuse of Domain Theory models. The reuse process is divided into two subprocesses, design for reuse and design by reuse. Design for reuse involves a domain analysis to specify the reuse library components followed by development of the components and documentation. Components are described and indexed to facilitate future reuse. Development of the reuse library also necessitates specification of reuse support tools. Design by reuse starts with requirements analysis in the new application domain, followed by component matching and retrieval. This leads to design of the application architecture and specialization of components where necessary. The system is then integrated and tested.

A key concern in design for reuse is generalizing components. Four treatments for abstraction were described. The first was cohesion analysis, which assesses the contribution of the component's methods and actions to a single goal. Second, coupling analysis investigates the degree of dependency between the component and other modules, that is, low-level data coupling that makes few assumptions about other components and is more effective for flexible reuse. Third, data abstraction is produced by normalization, reducing domain-specific references and creating more general classes; heuristics for data abstraction were proposed. Finally, guidelines for procedural abstraction were described, including design of flexible algorithms. The process of generalization at the knowledge level was discussed briefly.

The process of reuse by means of the Domain Theory was introduced as a specialization of the general reuse approach. Requirements analysis is followed by identification and retrieval of appropriate domain models of the application. Matching heuristics were proposed with a walkthrough method to discover appropriate Domain Theory models. Once the models have been located, they are combined into an integrated, but abstract, model of the new application, and then knowledge attached to the models as design rationale, claims, and generic requirements is transferred. The process of reuse was illustrated by a case study of the London Ambulance Service to demonstrate where the domain models specified system requirements and the reusable knowledge pointed to solutions that could have prevented problems that actually occurred in the real-life system.

Reusing Knowledge
and Claims

In this chapter the method is extended to deal with claims-based reuse. In the case of claims, the reuse library is open ended, as new design knowledge is being constantly created. The method starts with design for reuse or generalizing claims. Once generalization and retrieval have been addressed, the process of design by reuse with claims is reviewed, which integrates use of domain models and claims-based design knowledge. Claims reuse is illustrated by a case study that starts with the generation of claims in a parent application—INTUITIVE, an information retrieval database front-end environment—and subsequent reuse of generalized claims in a second application, Multimedia Broker, for Web-based information searching and brokering services. First, methods for general knowledge management are reviewed to set the context for the claims reuse.

8.1. KNOWLEDGE REUSE PROCESS

Knowledge-management tasks imply four roles in the process: a *knowledge harvester*, who solicits knowledge, designs it, and records it for reuse to complete the documentation activity by other personnel; a *knowledge documenter*, who is responsible for encouraging the documentation of reusable knowledge and then formatting and indexing it for the library; a *retrieval assistant*, who helps users find the appropriate knowledge, explains searching tools, and assists retrieval; and a *knowledge manager*, who has overall responsibility for the process and reuse library and who has strategies to encourage reuse. Knowledge reuse, as with design reuse, requires a culture of acceptance to be built up and a critical mass of knowledge to be created in the first place so that users can find appropriate content. Validation is also important so that managers build up trust in the library. This can be facilitated by sharing the experience of knowledge reuse with early success stories and by making the reusable components evolve over time. Annotations allow reusers to document their experiences with knowledge reuse and add their own advice or extensions to the original components.

Knowledge reuse is closely linked to organizational learning (Argyris, 1999), so the process not only involves familiar tasks such as acquisition, formatting, indexing and retrieval, and exploitation, but also metaprocesses for improving the original approach to knowledge management. This involves reviewing knowledge reuse, assessing its benefits, critiquing problems, and proposing improvements. The relationship between the initial process cycle and the reflective metaprocess is illustrated in Fig. 8.1.

Organizational learning can itself be encouraged by management structures that create task forces to harvest knowledge and encourage its reuse, including pilot projects to demonstrate success. These task groups should spread the reuse culture so that it permeates the whole organization, and in doing so transform their own role into a discussion forum for swapping reuse studies and discussing format and ways of improving capture and exploitation.

Knowledge reuse may be intraorganizational or interorganizational. The source of knowledge implies some difference in costs of acquisition and the processes used. In intraorganizational reuse, knowledge is harvested from employees; documentation time and resources have to be planned to ensure that the normal operational demands of work do not consume time set aside for reflection and documentation of experience. In interorganizational reuse, knowledge is acquired from external sources by literature searches, subscription to information vendor–business intelligence services, joining trade associations, and site visits to other companies. Costs here are funding information searcher roles. Most reusable knowledge is documented as informal narrative text; however, this can hinder effective retrieval. Claims provide a structured format for knowledge reuse that also promotes reasoning during the process.

8.2. GENERALIZING CLAIMS FOR REUSE

Two methods are required for claims reuse: first, designing claims for reuse; second, the method for reusing claims knowledge in design and decision making. The *factoring* process for generalizing claims is dependent on the maturity of the

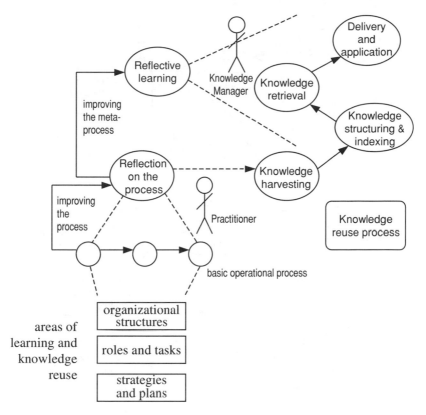

FIG. 8.1. Process cycle in knowledge management, including processes for organizational learning.

investigation and the level at which the claim is stated. Generally claims analysis should progress through several generations before generalization is attempted, because encoding immature knowledge is likely to lead to incomplete and ambiguous descriptions. However, the act of factoring can itself stimulate further investigation and theory development, so the interleaving of generalizing and evolving claims can yield productive insights.

The method stages are summarized in Fig. 8.2. The starting point is a specific claim developed by claims analysis and usability evaluation of a design. The first step is to factor the claim to discover any hidden "child" claims. This involves separating the functional and interactive aspects of the claim. Many claims are intended to support a user's task, entertainment, or learning and provide psychologically based design rationale that advises on the functionality that should achieve the stated goal. However, claims may include some specification of the interactive system dialogue and presentation that support a functional goal. The user-interface detail is implicit in the accompanying artefact even if it is not explicitly

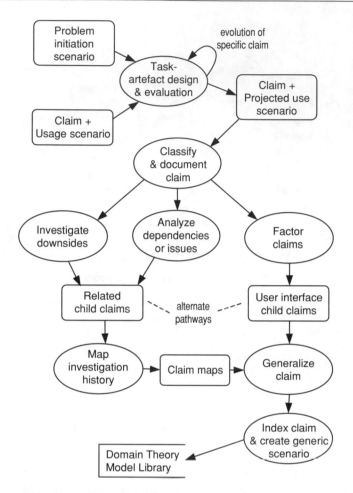

FIG. 8.2.   Method outline: generalizing claims for reuse.

stated in the claim. Consequently, the first two stages of the method aim to separate these issues and evolve a set of related, yet more abstract, child claims from the original parent.

8.2.1.   Factoring Issues

Analysis follows the principle of cohesion (Yourdon & Constantine, 1978). Questions are based on scenario analysis techniques (Potts, Takahashi, Smith & Ora, 1995) to tease apart the possible intentions that lie behind the claim. The questions probe the claim's design to indicate which domain models the claim should be indexed to. The claim description, scenario, issues, and effects clause (if documented) are investigated with the following probes.

What impact should be achieved as a result of applying the claim? If the claim has been documented according to the extended schema in Fig. 6.4, the answer to this question will be in the effects slot. However, not all goals necessitate change in the world to achieve a new state. Will a state be maintained as a result of applying the claim? Maintenance functions keep a system in a steady state. Does the claim solve problems stated in the usage scenario? Claims are frequently motivated by solving an observed usability problem rather than by fulfilling a stated goal or requirements. The effect will be the same, as application of the claim should solve the problem and achieve a system goal. Does the claim explicitly refer to helping the users, such as improving learning, ease of use, entertainment, or motivation? User-oriented claims belong to the user-interface Design or Education metadomains. Does the claim explicitly refer to support for activity of a single user or to supporting multiple users? Single user activity tends to be oriented toward generic tasks, whereas multiuser activity often indicates transactions and support for organizations. Does the claim propose a design that supports a complete user task or subgoals within it? Some artefacts may be necessary for the whole task, such as maps for navigation, whereas others support a discrete goal, such as a bird's-eye view for locating self in orientation.

Questioning claims may lead to the discovery of subgoals or hidden intentions, in which case the original claim will have to be split into two or more child claims, each addressing one specific goal. Reference to the Domain Theory models can indicate where multiple goals are present in a complex claim and also give an early indication for linking claims to domain models (see section 8.2.5).

8.2.2. Factoring Contributions

This stage takes claims that have a single cohesive goal and investigates the dependencies between the goal and user-interface features that are explicit in the claim or implicit in the artefact. This frequently leads to discovery of child claims that belong to the user-interface design family. The model (Fig. 8.3, after Norman, 1986) describes a cycle of user–system interaction that can be "walked through" by the claims author with question prompts at each stage that indicate the type of new claim that may be implicit in the original description or artefact.

By definition, claims refer to particular features, but factoring claims may suggest extensions or generalizations of the original claim, new artefacts, descriptions, upsides, downsides, scenarios, and so forth. The questions illustrated in Fig. 8.3 are used to step through the task described in the claims originating scenario. Each task initiates an interaction cycle that should achieve its goal; however, goal-related questions may suggest subgoals in the task structure. The original goal may, for instance, be underspecified, or a different means of supporting the task may become apparent. Questions within each cycle focus more directly on the user-interface components rather than task-support functionality. Hence if the artefact is primarily intended to support formation and monitoring of users' goals, it has a goal task

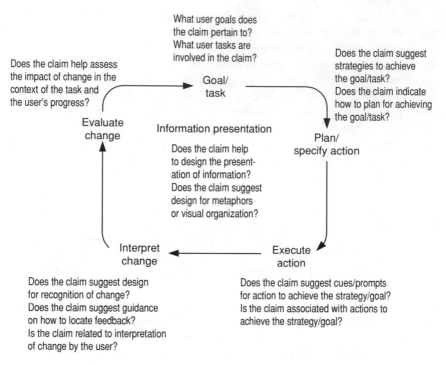

FIG. 8.3. The claims factoring walkthrough method, composed of questions attached to stages in the process model of interaction. Norman's (1986) stages to recognize and interpret change have been merged because they tend to implicate the same artefact components.

contribution; whereas a display feature is more likely to support interpretation and evaluation of change, or presentation of information.

8.2.3. Example of Factoring

Assessment of one artefact may result in discovering or deriving several new "child" claims with accompanying artefact features from the parent. With the Color-Coded Telegraphic claim, the walkthrough elaborates the following potential contributions. Using the cited scenario, the domain task goal "the learner is trying to create an UpperCaseTextPane" is composed of a subgoal that the system supports, "locate appropriate class for reuse," and a learning task goal, "explain next goal in the design task." The system infers that the learner is "searching for relevant classes and methods" and posts this phrase in the GoalPoster. The learner selects the posted goal to display an expanded explanation about why the goal should be pursued. Factoring so far has exposed a complex goal structure in learning a program design task. Note that the claim is related to the domain task as well as the learning task, so we may suggest that the GoalPoster artefact may (a) support software reuse by helping users find reusable components and (b) help programmers learn design by reuse in Smalltalk. Theoretical underpinnings suggest the claim belongs more closely to the latter. Following the "explain next goal in the domain task," the factoring questions point first to how the artefact supports strategy formation. This is achieved by the GoalPoster tree that displays a map of the tasks for the user to follow and highlights the next goal. Execution is not directly supported in the GoalPoster, as this is carried out in the domain by users selecting the appropriate class. Interpretation is supported by updating the goal tree on successful completion of action; in addition, expansion of the telegraphic text promotes understanding about the effect of action. Finally, evaluation is helped by placing the user's progress in the context of the overall domain task by highlighting achieved goals on the tree diagram. Presentation of information indirectly supports most interaction stages by providing an adaptable presentation that can be expanded to supplement the user's understanding for either planning or interpretation. The walkthrough produced the following list of explanations of the GoalPoster's contribution at different stages of the "explain next goal" task.

- Artefact: GoalPoster tool.
- Goals–task: learning Smalltalk; explain next goal.
- Planning–strategy: the goal tree and status indicator enable tracking of the user's progress, and hence planning future learning strategy.
- Execution: no direct support, but domain task actions are registered to update the user's progress on completion of learning subtasks.
- Interpretation: labels on the tree display help monitoring progress in a learning task; expansion of the telegraphic text display helps users understand the learning goals in more depth.
- Evaluation: providing a goal tree of the learning task helps the user understand how much of the task has been completed, the next steps to achieve, and where to backtrack to if necessary.
- Presentation: telegraphic text is a mnemonic cue for the goals, yet economical in screen real estate; color coding is used to segment the goal tree into substructures and indicate the user's current position. Expansion of telegraphic text provides an adaptable presentation for more detail.

The effect of the walkthrough is to assess the claim's contributions and derive new contexts for reuse. New claims arise from this process either within the same domain as new ways of supporting task subgoals are discovered, or more general claims evolve that are related to user-interaction support rather than a task. The walkthrough is suitable for derivation of child claims for user-interface artefacts from claims that have a wider, more functional scope. Claims that identify functions in their upsides often rely on complex artefacts to deliver their functionality. The walkthrough investigates how different aspects of the user interface contribute to delivering the functionality. Consequently, child claims may not require all components or the original artefact, so the feature most closely implicated in fulfilling the new claim's effects are investigated.

For high-level claims the feature may be synonymous with the product, but in many cases the issues clause may refer to design of a discrete user-interface component, hinting at a new claim–artefact combination. Indeed, the issues clause in the original claim often gives a valuable pointer toward factoring analysis. Note that the component may not be visible at the user interface, such as a dialogue strategy. This process may iterate as child claims are derived from the parent, although claims that are already associated with user-interface components will probably not be amenable to further factoring. Once the factoring is complete the scenario and feature descriptions are revisited to document the scope of the claim's future applicability. To illustrate the process, the evolution of the GoalPoster artefact and its associated claim into a new task–artefact combination is described.

Notice that the Color-Coded Telegraphic claim was motivated by support for learning; however, the factoring suggested a new, more general, artefact as a progress monitoring tool that may be suitable for a wide variety of user interfaces. The GoalPoster tool constitutes a generalizable feedback display that monitors user progress in a task and then provides feedback for interpretation and evaluation. Furthermore, the Color-Coded Telegraphic display provides a novel design concept for presentation. Classification and factoring proceed hand in hand to produce new claims.

Claim ID:	PTDisp
Title:	Progress Tree Display claim.
Author:	Sutcliffe, A. G.
Parent claim:	Color-Coded Telegraphic Display.
Explanation:	Users need to track their progress through a complex task and may lose their place. This hinders task completion as they lose the thread of the goals they have achieved and have to backtrack. A progress indicator display of a goal tree prevents the users from losing their place.
Upsides:	Provides persistent feedback on status of user action within a tree-structured task as well as access to further information; supports effective work by relieving user's working memory from progress tracking.
Downsides:	Users must learn the tree structure display and goal labels; the current location may be difficult to find in massive trees.
Artefact:	Tree monitor tool (link to artefact).
Projected use scenario:	The user interface presents a tree structure of the user's task with a status indicator showing the current subgoal. The user is distracted by a colleague's asking questions

and forgets where he was in the task. The user looks at the progress tree display and recognizes where he was in the task; however, the next step cannot be remembered, so the user expands the currently highlighted telegraphic goal by double clicking on it. The system provides a longer description of the task step as well as shorthand feedback on current status; the user remembers the task and continues.

Effect:	Improved provision of appropriate feedback on task progress.
Dependencies:	Detecting the user's progress in a task, known goal structure.
Issues:	What sort of feedback displays are effective and under what circumstances? Is color coding effective for indicating the three-way distinction among achieved subgoals, apparently correct subgoals, and apparently incorrect subgoals? Is a tree structure the most effective means of visualizing progress in a task?
Theory:	Observability principle (Thimbleby, 1990); see also ISO 9241 (ISO, 1997), part 10.
Scope:	Progress tracking generalized task; user-interface design user support subfamily.

The above claim has evolved from its original motivating example into a more general and widely applicable claim for user interfaces of any system with hierarchical, deterministic tasks. Note that the newly identified claim includes a projected use scenario that represents the designer's expectation for how the child claim and its associated artefact will function; it may also be viewed as a problem initiation scenario that summarizes the need for further investigation in a new task–artefact context. The issues clause indicates further directions in which the claim might evolve; for instance, there are issues of color coding the display for structure and indicating status; design of telegraphic, yet mnemonic goal names; and visualization of the goal tree itself.

8.2.4. Generalizing Claims

At this stage the claim description, usage scenario, and artefact will still be specific. Generalization involves removing as much detail as possible while preserving sufficient knowledge in the claim to make its reuse attractive. The stages for generalization are as follows.

Develop a generic scenario of use by investigating the similarities between the appropriate Domain Theory model and the originating scenario. Create a generalized activity script to describe the objects, actions, agents, and their roles. Grounded domains and generalized tasks have interaction models that resemble use cases, so these can form the basis for a generalized scenario. Metadomains, however, do not have use cases so the scenario is generalized by eliminating detail as described in the next step.

Generalize the scenario by substituting specific references as follows.

Names of people, users, actors → general roles.
Identities of objects → classes or categories of objects.
Specific actions → generalized actions from the associated task model.
Preconditions → eliminate or make tests refer to general states.
Application context → delete details or include in general preconditions if vital for understanding the claim.

Generalize claims by following the same substitutions in scenarios. Each clause in the claims schema (issues, effects, etc.) should be inspected in a similar manner.

If appropriate, develop a general design pattern to illustrate the claim. The role of the artefact in the originating claim is the most problematic. One option is to include the artefact as a concrete example of the claim with an explanation of how the specific design reflects the rationale expressed in the claim. Alternatively, if the claim rationale refers to the artefact's architecture or behavior, then a general pattern for its structure or behavior could be derived.

Once a set of generalized claims have been produced, they are indexed on the domain model. This sets the scene for the reuse process that starts with retrieval of claims by means of the Domain Theory models.

8.2.5. Linking Claims to Domain Models

Once the appropriate domain model for a particular claim has been identified, the next step is to link the claim to the relevant component. Some claims may suggest a design solution for the goal of the whole model (e.g., support a generic task), whereas others relate to particular components (e.g., support a single action). Where possible, claims are linked to actions or subgoals within generic or generalized tasks, architecture components in metadomains, and interactions within grounded domains.

Claims may be reused either solo or in association with other components. The process of reuse depends on the claim's scope and origin. Management-level claims are not associated with artefacts and designs, so reuse of these claims is by transfer of the knowledge alone. Knowledge reuse is more sophisticated in claims compared with other knowledge-management formats, because the claims ground their advice with a scenario of use and context and draw attention to the advantages and disadvantages of following the advice.

Non-management-level claims provide a comprehensive packet of knowledge for reuse. First there is the claim itself, expressing theory-motivated design rationale, dependencies, effects, and unresolved issues. The scenario grounds the claims in a context of use, whereas the artefact gives a concrete example of the claims application that may itself be reusable. Finally, if the claim has been generalized, it will have a design-associated pattern with one or more Domain Theory models to provide a design context.

Claims are associated with each other by being indexed on to domain models. Several claims may be associated with each grounded domain to describe several problems inherent in the abstract model. Claims are associated with reusable solutions in the artefact that may contain either specifications, designs, or actual software code. This enables the designer to trace from problem states to design knowledge in claims and a potential solution as an artefact or design pattern. Claims also provides suggestions about functional requirements for different task designs, with trade-offs for nonfunctional requirements, from their associated generic and generalized tasks; for example, one problem that appeared in the Information Retrieval generalized task and interaction pattern (see Fig. 6.7) was how to refine the user's need. This could be addressed by claims for preformed queries, concept maps, or an active thesaurus that have different trade-offs for novice–expert users and predictability–shareability of information needs.

8.3.   CLAIMS NETWORKS

Claims may also be related directly to each other as *genres*. Genres are structured to follow the derivation of claims as they evolve during a research project or over several years' refinement in design practice. Alternatively, genres can be given a more functional classification. The net effect is to associate claims into families, either by association with domain models for a context of application or by other classification schemes used by the library author. Claims families and genres are equivalent to pattern languages (Alexander et al., 1977), that is, collections of design advice structured in a hypertext network that allows many solutions to be recruited for a large-scale problem.

The relationship among a claim, its derivation history, and background theory can be understood from a map of the investigation history that gave rise to the claim. New claims may arise by one of three routes: first by factoring, second by research to address the downsides or design issues in the parent claim, and finally by generalization. Whatever the derivation, claims maps illustrate the motivation for each investigation that led to a claim and show associations between related claims. Figure 8.4 illustrates the point with a map of claims produced by the downside route.

The Color-Coded Telegraphic Display claim arose from research into the problem of feedback provision in an active tutoring environment for Smalltalk programming, the MoleHill tutor (Singley & Carroll, 1996). Subsequent investigations were motivated to solve downsides of the initial, identified claim. Three parents were linked to the Color-Coded Telegraphic claim. First, the system-generated goals described display design trade-offs for making the user's learning goals clearer. This claim can be traced back to *full planning languages*, which described

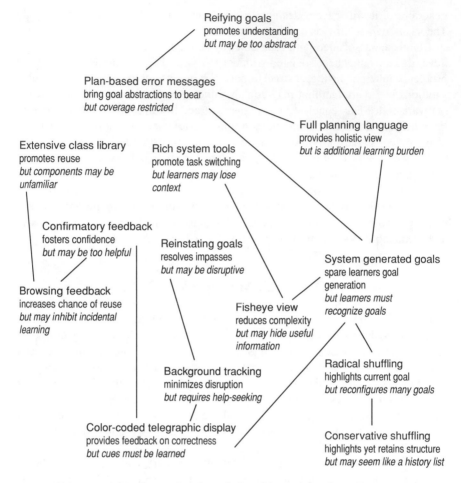

FIG. 8.4.   Map illustrating the relationships arising from investigation into Smalltalk programming support tools. Interclaim links are
represented in the relationship slot of the schema.

the trade-offs for explicitly expressing a plan of what the user was to learn, and
plan-based error messages, which advised giving users error messages when they
make mistakes and showing where they have made mistakes in the context of the
learning plan. In this manner the parentage of a claim can be traced back through
a history of investigation to help understand its motivation and the evidence on
which it rests. The second parent, *background tracking*, is motivated by a pedagogical concern to provide feedback on the correctness of the user's actions, but it
does so in a separate window to minimize disrupting the user's task. The motivation for the third parent, *confirmatory feedback*, can be traced back to support for
browsing and retrieving reusable components from the Smalltalk class library. The

design gave feedback on the relevance of a class for the user's current problem, and confirmatory feedback helps guiding the user's choice of components although it may overdo the effect and inhibit exploratory learning.

The Color-Coded Telegraphic claim was motivated by a display design problem; namely, how to give feedback that is clear and updateable but not too intrusive, while supporting two different parts of a tutoring environment. The claims map makes reference to a substantial investigation history that is anchored by the theoretical motivation of minimalist instruction (Carroll, 1990).

Generalizing claims illustrates some of the problems in designing HCI knowledge for reuse. Claims are anchored in a history of investigation that shaped design solutions for a particular problem. However, the solution involved several components and may recruit different theories and claims during the investigation. For example, the fisheye view claim rests on research by Furnas (1986), motivated by display design rather than learning support systems. If claims can be exported from one task–artefact cycle to another, this raises the question about which "seeding artefacts" are exported and how claims are attached to them.

The original artefact should retain its links with the child claim, but reference should be made to the contribution of the artefact in the claim's explanation, dependencies, and issue slots. One artefact may serve as an example for several claims. This is acceptable when the motivation for developing a claims repository is to reuse HCI knowledge alone. However, when software as well as HCI knowledge reuse is intended, artefacts for child claims will have to be designed de novo. The relationship between claims and software artefacts depends on the artefact's software architecture. For instance, in a modular design it may be possible to separate code from a parent artefact that relates to a child claim. When this is not possible a new artefact may have to be designed, or the scope of application of the original artefact to the new claim made clear in accompanying documentation. Taking the GoalPoster example, one sees that the child claim uses most of the parent artefact's components, that is, a mechanism for detecting user actions, display of a goal tree, and an updating component that highlights the next goal in a task sequence. Hence the artefact redesign may only require making the software more reusable, for instance, by facilities to customize the action detection mechanism and task hierarchy displays. As illustration of the need for more radical redesign, if factoring were taken further to evolve a child claim that addressed the usability of the expandable telegraphic display alone, then a display artefact would be designed with functionality for expanding telegraphic text in goal trees.

The Color-Coded Telegraphic Display can be reused more generally for display artefact design. However, this claim contains information that is not explained; for instance, the role of color coding is used to indicate the user's current location in a goal tree. Explaining a color image of the artefact may bring this information to the user's attention; but a safer approach is to illustrate and document implicit knowledge as dependencies and design issues. Alternatively, we may wish to refactor the claim by documenting its (and the artefact's) contribution at different stages of interaction; for example, color coding, alphanumeric mnemonic coding, tree structure feedback indicators, all contribute to interpretation and evaluation in progress monitoring. This leads to evolving claims at different levels of abstraction such as user-interface functions and task–domain support (Sutcliffe & Carroll, 1998). The claims map can be used to trace claims from one task–artefact context to another, enabling traceability back to a claim's original motivations and providing the designer with a view of the maturity of the investigations.

8.4. CLAIMS REUSE PROCESS

Reuse of claims has only three stages and uses a subset of the process for domain model reuse. First the appropriate claims must be found for the new application problem, either by tracing links in the claims–domain model library or by searching for claims directly. Then the claims knowledge is applied to the new design context, having established that it is appropriate. The final stage is to reflect on the usefulness of the knowledge transfer, which is valuable in two ways. First it acts as a reality check that the claim's advice really was correct, and second it leads to claims evolution. The act of problem solving usually stimulates new, potentially reusable ideas.

8.4.1. Retrieving Claims for Reuse

Retrieval can be effected by two routes, either by browsing the Domain Theory–claims library to find claims associated with a model or by querying the library. The Domain Theory–claims library is designed to support flexible access by means of two pathways.

The first pathway is access by means of domain models. In this case the developer has a target application in mind and can match it to one or more abstract domain models. The developer browses the domain library to find the relevant model(s) and then inspects the claims attached to the model to decide which claims are reusable. The localization of claims in domain model components helps to home in on the appropriate advice. Matching new applications to generic models in the library is the most difficult step in the process. The retriever-matching tool, described in chapter 4 and in Sutcliffe and Maiden (1998), can be used to find appropriate grounded domain models given a minimal input description of the new application. An alternative is to follow the heuristics described in chapter 7. Access by this route has the advantage that the designer obtains a rich set of contextualized knowledge as several related claims are attached to one domain model. Furthermore, the domain model itself provides reusable patterns that can be incorporated in implementation of the claim.

The second pathway is access by other paths. If the designer does not have a clear image of a new application and hence cannot follow the model's route, then the claims library can be queried directly. Designers can also access the library by following hypertext links. Each facet of the claims schema is queryable by simple keyword-matching search engines. Combinations of different facets can narrow searches effectively. However, if the designer is unable to think of appropriate query terms for direct searches, the Latent Semantic Indexing (LSI) algorithm (Landauer & Dumais, 1997) provides matching of claims by similarity, so scenario or claim descriptions can be entered for "find similar and related" type searches. The appeal of LSI is that it does not depend on lexical matching; instead it uses a statistical density of matched keywords throughout a document set, so, having found some lexical matches between two documents, it can infer possible matches between others on the basis of structural similarity and word-density distributions. This enables searches to be submitted as specific scenarios of use that are matched to generic scenarios on the basis of similar script structures. However, there is no complete escape from lexical matching; similarity-based searches using specific scenarios have to be seeded by substitution of specific identifiers with more abstract descriptions of agents, objects, and the like. This allows a search to progress from a specific description of a new application context toward more abstract models and hence to identify appropriate generalized claims.

8.4.2. Knowledge Transfer

Once appropriate claims have been retrieved, the knowledge contained within the claim can be exploited by the designer. Claims, however, offer no magic bullet. Indeed, the converse is intended. Claims deliberately express a tension in design, as do many patterns (Borchers & Muhlhauser, 1998; Coplein, 1999) to alert the designer to the dangers of jumping to conclusions. Other facets in the claims schema prompt further reasoning about the design problem, in the following slots.

- Downsides: these point to side effects that the claim may induce. The designer needs to decide whether these side effects will be serious in the new application context.
- Effects: what are the measurable outcomes of applying this claim?
- Dependencies: these point to other design problems that have to be solved, or resources acquired, for successful application of the claim.
- Issues: these alert the designer to other possible side effects that are more general than the downsides, such as impacts of the design on nonfunctional parameters of security, performance, and so on.

The scenario, generalized pattern, and artefact (if present) all help to contextualize the claim so that the designer can reason about how the knowledge will apply in a specific situation. The artefact and scenario juxtapose the specific with the abstract. The designer has to take these contrasts and reason by example and counterexamples to establish the validity of knowledge transfer with the triangle of knowledge illustrated in Fig. 8.5.

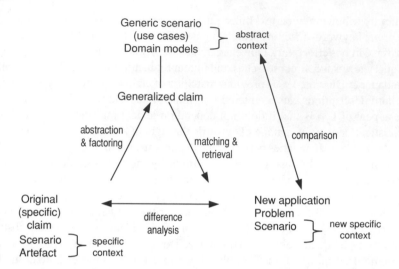

FIG. 8.5. Triangle of knowledge transfer, from specific scenarios of origin and intended use to generalized knowledge and back to specific situations in the new application.

The main problem is comparing specific scenarios from the new application context with the claim's generalized scenario. More scenarios help in comparing abstract models implicit in both the claim and the new application. The claim may contain references to theory underpinning its origins and having links to many related claims and abstract models. In this manner, transfer of claims knowledge is analogous to spreading activation in human memory. You start with one focus and then spread outward by following links to related knowledge to develop a more complex mental model of the design problem. The flip side of the rich schema is complexity. Designers do not always want sophisticated knowledge representations; indeed, more often the need is for the quick fix. Claims can accommodate this need by a layered approach that gradually reveals more knowledge as the designer demands. This follows the philosophy of the minimal manual approach to learning (Carroll, 1990), in which knowledge is gradually unfolded in tandem with the user's understanding of the problem. Hence in claims a three-layer unfolding is as follows.

- Layer 1: the claim description, scenario, upsides, and downsides.
- Layer 2: the claim as in layer 1 but adding the artefact–pattern, effects, dependencies, and issues.
- Layer 3: the claim plus the links to theory, other claims, and domain models.

Once knowledge transfer has been completed and the claim reused in design or management, the designer needs to reflect on its utility and validity. Reflection on design helps generalize the practice (Schon, 1983) and codify reusable experience. It also helps test the boundaries of application. One of the dangers of reuse is false transfer. This can be a particular problem for claims where the advice is expressed informally in natural language. In spite of comprehensive knowledge structures to promote reasoning, natural-language explanations will always be prone to misinterpretation. Reflection, especially testing the abstract with the concrete by examples and scenarios, is a useful check on misinterpretation. This process also leads to new design ideas that can be used to define claims or generate new ones.

8.5. CASE STUDY: CLAIMS REUSE

In this section the reuse and evolution of claims is reported from developing claims in the INTUITIVE project (Sutcliffe & Ryan, 1998). First the reuse of claims that originated in several investigations in INTUITIVE is described, followed by the transfer of claims that originated in INTUITIVE to a new application in the Multimedia Broker project (Sutcliffe et al., 1995).

The INTUITIVE system consisted of a set of reusable information retrieval services that could be embedded in a variety of applications. Two demonstrator applications were developed. The first version was a decision-support system for shipboard emergency management, and the second was a training system for shipboard emergency management. The first step in reuse is to establish the generic domains and tasks within the application. There are only a small number of metadomains, which are easily identified from their descriptions, in this case Education–Training. Generic tasks are discovered by examining task specifications for similarities with the generic models and by investigating the dependencies and issues clauses in any specific claims. The application tasks were diagnosing the problem that caused the emergency; planning the response to deal with the emergency; searching for information on the hazards, dangerous cargo, and emergency procedures; and planning training sessions. The grounded domains were Object Sensing to detect the emergency, Agent Control to plan and deal with the emergency, and Message Transfer to describe the communications between the captain and crew.

Taking one grounded domain as an example, the Rare Event Monitor claim was attached to the Object Sensing part of the application. The claim originated in research on safety critical specification methods with a case study on gas chromatograph analyzers (Sutcliffe, 1998). It was generalized to create a claim for monitoring hazards in safety critical applications. The sensing system user-interface functions and the scenario of use appears to be a good match with the Rare Event Monitor claim, so the claim could be reused in a new application that shared the same abstraction. This claim highlights design trade-offs for automatic detection of hazardous events that may be transferable from the voltage fluctuations in a laser chromatograph control system by means of the generalized claim for monitoring rare but hazardous events to a fire detection artefact in INTUITIVE.

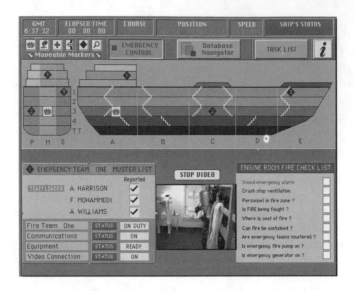

FIG. 8.6. INTUITIVE shipboard emergency management system, showing the checkbox artefact (bottom right) and preformed
queries as diamond icons leading to the answer box (bottom left).

Both artefacts have the functionality of rare event detection and signaling the
locus of the event on a diagram, although the originating artefact detected several
events of different types. The downside draws attention to problems of reliable detection of dangerous events and the danger of false warnings. Detection reliability
could be dealt with by tuning the sensor to prevent false alarms and using different
sources of evidence, for instance, using heat and smoke sensors to detect fire. The
new artefact gives the warning by a fire icon symbol displayed on the diagram of
the ship (see Fig. 8.6), so the feedback is presented with context information to
mitigate the claim's downside of lack of situation awareness. Other suggestions
were detecting different event types, such as types of fire and other shipboard
hazards such as chemical spillage (prompted by the artefact), and using multiple
sources of evidence to improve event detection reliability, such as using smoke and
heat to detect fires (prompted by the dependencies). However, the claim–artefact
combination has user-interface features that are not easily transferred. For instance,
the original display used a diagram of the gas chromatograph to locate the fault.
This was generalized to recommend a diagram for display but no format was specified. Clearly, the domain-specific information is inappropriate for fire location on
ships. In spite of this clash the HCI knowledge contained in the issues and dependencies clause can be reused (detecting locus of events, or giving contextual
feedback to the user). In the new design, the locus of the event is depicted by a
fire icon on the ship diagram, but this will require usability testing to validate the

claim's effect in the new design. This illustrates one of the problems of reusing claims. Whereas the HCI knowledge embodied in the claim may transfer across domains, this is less certain for claim–artefact combinations because the artefact's user interface frequently contains domain-specific details.

For the training version of the application, claims indexed on the Education–Training metadomain were matched by using design issues, agents, and their associated tasks. This is illustrated with the Color-Coded Telegraphic Display (Singley & Carroll, 1996). The desired effect of the design is to improve learning by provision of summary, but expandable, feedback; however, this depends on tracking the user's progress in learning tasks and a known goal structure. The learning task subject matter in this case is the fire-fighting procedure and the artefact consists of a monitoring process that tracked the users' completion of an operation and signalled progress in a simple checkbox display (see Fig. 8.6).

The preformed query claim, derived from the original artefact shown in Fig. 8.6, is given as follows.

Claim ID:	PQ1.
Title:	Preformed query claim.
Author:	Sutcliffe, A. G.
Artefact:	Preformed query library (INTUITIVE class) and UI menu selector.
Description:	A preformed query is attached to an icon or placed in a menu.
Upsides:	Provides rapid access to information; saves users effort in articulating queries.
Downsides:	Finding queries in a large library can be difficult; queries are inflexible, cannot be adapted.
Usage scenario:	The user interface presents a menu of queries that can be reused. The user selects a query that matches his or her need by selecting an icon or a menu option, and the system retrieves the information for presentation.
Effect:	The user can retrieve information by reusing familiar queries.
Dependencies:	Information needs and queries must be known; future information needs must be predictable.
Issues:	Query format, customizability of values and constraint clauses, addressing queries to different databases.
Theory:	Models of information searching (Ingwersen, 1996).
Scope:	Information retrieval tasks with predictable needs.

The GoalPoster tool and its companion claim could be reused to improve the checklist display; however, the dependencies point out that detecting updates in the task may be a problem. If updates can be easily recorded, the display will give improved feedback for the user (the ship's captain), but the downside is that the captain will have to learn the cryptic labels and display color coding. This might not be appropriate for the decision-support task of emergency control, although it could be acceptable for the tutorial system. Notice that the original claim was motivated by support for learning. The check box display in the training system was also used in the decision-support version. Evaluation of the artefact demonstrated that the progress tracking checklist was a useful aide-memoire for ships' captains during training and ordinary task operation.

Research on INTUITIVE created a toolkit of reusable classes that provided information retrieval services such as query facilities, navigation maps, browsers, and presenters for displaying results. Developing and evaluating these artefacts resulted in specification of claims for the Information Retrieval generalized task (see appendix C).

Design exemplars that explain application of the claim are referenced either as artefacts as examples, such as the INTUITIVE map displays of searchable resources and query templates (Sutcliffe et al., 1995); or to design patterns to address the problem (Sutcliffe & Dimitrova, 1999); or as research on how to solve the problem, in which case how a model may be used to help users articulate queries and refine their needs (Ingwersen, 1996).

The preformed query from the INTUITIVE claim was reused in the Multimedia Broker system, a Web-based broking application (Sutcliffe & Carroll, 1998). The prototype embodying this claim is illustrated in Fig. 8.7. In this case not only the claim but also its associated software artefact could be reused by customizing the INTUITIVE class. The basic functionality of the reusable query class and its components, that is, a library of queries, a selection mechanism for the user, and a means of submitting the query to a database, were transferred to the Multimedia Broker; however, the new requirements specified tailorable queries.

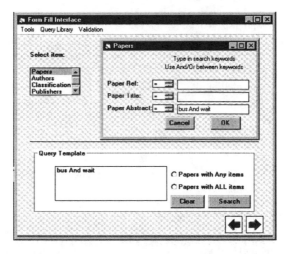

FIG. 8.7. Multimedia Broker implementation of the generic preformed query claim to support the user's Information Retrieval task.

The user interface for preformed queries in INTUITIVE was icons that enabled hypertextlike query by pointing. The user-interface manifestation of the preformed query is different in the Broker system, as the query buttons were redesigned as minimenus allowing the user to enter a limited set of keywords to customize the query. This mitigates one of the claim's downsides (inflexible queries), but the claim now appears in a different user-interface context and has new functionality in the keyword additions.

This indicates that a new child claim may have to be developed from the preformed query parent. When to evolve new claims is a matter of judgment about how the original claim and artefact fits the new application requirements. If reuse initiates functional redesign, it will require usability evaluation of the new task–artefact combination, and this will initiate a new task–artefact cycle. The usability payoff of the original claim may be compromised by changes in the user interface; however, the continuity of the artefact design for a similar task context gives reasonable confidence, if not a guarantee, that reuse in Multimedia Broker would pay off. Subsequent evaluation justified this decision and validated the new claim for customizable preformed queries (Sutcliffe, Ennis, & Hu, 2000).

8.6. SUMMARY

The claims reuse process commences with factoring the contributions of complex claims and artefacts. A walkthrough method based on Norman's model indicates where contributions are located for different stages of interaction. This leads to specification of new child claims. Generalization of claims involves removing domain-specific references and then attaching them to Domain Theory models. The models provide a general context for reuse. Reuse commences by retrieving claims. This is effected either by searching for appropriate domain models or by searching claims directly by using keywords or similarity search with LSI. Claims provide advice on pros and cons of an argument, issues, and dependencies. The advice can be revealed in increasing layers of complexity to suit the designer's needs. Claims are reused by interpreting the design advice and customizing the associated artefact. The process of reuse from one project to another related information-retrieval application resulted in claims evolution.

9

New Concepts

9.1. INTRODUCTION

This final chapter reflects on how software might be developed in the future by component-based engineering, and it speculates about the merits of different approaches to the reuse problem and which ones are likely to succeed. The tension between knowledge reuse and creative thought is investigated, and the framework for reuse introduced in chapter 2 is revisited to compare different approaches. However, first some time is spent in summarizing the problem.

The world of business, indeed the world in general, is changing at an increasingly faster rate. Businesses struggle to bring products to market, and we all struggle to deal with new technology and ways of working. Software has to keep pace. However, we find software legacy systems hard to change, and some software systems that take years to develop become obsolete before they are implemented. Software systems in the future will have to evolve. There are two main responses to this problem: either build generator systems that evolve by creating new versions from high-level descriptions of requirements, or develop component-based engineering in which new versions can be designed by flexible assembly of reusable components. Of course, there are approaches in between that incorporate ideas from both directions.

Software systems are currently inflexible monoliths or unreliable hastily produced applications. Time to market is an ever-pressing mantra for software developers who have less time to think and clarify requirements as well as less time to construct well-designed software. The result is poorly designed software that no one wants and everyone has to struggle with. Given the time pressure on developers, software reuse rather than reinventing the wheel seems to be an obvious solution. Unfortunately, this has not been the success story many had expected.

9.1.1. Reuse History Revisited

Even though reuse might not be an all-pervasive design practice, there are commercial success stories in ERPs and to a lesser extent application frameworks. Unfortunately, reuse of ERPs is not easy. Considerable effort has to be spent on adapting generic ERPs to the requirements of a business; even then the design is somewhat inflexible, so that business and people have to adapt to the software rather that the software being fitted to the user. The design of each ERP module assumes that it encapsulates software support for business best practice in a sector, for example, manufacturing, planning and control, payroll, logistics, and so on. However, even with globalization causing convergence on an American view of best practice, this is not acceptable in a variety of cultures, so the ERP view that one size fits all may not work in the long run. Although ERPs have been a great success to date, they are struggling to keep up. The Internet demands flexible and rapid service delivery, which is stressing the connection to ERP "back end" systems in many countries. SAP and other ERP vendors have recognized the need to adapt to the fast-moving Internet marketplace, but they may just be stuck with their own legacy problem: large monolithic general application systems.

The patterns community has made an impact in a less commercial manner. Object-oriented patterns have been shared since the "gang of four" launched them into the developer community (Gamma et al., 1995). A large number of program design patterns have emerged from PLOP conferences (Harrison et al., 1999; Rising, 1998), and patterns have diversified into human–computer interaction design (Borchers, 2000; Borchers & Muhlhauser, 1998; Tidwell, 2000), the Education metadomain with pedagogical patterns (Pedagogical Patterns Project, 2000), project management, and organization design (Coplein, 1999). The patterns community has evolved as bottom up, self-motivated initiative by groups of like-minded people who wish to share knowledge. Indeed, the development of patterns mirrors the evolution of the Internet and is probably a consequence of it. Patterns are typically published on websites rather than as scholarly papers. Some discipline and consensus is encouraged by writer workshops and pattern language conferences. Pattern authors submit their work to a group of peers to critique and improve before it is "published" or released. In the PLOP conference series, authors are assigned a shepherd or mentor who helps to edit and revise the pattern. The mentoring–critiquing process continues at writers' workshops; however, these rarely cause radical restructuring of patterns. Improvement helps clarity but the pattern content is mainly determined by the author's input, and the guarantee for its effectiveness and validity lies with the author's integrity. Patterns are a democratic movement that is very worthwhile, but it suffers from inconsistency and lack of standards. A patterns Tower of Babel has evolved. The original gang of four patterns have become a de facto standard, but there are not very many of them and they apply to a single domain: the design of object-oriented software. This has facilitated effective reuse. The same cannot be said for the plethora of other patterns. The Tower of Babel may evolve into tribes who can effectively communicate in certain domains, for instance telecommunications software, but this process will be limited by the motivation of small groups of like-minded people.

Application frameworks (Fayad & Johnson, 2000) have attempted to create some standardization but only within the area of each framework, for example, communications software, GUI components, and the like. Sharing components and reuse has been limited as a result. Non-object-oriented component libraries have fared little better. When there is a narrow domain that is well understood by a community of designers, reuse works. The original designers and the reuser–designers share sufficient knowledge that components can be understood and reused effectively. Furthermore, the range of components is usually modest (100–200; Arango et al., 1993; Tracz, 1995). One reaction to the reuse problem is standardization. If only everyone agreed on a common format for sharing patterns, components, and knowledge then, surely, reuse would be easier. The knowledge-engineering community realized this some years ago and came up with the solution in the Knowledge Sharing effort, Ontolingua and the Knowledge Interchange Format (KIF; Gruber, 1993a). Unfortunately, agreeing a format does not standardize content and granularity. The influence of a representation language on abstraction is also limited. The upshot is that formal knowledge reuse has been slow to spread. It is restricted to communities of researchers who agree on more detailed formats for content and message structures (e.g., KADS; Tansley & Hayball, 1993).

Knowledge reuse in business has been successful at the informal level, but attempts to format and structure knowledge for more effective reuse have not met with much practical success. People, particularly managers, like their knowledge in informal natural language that they can comprehend without much effort, even if they have to put up with the pain of ambiguity and misinterpretation. Knowledge reuse is like learning a foreign language: most of us will avoid it if we can get the material we want in our own. Only when we realize that to understand the material in depth brings additional rewards will we make the effort of reading a text in a foreign language. Formatting and representing knowledge for reuse is similar. The perceived, additional benefit of encoded, structured knowledge is not immediately apparent.

From this perspective, the future of reuse may seem to be uninspiring, but that may not be true. In the next section I propose how and why reuse may prosper.

9.1.2. New Approaches

So a new vision is needed. One view is to see software as a service (Brereton et al., 1999). Software becomes a set of downloadable services that can be composed to create applications. Software is almost a consumable in the marketing definition: you download it, presumably pay for it, and then throw it away. But what happens when we unpack this vision? First it begs the question of what a service is. Ideally software should act as a well-trained servant who understands one's requirements perfectly and then delivers the required goods or request efficiently but unobtrusively. So at the core of the concept is understanding requirements. There is the assumed intelligence of finding the appropriate solution for the request and delivering the service in an efficient manner. Implicit in the idea is reuse by composition, because only by composing applications from a larger number of smaller components can flexibility in responding to demand be achieved.

The aim for all design is to achieve an optimal fit between the product and the requirements of the customer population. Leaving aside the problems of market development and customer education, generally the better the fit between users' needs and application functionality, the greater the users' satisfaction. Product fit will be a function of the generality–specialization dimension of an application. This can be summarized in the law of user satisfaction.

- The user satisfaction supplied by a general application will be in inverse proportion to its complexity and variability in the user population.

The ideal is to have applications composed to fit our individual needs; general products become progressively less satisfactory as they try to cater for more and more users with diverse needs. The consequences flowing from this law are that design by reuse will be more difficult with a heterogeneous user population, because getting the right fit for each subgroup of individuals becomes progressively more challenging and expensive. The second consequence is that larger-scale and hence more complex components will be more difficult to tailor to users; also, people have a larger learning burden with complex products. The implications are that complex general products tend to make us frustrated because we cannot easily get them to do what we want. Furthermore, the more different types of user there are in a population (gender, age, different cultures), the harder it is for a general product to suit all. The reaction of designers is to strive for adaptable products, but that just increases complexity either overtly by giving users extra work filling in extensive profiles, or covertly by intelligent adaptive interfaces that rarely guess exactly what we want. The second law relates to the effort users will be willing to devote to improving the fit between their requirements and the product.

- The effort a user will devote to customizing a software product is inversely proportional to its complexity and the variability in the user population.

This implication follows on from the first law, in that the more complex a product is the more effort we have to devote to customizing palettes, user profiles, setting parameters, and so on. Furthermore, general products may not motivate us to spend much time on customization because the utility they deliver is less than a perceived ideal of our specific requirements. We can formulate this problem as a third law.

- User effort in customizing and learning software is proportional to the perceived utility of a product in achieving a job of work or entertainment.

People will devote considerable effort to learning how to use a product even if it is poorly designed, as long as they are motivated. Motivation itself is a complex subject. Classical models (Maslow et al., 1987) point toward several layers of motivation directed toward different rewards, ranging from basic needs (hunger or sex) to higher-order self-esteem and altruism. Teenagers already spend considerable time learning and adapting games software that rewards them with excitement; however, most business software only rewards us by getting a job done. Any effort expended in customizing software is not motivated by a direct reward, so we tend to resent this imposition on our time. Our motivation will depend critically on perceived utility and then the actual utility payoff. For work-related applications we are likely to spend time customizing and configuring software only if we are confident that it will empower our work, save time on the job, and raise productivity. Unfortunately, we rarely have any confidence that customizing a product will help. For personal productivity tools, the motivation may be higher than for more general-purpose business software that is regarded as part of the job. Technology acceptance models (Davis, 1993) point out that decisions to adopt technology depend on utility, usability, and possibly fun. Given that fun is going to be limited in many work domains, utility and ease of use will be critical for competitive advantage. However, these have to be offset against the effort of learning. Some adaptation–customization effort may be offloaded on to the customers, but only when the perceived utility (i.e., the customers' expectation for the product before they have used it) is high.

Adaptation causes users work. Software should therefore spare us the burden. Intelligent agents can automatically detect our requirements and provide appropriate services. Unfortunately, adaptation is a double-edged sword. It is fine as long as the adaptation is accurate and fits with our requirements, but when the machine makes mistakes and adapts in the wrong direction, it inflicts a double penalty because incorrect adaptation is perceived as a fault. First we have to understand what has happened as the new dialogue, feature, or function is unexpected. Then we have to adapt our behavior to work around the system's misguided initiative. If this were not bad enough, we also feel resentment at the "damned machine" taking initiative and getting it wrong. This soon gives an adverse image of the computer and lowers our motivation to use it effectively. This leads to the fourth law.

- The acceptability of adaptation is inversely proportional to system errors in adaptation, with the corollary that inappropriate adaptation inflicts a triple penalty on our motivation (cost of diagnosing mistakes, cost of working around, and negative emotions about system usurping human roles).

Hence adaptation cannot afford to be wrong, but adaptation is one of the most difficult problems for machines to model, as pointed out in chapter 2. Even if the system could gather perfect knowledge of its environment and had perfect interpretation, other (human) agents could change their minds. Such change cannot be anticipated short of clairvoyance. Some system mistakes are therefore inevitable in adaptation. Given the heavy penalty for maladaptation, this approach to software evolution may be ill advised unless there is a high user motivation that will tolerate mistakes. An interesting aside on the adaptation problem concerns safety critical systems. In dangerous or time critical systems, software has to adapt to events in the environment and make decisions when humans are too slow. Adaptation is taken on trust in many cases but, when the consequences of machine mistakes become apparent in unusual circumstances, the results can be catastrophic. This has led many to distrust complex command and control systems for avionics, nuclear power plants, and the like.

If only we could express our requirements in the first place, then maybe the application could be composed to fit our needs without having to be adapted or customized. The ideal in this case is to have a natural-language understanding system linked to an application generator. Unfortunately this implies considerable artificial intelligence and currently intractable problems in general purpose natural-language understanding, as demonstrated by the CYC project (Lenat, 1995) that has devoted many years' research to natural-language understanding and commonsense reasoning, without much success. However, more specialized, domain-specific sublanguages may hold the answer (Grishman & Kittredge, 1986). The trade-off is between the constraints imposed on users in restricting their means of expressing their needs and the accuracy of requirements statements for machine interpretation. At one end of this dimension are formal requirements languages that have been developed for specific domains (Freeman, 1987; Liete, St Anna, & De Freitas, 1994; Neighbors, 1984), or more general-purpose expressions in Taxis–Requirements Modeling Language (RML; Greenspan, Borgida, & Mylopoulos, 1986). These impose a learning burden on users who have to translate their requirements into an essentially foreign language. An example of these complex requirements languages is the plan calculus in the Requirements Apprentice (Reubenstein & Waters, 1989), which could be used to specify detailed requirements for library systems but not in a form that users could comprehend. In some cases the language has been used to create a domain analysis to specify a library of rules, components, and constraints to generate applications in particular areas such as air traffic control scheduling and flight planning (Smith, 1992).

Closer to the user are sublanguages that do not require learning a foreign vocabulary or syntax. Sublanguages are subsets of natural language that have limited vocabularies, restricted syntax, and telegraphic expressions to code specific meanings (Grishman & Kittredge, 1986; Harris, 1989). An example is the language of air traffic control, which is terse and ritualized. Instructions are easily understood by the professional in the domain, for example, "BA 3450 turn right heading two five oh, descend 10000" will be understood by the pilot of the British Airways flight as an instruction to turn right on to compass heading 250 (southwest) and descend from the current height to 10,000 ft, but no further. Sublanguages are familiar to professionals and sufficiently terse for limited natural-language processing. The narrow domain enables an expert system to be built so that statements can be interpreted accurately. Indeed, many commercial expert systems exist in sublanguage domains. However, the domain restriction is the Achilles' heel of the approach. Many system generators have to be developed, each targeted on a specific domain. Strangely, this approach has seen little research in software engineering. The only successful generative technologies exist for design domains where the users will accept a specialist requirements language and the domain knowledge is well known. Some examples are high-level hardware definition languages that allow automatic creation of electronic circuits and chips (Edwards, 1995), transformation of database schema definitions into database implementations (Batory, 1998), and automatic transformations of UML specifications into executable code (Kennedy-Carter, 2000). These specialized generator applications have not enjoyed commercial success compared with general-purpose application generators, which have grown out of the fourth-generation language movement (e.g., Powerbuilder). Although these products impose considerable burdens on users who have to learn a new (programming) language, end-user computing empowered by such languages is one rival for reuse-driven approaches.

In summary, reuse by application generators is but one of the competing approaches for the future of software engineering. As with many endeavors in life, there is a trade-off between process-oriented and structured approaches. The structured approach is exemplified by reuse patterns and component libraries, whereas the process approach starts with linguistic expression of requirements and then automatically generates applications. The choices and their trade-offs are as follows. In reuse by component libraries and patterns, and design by composition, there is a high cost of design for the library and some design cost in reuse; however, the user–task fit is potentially good. In application generation from requirement languages, there is a high design cost for the generator but low design costs for each application; the user–task fit depends on language expressibility, but there are domain limitations.

The laws of functionality and adaptation-related costs apply to general features of design, so the next step is to elaborate the framework for software reuse that enables competing approaches to be compared.

9.2.   FRAMEWORK FOR
SOFTWARE EVOLUTION

Software will always have a cost. It is knowledge intensive and people intensive to construct. There are some approaches in the gift economy where software is freely distributed, Linux being a well-known example; however, it is unlikely that most software houses will follow Torvas Linvald's example. Like most products, software has a perceived utility that governs the price people are willing to pay for it. We can apply marketing theory to any software product and predict that a product's success will depend on

- *Price*: in relation to the perceived utility and competitor products;
- *Population*: of purchasers of the product;
- *Place*: the localization of the market, the spread of publicity, and knowledge about the product; and
- *Promotion*: advertising and the level of education of potential customers about the merits of the product.

Clearly these factors interact, as knowledge of the product spreads by publicity, the market place becomes more educated, and more potential purchasers are available. Early entry products sometimes fail because of insufficient market education, leaving a successor product to reap the rewards (e.g., the Xerox Star workstation that Apple capitalized on with the Macintosh). Early products tend to compete on functionality and features and have few competitors, whereas more mature products face many competitors, compete more on usability than functionality, and have lower price margins (Norman, 1999). This digression into marketing theory has a point. The appeal of a development approach may depend on the maturity of the product. Innovative applications will always be designed de novo, even if their design depends on reused components. Innovative products are unlikely to be developed by the generative approach because it would take longer to develop the generator for requirements in a new domain than it would to develop the product from scratch. Another implication is the impact of perceived utility and the importance of usability. Users in immature markets tend to have higher expectations of perceived utility, particularly early adopters, so they will put up with design and customization burdens. The fit between the users' need and product functionality has more tolerance. This is less true in mature markets, in which supplier reputations have developed and users place more value on usability and an exact fit to their needs.

Therefore we need to consider not only costs of the product but also costs of adoption by the user. Technology acceptance models (Davis, 1993), based on the theory of adaptive decision making (Ajzen & Fishbein, 1980), assert that purchasing (or any other) decisions are governed by weighing the merits of attributes of rival products. Thus the question is, What will those attributes be? I propose that they will be the following.

Perceived utility is the expected value to the individual in saving time, increasing performance or quality, and achieving the user's goal for work-oriented software; for entertainment applications this will be the perceived potential for excitement and fun. Actual utility is the value experienced by the individual accumulated over time, which may be very different from expectations. Usability is the ease of learning and ease of use, which will be more important in mature markets. Cost of purchase is the acceptable cost that will be influenced by the perceived and actual utility and the individual's (or organization's) relative wealth. Brand identity and reputation: purchasers often prefer supply from a reputable source. Finally, convenience is the ease of setup and the time to effect use.

These variables will have complex relationships. For example, Media Communication Theory (Daft, Lengel, & Trevino, 1987) points out that information about products can be obtained from broadcast or narrowcast sources. Advertising is broadcast whereas word of mouth recommendations are targeted advice. Product surveys and reference sites fit in between. Brand identity, trust, and perceived utility may be acquired from several sources and the importance attached to this information will vary according to the users' trust of the source. The transformation of perceived utility into actual utility depends on experience, but experience may have a history. If the customer has experience of similar products from the same supplier, and those experiences have been positive, then trust will have been created. Moreover, this will have a positive effect on perceived utility for the next generation of products. Conversely, if the experience was negative, then trust and perceived utility will be affected adversely. So the success of a development approach will depend on the perceived utility of the generator or component library and the usability of each approach. Usability may be reflected in the trade-off between understanding a requirements language or a design support tool.

Purchasing decisions will be a function of cost–benefit trade-offs. Cost will be incurred by a less than perfect task fit for the customer population in question, design and configuration effort incurred to improve the task fit, cost of failures (software reliability and usability errors), and convenience costs in setup. Set against these costs, the benefit side of the equation is composed of perceived utility, plus actual utility for repeat purchases, and values established by trust of the supplier and brand identity. These can be summarized as follows.

$$\text{Value} f (\text{PercUt} + \text{Brand}) - \text{Costs}(\text{Design} + \text{Task-fit} + \text{Usab} + \text{Reliab} + \text{Conv} + \text{Errors}).$$

Acceptability and purchase will depend on the value–purchase price balance for any one user or organization. Thus if brand identity and perceived utility are low, lowering reuse design, usability and convenience costs will not dramatically increase the relative value, and purchase is less likely. Note that perceived utility, usability, and convenience are all a function of experience, which may be adverse, so use and acceptance may not follow purchase when the actual utility and convenience do not agree with expected values. Clearly the value placed on the variables will be different in corporate and individual purchasing decisions. Individuals will value usability and convenience more, whereas managers may (but shouldn't) place more weight on utility. In mature markets, users will place more weight on the costs so products will have to minimize these by better usability, reliability, and convenience with excellent task fit and low design costs.

Another factor in the purchasing equation is reputation. This is the collected wisdom of other users that relates to usability and actual utility. As the Internet lowers the costs of spreading information in electronic fora and catalogues, reputation information will feed back more rapidly and poor products will become eliminated. For reuse libraries the key factors are going to be the utility, usability, and convenience side of the equation. These will be influenced by the development cost factors described in chapter 2. Adaptable products, in theory, should outscore other approaches, as they could ideally adapt functionality to suit the users' actual utility needs, improve usability by adapting to users' characteristics, and reduce convenience costs by autoconfiguration. Unfortunately, adaptable products often make mistakes in interpreting users' requirements, whether input as a sublanguage or inferred from user behavior. The sting of high error costs makes adaptation a risky strategy. Reuse and component-based engineering will increase design costs for the user and reduce convenience, so they will only be acceptable to end users if they achieve good utility and usability. Unfortunately, component-based engineering has no easy means of persuading users to climb the hump of motivation and effort to reap the rewards of design by reuse (Fig. 9.1).

9.3.   MODELS OF EVOLVING SOFTWARE

The two reuse paradigms are investigated in more depth to set out the requirements that generative software architectures and components engineering will have to achieve to succeed in delivering cost-effective software evolution.

9.3.1.   Component Engineering

This paradigm assumes that software will be composed from components. Design might be achieved by designers working directly with component libraries, but more probably they will build applications from a high-level specification–requirements language with automated support for component selection. Reusable components may be specifications, designs, possibly code, and, for claims and design rationale, information about generalized design principles and a history of design decisions. In the future, products of the design process (specifications, etc.) and products themselves will be integrated. As components may be reused in many different contexts, organizations, and applications, metadata or descriptions about

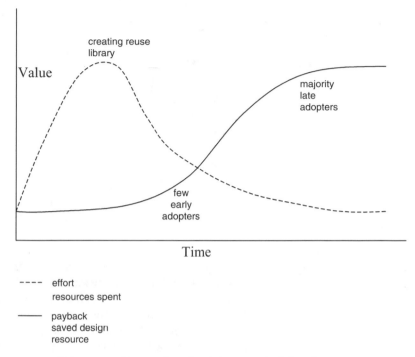

creating reuse
library

Value

majority
late
adopters

few
early
adopters

Time

- - - - effort
resources spent

——— payback
saved design
resource

FIG. 9.1. Effort and payback in reuse-led development.

the components' capabilities, limitations, and design features should accompany it. Thus a future reusable component might be as illustrated in Fig. 9.2.

The component has an onion layer structure of high-level explanation of its functionality, design history, and potential application contexts on the outside. The metadata layer might contain goals for functional descriptions, design rationale, claims, and scenarios of use. The next layer contains detailed design information as specifications of the components, user interfaces, data structures, and algorithms. The inner layer consists of software code, possibly with adaptation mechanisms that can be acted on by an application generation environment.

The first approach is largely passive. Components are contained in a library, retrieved according to their description, and then used to compose applications either manually or automatically by a component interpreter–composer. The second model assumes more active, agentlike components. These embed intelligence in each layer, so explanations for designers can be customized and reusable agents can collaborate with each other and application generation environments. This model begs the perennial question of distributed computing: What degree of centralization and standardization is required within a set of distributed resources? Clearly component agents are going to require a *lingua franca* to communicate. That much has been realized by standardized knowledge exchange languages

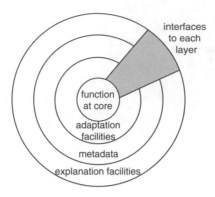

FIG. 9.2. Model of an active reusable component that is wrapped with adaptation facilities and metadata so it can explain its functionality and adapt to new application environments.

such as KIF and Ontalingua (Gruber, 1993a, 1993b). However, even if agents can exchange data and information, they still have to interpret messages. This leads back into the knowledge-acquisition and adaptation trap. Each agent needs to embed a model of its environment so it can interpret messages from that environment. This revisits the embedding models of the world dilemma that appeared in chapter 1. The more a software design tries to embed a model of the external world within itself, the more complex it becomes and the problem of maintaining an accurate picture of the external world gets worse. Dividing the system into agents hasn't made the problem go away. Each agent now needs a model not only of the external world but also of all the other agents in its designed world (Fig. 9.3).

Thus the multiagent peer group with intelligent components as a strategy for software evolution is fraught with some danger. It may succeed in narrow, prescribed domains where agents and their responsibilities can be well defined. In narrow domains the necessary knowledge of each other and the world might be embedded in a population of different agent types. Unfortunately, reuse has to transgress narrow domain boundaries. This will give distributed agents the CYC problem, how to learn enough about the world to interpret it. Distributed learning machines may solve this problem in the future, but current learning systems favor a centralized architecture approach, and even then progress is slow.

However, a compromise solution may be successful. Embedding some intelligence in component–agents may make the composition process more effective. If the agent has knowledge of its own competences, then it could interpret requests from a generation environment and suggest possible services and customization thereof, or warn about its limitations and performance requirements. The question is how much knowledge to embed. It will be easier to agree to the specification of sets of semi-intelligent reusable components than a set of intelligent agents with more complex and less predictable behavior. However, reasoning for reuse

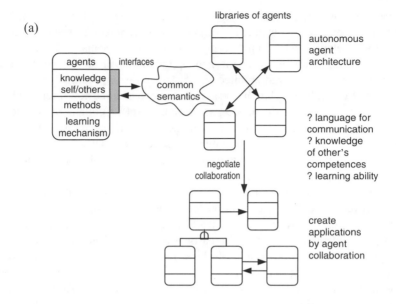

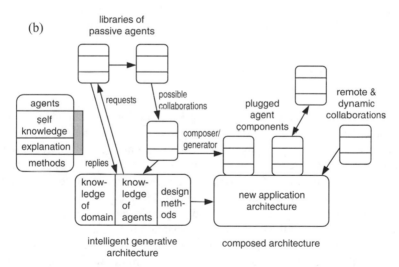

FIG. 9.3.   Intelligent components and agent-based reuse: (a) peer-group agents approach and (b) centralized control model.

depends on knowledge of the new application context. This will naturally be located with the generative architecture or composition mechanism. Hence it makes sense to restrict the ambitions of intelligent agent solutions because it makes the reuse problem worse. Knowledge of the new application will always be localized to an extent, so a centralized architecture that acquires requirements will be more efficient. A centralized solution also avoids the need to agree how inferential ability and design knowledge should be partitioned. A set of collaborating intelligent agents may take longer to discover each one's domain capabilities than actually cooperating. Furthermore, distributing intelligence creates worse incompatibilities and longer negotiations when two or more agents have slightly different versions of the same capabilities.

Responsibilities will be partitioned between agents that contain knowledge of design solutions and the composition–generation environment that has responsibility for domain knowledge. If architectures could be built that had wide-ranging domain knowledge, then they could reason about requirements and transform them into properties of desired design solutions. The generative architecture could then search for design components, interrogate them for their capabilities, and select the most appropriate ones. The key transformation is from application requirements from the real world to design requirements. This is where the Domain Theory models can play a role. They form an intermediate layer of knowledge that could be embedded as a knowledge base for transforming requirements into designs.

9.3.2. Programming for Adaptable Software

An alternative to component engineering is to develop programming languages that can create adaptable software. This approach has been researched for some time in aspect-oriented and subject-oriented programming languages (Czarnecki & Eisenecker, 2000; Kiczales, des Rivieres, & Bobrow, 1991). Aspects are common recurring properties of a program that appear in many places, essentially a variant of the common subroutine problem. Rather than calling the common routine in numerous places, aspect-oriented languages have compilers that offload this concern and adapt the code by late, dynamic binding at run time. Examples of aspects might be error-handling routines, communications protocols, adaptive handling of devices, drivers, and so on. The programmer writes references to the aspect at join points in the code, which cause the compiler to weave the aspects into the code at appropriate points.

A close relative to aspect languages is subject-oriented programming, developed by IBM. In this case the reusable component or concern is a highly cohesive, loosely coupled module. Subject-oriented programming environments facilitate the development of highly modular reusable code, so they go beyond aspect, which primarily address the common subroutine problem of cross-cutting functionality.

However, both aspect languages and subject-oriented programming are providing tools to facilitate reuse and generation of adaptable software. The tools are for software engineers, so they are little help for nonspecialists. For end users to be empowered, generative architectures and requirements languages are necessary.

9.3.3. Application Generation Architectures

Assuming a set of components are developed that encapsulate metadata about their own capabilities with limited explanation facilities, what might a component engineering architecture look like? The approach will depend on assumptions about involvement by human designers. One philosophy is to automate the process as far as possible so the user–designer specifies his or her requirements in a high-level language and the generative architecture composes a new application (see Fig. 9.4). The other approach is to make the process more transparent to the user with less automation. The consequences of each approach will be examined in turn.

Generation necessitates a soundly based means of expressing requirements. This has been researched for many years, and domain-oriented languages have been developed for specifying electrical circuits and formatting text documents; however, the scope of domain-oriented languages has not dramatically increased over the years. Unfortunately, domain-oriented languages do not really express

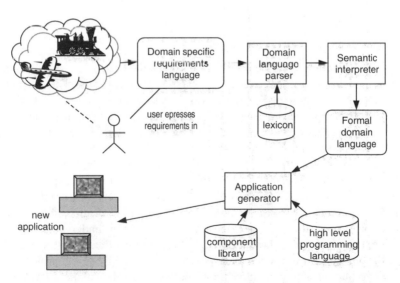

FIG. 9.4. The relationship among application domains, requirements languages, and generative architectures.

high-level requirements; furthermore, they require considerable knowledge of the language and its syntax to specify a design.

The question for designers of future generator environments is which requirements language to choose. Sublanguages based on natural language will be easier for users to understand, but these languages are restricted to narrow professional domains. Specialized technical languages will be more acceptable for users when the requirements language is already part of the users' knowledge. However, this still leaves a large class of applications for which no specialist language exists. For these, general-purpose requirements languages or end-user programming languages may be the answer.

For technical domains, application generation systems will be worth the investment if the domains are reasonably stable over time; for instance, in civil, mechanical, and other branches of engineering. In other domains in which sublanguages exist, generative architectures may also be worth the investment if reasonable stability can be assumed. This seems to be an opportunity for software engineering research, as many of these domains currently develop systems by informal software evolution over versions, for example, air traffic control systems and many other command and control systems. Generative architectures driven by sublanguage interpreters may be the answer; however, there is a danger in sublanguages. They usually express operational concepts in a domain, that is, command instructions and reports, rather than design requirements. Thus considerable human expertise is still going to be necessary to interpret the design implications implicit within sublanguage utterances.

9.3.4. End-User Programming or Component Engineering?

The future approach to software evolution comes down to a few simple choices. On one hand there is the language process approach in which users have to express requirements and automated processes do the rest. On the other hand there is the structural reuse approach: give users components and let them build applications by themselves. Both approaches impose some learning burden on users and designers. These costs are summarized in Table 9.1.

If designers follow the component engineering route, then they have to learn about the properties and facilities offered by components. Self-explaining components can reduce this burden partially, as can well-designed components for black-box reuse. However, this will only be possible in well-understood domains. The end-user programming approach imposes a different understanding cost, in learning the requirements language. If the language is already part of the users' or designers' technical vocabulary then these costs will be negligible, so end-user programming with generative architectures should be competitive in narrow technical communities. Implementation costs for end-user programming are minimal. Once the requirements have been specified, the system automatically creates

TABLE 9.1
Relative Costs for End-User Programming and Component Engineering

Approach	Understanding	Implemen.– Develop.	Initial Invest.	Payoff	Limitations
End-user program.	Requirements language	Expressing requirements	high: many generators	technical & general domains	Narrow domains
Component eng.	Component design & functions	Design & test; Expressing requirements	high: component library	technical domains	None if appropriate library exists

the product. In contrast, component engineering always incurs some design and implementation costs, even in black-box reuse. However, these costs could be hidden in a hybrid approach that generates applications from a requirements language using a component library.

Initial investment costs are considerable in both approaches. Component engineering has to create the reuse library and support tools, whereas the generator approach has to develop the application generator architecture and environment. If the ideal of a general-purpose requirements language were achievable, then economies of scale would favor this approach, but such an ideal is many years in the future. Practical application generators could be built for many separate and narrow domains, so there is an interesting economic balance between developing many generators for several domains, and component libraries with support tools that could cover a similar span of domains if the library is comprehensive and the level of abstraction offers good comparability.

The payoff between these two approaches presents a paradox. End-user programming from one viewpoint seems to be the superior approach. In narrow technical domains where sublanguages exist, users will incur few costs with this approach. Component engineering, in contrast, will always impose understanding and design costs, although these may be acceptable for technical users who are already familiar with the reuse library and design architectures. Component engineering is therefore likely to compete more effectively among designers rather than end users. Even with technical users, cost offloading by application generator front ends on component libraries may be appealing, but the loss of control over the final design may limit the spread of generators among designers. Accepting application generators means that designers abrogate their responsibility for design detail. This may clash with many designers' sense of professionalism. For end users this is not a concern. They just want to get a product that fits their needs as painlessly as possible. Component engineering may be acceptable for the more technically minded early adopters. These individuals will put up with the learning and design burden. However, for the majority late adopters, component engineering will never be the answer. The costs will always be too high.

The end-user programming approach appears to be the only acceptable way for most users, but it is likely to be difficult for several years to come. General-purpose requirements languages will be the semiformal expressions of designs, and end-user programming will indeed be programming rather than specification. In narrow technical user domains, sublanguages may be exploited more effectively, but this is no panacea for more open-ended domains.

So where is the future for component engineering? One prospect lies in the difference between software markets for individuals and for organizations. Corporate software tends to be more conservative. Cost reduction is a constant driver but so is reliability. Reuse libraries, once established, offer better guarantees of reliability and considerable cost reduction over bespoke development. End users, in contrast, will be more sensitive to imposed costs and product price. Either they will choose software as they currently do in the COTS (customer-off-the-shelf) market place, or more tractable requirements specification languages will evolve so that end-user programming and application generation become a low-cost (in cognitive and economic terms) alternative. However, I doubt this will happen in the near future. Natural-language processing and acquisition of sufficient domain knowledge for general-purpose reasoning are the barriers. In spite of these limitations there is still great potential for research into more generally applicable requirements languages, and application generator technology. The natural-language community has spent much effort in inferring facts, arguments, and even stories from natural-language texts in restricted domains (Cowie & Wilks, 2000; Humphreys et al., 1999). This research has to be integrated with software and requirements engineering. Initial attempts in this direction have solved the easy problems of deducing data structures and entity relationship models from natural-language texts. The more difficult problem of inferring functions, behavior, and goals from requirements expressed in natural language has yet to be addressed.

The final reflection on the future is how machine learning may play a role in software evolution. The difficulty of customizing and adapting designs to users' requirements has already been noted, but that does not mean the problem in insoluble. Building general-purpose learning machines is just as difficult as natural-language understanding. These problems are just different sides of the same artificial intelligence coin. To understand natural language you need to acquire large quantities of complex knowledge. To acquire complex knowledge takes time, and the only efficient way is to build learning processes. Acquiring requirements is a form of knowledge acquisition, so if applications could learn and then adapt to new circumstances, then this could solve the software evolution problem.

Some first steps have been taken in this direction in the concept of Requirements Monitoring (Fickas & Feather, 1995). If an application can detect changes in its environment and has an embedded model that enables it to interpret those changes, and furthermore the ability to infer the implications of those changes for design, then it could autoadapt its behavior for evolving requirements. This vision is not new. The human–computer interaction community proposed adaptive and adaptable systems some time ago (Browne et al., 1990), but progress has been slow. Unfortunately there is no simple silver bullet. Learning machines require embedded models of the world to improve efficiency of learning, as well as more sophisticated learning algorithms to infer deep knowledge for more surface-level information. This leads us back into the embedding models of the world in the machine dilemma we encountered in chapter 2.

Although general-purpose learning machines are still an open research issue, more humble adaptable components with limited ability to learn are feasible. The research questions are to find which changes in the environment are worth learning about and how to adapt to them. This will require a clear theory of abstraction that Domain Theory contributes toward. The next question will be to research how populations of agents might exchange experiences so they could help each other adapt. This is one of the grand quests of distributed artificial intelligence. Some glimmers of the future may reside in communities of artificial life in which autonomous agents compete with each other and adapt the competitive environment. If component libraries were composed of such semi-self-aware agents, then software evolution might be possible.

A means to this end is to apply the principle of Darwinian evolution to the problem. If software is to evolve then it should live or die by the laws of natural selection. These concepts have been applied to software in the form of genetic programming (Back, 1997). A population of slightly different programs is created and then run to create outputs. Survivorship criteria are applied to select only those variants that had optimal or acceptable results. The population is then allowed to evolve by adopting more lessons from biology. Programs can mutate in a semirandom fashion to create new variables, actions, or possible conditions. Crossover allows programs to exchange different segments, such as conditional tests or operations. The new population is rerun against the survival criteria, and variants that compete successfully survive to the next generation. In genetic programming these concepts are applied to microscale design changes, such as variables, ranges on conditions, and operations. Evolutionary programming has been successfully applied for deriving optimal solutions for a narrow range of algorithm optimizations, although it is less successful in generating new designs. There is an opportunity to apply such ideas to the world of requirements.

The final vision for an evolving software environment is shown in Fig. 9.5. If the generative environment became a selection mechanism for a domain then different design solutions could be run against sufficiency criteria imposed by the domain. The designs would have to be given an initial form. This would be the role of the component library. Application templates could compose a set of first-generation designs. These would be run in the domain environment, which imposes environmental constraints and sets performance criteria. The initial population of designs is reduced by (artificial) natural selection. The next generation of designs is created automatically by crossover of components between different slots in the application template, or by semirandom mutation to generate new components from the library. The mutation, crossover process would have to be controlled by rules that constrain allocation of component types to particular template slots,

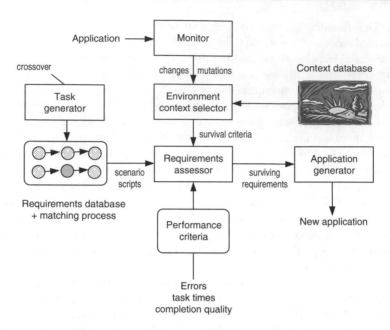

FIG. 9.5.   Software evolution environment.

but these rules are already part of many application architectures. The second generation of designs is run in the domain generation environment and natural selection takes its course. Over many runs with careful design of crossover and selection rules, the design population should stabilize with an optimal solution. The next step for software evolution is to make the domain environment capable of detecting and interpreting changes. It then changes its own survivorship parameters and triggers further design evolutions to fit with the changed requirements. This approach will not solve all reuse problems. For instance, composition rules will still have to be specified and the evolutionary mechanism will be constrained within some limits by the set of original components. Furthermore, the environment will have to be limited in scope so that a tractable set of survivorship parameters and composition rules can be specified. This approach is currently being researched in the ERSRC SIMP project for requirements evolution, with a restricted set of command and control applications. A progress report will have to await my next book on the Domain Theory's evolution.

9.4.   SUMMARY

The prospects for the future of reuse are reviewed. Two competing approaches are contrasted: first, reuse library component engineering; second, application generation by means of requirements specification languages. The costs of reuse approaches are elaborated in terms of a marketing model. Adaptation appears to be a risky strategy because of the potential cost of errors and maladaptation. Component engineering and application generation have lower costs but application generators will be more suitable for end users, whereas component engineering may prove to be acceptable for technical users and large organizations. A model of future intelligent reusable components is proposed with an application generator architecture that assembles applications from semiautonomous agents. However, this poses problems of distributing knowledge among agents, so a final vision for software evolution is to apply genetic algorithm approaches. An evolutionary application environment senses the world and sets survivorship criteria for evolution populations of applications. Both compositional approaches to reuse and requirements languages with generative architectures encounter the Tower of Babel problem. There is no escape from a *lingua franca* if reuse is to create a wide-ranging cross domain market place. Maybe standardization will take hold, but perhaps that is unrealistic. The future will probably lie in communities of reusers, domain tribes if you like, although I speculate that evolutionary programming and intelligent generative architectures may produce the eventual solution.

APPENDIX A

Specification of the OSM Library

A summary of the OSM families is shown in Fig. A. Some families in previous versions of the Domain Theory have been subsumed in others; for instance, Object Manipulation is now modeled by the Object Construction family, whereas the Object Containment family has been simplified by elimination of the Object Supply class, leaving three level 2 classes. Financial Object Exchange used to be a separate family, but as this was not identified individually in the validation experiments, it is now modeled in its appropriate structural home as a level 2 class (Accounting Object Transfer) in the Object Containment family.

Each OSM is illustrated as an informal diagram using the metaschema semantics, and as a corresponding model in UML notation (Rational Corporation, 1999); this shows classes, inheritance, aggregation, and instance relationships with message connections. Only key attributes and methods are included. Several OSMs are further illustrated with interaction diagrams.

Notation in the informal diagrams is as follows.

□   structure object
▦   agent
o   key object
➜   state transition

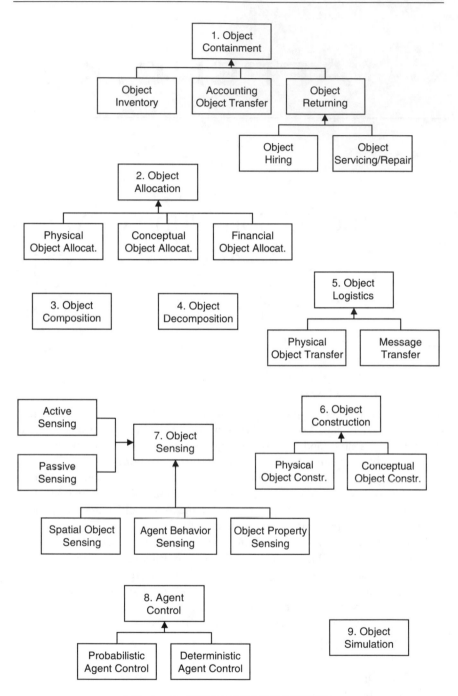

FIG. A.   Summary of the OSM families.

A1. LEVEL 1 CLASS: OBJECT CONTAINMENT

This family is characterized by the unidirectional transfer of key objects from an owning structure to a client agent who generated the request for the object. Transferred objects are moved physically into a different container and are consequently owned by a different agent. Familiar examples are sales order processing systems and inventory applications. The model has one structure object, two agents (resource requester, resource owner), one key object, and two transitions that model the request for the transaction and for delivery of the object (see Fig. A1). The common purpose of this class is the orderly transfer of resource objects from an owner to a client who requires the resource. The goal state asserts that all requests must be satisfied by transfer of key objects to the requesting client. Specializations of this class distinguish between transfer of physical objects; a separate abstraction is used for the monetary aspects of sales.

Goal state: to satisfy all resource requests by supply of resource objects.
Agents: client (requester), supplier.
Key object: resource.
Transitions: request, supply transfer.

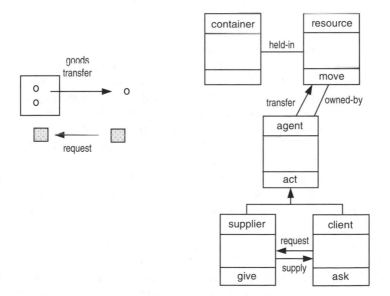

FIG. A1. Object Containment OSM.

A1.1.   Level 2 Class: Object Inventory

Synonyms: inventory management, stock control, materials supply.

This subclass family models a wide variety of inventory-type applications and is frequently aggregated with its sister class, Accounting Object Transfer, to model purchase and sales; on its own it models many systems where resources are transferred, such as internal supply or donations of resources. The key object is a physical good or a conceptual service; the structure object and agents are inherited from Object Containment. To differentiate between inbound and outbound stock control, a viewpoint concept is used. A supplier sees an outbound state transition while the receiving agent sees an inbound, stock-in transition.

Goal state:	to satisfy all resource requests by supply of resource objects.
Agents:	client (requester), supplier.
Key object:	physical resource, conceptual service.
Transitions:	request, supply transfer.

Modeling supply chains and inventory management systems is handled by aggregations of OSM models. For instance, a typical stock control system aggregates two OSM models so that one structure object models the supply of new objects, and the inbound state transition represents the transfer of objects from the supplier to the owning organization. The second OSM model represents the stock-out part of the inventory management and may be viewed in turn as a supplier to the next component in the chain. The purpose in this model (Fig. A1.1) is not only orderly transfer of objects to a client but also replenishment of resources from suppliers; hence the goal state is that all outbound requests by clients and requests initiated by the owning agent for inbound replenishment of key objects must be satisfied.

The interaction diagram shows the customer's request being clarified before the goods–product are delivered (Fig. A1.1a). This class is frequently associated with Object Allocation for product selection, Object Logistics for the delivery processes, and is coupled to the Financial Object Allocation subclasses to model the purchasing and selling financial transactions that accompany transfer of goods or services. Further associations are with transaction control generic and generalized tasks (e.g., validating orders; checking customer, i.e., Evaluate, Compare; matching customer requirements to goods and services; and planning scheduling delivery).

The requirements problems encountered with this class are as follows.

- Validation of orders, checking that details are correct.
- Allocation of stock–products to orders; when there is insufficient stock, or clashes in demand between different customers, allocation has to be rationed or prioritized. Solutions to these problems are to adopt a just-in-time rapid inventory replenishment system so that stock outages are rare, or to create

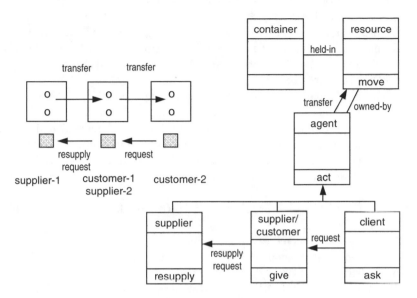

FIG. A1.1. Object Inventory OSMs in a supply chain to illustrate supplier–customer views. Agents are modeled explicitly as roles, although they could be depicted as two object instances of a class, as is the case with container.

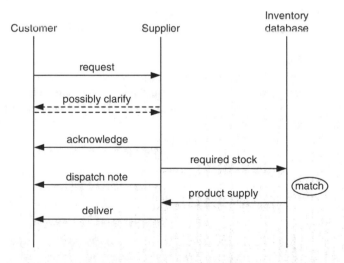

FIG. A1.1a. Interaction diagram for Object Inventory OSM.

a prioritization system so that favored major account customers have their orders allocated first.

- Ensuring the inventory database is an accurate reflection of reality, and informal allocation has not bypassed the system. This can be dealt with by frequent stock audits or automated picking systems so that informal allocation bypasses are ruled out.
- Ensuring adequate inventory levels to satisfy demand while not carrying too much stock that ties up working capital. This trade-off can be determined by forecasting functions that analyze the history of demand and project future needs based on past patterns and marketing estimates. Intelligent decision-support systems for demand forecasting in different product sectors provide solutions for these problems (Singh & Yang, 1994; Singh & Zeng, 1996).
- Managing the dispatch process; this involves coordination with the Object Logistics process.
- Checking that only creditworthy customers are supplied; this necessitates coordination with financial credit check and Accounting Object Transfer (payment) OSM.
- Checking that only reliable suppliers are used to replenish stock. The associated IR generalized task and generic tasks of selecting appropriate suppliers help to solve this problem.

Generic requirements associated with this subclass are as follows.

1. Validate orders, using range checks and look-up tables to ensure order details are correct.
2. Allocate products to orders, using matching algorithms (see generalized task).
3. Check supplier credit.
4. Demand forecasting for resupply.
5. Rapid resupply communications for just-in-time replenishment.
6. Monitor processes to check when stock levels are slow, hence triggering replenishment.
7. Audit of slow moving–unused stock.
8. Audit of actual stock, versus recorded levels.

A1.2.   Level 2 Class: Accounting Object Transfer

Synonyms: purchase ledger, bought ledger, sales accounts, accounts payable (payments outbound), sold ledger, accounts receivable (payments inbound); general ledger, cost center accounts (summary accounts).

Financial and accounting systems (Fig. A1.2) share many structural properties with other classes. Given that finance is a salient descriptor of business information

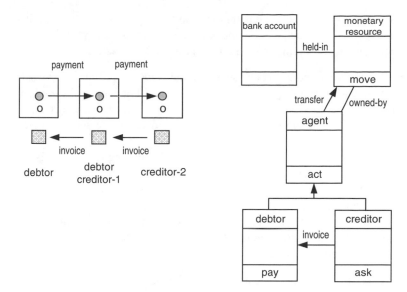

FIG. A1.2. Accounting Object Transfer OSM showing variations for accounts payable–receivable.

systems, this class is discriminated by possessing a conceptual (i.e., financial) key object. The goal state is similar to the Object Inventory Model, with the addition that a monetary value must be exchanged between agents and structure objects that model accounts. Viewpoints also apply to this class. Purchase ledger applications represent sending a purchase order by one agent to a supplier and then the transfer of a monetary key object from the owning agent's structure object (bank account) to pay for the goods. Viewed from the supplier's perspective, the same transaction is a sold ledger application that commences with dispatch of an invoice to the customer and ends with receipt of payment (i.e., a financial key object). This class is distinguished from Financial Object Allocation, which models book keeping transactions, by the object structure and transitions for internal (cost center) movements. In the Financial Object Allocation abstraction, no monetary key objects are transferred between owning agents; instead transitions are internal within the organization (structure object). Accounting Object OSMs are frequently associated with classification generic tasks.

Goal state: to satisfy all payment requests by supply of monetary objects as payment.
Agents: client (requester), supplier.
Key objects: money, financial documents.
Transitions: invoice, payment.

Further specializations of this class subdivide the structure object to represent cost centers and accounting units. These may be based on logical or physical units of the organizations. Cost center accounts are aggregated to model profit and loss accounts when all the payments inbound and outbound are reconciled and adjustments made for acquisition and amortization of assets.

Requirements problems associated with this class are as follows.

- Nonfunctional requirements: security, and fraud prevention.
- The need for accuracy and updating integrity of accounts. Failure to implement sound cross-posting procedures can result in inconsistent accounts, such as the total in the summary account does not match the balances in lower-level accounts.
- Validation of payments in accounts receivable; making sure money is securely transferred to prevent fraud.
- Prevention of false payments; checks to make sure payments are only made with proper authority.
- Explaining account movements to users. Accountants use conventions that are not always intuitive for users. Reports have to be tailored for professional accounts and lay users.

Generic requirements for this class are as follows.

1. Authorization checks for payments by using personal identification numbers (PINs), passwords, and other codes.
2. Validation checks for accepting payments to ensure money transfer is authorized.
3. Cross-posting functions, to ensure payments and receipts are aggregated into the appropriate higher-order accounts.
4. Cross-posting for double-entry book keeping; within an organization's accounts a debit on one account must have a corresponding credit in another, to record the origin and destination of the money.
5. Functions to calculate discounts and interest charges.

A1.3. Level 2 Class: Object Returning

The purpose of this object system (see Fig. A1.3) is the orderly transfer of reusable resources to a client and the return of those resources to the owner; hence this class specializes into hiring, servicing, and repair-type applications. The goal state asserts that all loaned key objects must be returned at some specified time in the future. This model is composed of a state transition outbound to the client agent from the owning object structure and a second state transition from the client returning the key object to the owning agent.

Goal state: to satisfy all resource requests by temporary transfer of
                resource objects and ensure the return of all transferred objects.
Agents: client (requester), owner.
Key object: owned resource.
Transitions: request, provide, return.

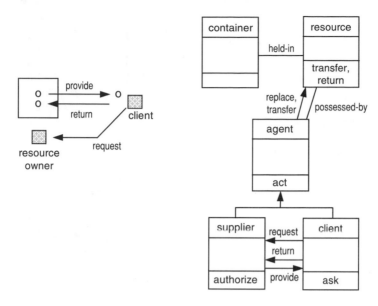

FIG. A1.3   Object Returning OSM.

A1.3.1.   Level 3 Class: Object Hiring

Synonyms: hiring, borrowing applications, loans, rentals.

The purpose of these systems is to control the loan, hire, or temporary transfer of ownership of some resource from an organization to a client who requests posses- sion of the resource. This object system (see Fig. A1.3.1) is characterized by one structure object, the owning organization, owner and client agents, one key object (the resource) and three transitions representing the request, loan, and return of the resource. The goal state is the same as for the Object Returning model. As with the Object Inventory class, aggregation with the Accounting Object OSM is used to distinguish between hiring applications (Object Hiring and Accounting Object Transfer) from free loans (i.e., as in library books) that is represented by a stan- dalone Object Hiring model. Subclasses of this model are specialized by possessing either physical or conceptual key objects. Financial loans are modeled as an Object Hiring concept abstraction that represents the loan aggregated with an Accounting Object Transfer for interest payment. Object Hiring models are also associated with matching generalized tasks to find the appropriate resource for a customer. Specializations of the subclass distinguish between hiring key objects with no per- ceived monetary value and those where there is a marketable value to the client.

Goal state:	to satisfy all resource requests by temporary transfer of resource objects and ensure the return of all transferred objects.
Agents:	client (requester), supplier.
Key object:	owned resource.
Transitions:	request, transfer, return.

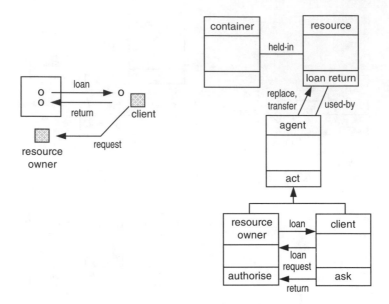

FIG. A1.3.1.   Object Hiring OSM.

The interaction pattern for the Object Hiring OSM is as follows.

Client agent

Expectations:	to gain a resource (book).
Knowledge structures:	identity of required resource.
Competences:	communication skills.
Responsibilities:	to return resource.
Role:	request, initiator; depends on resource holder agent.

Resource Holder agent

Expectations:	to loan a resource.
Knowledge structures:	available resource.
Competencies:	loan procedures, assessing client's needs.
Responsibilities:	to service client requests.
Role:	loan, responder.

In this case the interaction is closely anchored to the transaction. The resource requester has to ask for the items; this may be followed by a clarification subdialogue after which the conversation progresses to authorizing and recording the loan. A separate pattern handles returns and loan renewal.

The requirements problems commonly associated with this model are as follows.

• Ensuring the safe return of the loaned resource. Possible solutions are to enforce a financial penalty for late return or loss of the resource and to be proactive by sending out reminders before the return date becomes due. A delinquent client who fails to return the resource may be barred from the list of acceptable clients in the future, and a search task launched to track down and recover the resource.

- Having sufficient resources available to meet demand while not having too much capital locked up in resources. This balancing problem has similar solutions to those proposed for the inventory management abstraction: demand forecasting systems that projects demand based on historical data and market projections. An alternative is to form interorganization relationships for resource sharing to meet peak local demands.
- Ensuring only trustworthy clients are allowed to borrow resources. This implies an information searching generalized task to check personal and credit references.

Generic requirements are as follows.

1. Search and retrieval functions to find the appropriate resource for the customer.
2. Reservations: reserving a particular resource for a customer that may not be immediately available.
3. Loan recording: creating a database record linking the customer with the resources.
4. Validation checks on customer suitability, creditworthiness.
5. Loan authorization: special checks may be necessary for high-value resources.
6. Returns: checking that the resource has not been damaged; updating loan records.
7. Renewals: extending the loan period.
8. Recalls: requesting return of a resource before the due date because another customer wants it urgently.
9. Fines: calculating extra charges that may be imposed if the customer does not return the resource on time or it is damaged.

A1.3.2.   Level 3 Class: Object Servicing–Repair

Synonyms: repair, fixing, maintenance, treatment, curing defects–illness.

The purpose in this object system (Fig. A1.3.2) is to control the exchange of objects between a client and a servicing organization. This family describes service and repair applications in which the key object is in some way improved or has value added to it by the servicing agent. This subclass has the same object structure as in the Object Hiring model, but is differentiated by the concept of augmentation of the key object. This concept is represented by a relationship between the inbound and outbound state transitions and is specified in the goal state.

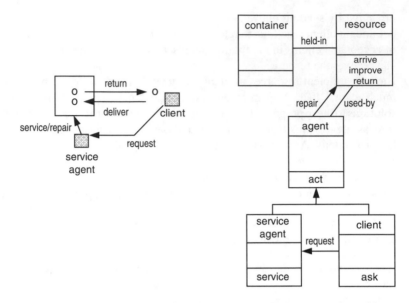

FIG. A1.3.2.   Object Servicing–Repair OSM.

Goal state:	to satisfy all the client's service requests by repairing the key object and returning it to its owner.
Agents:	client (requester), repairer.
Key object:	damaged resource.
Transitions:	request, transfer, repair, return.

Subclasses of this model depend on the triggering event. Ad hoc or emergency servicing has nondeterministic triggers, whereas regular servicing has a predetermined servicing schedule. The Object Servicing–Repair models are associated with a diagnosis generalized task to find out what is wrong, and with planning–scheduling for predetermined servicing. The activity of augmenting (repairing–servicing) the key object differentiates this class from Object Decomposition (taking the object apart prior to repair); Object Construction (if substantial changes are needed such as creating new parts); and Object Composition (replacing all the parts in working order).

Requirements problems associated with this class are as follows.

- Checking that the repair is acceptable. This implies generic requirements for quality assurance, with checking–validation and comparison (before and after) generic tasks.
- Selecting a suitable organization or agent for the repair; indicating a generic requirement for an IR generalized task to check references for the repair–servicing agent–organization.

- Checking that the repair will last. This can be dealt with by prolonging the period of quality assessment and proactively by checking the previous track record of the servicing organization–agent.

Generic requirements are as follows.

1. Functions to support diagnosis (see generalized tasks in appendix B2).
2. Identifying the object–agent for repair, accessing any repair–service history.
3. Quality assurance to check that the repair is acceptable.
4. Scheduling servicing–repair requests.

A2. LEVEL 1 CLASS: OBJECT ALLOCATION

Synonyms: matching, broking, goodness of fit.

This family models applications that create an object state change as a precursor to some other transaction, such as booking types of application. The purpose of such systems (Fig. A2) is to establish an association between a key object and a partition in a structure object according to the wishes of a client. A second, optional transaction may be added that is consummatory in nature when the allocated resources are used by the client; however, this will usually be modeled in a separate

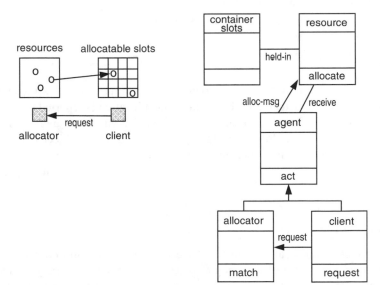

FIG. A2.   Object Allocation OSM.

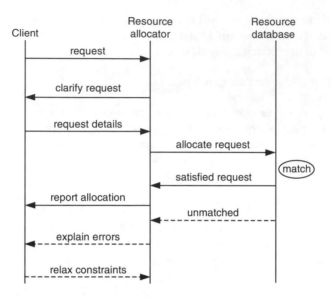

FIG. A2a.   Interaction diagram for Object Allocation OSM.

OSM family, such as Object Inventory. This class is modeled by two structures, the source of unallocated objects and the destination of allocated objects, with an agent that is responsible for determining the association.

Goal state: to place key objects in slots of a partitioned structure
                object, according to the client's request.
Agents: client, allocator.
Key objects: resources.
Transitions: request, allocate.

The interaction diagram (Fig. A2a) shows the user's request being clarified before the allocation task is executed. The result of the allocation is reported to the user. If allocation is unsatisfied, a constraint relaxation dialogue is initiated. This OSM family is closely coupled to the matching generalized tasks, Object Hiring, and Object Inventory models, either when demand exceeds supply and requests for more resources are generated or as part of the order-inventory management process.

A2.1. Level 2 Class: Physical
Object Allocation

In this subclass physical key objects have to be allocated into containers that are modeled as a partitioned structure object. This models a variety of sorting problems such as allocating parts to bins in stock control or sorting materials into appropriate groups. This class shares a partitioned structure with Object Logistics but is differentiated from it by a different goal state. In Logistics, the transport of an object to a remote location is the problem; in Allocation, sorting key objects into a partitioned space is the system goal.

A2.2. Level 2 Class: Conceptual Object Allocation

This subclass models allocation and booking types of applications. The destination structure is conceptually partitioned to model the structure of slots with which key objects may be associated; examples are seats and shows in theater booking, timetable slots allocated to lectures, and the like.

A2.3. Level 2 Class: Financial Object Allocation

In this class the key objects are financial entities or values and the structure object is a coding system. This models general ledger accounting in which financial transactions are allocated to expenditure codes and cost centers.

Requirements problems commonly encountered in this family are as follows.

- Not being able to satisfy the client requirements from the allocatable resources. This can be solved by increasing the available resources or imposing a rationing system. This leads to the next problem: prioritizing allocation.
- When resources are insufficient to meet demand, then setting priorities among the clients becomes a problem. This can be addressed by establishing a ranking among the clients according to merit or business criteria, such as most valued clients are processed first. Another solution is to adopt a constraint satisfaction approach and match fussy clients who impose more restrictive requirements first, then gradually work outward toward less demanding clients. As clients' demands often clash, a generic requirement is for linear programming or constraint-based matching algorithms to optimize the mapping between clients' constraints and properties of available resources. Configurable constraint-based algorithms allow the user to set override priorities.

Generic requirements are as follows.

1. Matching functions, as detailed in generic task description in appendix B2.
2. Criteria and functions for prioritizing clients.
3. Means of acquiring clients' needs.
4. Negotiation functions if clients' needs cannot be met.
5. Brought forward facilities so that clients who did not receive a full allocation in one batch are given priority in the next.
6. Constraint-based matching algorithms.

A3.   LEVEL 1 CLASS: OBJECT COMPOSITION

Synonyms: assembly, aggregation, building, putting together, packaging.

In this class the purpose is to aggregate key objects and thereby synthesize new ones, so the goal state is that all input objects should be composed into one or more new composite key objects. Concrete instantiations are a wide variety of manufacturing systems that assemble components into a product. This object system (Fig. A3) is characterized by two structure objects (the source of objects to be composed, and the destination of composed objects), two sets of key objects (components and composite objects), and one transition for merging component objects into composites. A controlling agent is responsible for organization of the process. Robotic manufacturing systems are matched to this family and aggregated with the Object Construction OSMs. This family is linked to modeling, planning, and scheduling generalized tasks.

Goal state: to compose one or more composite objects from components; all components are assembled into new key objects.

Agents: composer.

Key objects: components, composed objects.

Transitions: compose.

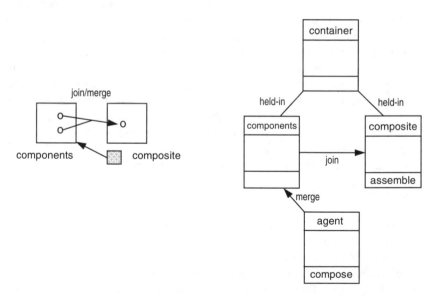

FIG. A3.   Object Composition OSM.

The requirements problems associated with this class are as follows.

- Selecting the appropriate components (or raw materials) for composition. This bill of materials problem indicates generic requirements for analysis and information searching tasks to specify the necessary components and obtain sources for them (Object Inventory model).
- Planning the composition sequence, which entails requirements for modeling, planning, and scheduling generalized tasks. Where composition requires several different processes for assembly or manufacture, those processes can be mapped to the capabilities of different machines. There is an implied association with the Object Allocation OSM and the matching generalized task to allocate jobs to machines.
- Handling exceptions to the composition process when components break, become damaged, or machines malfunction. The generic requirements for exception handling are dynamic planning tasks and backtracking procedures to reorder the composition process. The diagnosis generalized task may also be required to discover what caused the failure.

Generic requirements are as follows.

1. Acquiring the list of components or parts.
2. Functions for ordering and scheduling assembly sequence.
3. Means of allocating assembly actions to devices–operations that will execute assembly.
4. Control system to invoke assembly operations.
5. Monitoring function to check that operations are completed successfully (Object Sensing).
6. Backtracking and recovery procedures if operations are not completed successfully.

A4. LEVEL 1 CLASS: OBJECT DECOMPOSITION

Synonyms: disaggregation, disassembly, unpacking, or applications involving decomposition.

This is the opposite of composition; it maps to concrete examples of systems that disaggregate objects. In this case the goal state at the end of system activity is that no composite key object should exist. This system (Fig. A4) is characterized by a source and destination structure object, two sets of key objects, composites and components, and one transition representing decomposition. As with object composition, a controlling agent is present.

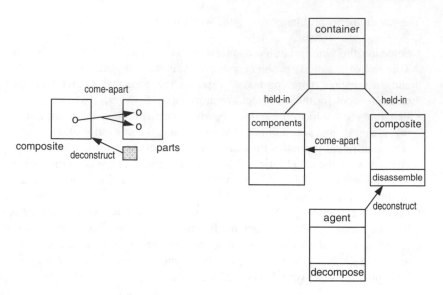

FIG. A4. Object Decomposition OSM. Note that the Domain Theory does not distinguish between destructive and nondestructive decomposition, so this family may decompose composites created by the Object Composition and Object Construction families.

Goal state:	to decompose one or more composite objects into their constituents.
Agents:	decomposer.
Key objects:	composed objects, components.
Transitions:	deconstruct.

Many requirements problems for this class are shared with the Object Composition family, although each problem is viewed from the opposite direction.

- Planning the decomposition sequence; finding the location to start.
- Controlling decomposition and knowing when to stop; recursive descent problem.
- Keeping track of all the components.

Generic requirements are as follows.

1. Functions for ordering and scheduling disassembly sequences.
2. Means of allocating actions to devices–operations that will execute decomposition.
3. Control system to invoke decomposition operations.

4. Monitoring function to check that operations are completed successfully.
5. Monitoring function to control when to stop.
6. Backtracking and recovery procedure if operations are not completed successfully.

A5. LEVEL 1 CLASS: OBJECT LOGISTICS

Synonyms: transport, transfer, translocate, transmission, move.

The purpose of this class is to move key objects within a partitioned structure object from a starting location to a destination goal set by the client agent. The OSM (see Fig. A5) is composed of key objects that must be translocated, structure objects that represent the topology or geography over which movement will occur, agents that are purposeful originators and receivers of key objects and, optionally, an agent that mediates transport. The goal state of this family asserts that all key objects must arrive at their destination; however, within subclasses the key object may be conceptual or physical.

Goal state: to transfer a key object from one structure object container to another; all key objects must arrive at their destination by a set time.

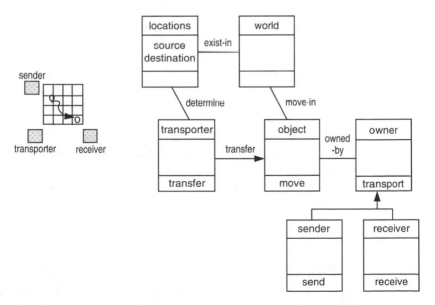

FIG. A5.   Object Logistics OSM. Movement or transport of object is modeled as transitions following a path through the partitions in the structure object.

Agents: sender, receiver.
Key objects: objects.
Transitions: send.

This family is associated with Planning–Scheduling, Navigate, and Communicate tasks.

A5.1. Level 2 Class: Physical Object Transfer

This subclass models delivery and transport systems. It is composed of an agent that effects the transport and a resource (e.g., truck, van, aircraft), as well as the transported object with sending and receiving agents. Further specializations model geographical constraints imposed on the path of transfer (c.f. three- and two-dimensional constraints in Object Sensing).

Goal: to transfer goods from one location to another; all goods must arrive at their destination by a set point in time.
Agents: sender, receiver.
Key objects: resources, goods.
Transitions: send.

Requirements problems are as follows.

- Optimal routing transfer through a transport network.
- Problems of obstruction in the network that require adaptive planning.
- Detecting obstructions on the route that may be physical blockages or traffic congestion (see Object Sensing, Monitoring).
- Navigating and route planning with uncertain information.

Generic requirements are as follows.

1. Planning and scheduling algorithms for optimal routing (c.f. the traveling salesman problem).
2. Information gathering for problems on transport network.
3. Navigating and wayfinding on route.
4. Checking despatch and arrival.
5. Progress tracking.

A5.2. Level 2 Class: Message Transfer

The class is characterized by one or more key objects (messages), structure objects representing the network topology through which communication takes place, and at least one state transition for exchange of messages. Specializations in this class distinguish between partitioned structure objects that model communication

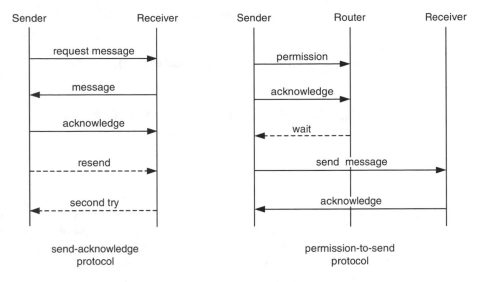

FIG. A5.2.   Interaction diagrams for Message Transfer OSM.

topologies (e.g., star, network, bus, etc.) and channel structures for broadcast or narrowcast communications (radio, television, telephone). Further subclasses add transitions with relationships to represent different communication protocols (e.g., simplex, half-duplex, full duplex, reply–acknowledge, etc.).

Goal state: to transfer a key object from one structure object container to another; all messages must arrive at their correct destination at a set time.

Agents: sender, receiver.
Key objects: messages, information.
Transitions: request, send, receive, acknowledge.

Two interaction diagrams are illustrated in Fig. A5.2. One shows a simple send–acknowledge protocol, and the second is a permission-to-send protocol for senders to access the communications channel.

Requirements problems are as follows.

• Bandwidth and network constraints on throughput.
• Detecting network congestion.
• Errors and loss of messages.

Generic requirements are as follows.

1. Access protocol for message transmission, such as token ring, CSMA/CA (Carrier Sense, Multiple Access/Collision Avoidance: the Ethernet protocol).
2. Adaptable route planning to avoid network congestion.

3. Error recovery protocols (acknowledge, resend).
4. Message preparation and formatting (packet protocols).
5. Message assembly.
6. Detecting message loss (packet headers, sequence codes).

A6.   LEVEL 1 CLASS: OBJECT CONSTRUCTION

Synonyms: building, synthesis, making objects, creating objects, manufacture.

The purpose of this class (see Fig. A6) is to build a new key object by altering components and possibly adding new elements during the construction process. Note that this class differs from composition in which an object is assembled by aggregation of clearly recognizable components. In this family the state transitions alter the fundamental properties of the key object itself. The state transitions model a change emanating from an agent that alters a key object and feedback conveying observed change. The goal state specifies that any change requests from the agent are imposed on the key object. No key object movement is involved in this abstraction; instead structure objects model the apparatus in which the change takes place and an agent models the human or device a machine or a computer,

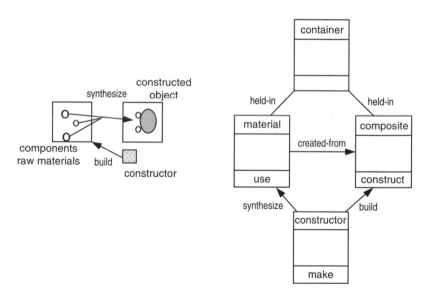

FIG. A6.   Object Construction OSM. The state transition alters the key object by adding new parts or by synthesizing components from materials input to the system.

which facilitates or carries out the change. This family is closely related to the Object Composition class but is distinguished by the presence of a synthesize transition. Object Composition models only aggregation in which the components are not altered; in Object Construction, components are changed. In manufacturing systems, Composition and Construction are usually interleaved. Construction is also related to Object Servicing, as both models possess a change transition and alter the state of the key object. Servicing is distinguished from Construction by the goal state. In Servicing the key object is damaged; hence the goal state is to return it to a previously satisfactory state; in contrast, Construction transforms the key object into a new state. Subclasses in this family distinguish construction of physical and conceptual key objects.

Goal: to build a key object from components or raw materials.
Goal state: constructed objects are created, and raw materials are consumed.
Agents: constructor.
Key objects: raw materials, constructed object.
Transitions: synthesize, build.

The OSM family is associated with many physical tasks that are not specified in the Domain Theory and a generalized task for Planning–Scheduling.

Requirements problems are as follows.

- Planning, ordering, and scheduling construction tasks.
- Controlling activity in the construction process, machine control or robots, or other devices (Computer Numeric Control).
- Acquiring and delivering raw materials for the manufacturing process (bill of materials, production planning).
- Detecting errors and quality defects in manufacture (Validation–Testing task).
- Adaptive planning of process when errors are detected.

Generic requirements are as follows.

1. Production planning–scheduling algorithms.
2. Allocating manufacturing jobs to appropriate machines or devices.
3. Monitoring production process for breakdowns.
4. Quality assurance of manufacture products.

A6.1. Level 2 Class: Physical Object Construction

The state transitions model a change emanating from an agent that alters a key object. The goal state specifies that any change requests from the agent are acted on by the key object. The purpose of this class is to build a new physical object from raw materials by a physical, chemical, or biological process. The agent causing the constructive change may be either a human, machine, or a natural agent; for example, an enzyme triggers synthesis of a new protein, and a catalyst triggers a chemical synthesis. The class consists of physical key objects for materials and products, a structure object, and a causative agent. The state transition changes the physical properties of the key object resulting in a new, synthesized object that is the goal state of the system. Some examples may lie on the boundary between Composition and Construction, such as welding to build a ship; however, the important difference is change to the materials and reversibility of action. Construction is not immediately reversible, whereas Composition is; hence welding is Construction but bolting components together is Composition.

A6.2. Level 2 Class: Conceptual Object Construction

This class represents a large family of applications including computer-based tools for word processing, graphics packages, decision support, design support, CAD systems, and so on. From the design viewpoint this class also contains all computer programs. These systems are characterized by a user agent who initiated change, and an implementor agent that carries out actions on the key conceptual object in a virtual structure object, that is, computer memory. Transitions in this class are edits or inputs that lead to updates, additions, and deletions that act on components or the composite. This class was modeled as Object Manipulation in earlier versions of the Domain Theory and is a similar abstraction to Jackson's workpiece problem frame. This class is frequently aggregated with Object Simulation in design.

The interaction diagram (Fig. A6.2) for this class shows interactions for creating, editing, and deleting objects.

A7. LEVEL 1 CLASS: OBJECT SENSING

Synonyms: monitoring, detecting, state changes.

The purpose of this class (see Fig. A7) is to monitor the physical conditions or movement of objects in the real world and record their relative state with respect to a spatial or physical structure object. This class has a sensing agent that reports on the key object. For this family, the goal state is that changes in key objects must be detected and signaled to the agent. Subclasses in this family are determined according to whether it is a property or behavior of the key object that is to be detected or spatial behavior, and whether the sensing agent is active or passive, such as spatial sensing by radar detection of air traffic; or property sensing applications, such as monitoring temperature or pressure in process control applications.

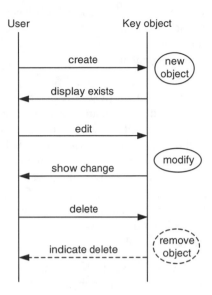

FIG. A6.2. Interaction diagram for Conceptual Object Construction OSM.

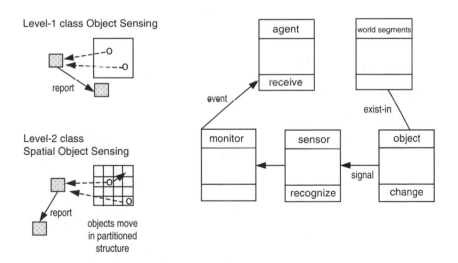

FIG. A7. Object Sensing OSM. The sensor agent may be a means of communicating events or an active detection device. The class model is the same for both the level 1 and level 2 classes, although the event and use of segment attributes in Spatial Object Sensing will be different.

Goal: to detect any state change in a key object and report that
                  change to an external agent.
Agents: sensor, client.
Key objects: changing components.
Transitions: signal, report.

The interaction diagram (Fig. A7a) shows the operator requesting the monitor agent for a discrete, as opposed to continuous, detection of change. The sensing agent reports changes on demand. Other models are continuous reporting without an explicit request. This family is associated with Interpret, Evaluate, and Communicate generic tasks. Subclasses in this family are divided into two subfamilies: the nature of the event being detected (property, behavior, change in the world) and the sensing mechanism (active–passive). To describe particular problems these subclasses are aggregated; for example, an active sensor with Object Property OSMs is used to describe a patient heart monitor.

Requirements problems are as follows.

- Fidelity of detecting events to avoid false alarms.
- Sampling rate and frequency of state change in the world to avoid missing rapid changes.
- Interpretation of events and the context of change.
- False events caused by oversensitive detecting devices.

Generic requirements are as follows.

1. Reliable event detector and interpreter.
2. Sampling rate control.
3. Tuning sensing mechanism to eliminate false alarms.
4. Interpreters–filters to eliminate false alarms.
5. Log file for history analysis of events.

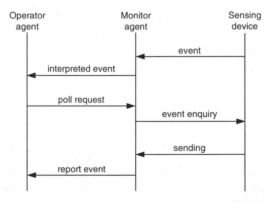

FIG. A7a.   Interaction diagram for Object Sensing OSM.

A7.1. Level 2 Class: Spatial Object Sensing

In subclasses of this family, structure objects model significant spatial components of the real world and can be partitioned, such as sectors within an air corridor. Key objects change within this structure and these changes are reported to the sensing agent as events. Further subclasses specialize the problem in either three-dimensional space (e.g., air traffic sensing) or two-dimensional sensing (vehicle traffic and shipping), and at the next level according to movement constraints placed on key objects, that is, constrained space (traffic on roads) versus unconstrained space (ships at sea).

Goal:	to detect the location and any movement in a key object and report that change to an external agent.
Agents:	sensor, client.
Key objects:	real-world objects.
Transitions:	detect, report.

A7.2. Level 2 Class: Agent Behavior Sensing

In this subclass actions of an agent are monitored, so the key object is replaced by an agent. Behavioral changes by the agent within a physical world or a conceptual task structure are detected and reported to the sensing agent as events. This class monitors action detail of an agent, in contrast to gross movement of the agent as a whole unit (Spatial Object Sensing), and change in an agent's state (Object Property Sensing).

Goal:	to detect the behavioral detail carried out by an observed agent and report that change to an external agent.
Agents:	subject, sensor, client.
Key objects:	subject agent.
Transitions:	behave, detect, report.

A7.3. Level 2 Class: Object Property Sensing

The subclass detects properties of a key object such as temperature, size, density, and weight, that is, any information about an object except spatial semantics of movement, position, and direction. Typical applications are sensors in process control, chemical plants, and equipment monitors.

Goal: to detect any state change in a key object's attributes and
                   report that change to an external agent.
Agents: sensor, client.
Key objects: real-world objects.
Transitions: detect, report.

A7.4.   Level 2 Class: Active Sensing

This subclass models sensors that emit a signal in order to detect change, such
as radar transponders, and another transition is added to model the echo returned
by the sensed object. Further specializations of this subclass differentiate between
agents that emit sensing signals continuously and domains in which the key object
emits a detectable signal only in response to another event, such as an aircraft
transponder.

A7.5.   Level 2 Class: Passive Sensing

Applications in which the device detects chemical or physical change in the environment but the key object does not emit a signal are modeled as passive sensors.

A8.   LEVEL 1 CLASS: AGENT CONTROL

Synonyms: ordering–obeying, executing authority, commanding, directing.

   This OSM family models command and control applications (see Fig. A8). The
class is characterized by a controlling agent and one or more controlled agents
contained in one object structure. In this class, key objects are agents contained
within a structure that models the real-world environment where behavior takes

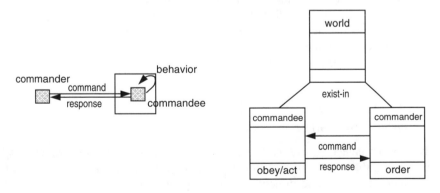

FIG. A8.   Agent Control OSM.

place, such as airspace in air traffic control. The transitions represent messages passed from the controlling agent to the controllee to change its behavior in some way. The goal state asserts that the controlled agent must respond to the commander agent in a satisfactory manner. Specializations of this class are determined by the nature of the controlled agent, which may be either deterministic or probabilistic in its response. Complex networks of commands can be built up to model distributed command systems and hierarchical chains of command.

Goal state:	for one agent to control the behavior of another; all commands issued by the commanding agents have to be responded to in some manner by the controlled agent.
Agents:	controller, controllee.
Key objects:	as for agents.
Transitions:	command, respond.

Agent Control OSMs are associated with the Object Sensing family and Interpret and Evaluate generic tasks.

Interaction between the commander and the subordinate consists of a three-part order–acknowledge–report protocol (Fig. A8a). More elaborate protocols are found in the Probabilistic Agent Control, where a course of action may be negotiated (see section 5.2, Generic Dialogues).

Requirements problems are as follows.

- Expressing commands clearly so that subordinates understand.
- Directing commands to the appropriate agent.
- Interpreting commands by the subordinate agent.
- Ability to act and execute commands; assignment of responsibility.
- Communication protocols for reporting commands are received, understood, and carried out.
- Depth of the command hierarchy resulting in confused translation of commands between levels.

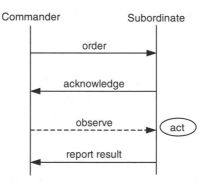

FIG. A8a.   Interaction diagram for Agent Control OSM.

- Breadth of the command hierarchy so that the commander has too many subordinates, leading to overloading.
- Ambiguous or ill-defined lines of command.
- Motivation of subordinates for obedience.
- Communication problems and indecision (order, counterorder, disorder).

Generic requirements are as follows.

1. Command structures that balance breadth with depth.
2. Appropriate allocation of roles and responsibilities.
3. Clear command vocabulary.
4. Command received and report back protocols.
5. Incentives to motivate subordinates to obey.
6. Clear feedback on progress to commander.
7. Automated feedback and progress reporting.

A8.1. Level 2 Class: Probabilistic Agent Control

This class models controlled agents whose response cannot be guaranteed, such as intelligent agents and people who may or may not obey commands. Command events in this class may not always be matched to the agent's response. Autonomous models of command (see appendix B3, Generic Dialogues) may be more appropriate with monitoring tasks.

A8.2. Level 2 Class: Deterministic Agent Control

This subclass models controlled agents that are designed to respond to commands in a predictable manner, such as robots and most machinery that exhibit predictable responses (e.g., cars, aircraft, engines). The command and response set of the commanding and commanded agents is therefore finite and predictable.

A9.   LEVEL 1 CLASS: OBJECT SIMULATION

Synonyms: demonstrations, interactive models, presentations.

The purpose of this class is to represent a model and its behavior to an external agent (see Fig. A9). The class is composed of a structure object and the modeled world that contains one or more key objects, representing components in a real-world domain or a design. This family represents a wide range of simulation

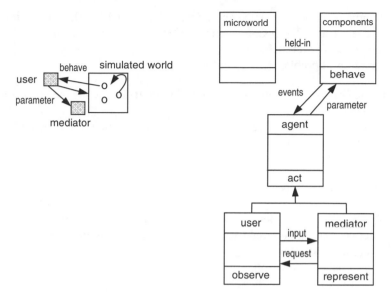

FIG. A9. Object Simulation OSM.

and display applications, including multimedia presentations, simulations, inter-active microworlds, and virtual environments. The architecture follows the Model View Controller abstraction (Krasner & Pope, 1988). The model may represent phenomena in the real world (e.g., model of a pond ecosystem) or designed arte-facts. The client agent sends input events to the key object that responds with output behavior. A mediating agent may be present to handle the external representation of the model's output. This family models simulations in which a model is run or interacted with by the user. No change is caused to the model itself by the state transitions; however, the user agent may input parameters that change the model's behavior. Substitution of intelligent agents for objects in the model extends the range of behavior. The external agent may also have a simulated presence in the modeled world, such as avatars in virtual-reality applications. The goal state dif-ferentiates Object Simulation from Object Construction by allowing only change, creation, or deletion of key objects in the latter. A simulation construction kit is therefore an aggregate of Object Simulation and Construction, whereas simula-tions that are run but not edited belong to this family. Simulations for decision support and design environment fall into this class, as do most computer games.

Goal state: to represent properties of a modeled object to an external agent; all events input by the user agent are responded to, and all transitions in the internal agent's script are completed.

Agents: viewer, mediator.

Key objects: model.

Transitions: input manipulations, model responses.

This family is associated with Analysis–Modeling and Validation–Testing generalized tasks, and Object Construction OSMs when the products of manufacture are run to observe their behavior.

Requirements problems are as follows.

* Choice of media to represent the simulation, including the metaphor for the modeled world.
* Display devices and degree of physical representation; the choice between augmented and virtual reality.
* Script interpreter to run the simulation.

Generic requirements are as follows.

1. Presentation controller that integrates media rendering devices.
2. Media presentation rendering devices: speech, sound, moving image, graphics, and so on.
3. Script behavior controller.
4. Functions that create the simulated system.
5. Input for parameters and controls for running the simulation.

This is the breadth of the Object System Model space as it currently stands. Further analysis of applications may lead to discovery of new OSM families; however, the set described herein has remained stable over successive analyses of applications from real life and case-study descriptions taken from the software engineering literature.

A10.   INFORMATION SYSTEM MODELS (ISMS)

A set of seven generic information system classes have been modeled; some examples are reporting values and states, counting individuals, matching criteria, list duration, and progress tracking. Information System Models extract data about objects and agents in OSMs. Unlike OSMs, ISMs do not have any correspondence with a physical world, apart from the databases and computers that implement them. Indeed, the basic abstraction of all ISMs is a database key object, contained in a computer structure object with a reporting agent that is the program for data access, report generation, and online query. The main focus of ISM abstractions is to describe how information is handled and reported to an external agent.

A10.1.   ISM: Information Reporting

This family models all computer programs that generate reports and online queries. The model consists of a database and a reporting agent that accesses the database and creates an external representation of the data that is sent to the external user agent. Specializations of this class differentiate between batch and online queries. Considerable processing of the data is possible after access, for instance by sorting and mathematical operations for calculations. It is not the remit of the Domain Theory to describe such functions; however, certain patterns for extracting and treating data are specified. These patterns are described as separate classes, which in practice are aggregated with Object Reporting to create different data treatments.

Goal state: to represent properties of key objects or agents in an OSM to a user agent; all user requests for information are processed.

Agents: user, mediator.

Key objects: OSM objects and agents.

Transitions: information request, report.

Subclasses in this family are as follows.

- *Category-sorted reports*. The information is grouped by Classify generic task into higher-order units. This is the default case in which most reports are organized in a classification structure, such as countries, regions, areas, branches.
- *Time ordered reports*. Information is ordered in a time line or history. Dates or time periods form the organizing principle for these reports, which are closely associated with the Progress Tracking ISM. Time-ordered reports imply graphical representations as bar charts, or date-ordered sorting.
- *Trend reports*. These reports are related to the time-ordered variety because trends are frequently ordered over time. However, trends may be observed over space and within a non-time-ordered sequence. The basic abstraction of trends is the comparison of information values along a dimension.
- *Difference reports*. Most monitoring and deviation reporting falls into this subclass, such as plan versus actual, observed versus expected, performance comparisons. The essence is one set of values that can be compared with another, or values that can be compared against a reference point.

Subclasses in the report family are frequently aggregated so difference-trend reports will model a multiple trend line graph that draws attention to the differences at each plot point. This family is associated with the IR generalized task and the Interpretation, Compare, and Sort generic tasks.

Requirements problems are as follows.

- Selecting information that fulfills the users' requirements.
- Accuracy and timeliness of information.
- Establishing criteria for sorting reported items into groups.
- Ordering and sorting items and groups.
- Report formatting for clarity and providing information appropriate to the users' needs and tasks.
- Distributing reports to appropriate users.

Generic requirements are as follows.

1. Data selection for report.
2. Media selection for representing data, such as tables, graphs, and formatted text.
3. Formatting reports.
4. Adding status information, date, and page numbers.
5. Report distribution mechanisms.

A10.2.   ISM: Progress Tracking

This class reports on any object that has an ordered history and is subjected to sequential updates. The composition of the class is the same as the Information Reporting model; however, the output structure is segmented into slots that record counts of object instances that have a certain historical status, such as age of debt or location in a pathway.

Goal state: to represent time sequence and history states of key
                objects or agents in an OSM to a user agent; all user requests
                for information are processed.
Agents: user, mediator.
Key objects: OSM objects and agents.
Transitions: information request, progress report.

A10.3.   ISM: Categorization

This models all sorting applications that order object instances into a hierarchical structure and uses Sort and Clarify generic tasks. It is related to the Object Allocation OSM, except in this case the system aim is simply to categorize objects without any transactional purpose in view. The output structure is composed of hierarchically arranged slots that contain counts of objects whose properties match the definition of each slot.

Goal state: to sort key objects into categories; all objects belong to at least
                one category.
Agents: user, mediator.
Key objects: OSM objects and categories.
Transitions: place.

A10.4.   ISM: Information Search

This models information reports resulting from searching any database or library. The goal is that information requests must be matched to the conceptual object contained in a database structure object and that those objects that match are retrieved for the user. This ISM uses matching and goodness-of-fit algorithms and is aggregated with the IR generalized task. The information items in the report are ordered according to their relevance to the user's query.

Goal state: to match and retrieve information objects from a database according to a user agent's request; all user requests for information are processed.

Agents: user, search engine.

Key objects: information objects.

Transitions: information request, retrieved objects.

APPENDIX B

Generic and Generalized Task Models, Dialogues, and Argumentation Schema

B1. GENERIC TASKS

The task families are as follows.

Action:	B1.1–B1.6
Information Processing:	B1.7–B1.15
Communication:	B1.16–B1.18
Exploration–Sensing:	B1.19–B1.22.

B1.1. Plan

Precondition: intention–subgoal present.
Action sequence:
    Load actions into working memory.
    Locate external affordances (objects) for action.
    Interpret affordances.
    Order actions into procedure.
Postcondition: procedure present in working memory.

Note that the task schema only specifies an idealized sequence; for example, if the affordances were ambiguous or inappropriate for action then the task would not be completed, leading to a search for new affordances or replanning.

B1.2. Interpret

This is making sense or comprehending a change in the environment, or ascribing meaning to a state change.

Precondition: a state change is perceived.
Action sequence:
    Recognize change.
    Map change to object in memory.
    Create working memory schema of change stimulus with associated memory components.
Postcondition: a state change is understood or the change is incomprehensible.

B1.3. Evaluate

Precondition: a perceived state is not known.
Action sequence:
    Map change to associated memory schema (procedural, episodic, categorial,) etc.
    Create mental model of change with associated memory components.
    Assess consistency of change with respect to memory.
Postcondition: the implications of the state change are evaluated as being either compatible or incompatible with memory.
Exception conditions: change is unexpected, does not conform to memory, triggers problem solving–causal analysis.

Evaluation assesses the implications of a state change with respect to progress through a task or a perceived state of the world. Evaluation has two subtasks: one covers state change evaluation and the other covers evaluation of the properties or qualities of an object.

B1.4. Assemble

Precondition: objects or parts to be assembled are available.
Action sequence:
    Plan assembly sequence.
    DO WHILE parts left.
    Identify part(s) for aggregation.
    Join parts or place in same container.
    END.
Postcondition: parts are organized so that a new composite object is recognizable.

In Assemble, parts or components are placed together so they make a coherent whole. Assembly of physical items is a spatial task; however, conceptual items may also be assembled, such as topics for an essay plan. This generic task is strongly associated with the Object Composition OSM. Variants are hierarchically organized assembly with substructures.

B1.5. Disassemble

Precondition: composite object exists.
Action sequence:
    Plan decomposition.
    DO WHILE composite exists.
    Select initial part for removal.
    Remove part.
    END.
Postcondition: object and parts are isolated and the composite structure no longer
                 exists.

Disassemble is the opposite of Assemble when a composite object is taken apart. This task may also function to disassociate or break a relationship (see Associate). This task is strongly associated with the Object Decomposition OSM; however, it should be noted that there is a subtle distinction between Disassemble that takes apart a composite structure and decomposition in a biological sense that reduces an organized life form to its elemental constituents.

B1.6. Transform

Precondition: facts to be changed are held in working memory.
Action sequence:
    Select transformation rules.
    Apply rules to each fact–object.
    Record transformed fact in new structure.
Postcondition: a representation is produced that conforms with problem solution
                 criteria.

Transform changes one representation of a problem into another, usually representing the solution. Specific examples might be translating one language into another, transforming expressions in mathematics, or changing a representation to solve a problem. Transformation usually embeds generic problem solving and reasoning.

B1.7. Model

Precondition: a set of facts are known but unorganized.
Action sequence:
    Evaluate associations between facts based on memory.

Identify relationships between facts.

Order relationship to create a mental model.

Postcondition: a semantic network of associated facts are held in memory to enable reasoning.

Modeling is constructing a mental model of the problem at hand, the environment, or other phenomena (agent's beliefs, roles) implicated in reasoning. Modeling in the software engineering sense will involve analysis (interpretation and evaluation) to understand the facts, then building the internal mental model, and then recording the model externally as a diagram or specification.

B1.8. Sort

Precondition: facts to be sorted or ranked and the ordering criteria are available.

Action sequence:

Select sort criterion.

Arrange objects in order according to criterion.

Resolve any ties.

Postcondition: objects are organized according to a scalar dimension that expressed ranking criteria.

Sort is closely coupled with Classify that groups instances into sets. Sorting, ranking, and prioritizing are treated as one generic task because they all reflect subgrouping with increasing constraints. The difference between sorting and ranking is that ranking has a dimension or metric that allows ordering of sorted groups. More complex sorts can have two or more criteria and suborders within the major order, such as rank by date with an alphabetic order. Sorting is related to comparison but the end state is an ordered list expressing priority, preference, or importance, whereas comparison stresses the difference rather than the similarity between objects.

B1.9. Classify

Precondition: facts to be classified are available.

Action sequence:

Select shared attributes.

Identify categories and sort criteria.

Classify objects into categories.

Resolve boundary cases.

Postcondition: objects are grouped into one or more categories.

Classify takes a collection of items and organizes them into categories according to rules that explain their commonalities. Classification tasks are closely related to sorting and may have an iterative sequence in hierarchical classification. Variants of this generic task are classification that assigns each object uniquely in one category, and categorization, when set membership is decided by the number of attributes an object shares with the category-type definition. This is often called faceted classification.

B1.10. Associate

Precondition: two or more objects or facts exist.
Action sequence:
    FOR each pair of objects DO.
    Identify shared attributes,
    Select relationship type,
    Record relationship.
    END.
Postcondition: two or more facts–objects are connected by a relationship.

Associate forms a relationship between two or more items. This task is related to Compare and differs from categorization in that the relationship or the type of association is important rather than group membership. Association may also allocate individuals to each other, resources to agents, and so on, and it is strongly related to modeling. Variants of this task are discovering relationships according to external criteria rather than similarities and shared attributes between the objects. Associate has a mirror image generic task, Disassociate, which undoes a relationship.

B1.11. Select

Precondition: two or more objects and selection criteria exist.
Action sequence:
    Identify object set for instances that match selection criteria.
    Mark instance or extract instance from set.
Postcondition: an object instance is selected from a set.

This generic task is closely associated with Search and Identify. Select may be effected by marking one or more objects for conceptual selection or physical removal of the selected object from a set.

B1.12. Identify

Precondition: the object to be identified is inspectable.
Action sequence:
    Select key attributes.
    Identify object instance.
    Assign identity label.
Postcondition: an identifying label is attached to an item.

Identification is the process in which the name, label, or category of an item is established by examining its attributes or properties. This task is related to Interpret, because Identify usually uses memory; and to Classify, because items have to be identified before they can be assigned to categories.

B1.13. Compare

Precondition: facts to be compared are available.
Action sequence:
    Select basis for comparison.
    Evaluate difference in attributes.
Postcondition: a relative assessment of the similarity or difference between two
                objects has been made.

Compare is a specialization of Evaluate in which judgment is made between two or more phenomena (events, agents, and objects), either relative to one another or against an external benchmark standard.

B1.14. Decide

Precondition: object–agent–event and its attributes are known; external criteria
                given.
Action sequence:
    Select attributes relevant to external criteria.
    Rank good–bad value of attribute with respect to external criteria.
    Sum rankings to arrive at overall judgment.
Postcondition: an event, object, or agent is labeled on a good–bad dimension.

This task is referred to as judgment and valence assessment in psychology. It involves assessing an object or action as good or bad or gradations in between. The Decide generic task is embedded within the more complex generalized task of choice and decision making that involves not only judging but then taking action based on that judgment.

B1.15. Test

Precondition: a model or proposition exists,
Action sequence:
    FOR model DO
    Identify test success criteria,
    Select test data,
    Evaluate model–propositions against test data,
    Establish model–proposition correct or incorrect.
    END.
Postcondition: Valid–invalid model, suggestions for improvement.

Test checks a hypothesis, model, or proposition to assess whether it is true or consistent with a set of facts. Testing is the validation stage of generic problem solving. This task is related to Evaluate, which established more knowledge about a particular object. Associate may also allocate individuals to each other, resources to agents, and so on, and it is strongly related to modeling. Testing appears in Analysis, Diagnosis, and Validation generalized tasks.

B1.16. Record

Precondition: a semantic network of associated facts are held in memory.
Action sequence:
    Select mapping of mental model components to external notation element.
    Write, draw, or create external notation element.
Postcondition: facts and models are represented in a permanent medium.

Record transfers a model or collection of facts into a permanent medium, such as writing text or drawing a diagram.

B1.17. Communicate

Precondition: facts to be communicated are held in working memory.
Action sequence:
    Select medium.
    Plan message structure.
    Compose message by using rules of language (or notation) syntax.
    Express message elements in medium.
Postcondition: a message is transferred to another party.

Communicate sends messages to another party, either by speech or by use of another medium. This generic task is specialized by dialogues that describe the turn-taking structure and possible content.

B1.18. Explain

Precondition: facts to be communicated are available in external or working memory.
Action sequence:
    Plan explanation sequence.
    Introduce.
    Deliver content.
    Summarise topics.
    {Provide supplementary information}.
Postcondition: information is understood by the other party.

Explanation and advising provide facts and information to a requesting agent with reasons and supplementary information and may be associated with Communicate for answering problem-related questions, resulting in providing supplementary information. Explanation may take many forms, such as causal and procedural explanation with demonstration, which transform explanation into a more complex generalized task of Explanation–Advising. The possible content of Explanation tasks is elaborated in argumentation schemas.

B1.19. Monitor

Precondition: environmental events are detectable.
Action sequence:
    Detect event.
    Interpret event in context of world model.
    Signal interpretation to agent.
Postcondition: event is detected and an interpretation is sent to the monitoring agent
                for a reaction.

Monitoring observes the environment for state changes of interest. Monitor will involve the primitive tasks for Interpret and Evaluate change but is itself the act of observing and searching for events. Monitoring task variants depends on the nature of the event to be detected, which may be discrete (a single change such as a gunshot) or continuous (gradual temperature change). Events may be located in space and time, involve the movement of objects, or record changes to the attributes of objects and properties in the environment. This generic task is strongly associated with the Object Sensing OSM.

B1.20. Search

Precondition: object or fact to be found is identified.
Action sequence:
    Select search space.
    Match objects to target.
    Select matched targets.
Postcondition: the objects or facts of interest are located.

Searching is detecting (usually looking for) items of interest in the environment, either visually or by using other senses (audio, olfaction). Search is related to Monitor when the environment has to be actively scanned for events.

B1.21. Locate

Precondition: environment is perceivable and the search target is known.
Action sequence:
    Scan environment.

> IF object in proximity THEN establish location;
> ELSE
> REPEAT UNTIL object located.
> Move to next area.
> Scan.
> Postcondition: object or search target has been located.

Locate is finding the spatial position of an object in a space. Locate is frequently associated with perceptual actions not described in the Domain Theory (e.g., scan, recognize) and the Identify generic task.

B1.22. Orient

> Precondition: environment is perceivable and directional criteria are known.
> Action-sequence:
>> Scan environment for cues that match criteria.
>> Select direction.
>> Change posture and position of self to new direction.
> Postcondition: agent is oriented in the desired direction for travel, or location of a
>>   desired object is established.

Orienting is finding a location for travel or an object in an environment, including finding orientation cues. This primitive task is related to searching but differs because the orientation is with respect to a reference point of one's self. Variants of this task are an agent that is oriented towards an object rather than orienting the viewpoint of the agent itself. Orientation is part of the Navigation generalized task, which contains movement, navigation planning, find location, and orientation.

B2. GENERALIZED TASKS

Generalized tasks may have a deterministic structure, so their composition from primitive generic tasks can be specified with some confidence; however, more often, generalized tasks have a less determined structure so that only a typical sequence can be described. The following list of generalized tasks is not exhaustive. Generalized tasks are represented as a *goal hierarchy*, with notes on the variations that may occur. Generic requirements, claims, and requirements problems are attached to generalized tasks to guide the designer in functional allocation and specification of task-support functionality. Where tasks tend to involve interaction between two or more agents, a typical interaction pattern is given. An interaction pattern is a generalized template for conversation between agents that achieves a task goal. The purpose of these templates is to provide information on the agents involved and the conversation exchange, which will become an outline specification for the human–computer dialogue. First the participating agent's properties are specified to provide more information of their abilities.

Agent properties

Expectations:	beliefs held about the purpose of the transaction in the domain of interest.
Knowledge structures:	relevant information–memory held by the agent.
Competencies:	skills or abilities to discharge the obligations in the domain.
Responsibilities:	obligations placed on the agent to achieve the task.
Role:	tasks and actions they carry out and their role as initiator or responder in a conversation.

Interaction patterns integrate discourse acts with cognitive and physical actions to describe the communication components of generalized tasks. Because communication and action frequently proceed in parallel, interaction patterns and generalized task models form two interlinked threads of activity performed by the participating agents. The interaction pattern is composed of the agent descriptions and a diagram that illustrates the conversation as a sequence of acts between the agents. In contrast, generic tasks are carried out by a single agent and therefore do not have associated interaction patterns; however, the Communicate generic task does have a family of dialogue patterns that specialize it.

Notation in the goal hierarchies is as follows:

$\triangle$:   or
$\wedge$:   and
$\bigcirc$:   iteration
$\star$:   variation points

B2.1.   Information Acquisition

This task covers fact finding, eliciting, and acquiring information from people or documented sources. It therefore involves the Communicate generic task and dialogue patterns for questioning, clarifying, and summarizing. The goal hierarchy is shown in Fig. B2.1. The first two subgoals are to scope the information that is required and then locate sources of information. This is followed by choice of the information-gathering approach, which may involve interviewing, observing, or more specialized techniques such as laddering, repertory grids, or, more conventionally, questionnaires (Maiden & Rugg, 1996). Interviews and questionnaires are the least resource-intensive techniques that can be applied to acquire most types of information; card sorts and repertory grids are useful for eliciting categories and classifications; laddering can help capture goal hierarchies and plans; and observation is useful for processes, work context, and tasks. Documentation analysis supplements information acquired from people, and the final subgoal is to record the elicited information. Information acquisition is a human-oriented task because it involves communication; however, some automated support can be provided as for recording and representing information.

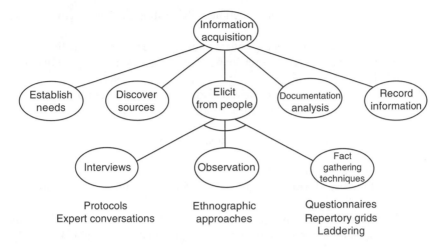

FIG. B2.1. Goal hierarchy for the Information Acquisition task.

Information acquisition is usually associated with Analysis–Modeling and Validation–Testing generalized tasks, and all three form the requirements analysis phase in software engineering. Interaction patterns for this task are very variable and depend on the structure of information-gathering dialogues. These are documented in the Generic Dialogues (appendix B3). Information acquisition is a complex task that requires human abilities to communicate and take on the spot judgments, so the requirements problems point to social issues that frequently do not have a technical solution. Computer system support in the generic requirements suggests functions for documenting requirements and analyzing information. Some of these tools will overlap with support for the Analysis–Modeling generalized task.

Requirements problems are as follows.

- Locating appropriate sources for different types of information; for example, senior managers are necessary for high-level strategies and junior managers are needed for tactics and operational procedures.
- Acquiring tacit knowledge: people frequently do not report facts they regard as obvious. Skill and well-known knowledge are assumed. Techniques such as verbal protocols or expert dialogues can help elicit tacit knowledge.
- Acquiring contextual knowledge: people often forget important facts when they are interviewed away from the work setting. Interviews in the workplace enable the analyst to ask about artefacts involved in work (Beyer & Holtzblatt, 1998).
- Eliciting informal knowledge and workarounds: many systems have an official set of documented procedures and a set of undocumented workarounds

that people use to deal with exceptions. Observation can help uncover undocumented procedures.

- Acquiring politically sensitive information. People are often unwilling to disclose information for fear of retribution. Creating an atmosphere of openness can help.
- Dealing with private and sensitive information, where disclosure could have adverse social or economic consequences.

Generic requirements (task-support functions) are as follows.

1. List managers to record facts and requirements management tools.
2. Function for indexing facts and information, and repository–database management facilities.
3. Traceability functions, so information can be indexed with authors and source and retrieved so the source of requirements or reusable knowledge can be traced.
4. Password protection and other security functions to protect sensitive information.
5. Query tools and IR functions.
6. Hypertext and information visualization tools to enable an overview of an information space.
7. Diagram and sketching tools to record nonverbal information.
8. Text analysis–search tools necessary for locating information in interview notes, documents, and transcribed protocols.
9. Voice capture and speech-recognition software: taking handwritten notes is laborious; voice notes are quick but have to be transcribed automatically.
10. Image capture, via digital camera; documenting physical information and contexts is quicker by photographs or video.

B2.2. Analysis–Modeling

Synonyms:　specification, investigation, researching.

This generalized task involves organizing facts in a coherent representation (i.e., modeling) and then inferring interesting properties of the modeled phenomena (see Fig. B2.2). Although analysis may be separated from modeling, in most cases the two tasks are closely coupled. Note that Analysis often forms part of Diagnosis, so generalized tasks may form aggregations; however, Analysis can be performed without diagnosis, for instance, analyzing the structure of a symphony. The template sequence is as follows.

- Classify and organize facts (Classify, Sort).
- Select modeling representation (Model, Select).
- Represent facts in model (Model).

FIG. B2.2. Goal hierarchy of the Analysis–Modeling task.

- Analyze categories, relationships, and sequences (Sort, Classify, Evaluate).
- Edit–augment model to record results (Model, Record).
- Repeat until analysis and modeling are sufficiently detailed.

The task structure illustrates specialization points for analytic techniques and representing the model. There are a wide variety of analytic techniques: some are general and others are specific to particular areas of science, such as finite-element analysis in civil engineering, or normalization of data models in computer science. Many detailed analytic techniques are dependent on the representation used; for instance, set theoretic notation allows membership and relationships to be assessed, whereas expression of facts in logics enables truth values, behavior, and obligations to be analyzed. These specific techniques are not described in the Domain Theory. Other more general analysis techniques are as follows.

- *Causal analysis*: establishing the reason why an event happens, or how something works. This uses pathway tracing and investigation of relationships.
- *Sequence analysis*: investigating the ordering of facts and their dependencies.

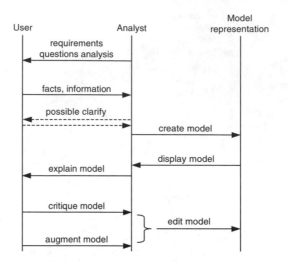

FIG. B2.2a.   Interaction diagram for the Analysis–Modeling task.

- *Temporal analysis*: a specialization of sequence analysis in which the ordering is in the time dimension. Temporal analyses can also concern durations and clustering of events in time intervals.
- *Set membership*: classification of facts, objects, and the like into classes (Classify generic task).

The interaction diagram for this task is illustrated in Fig. B2.2a. Questions and clarification dialogues refine the analysis with the user, followed by modeling. The model is then explained to the user, leading to critiquing and more analysis.

Analysis and Modeling tasks often co-occur with Validation–Testing. Functional allocation for analysis and modeling has software support for modeling, whereas analysis requires human reasoning and problem-solving abilities. Some analytic procedures can be automated, such as pathway tracing; however, most analyses are more suitable for people because they possess the domain knowledge to understand the system.

Requirements problems are as follows.

- The degree of support for the analytic process. In well-known deterministic domains, analysis can be completely automated as an expert system, such as structural analysis of stress failure in building materials by finite-element analysis. In less well-known domains, only partial analysis is possible so that the system functions support the user's task by preprocessing information; for example, to analyze the effectiveness of a drug treatment in a clinical trial, the system sorts all the observations according to their effect by patient group.
- Support for representing the problem (modeling). Modeling notations vary from informal but accessible diagrams and sketches to formal notations. Choice

of representation will depend on the user population. Informal notations help communication with users and customers; formal notations are more concise for experts. Explanations that link formal and informal notations are necessary when models have to be shared between experts and end users.

• Communicating the results. The consequences and implications of the analysis may be clear for the participants but not so clear to outsiders. The consequences of analysis have to be made clear as summary points, explanations of consequences, and animations of models.

Generic requirements (task-support functions) are as follows.

1. List managers for recording the initial facts.
2. Diagram drawing and sketching tools to represent the problem space.
3. Modeling tools that support more formal diagramming with embedded rules for syntax checking.
4. Functions for recording results and list managers, with sorting, prioritization facilities.
5. Automated analysis functions, pathway tracing, and specific techniques.
6. Explanation facilities for automated analysis tools so their reasoning can be checked.
7. Simulation tools so models can be represented with embedded rules encapsulating domain knowledge. The analysts can then try out "what if?" hypotheses with the simulation.
8. Consistency checking to ensure that the recorded model obeys laws of the modeling language.

B2.3. Validation–Testing

This task checks that a design or a problem solution satisfies a set of sufficiency criteria (see Fig. B2.3). The criteria may be precisely specified so assessment can be measured and possibly automated (i.e., testing) or rely on human judgment (i.e., validation of requirements). Validation uses the Compare primitive task to test that a model is acceptable according to a set of criteria. As with Analysis, there are many possible tests and validation techniques that the Domain Theory does not detail. A high-level view of validation is checking that a model of a design accords with users' requirements, or that explanation of a theory agrees with observed facts. The essence of the task is testing aspects of a model against an external set of facts, observations, or criteria.

The typical task structure is thus as follows.

• Establish validation criteria or test observations (Select).
• Select properties of the model or explanation to be tested (Model).
• Test explanation–design against external criteria (Compare, Evaluate, Classify).

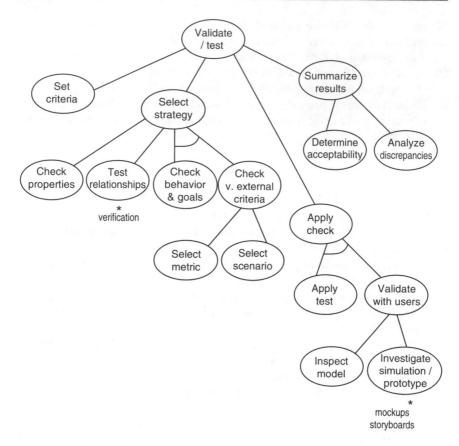

FIG. B2.3. Goal hierarchy for the Validation–Testing task.

- Establish reasons for any discrepancy (Diagnosis, Analysis–Modeling).
- Summarize test failure and successes.
- Determine overall acceptability of explanation–design (Evaluate).

Validation is closely linked to Analysis–Modeling, which provides the subject matter input for the task, and with Diagnosis, which is necessary if part of the model fails the validation test. Validation has specialization points for communicating the design to customers–users that can use a variety of techniques, such as mockups, prototypes, or specifications. The structure of testing varies from walkthroughs to more formal critiques or interaction with prototypes. The interaction diagram (Fig. B2.3a) has a cycle of explaining the design to the user, getting feedback, noting changes, and then progressing on to the next stage in the validation walkthrough.

In practice, Validation is interleaved with Analysis–Modeling and Negotiate in the design process, so the boundaries of this generalized task are hard to set. In

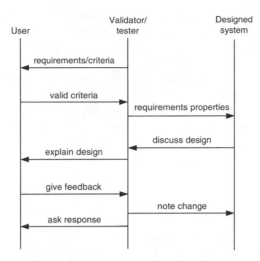

FIG. B23a. Interaction diagram for the Validation–Testing task.

software engineering, validation is often conflated with verification (formal model checking). This involves checking the internal consistency of the modeled design or theory. Verification may test model properties such as the following.

- Checks that appropriate components are connected by a specific relationship type.
  check {detects dyadic component relationships};
  model morphology: component (x), relationship (y), component (z); schema laws:
  (component type (i) component (x), mandatory);
  (component type (j) component (y), mandatory);
  (relationship type (k) relationship (z), mandatory).
  For example, check that all tasks are controlled by at least one agent. First a consistency checking tool finds all nodes with a component type = agent, then finds all the nodes connected to that agent that are tasks, and finally whether the relationship that connects the two nodes is of the correct type = control.
- Checks whether two components participating in a relationship have specific properties.
  check {detects components in a relationship have the correct properties}
  model (component (x), property (w), relationship (z), component (y), property (v));
  schema laws:
  (component type (i) component (x), mandatory);
  (component type (j) component (y), mandatory);
  (relationship type (k) relationship (z), mandatory);

(component (x) property (w), mandatory);

(component (y) property (v), mandatory).

In this example the consistency check is that all use cases with a <decision> property are linked to an agent that has an <authority> property. In this case the verification–checking tool has to search for nodes with a type = agent, and then it tests all the relationships connected to the agent node. If any of these relationships is connected to a node type = use case, then the tool reads the property list of the use case and the agent. If the agent does not have an "authority" property when the use case has a "decision" property, then the model is inconsistent with the schema laws.

Other checks are tracing relationships and pathways through the model to ensure the system will work correctly. More formal approaches to model checking involve verification by using formal methods to determine that constraints are not violated or that the desired states will be the outcome of executing procedures. Functional allocation in validation automates the verification parts of the task, whereas the interactive part of checking user requirements has a collaboration between the computer providing simulations and prototypes that are then explained by people. Validation requires human communication to explain the design and gather feedback.

Requirements problems are as follows.

- Choice of representation for promoting user comprehension.
- The form of problem representation influences the process. For validating designs, interactive simulations and prototypes are superior to written specifications because they engage the users in problem solving (Maiden et al., 1995; Sutcliffe, 1997). However, when formal theories are validated, specialized representation to support critiques may be more suitable.
- The degree of automation achievable. Although the essence of validation is user involvement to assess satisfaction, some automatic checking may be possible for the verification side of this task (see tests described herein).
- Representing results. The conclusions from validation have to be recorded so the design features that have to be fixed are clear.
- Impact assessment. Validation will detect all sorts of problems, some of which may be trivial or have only a minor impact. A means of determining the severity of the problem is necessary. The quick way is to ask users to rank problem severity.
- Coverage problem. Validation is time consuming, and complex systems are difficult to test exhaustively.

Generic requirements are as follows.

1. Representing the design as a storyboard, simulation, or prototype. The more interactive functionality that can be provided, the better.
2. Representing design and specification documents that may have to be cross-referenced with prototypes when faults are found.

3. List managers for recording results, problems encountered, and means of ranking problem severity.
4. Automated checking functions in which the validation criteria can be precisely specified.
5. Functions to handle feedback from several users, sort by viewpoints, and identify common concerns.
6. Consistency checking in models and with external criteria.
7. Scenario test data generation or capture functions to increase test coverage.

B2.4. Progress Tracking

This task involves analyzing how a process is operating or how an object–agent has progressed through states in a life history. This composite task is an aggregate of Monitoring, Evaluate and Model, with ordering of the output (see Fig. B2.4).

- Establish progress measurement criteria (Select).
- Develop progress-tracking structure, time line, sequence (Model).
- Gather information on relevant objects or agents (Classify).
- Allocation each individual to a slot in the progress track (Associate).
- Identify any delinquent with respect to criteria (Evaluate, Select).
- Create report.

This task is closely associated with the ISM of the same name. It has a regular structure with some variation coming from the criteria that were given for determining the report and the ability to detect all the objects in the domain of interest. Progress tracking tends to be an automated task.

Requirements problems are as follows.

- Detectability of all the instances that have to be tracked.
- Accuracy of the objects' status information; detecting granularity of each time or sequence step.
- Deciding boundary cases.

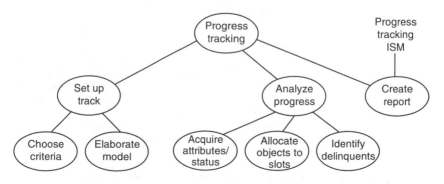

FIG. B2.4. Goal hierarchy for the Progress Tracking task.

Generic requirements are as follows.

1. Means of detecting objects (see Monitor).
2. Detecting exceptions and missing items.
3. Detecting inconsistent progress or static items.

B2.5. Planning–Scheduling

This is the act of organizing some resource or event so that it should happen at a certain time or occur in a specific place (see Fig. B2.5). The essence of planning is ordering the future. In the Domain Theory, planning is interpreted in the cognitive sense of creating a memory structure of intentions, that is, a task goal structure that describes a high-level approach to solving a problem or carrying out an activity (see Task Knowledge Structures; Johnson, 1992). This contrasts with the AI sense of planning that is the process of searching a goal tree to determine a course of action or composing lower branches of a tree from plan components in response to

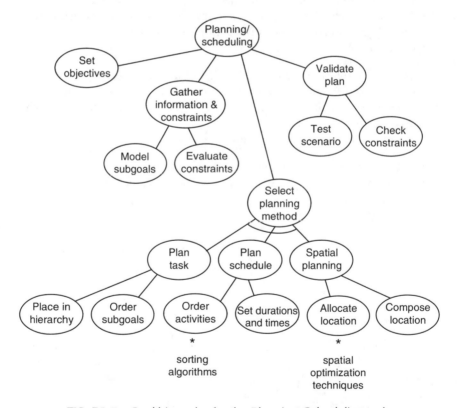

FIG. B2.5. Goal hierarchy for the Planning–Scheduling task.

environmental change (dynamic planning). Human planning has variations such as spatial planning layouts of objects, temporal planning of schedules, and planning that involves allocation. Scheduling involves planning with sequential or temporal constraints. Temporal planning involves the additional complexity of sequencing and synchronizing activity. The major problem in Planning is uncertainty. In deterministic domains in which the behavior and properties of objects are known, plans can be formed in detail. In nondeterministic domains, no planning may be possible because of the high level of entropy. In between are most domains in which change is a fact of life but some regularity exists. Plans, therefore, usually have to start with a default or idealized version and then expect to be revised in light of experience. Planning can be fully automated if detailed knowledge can be captured; however, in domains with heuristic and informal knowledge, humans carry out the planning with computer support in the form of lists of goals, operations, constraints, and plan templates, with sorting and ranking functions.

As Planning has to respond to change, this generalized task is associated with Analysis–Modeling, Monitor, Interpret, and Evaluate generic tasks.

Requirements problems are as follows.

- Criteria for ordering actions may be ill defined or ambiguous.
- Concurrency within plans and how to control it.
- Synchronization between tasks.
- Prioritizing tasks in nondeterministic sequences.
- Dealing with change and updating plans.
- Allocating resources and capable agents to goals or tasks. In HCI design, this becomes functional allocation.

Generic requirements are as follows.

1. Constraint-based problem solver; most plans involve ordering goals within a set of constraints.
2. Plan execution controller, a mechanism that connects plans to their realization as procedures, actions, and so on.
3. Synchronization and timing mechanisms that interact with the execution controller.
4. Multitasking scheduler that controls synchronization and execution in less deterministic environments. This requirement has subrequirements for task status indicators and switching mechanisms.
5. Monitors to analyze change in the environment.
6. Plan-revision mechanism to respond to environmental changes.
7. Simulation tools to explore alternative plans.
8. Sorting, classifying, and modeling tools to support human planning.
9. Visualization tools for models and ordering (e.g., Gantt charts, Pert charts).

B2.6. Navigation

This task can have many meanings (see Fig. B2.6). It involves planning where to go, executing movement (physical primitive action), and monitoring the environment to assess progress and deciding when the destination has been achieved. Navigation also uses orientation to locate cues and elect a direct for travel. The complexity of navigation is increased when symbolic representations of the navigable space (maps) are used.

The interaction diagram for this task (Fig. B2.6a) shows three dialogues between the navigating person and an information provider for a bearing or pathway, pointing out the person's location, or the location of the target.

Maps improve the efficiency of navigation but they increase the user's cognitive load because they have to be interpreted in terms of the perceived reality and a mental model of the navigable space. People's mental models of navigable spaces, even when they are familiar with their environment, show considerable

FIG. B2.6. Goal hierarchy for the Navigation task.

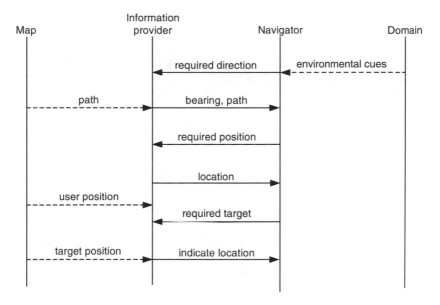

FIG. B2.6a. Interaction diagram for the Navigation task.

individual differences and distortions (Gould, 1987). Most people find navigation a difficult task in an unfamiliar environment, but with familiarity it becomes an encoded skill so we are not aware of having to find our way through areas we know well. Navigation relies on landmark memory in which we encode specific objects as salient locations with an approximate distance between them. Coordinate memory for areas and reference points is less natural and not accurate, so people navigate by landmarks and by associating objects and areas within their proximity (Kosslyn, 1980). Functional allocation in navigation has computers providing route planning and directions with map displays to indicate directions and locations. Humans are responsible for movement and sensing location in the environment; however, in many navigation domains the whole process can be automated as autopilots.

Navigation has several variations. First, the user may not have a specific target, in which case Navigation becomes a series of somewhat arbitrary procedures of scan environment–select direction–move. Second, the user may be lost, in which case the structure is as follows.

```
REPEAT UNTIL location found.
    Backtrack to previous known location.
    Scan environment for waymarks and clues.
    IF identified move toward known location.
    ELSE move and scan using a search technique.
```

Requirements problems in Navigation are as follows.

- Provision of an accurate map of the environment.
- Forming a mental model of the navigable space.
- Locating oneself within the navigable space.
- Linking perceivable features in the environment with symbolic representations on maps.
- Orienting maps with the direction or travel and view in the perceived world.
- Establishing one's orientation with respect to features on the symbolic representations (map, plan, diagram).
- Planning an optimal course to the desired location.
- Avoiding obstructions and hazards en route.
- Judging scale, speed, and direction during motion.

Navigation is usually a solo agent generalized task, although this task may make use of social navigation information such as visit lists of popular locations.

Generic requirements are as follows.

1. Controls to gives users flexible navigation, such as. six degrees of freedom in virtual worlds.
2. Functions to set viewpoints in maps–symbolic representations.
3. Ability to view maps at different scales or zoom–pan over large area maps.
4. Overview function to get a bird's-eye view.
5. Self-location indicators.
6. Search for landmark–environment feature.
7. Course–route planning functions (see Planning).
8. Autopilot for navigation in large spaces with complex routes.
9. Visit lists and pathway trace of movement.
10. Collated visit lists from selected population (social navigation feedback).

B2.7. Diagnosis

This is a complex generalized task that has two major substructures: causal analysis and repair (see Fig. B2.7). Diagnosis uses several generic tasks, such as Model, Interpret, Evaluate, Compare, and Sort. It has subclasses for the diagnosis of problems with living things, designed artefacts, and complex systems. The generalized model of Diagnosis is derived from a fault-finding task described by Rasmussen (1986).

The Analysis subtask is as follows.

- Identify failure event (sign, symptom; Evaluate, Identify).
- Gather fault context information (Model).
- Locate area of failure (Locate, Identify).

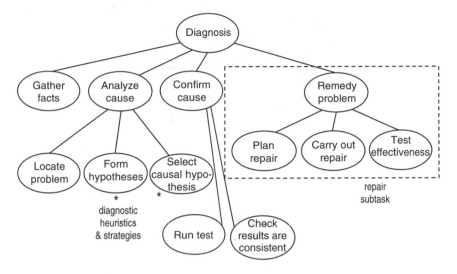

FIG. B2.7. Goal hierarchy for the Diagnosis task.

* Propose causal hypothesis (Sort, Evaluate, Classify).
* Check hypothesis against evidence (Compare, Evaluate).
* Select causal explanation (Select).

The Repair subtask is as follows.

* Plan repair–treatment (Plan).
* Prepare object for repair (possible Disassemble).
* Remove faulty component or repair fault.
* Test repair works (Evaluate).
* Return object to normal working condition (Assemble).

Diagnosis is closely associated with either communicating with people to gather information (symptoms in medical diagnosis) or manipulating designed artefacts to find out why they have failed. Requirements for this generalized task are for information on signs and symptoms for determining courses and appropriate treatments. In deterministic cases, when diagnostic knowledge can be captured and modeled as formal rules, the whole task can be automated as an expert system (e.g., electronic equipment fault finding and repair). However, most diagnostic tasks are cooperative in nature, as illustrated in the typical interaction pattern, given in Fig. B2.7a. The interaction pattern shows a general view of communication that is necessary for gathering signs and symptoms of the problem, posing follow-up questions, and then testing that the repair has worked. Functional allocation in diagnosis varies for near complete automation in deterministic domains (e.g., electrical fault finding) to collaborative models in less deterministic domains

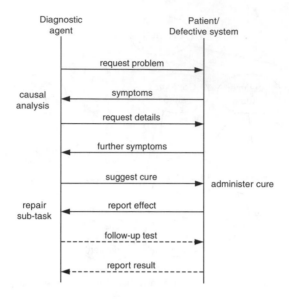

FIG. B2.7a. Cooperative diagnosis interaction pattern.

(e.g., medical diagnosis). In the latter, the computer supplies information on the faulty system, lists of potential faults, signs, and symptoms of problems, and lists of possible causes, with repair strategies for fault types.

Requirements problems are as follows.

- Gathering information for diagnosis when the signs might not be immediately accessible.
- Structuring facts to create a model of the problem.
- The degree of automation, as with most tasks, is dependent on the domain. In well-known determinist domains, diagnosis can be completely automated as an expert system, such as faulting finding in car engines from electronic tests. In less well-known domains only partial support for the user's task is possible by preprocessing information, such as screening out hypotheses that do not match with known observations.

Generic information requirements are as follows.

1. Components, subassemblies of the artefact, machine, or agent being considered.
2. Fault failure history for the object–artefact instance.
3. Typical faults found with the class of objects–artefacts.
4. Heuristics or rules for forming diagnoses from the observed evidence, differential diagnosis hints.
5. List of treatments coupled to diagnosed causes.

Generic functional requirements are as follows.

1. Preprocessors to sort and rank symptoms and observed problems in order of severity, importance, time, and so on.
2. Question checklist dialogues to ensure full capture of diagnostic information.
3. System model simulations to locate problems and support diagnostic reasoning.
4. Expert system inference to diagnose possible causes from observed signs.
5. Interactive microworld system models with "what if?" testing facilities.
6. Automatic implementation of treatments for identified problems.
7. Suggestions for potential cures–treatments.
8. Facilities for follow-up tests to confirm diagnosis.
9. Guided assistance for repair strategies and procedures.

B2.8. Information Retrieval

This task involves searching for information items but also deciding the strategy for searching (browsing, use of query language), selecting search terms, and evaluating the relevance of search results (see Fig. B2.8). The steps and embedded generic tasks in goal-directed information searching are as follows.

- Ascertaining the information need (Communicate, Identify).
- Clarifying the search request (Explain, Identify).
- Transforming the search request into a query (Model, Transform).
- Carrying out search (Navigation, physical action).
- Evaluating the relevance of retrieved items (Evaluate, Sort, Select).
- Extracting relevant information from the retrieved items (Interpret, Evaluate, physical action).
- Delivering the result to the requester (Communicate, physical action).

How a search is implemented depends on the available technology. In manual searches the user scans and explores the information resource by following navigation cues, such as looking for shelf marks in a library and hunting for a book by its title. In automated systems, submitting the query to a search engine to find the document (physical action) is one means of carrying out a search, but it could also be executed by following links on a hypertext.

Information searching consists of a cycle of refining searches as the results from one search help refine the query for the next and so on until the user homes in on the target. The early phase is similar to Analysis–Modeling when a picture of the user's information need is constructed. This is followed by translating the need into a language suitable for an automated search engine. Finally, once results are retrieved, they have to be interpreted, evaluated, and sorted before the relevant subset can be passed on to the user. The instantiation in this case depends on the type of search system being used, for example, keyword search, hypertext, or SQL;

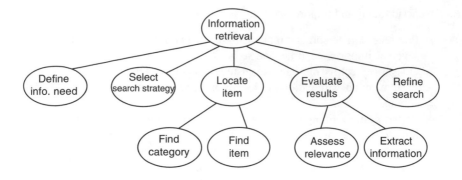

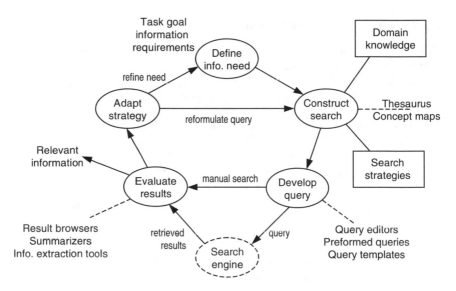

FIG. B2.8. Template structure for Information Retrieval, showing goal hierarchy and execution cycle views.

for instance, hypertext will involve the Search primitive task to find link cues on an interface.

In browsing, search is less goal directed, so the steps become as follows.

Scan information space for categories or items of interest (Interpret).
Move to new location of interest.
Assess available information (Evaluate).
IF interesting THEN
    Explore in more detail

EITHER
    Extract useful information (Select)
OR
    Place bookmark reminder (Select, Record)
ELSE
Continue.

The browsing-style information search may explore the metadata or structure of the information space, or it may be directed to the content of the database. As with goal-directed search, the execution of browsing depends on the available technology; for instance, a query language may be used for browsing sample queries or by picking items on a hypertext map. More detailed models of the IR task can be found in Sutcliffe and Ennis (1998). The interaction pattern, which may be specialized to two human agents (expert intermediary) or one human and one machine (IR system) agent, is depicted in Fig. B2.8a (see Kuhlthau, 1991; Marchionini, 1995).

Requester agent
    Expectations: to gain knowledge.
    Knowledge structures: domain of interest (may be partial knowledge of).
    Competencies: articulate request.
    Responsibilities: to be accurate and honest in articulating request (Grice's maxims).
    Role: articulate request, formulate query, evaluate results.

Search Assistant agent
    Expectations: to supply knowledge.
    Knowledge structures: available knowledge, location thereof.
    Competencies: search strategies, procedures.
    Responsibilities: to service requests.
    Role: retrieve and display results; check query and information needs.

The interaction pattern has two nested iterations for search refinement and clarification within each search. The interaction pattern follows the procedures in the task and associated claims, and it indicates how task-support processes should be designed and ordered within a dialogue. For instance, the assess need process carried out by the librarian may be partially automated by providing a thesaurus; likewise, formulating a query can be helped by a form-filling dialogue. See appendix C.

    Functional allocation for IR automates the search process but leaves identifying and articulating the search need with people. Some support for this task can be given by term suggestion facilities and thesauri. People are also necessary for assessing the relevance of retrieved items, so a collaborative model is needed in which an automated search algorithm is tuned in reponse to user feedback.

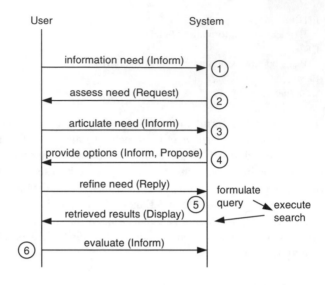

Claims

1. Preformed queries
2. Conceptual maps
3. Active thesaurus
4. Intelligent strategy planner
5. Feedback/browser presenter
6. Relevance feedback

FIG. B2.8a.   Interaction pattern for the IR generalized task. Claims (see chapter 6) are attached to either the whole task or specific components, depending on the original task–artefact context.

Requirements problems are as follows.

- Articulating the search need; most users find identifying search terms difficult.
- Identifying the search target, as this may change during the search process (Belkin, 1987).
- Finding the appropriate information resource to search, as many databases may contain the necessary information.
- Composing queries.
- Search tactics, especially how to exclude unwanted items (NOTs) and use of Boolean operators.
- Interpreting null results, which may mean that the database does not contain the desired item or that the query was inadequate.
- Evaluating large volumes of retrieved data.

- Assessing relevance of retrieved data.
- Reformulating queries in light of retrieved results.
- Extracting information from retrieved documents.

Generic requirements are as follows.

1. Conceptual maps of the available information resources.
2. Controlled vocabularies or thesauri of information resources, preferably displayed as maps (see Information Visualiser; Card et al., 1991).
3. Query terms suggest facilities; this is essentially a means of querying the thesaurus.
4. Syntax directed editors or fill in template editors for query languages.
5. Restricted natural-language query interfaces.
6. Structured keyword lists to support "drill down" search refinement.
7. Query by example or scenarios with similarity-based searching (Landauer & Dumais, 1997).
8. Reusable query libraries and generic templates for query types.
9. Query formulation advisors, which guide on the use of Boolean operators and choice of terms.
10. Results summarizers and browsers to deal with large volumes.
11. Results postprocessors that apply filters (query extensions) to reduce size of results sets.
12. Relevance feedback by marking query terms in retrieval document or summarizing hit density of terms (Moran & Carroll, 1996).
13. Query reformulation strategy advisors that guide on revising queries according to the volume and relevance of the retrieved results (Sutcliffe & Ennis, 1998).
14. Relevance feedback facilities that encourage selecting terms from relevant documents to be added to the subsequent query (Robertson & Beaulieu, 1997; Robertson, Walker, & Beaulieu, 1997).
15. Information extraction facilities that search for word phrases and sentence structures.

Further generic requirements could be added to describe the wide range of different search engine technologies that automate the database search task, such as Latent Semantic Indexing (Landauer et al., 1997) and other statistical–probabilistic search mechanisms. The TREC conference series, for example, Robertson et al. (1997), gives further details.

B2.9. Judgment–Decision Making

Decisions may concern a course of action (policy adoption), accept or reject one option (unitary decisions), or select one or more objects from a set of possible options (multiple decisions). This task has two main variants:

- fast-path attitude or memory-bound decision making, which is closely related to the decide generic task; and
- slow-path reasoned decision making, in which a mental model of the decision space is made and a systematic process is followed to establish the best decision in the circumstances.

Fast-path decision making takes the attributes of two or more competing objects or agents and selects one of them based on the more salient or favored attributes. Slow-path decision making can apply several different reasoning strategies according to the problem at hand and the user's knowledge (e.g., Beach & Mitchell, 1978; Payne et al., 1993). The goal hierarchy for this task and its variants is given in Fig. B2.9.

Gather facts.
Form mental model (Model).
Establish elimination criteria.
    Filter unsuitable options using criteria (Compare).
For remaining options,
    Match attributes against decision criteria (Compare, Evaluate).
    Sort and rank options on goodness of fit (Sort).
    Select best fit option (Select).
    Validate choice against original criteria (Evaluate).

Other variations in the Decision Making task are continuous judgments in perception motor coordination, such as keeping to a constant speed when driving a car (theory of reasoned action; Ajzen & Fishbein, 1980) and deciding whether to follow a particular course of action or adopt a policy. Decision making and judgment tends to be allocated to people with computers providing support processes of information ranking and sorting with simulations for what-if exploration options. In deterministic domains decisions can be automated as an expert system; the user just sets parameters and leaves the system to make the decision by using logical or probabilistic reasoning.

Requirements problems are as follows.

- For the fast-path model, presenting the necessary attributes in a ranked order to facilitate judgment.
- For the slow-path model, presenting information to allow the user to form a mental model.
- Formation of inaccurate or incomplete mental models.
- The degree of automated support to provide. In well-known and deterministic domains, the decision-making process may be automated; however, in most domains cooperative task support has to be designed. This may be filtering out poor options against baseline criteria, providing ranking and sorting functions, or what-if functionality.

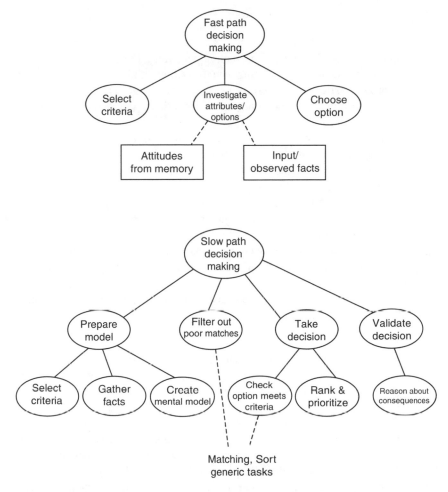

FIG. B2.9. Goal hierarchy for the Judgment–Decision Making generalized tasks, showing slow and fast route variations.

- Counteracting human biases in judgment, such as confirmation bias (using only positive evidence to validate a decision; not looking for counterexamples), encysting and halo effects (can't see the wood for the trees; bias of limited evidence).
- Counteracting human biases in probabilistic judgment, such as belief in small numbers (inadequate samples; Kahnemann & Tversky, 1982).
- Preventing jumping to conclusions (Reason, 1990), and judgment failures under time pressure and stress, caused by frequency and recency effects (go with the most familiar solution without thinking about it).
- Poor validation of decisions.

Generic requirements are as follows.

1. Functions for selecting and presenting decision criteria.
2. Alternative means of presenting data to counteract biases, such as graphics for probabilistic data (Gigerenzer & Goldstein, 1996).
3. Advice on human bias with heuristics on gathering evidence to refute hypotheses (confirmation bias).
4. Presentation of choice options, decision tables, and trees.
5. Filtering out options that do not meet basic criteria.
6. Sorting and ranking other remaining options.
7. Automatic selection of options against criteria.
8. Simulation models for slow-path decision making.
9. What-if decision support by changing weights on criteria in decision tables (Hauser & Clausing, 1988).
10. What-if decision support by changing parameters in simulations.
11. Decision support for probabilistic reasoning, such as Bayesian belief networks (Fenton & Pfleeger, 1997).
12. Interactive microworlds of the decision domain to support exploration of alternatives and validating decisions.

More complex decision-support techniques that support several generic requirements are card sorts and repertory grids for categorization-type decisions; the analytic hierarchy process for ordering options; Dempster Schaefer theory, Bayesian belief networks, or fuzzy logic for judgment under uncertainty; and finally MCDA (Multi Criteria Decision Analysis), which provides Rolls Royce support for multivariate decision making, where variables can be ranked, weighed, assigned importance with adjustable relevance ranges, and so on to create a complex mathematic model of a decision domain (Fenton & Pfleeger, 1997). General mathematical modeling tools can be used for the same purpose to create a wide variety of decision-support tools for financial forecasting, such as the IVM (Inclusive Value Manager) for value-based system assessment (M'Pherson, 1999).

B2.10. Explanation–Advising

This generalized task is closely associated with the Learning and Tutorial meta-domain, but it also occurs in tandem with many other tasks. Explanation has a process component that is described here and a content component that is specified as explanation patterns in the next section. Explanations can either be preplanned or scripted (see sections B3.1 to B3.6), or they can be composed dynamically as illustrated in the template in Fig. B2.10.

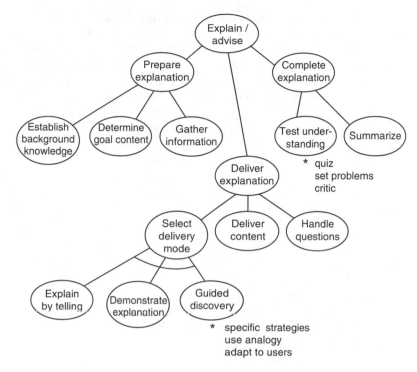

FIG. B2.10.   Goal hierarchy for the Explanation–Advising task.

This has three main phases: planning the explanation, delivery, and then follow-up.

Acquire recipient's background knowledge.
Select content.
Select means of delivery, for example, explanation by telling, use analogy, demonstration, guided discovery (Plan, Select).
Plan explanation script (Plan).

Deliver explanation (Explain).
Handle questions (Communicate, Request).
Test users' understanding (Check).
Clarify misunderstandings (Clarify).
Provide follow-up explanation (Explain).
Summarize explanation.

Planning explanation is complex. Even scripted explanations have to account for the user's prior knowledge and needs. However, explanations should also be interactive so the student can interrupt and ask questions. The system has to interpret the question and compose the answer. This usually takes considerable artificial intelligence and natural-language processing; however, the problem can be simplified by adopting question-type taxonomies and reply plans (see Feiner & McKeown, 1990; Maybury, 1993; Moore & Mittal, 1996). The boundary between explanation and pedagogical design is hard to draw. Explanation templates can easily expand into a whole book on teaching styles and different pedagogical approaches. This section and the description in the Education metadomain in chapter 5 give only a brief summary. Explanation still requires human talents for a flexible, question-answering response. Functional allocation judgments depend on analyzing regular explanation patterns (see appendix B4). Regular explanations can be scripted for automated delivery, but tailoring to individual needs requires human judgment. Automated systems can do a partial assessment of learning and primitive adaptation; however, progress toward completely automated intelligent systems has been slow.

Requirements problems are as follows.

- Acquiring the user's background knowledge and information needs. Acquisition dialogues are intrusive, but the alternatives are either using stereotype user models or trying to infer what the user knows from records of interaction. Both strategies are prone to error.
- Tailoring the explanation to the student's background. Tuning the explanation content to suit the level of prior knowledge is usually possible, but adapting the means of delivery is more difficult.
- Choosing the appropriate delivery mode for the subject matter. Some content suggests particular explanation approaches; for instance, procedures and causal explanations (see B4.4–B4.5) are better explained by using examples, demonstrations, and simulations. Delivery modes for other types of content are less clear cut.
- Choosing the appropriate representation for the content; some material may be expressed better as a diagram or a simulation (Sutcliffe, 1999).
- Initial explanations are rarely adequate so users often need to ask follow-up questions. These are difficult to answer by machine-based explanations systems (Moore & Mittal, 1996).
- The degree of expert initiative in explanation. The explainer may be dominant and give the user no chance to ask questions, active and take the initiative most of the time but allow questions, or passive for user-driven explanation by questioning.

Generic requirements are as follows.

1. User needs acquisition dialogue to find out what the required explanation topic is.
2. Dialogue to acquire user background knowledge; this will have to be structured according to the system's domain knowledge.
3. Explanation planner that can be configured with a delivery script.
4. Demonstration–simulation facility if appropriate for the content.

5. In guided discovery explanation, a monitor is necessary to track users' actions and mistakes.
6. An interpreter to analyze users' mistakes.
7. Critiquer to explain mistakes and provide suggestions for correction.
8. Function to assess users' progress, usually implemented as a quiz.
9. Question handler; this can be a very complex requirement if free-form natural-language questions are allowed. More often a menu of frequently asked questions linked to preformed responses is provided.
10. Adaptation mechanism that tracks users' understanding and adjusts the explanation content accordingly.

B2.11. Matching

Matching is the process of finding the goodness of fit between a set of requirements and properties of objects that might satisfy those requirements. In computation terms this problem is solved by constraint-based problem solvers and linear programming algorithms. This generalized task is closely related to the Object Allocation OSM and uses the Associate generic task. Matching can be achieved by several strategies, and these have important implications for requirements. In an ideal situation all the client requirements can be satisfied so that everyone gets what they want. More frequently there is an insufficient supply of resource objects, so Matching has to be a compromise. Matching extends the Compare generic task to establish the goodness of fit between a set of criteria and the properties of one or more objects.

Matching strategies depend on how clients are handled. For instance, processing can be first come first served, but that may be unfair to clients later in the queue. Another fairer strategy is to ration all clients to a proportion of their requirements according to the stock at hand. If volume is not a consideration, satisfying clients with many constraints (awkward customers) first maximizes satisfaction; however, satisfying low-constraint customers makes for more efficient processing. Matching can be made multiple pass, taking on simple constraints first and more stringent ones in later passes. Functional allocation for this task depends on the flexibility of the matching process. In deterministic domains the whole process can be automated, but where matching relies on human judgment the task is supported by preprocessing information (ranking sorting resources) for human judgment. The outline goal structure of the Matching task is shown in Fig. B2.11 with notes on where strategy variations may occur.

Requirements problems are as follows.

- Determining priorities when demand exceeds supply.
- Assessing priorities among matching criteria.
- Handling excessive constraints: constraint relaxation.
- Handling multiple matches and prioritizing clients who were not satisfied for the next batch.

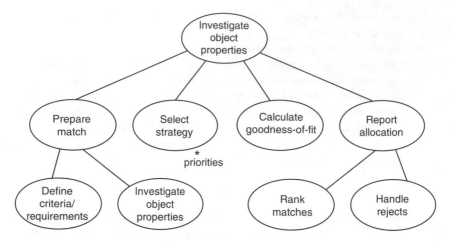

FIG. B2.11.   Matching generalized task and strategy variations.

- Order processing to achieve fairness or efficiency.
- Accurate information on resources.

Generic requirements are as follows.

1. Constraint-based matching algorithm, with search optimization heuristics.
2. Constraint acquisition and feedback dialogue to encourage constraint relaxation.
3. Displays to present goodness-of-fit indication between criteria and objects.
4. Prioritizing and sorting functions for supporting multiuser matching.
5. Interbatch handling facilities.
6. Flexible matching algorithms for single- or double-pass processing.

B2.12.   Forecasting

Forecasting predicts a future state by extrapolating from current data and history (see Fig. B2.12). The first subgoal is to gather data; this is followed by creating the model or theory that will predict the future and then the model is run to produce output. The forecasting task is related to Analysis and Planning–Scheduling. It depends on a model of the represented world and algorithms or inferential processes that extrapolate from current data to the future. Forecasting algorithms usually have a mathematical basis that deals with complex multivariate interactions over a time series to predict future states. The accuracy of the forecast is a function of the sophistication and validity of the model, the algorithms, and the reliability of available data.

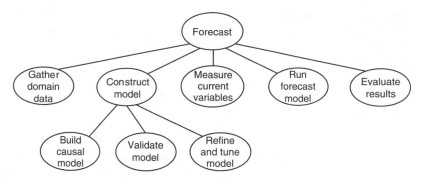

FIG. B2.12.   Goal hierarchy for the Forecasting task.

Requirements problems are as follows.

- Creating an accurate model of the world for forecasting.
- Gathering sufficient reliable data for forecasting.
- Hidden unexpected effects, such as exponential runways.
- Unforeseen interactions between variables.

Generic requirements are as follows.

1. Forecasting algorithm or inferential process.
2. Causal model of domain for forecast.
3. Validation data.
4. Data set for use in forecast.
5. Representation and interpretation of results as charts or graphics.

B3.   GENERIC DIALOGUES

Interaction schemas (chapter 5.3) described prototyping exchanges between agents in a task-related context. This view is refined at a lower level to propose patterns for the Communicate generic task that specify how a dialogue between two agents should take place to achieve a particular communication goal. In linguistics, conversations are composed of discourse acts structured into moves and exchanges that specify a sequence of conversational turns between two parties. Dialogue patterns are composed from the following set of discourse acts (Sutcliffe & Maiden, 1991).

Request (question),
Inform (provide information, answer),

Acknowledge (communication received),
Check (belief),
Confirm,
Propose (action),
Command,
Agree,
Disagree,
Correct.

Conversations have goals that are set by the tasks, so interaction patterns are structured to provide the means to achieve these ends. Primitive conversation patterns were originally described in conversation analysis by Sacks et al. (1974), whereas larger patterns associated with tasks were specified in the conversation for action research by Winograd & Flores (1986). Although natural human discourse is very variable even when associated with specific task goals such as buying and selling goods, the patterns have utility for planning computer agent–user conversations and interpreting users' speech in natural-language processing.

B3.1. Questioning

This pattern requests information by one party from another. The dialogue has many different surface manifestations, such as Wh* questions (where, why, who, how, when, etc.), verb inversion ("So can I find it?"), and rhetorical formats ("The purpose of the pattern is to give a typical sequence, isn't it?"). The underlying abstraction between participants A and B in discourse acts is

    A: Request (question).
    B: Inform (answer).
    A: Acknowledge and evaluate.

This pattern is elaborated in Fig. B3.1 to show Questioning and the related Clarification pattern.

B3.2. Clarification

This pattern (see Fig. B3.2) tests understanding about beliefs or facts, so agent A can ascertain that he or she shares the same knowledge with agent B. Clarification or checking understanding may be carried out by overt questions or by statements that assert a belief to be confirmed or denied; for example, "so patterns can be used to construct user computer dialogues" is a statement that you might either agree or disagree with.

    A: Check (assert belief); may be Request or Inform act.
    B: Confirm or Disagree, with a possible Correct.

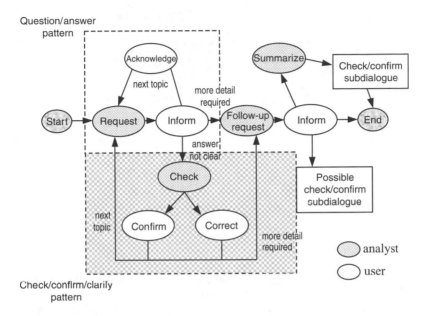

FIG. B3.1. Typical Questioning dialogue with an associated Clarification pattern that handles follow-up questions.

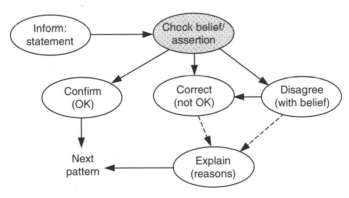

FIG. B3.2. Clarification dialogue pattern.

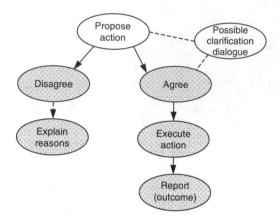

FIG. B3.3.   Propose action pattern with related dialogue.

B3.3.   Propose Action

Proposals are suggestions for action in collaboration with another party (see Fig. B3.3). The initial proposal invites agreement or disagreement. In the case of agreement there should be a commitment to future action, either immediately or in the future, thus building an action ladder from communication to intent to behavior (Clark, 1996). The patterns structure is

> A: Propose (action–strategy–goal).
> B: Agree or Disagree.
>> IF agree
>>> B is committed to action.
>> ELSE
>>> B: Clarify or Propose (alternative).

This pattern is related to Command, but it has less binding force on the recipient to act.

B3.4.   Propose Idea

This pattern is closely related to the previous one, but the proposal differs (see Fig. B3.4). In this case it is an idea-building dialogue that invites the other party to contribute ideas to the original proposition or to refine a proposal. This dialogue is common during analysis–modeling, design, problem solving, and brainstorming.

> A: Propose (idea–concept–design).
> B: Inform (augment proposal)
>> or Propose (offer counter proposal)
>> or Clarify (original proposal)
>> {iterations of proposal building UNTIL}

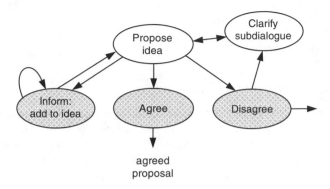

FIG. B3.4. Propose idea dialogue pattern.

A/B: Agree or Disagree
  IF agree
    B is committed to ideas—concept.
  ELSE
    B: Clarify or Propose (alternative).

B3.5.   Command

These patterns are perlocutary acts in Searle's (1969) terminology. The goal of the initiator is to get the other party to follow instructions and carry out some action. Command patterns are associated with the Agent Control OSM and Analysis–Modeling generalized tasks, and they are related to making proposals, reporting facts, and explanations and patterns associated with negotiation. In the Command family the patterns are specialized according to the coupling between the agents and the constraints imposed by the command on the subordinate's action. [The variations in this pattern are illustrated in Fig. B3.5.]

B3.5.1.   Formal Command

In strict hierarchies the command should be followed to the letter of the law, and the only response expected is acknowledgment of the command and reporting back on completion.

A: Command (instructions to act or belief to hold).
B: Acknowledge and subsequently follow instructions.
B: Inform (report back to A).

B3.5.2.   Informal Command

In less hierarchical situations, the subordinate has the choice to clarify the command first, possibly refine the course of action, then carry out the action, and report back. As the power balance between the parties becomes more equal, the command pattern evolves into the proposal liaison pattern in which one party makes a suggestion, they both discuss it, and both agree on a plan of action.

A: Command (action or belief to hold).
B: Acknowledge and possibly Clarify.
B: (subsequent action).
B: Inform (report back).

B3.5.3.   Constrained Command

Commands not only have different forces but also impose constraints on action. The recipient may either be told to carry out an action in some detail, or may be given a higher-level goal with considerable freedom to interpret the plan of action on his or her own. A middle ground would be giving the subordinate the goal and some guidance about how to plan the action. Other variations depend on the group structure. A command might involve a single agent, or it might ask one agent to coordinate the work of others. The degree of autonomy influences the pattern structure.

A: Command (action plus constraints).
B: Acknowledge.
B: Command (subordinate, transfer instructions).
C: Acknowledge (act); Inform (report back to B).
B: Inform (report back to A).

B3.6.   Negotiate Position

There are many tactics and strategies in negotiation, and this pattern has many variants according to the nature of the proposition and how it is represented, for example, negotiating about one choice among many, reaching a consensus from conflicting viewpoints, and so on. This pattern is closely related to the Judgment–Decision Making and Validation–Testing generalized tasks. The template is as follows.

A: Propose (position, belief, action).
B: Propose (alternative, position).
A&B: Inform (justifications and evidence to support positions).
A&B: Clarify (positions and arguments).
A/B: Propose (common ground).
A/B: Agree or Disagree.

The dialogue pattern with variation points is illustrated in Fig. B3.6.

B4.   ARGUMENTATION SCHEMAS

Argumentation–explanation patterns owe their heritage to functional theories of language, notably Rhetorical Structure Theory (RST; Mann & Thompson, 1988). RST specifies a schema of relationships that express the nature of the argument

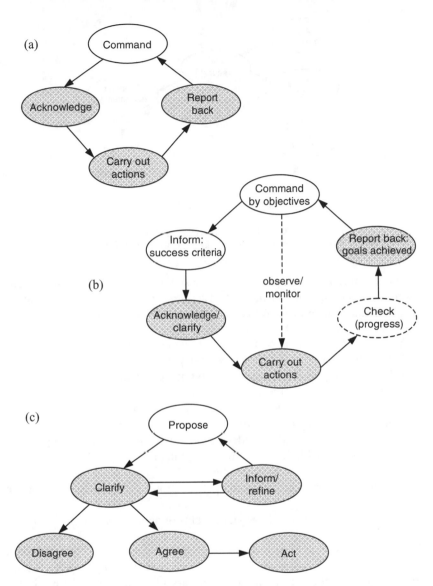

FIG. B3.5.   Variation in the Command pattern with (a) a strict hierarchy, (b) local autonomy, and (c) informal–liaison pattern.

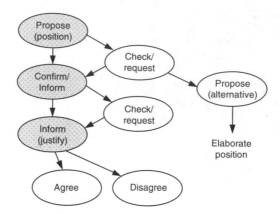

FIG. B3.6.   Negotiation dialogues showing the structure of acts in opening positions, exploration, and resolution phases.

linking two information components; the first subject is referred to as the *nucleus*; the second supporting component is called the *satellite*. RST describes 22 relations all told, of which the more useful are as follows.

- *Enablement*: procedural or how-to-do-it explanation.
- *Elaboration*: adds detail to describe an object–agent–event.
- *Solutionhood*: proposes a means of solving a problem.
- *Summary*: précis of a preceding argument or conversation.
- *Result*: describes the postconditions of an event or causal sequence.
- *Cause*: explains the reasons why an observed event (the result) happened.
- *Motivation*: encourages the reader–listener to accept an argument or proposal.
- *Justification*: provides evidence for an argument or proposal.
- *Background*: adds general description of the subject matter.
- *Circumstance*: provides contextual information relating to an event, action, or location.
- *Comparison*: compares two objects, events or agents.

RST relations can be applied just as well to define the content of each node in an argument, and this has been a common use in AI planning systems that automatically construct explanations from a library of components (Andre & Rist, 1993; Feiner & McKeown, 1990; Maybury, 1993). The Domain Theory uses RST components to describe argumentation patterns that are based on observations of human–human explanations (Sutcliffe, Maiden, & Cooper, 1992).

Following the usual tenets of the Domain Theory, argumentation patterns consist of a set of components that achieve a single goal, such as the goal of the Explain generic task specialized to a topic. These patterns are a sequence of arguments that convey understanding about a body of facts to the reader–listener, so they

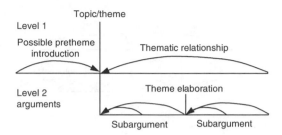

FIG. B4. Schema of an argumentation pattern showing composition of content and RST relations.

are larger units than simple factual statements. Explanations have a hierarchical structure of subarguments that contribute to the overall theme and a sequence that represents the presentation script. These patterns are illustrated as a hierarchy of arguments; reading along the base of the tree gives the sequence of components in a presentation order; see Fig. B4.

B4.1. Classification

The purpose of this pattern is to explain how objects can be assigned to categories according to a set of rules. The pattern is based on categorial models of memory (Rosch, 1985). Classification explains how instances of objects, agents and events belong to general categories. First the category is introduced, and then examples of well-formed members are given, followed by poor examples and members of related categories. The pattern concludes by summarizing the classification rules and may also include an overview of the class hierarchy. This pattern is associated with the Classify generic task.

- Elaboration introduces the category, its attributes, and its position in a taxonomy (Circumstance).
- Comparison describes a good member by pointing out the member's features that agree with the category's attributes.
- Comparison explains a related category member or counterexample.
- Summarizes the classification rules, supplemented with an Elaboration for a large taxonomy.

The content structure for the Classification pattern is shown in Fig. B4.1. Classification may be illustrated by examples of good and bad members of the set. Variations of this pattern are strict classification in which rules are given that assign each object to a unique class without doubt, and categorization when some doubt exists and assignment is made by judgment on how many attributes an object shares with the class definition.

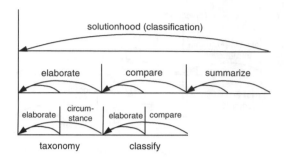

FIG. B4.1.   Classification pattern.

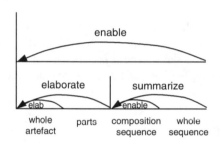

FIG. B4.2.   Composition pattern.

B4.2.   Composition

The Composition or whole–parts pattern explains the composition of physical or conceptual objects in terms of components and how they fit together. The pattern can be specialized to illustrate Decomposition rather than Composition, and it is linked to the Composition–Decomposition grounded domain OSMs.

- Elaboration introduces the whole object and describes its role or function.
- Elaboration then describes or shows the parts.
- Enablement is used to illustrate the composition–aggregation sequence from parts to substructures and the whole object.
- Summary is used to recap facts about the object and its parts and to point out major subcomponents.

The template structure shows the iterative top-down nature of this explanation (see Fig. B4.2).

B4.3.   Task-Based (How-To-Do-It) Explanation

The task sequence given here is specialized for physical or abstract cognitive tasks. The sequence is organized to first provide the task goal (purpose) and then give details of the procedure steps, followed by a summary.

- Enablement introduces the overall plan and explains the task goal. This may be accompanied by a diagram of the plan.
- Circumstance gives the preconditions for the task to commence.
- Enablement describes the task steps.
- Summary integrates the explanation and describes the postconditions for task completion.

Conceptual (i.e., cognitive) tasks are explained in the same manner, and both benefit from use of an example to elaborate each step (see Fig. B4.3).

B4.4. Causal (Why-How It Works) Explanation

This pattern starts by introducing the domain, important objects, and concepts; then the causal model is explained, followed by background knowledge to back up why the events happen. A summary concludes with key events and their causation. This script is closely associated with Analysis and Diagnosis generalized tasks (see Fig. B4.4).

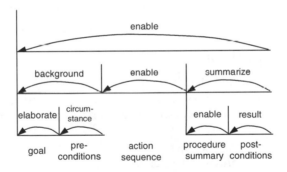

FIG. B4.3. Task-based explanation pattern.

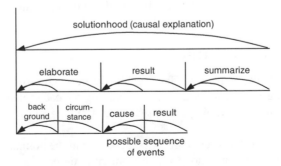

FIG. B4.4. Causal explanation pattern.

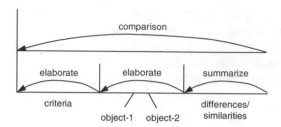

FIG. B4.5. Comparing objects pattern.

- Elaboration introduces the domain and important objects.
- Cause followed by Result describes the sequence of cause and effect, possibly supplemented by Background to explain key facts and background knowledge.
- Summary is used for key events and causal explanation if the explanation concerns natural phenomena, or Solutionhood if the explanation concerns a how-something-works problem.

Causal explanation benefits from demonstrations and simulations so the user can discover associations between causes and effects. This pattern may require an interactive microworld to help the user understand the content as well as a scripted presentation.

B4.5. Comparison

Comparison is intended to show the differences or similarities between two or more objects (see Fig. B4.5). The structure indicates juxtaposing of two or more objects for comparison in displays so that the user can scan them during the task.

- Elaboration: comparison criteria.
- Elaboration: similarities and differences.
- Summarize differences.

The pattern draws attention to the need to highlight the relevant features for comparison if these are known beforehand.

B4.6. Sequence Tracing

This pattern explains a sequence of facts within a representation or shows a pathway for navigation tasks. The structure involves picking out each segment in sequence and then explaining the whole path or sequence (see Fig. B4.6).

- Background explains segments or components in the domain.
- Elaboration draws attention to each segment in order.
- Summarize whole sequence or pathway.

B4.7. Motivation

This pattern encourages the recipient to accept a proposal, belief or argument. It is related to design rationale representations and the negotiation dialogue pattern. The structure sets out the argument and then presents evidence (see Fig. B4.7).

- Elaboration: proposition, belief, argument.
- Motivation: argument in favor.
- Justification: additional information to back up motivational arguments.
- Circumstance: evidence why the proposition is worthwhile.

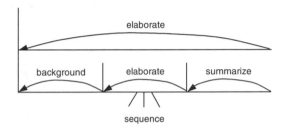

FIG. B4.6. Sequence tracing pattern.

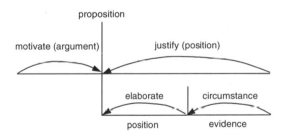

FIG. B4.7. Motivation pattern.

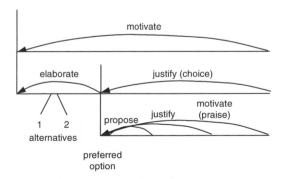

FIG. B4.8. Persuasion pattern.

As with many patterns, there are substantial variations. In motivation the subtleties are how the content is selected and expressed, as well as how those selections are made with respect to the model or the recipient of the argument. The more that is known about the recipient, the better the argument can be tailored to his or her motivation.

B4.8. Persuasion

This pattern is a specialization of Motivation. The difference lies in the aim of Persuasion to make the recipient take a course of action, accept a belief, or make a particular decision. Persuasion is closely associated with the Judgment–Decision Making generalized task. The sequence is illustrate in Fig. B4.8.

- Elaboration: choices or alternatives.
- Proposal: choice or preferred action.
- Motivation: choice with supporting arguments.
- Justification: choice by evidence.
- Motivation: praise recipient choice.

Praising the recipient's choice, even though it might sound sycophantic, does have a positive effect. Most people feel better and well disposed toward others who praise them (Reeves & Nass, 1996).

APPENDIX C

Claims Library

This library is collated from my work, joint papers with Jack Carroll, and Jack Carroll's own papers. Most claims come from the last source. Claims in sections C1–C3 predate development of the extended schema and are therefore documented in the minimal schema, comprising only a brief description, upsides, and, expressed in the *but* clause, downsides. Additional claims can be found in chapters 6 and 8.

C1. METADOMAIN: DESIGN

C1.1. HCI Design: Information Presentation Family, Multimedia Claims

Video Information claim: video information
Artefact: Lincs project multimedia tutorial environment.
* a very rich, intrinsically appealing medium
* *but* difficult to search and must be viewed linearly in real time.

Fast-forward claim: fast-forwarding video information
Artefact: Lincs project multimedia tutorial environment.

- allows the viewer to more rapidly scan and evaluate clips
- *but* destroys intelligibility of the sound track and the "feel" of the real-time visual information.

Stand-alone Clips claim: decomposes the project history into a pool of stand-alone video clips

Artefact: Lincs project multimedia tutorial environment.

- facilitates analysis of the system from diverse perspectives
- engages the person by allowing him or her to "construct" an overall view of the technical rationale and design process from diverse pieces
- *but* people may find it difficult to integrate conflicting bits of information into a coherent overall concept.

C1.2. HCI Design: Information Presentation Family, Visualization Design Claims

Time-line claim: the time-line interface control

- encourages a user to take a historical perspective or to consider historical or process issues
- *but* the time periods may not resolve the history finely enough
- *but* the relative model of time may not support the user's concerns (e.g., a "when" question).

C1.3. HCI Design: Dialogue Control Family, Control Widgits Claims

Control panel interface claim: a simple control panel interface

- directly conveys the content categories of the database
- encourages direct interaction
- *but* precise or complex queries may be difficult to directly articulate.

C1.4. HCI Design: Collaboration Family, Strategy Claims

Social conformity claim: articulating one's beliefs and engaging in action in a social context

- provides a highly responsive setting for testing and refining one's beliefs and behavior, and for building group consensus
- *but* encourages actions and beliefs that are group normative and consistent with the actions and beliefs of powerful others (e.g., group leaders), and thereby can inhibit diversity.

C1.5. HCI Design: Collaboration Family, Controls Claims

Human issues claim: the human issues button, the team members' buttons, and the appearance of team members in the clips
  • suggest questions about collaborative dynamics among team members
  • *but* may evoke questions for which there is no information in the database.

C2. METADOMAIN: EDUCATION

C2.1. Learning Strategies Component, Subject-Domain Object-Oriented Programming

Claims in this section refer to the Smalltalk tutoring environment (Carroll, 2000).

Claim: searching for code with the class hierarchy browser
  • directs attention to inheritance relationships among objects
  • *but* may reduce attention to other important object relationships (such as sharing instance variables)
  • *but* gives no application view in which objects that work together in an application
  • appear together in the code library
  • *but* the number of classes in the class hierarchy may overwhelm new programmers.

Claim: tracing references to classes in method code
  • allows learners to analyze run-time relationships among application objects
  • *but* many run-time relationships are not obvious just from the code as a text (e.g., user-interface code is especially hard)
  • *but* finding a class referred to leaves open how *that* class works (which in turn involves understanding all of its methods)
  • *but* reconstructing a network of class references in various methods may not reveal the overall application design.

Claim: the View Matcher breakpoints
  • parse application execution into coherent episodes for analysis
  • *but* may interrupt interaction sequences
  • *but* it can be difficult to make sense of an application in the midst of a message send.

Claim: application-filtered Class Hierarchy Browser (Bittitalk Browser)
  • focuses attention on inheritance relationships among application objects

- encourages and supports opportunistic analysis of the application design
- *but* may reduce attention to other important object relationships (such as sharing instance variables)
- *but* other classes in the class hierarchy cannot be accessed.

Claim: the object communication summarized in the message execution stack
- helps learners to decompose application functionality
- supports transfer from procedural programming experience
- *but* the object communication can be quite complex
- *but* learners may rely on a procedural model of computation to interpret the stack.

Claim: application-specific commentary for each message in the stack
- supports an application-oriented interpretation of object communication
- *but* is not general and may not apply well to other applications.

Claim: running the system demos
- captures the interest of programmers
- motivates programmers to learn by doing
- *but* noninteractive demos offer little for the programmer to do
- *but* programmers may have difficulty finding the demo code.

Claim: browsing and studying demo code in the Class Hierarchy Browser
- establishes basic Smalltalk programming skills
- provides model applications for programmers to analyze and extend
- *but* may reduce time spent on instantiating and analyzing objects (e.g., in a Workspace)
- *but* the demos are not paradigmatic Smalltalk applications.

Claim: permanent display and coordination of a filtered class hierarchy (Bittitalk view)
- encourages and supports opportunistic analysis of the application design
- simplifies access to the class hierarchy
- *but* other classes in the class hierarchy cannot be accessed or learned about
- *but* does not develop basic skills for accessing and managing the Class Hierarchy Browser.

Claim: playing and analyzing a paradigmatic interactive application (the blackjack game)
- captures the interest of programmers
- motivates programmers to learn by doing
- establishes basic Smalltalk programming skills
- provides model applications for programmers to analyze and extend
- *but* may encourage context-specific learning

- *but* people may spend too much time using the application and not enough time learning about it
- *but* the game may introduce learning burdens of its own if it is not sufficiently familiar to the learner.

C2.2. Learning Strategies Component, Procedural Training

Claim: decomposing learning objectives into sections and steps and directing each of these in turn
- allows complex concepts and skills to built up from parts
- *but* learners may become impatient, and may reject activities that seem trivial or irrelevant
- *but* following steps may not facilitate retrieval and performance in the real tasks.

Claim: keeping directive instructions and learner practice in lock-step contiguity
- allows the learner to know exactly what to do and when
- *but* does not promote reflection or analysis (the learner may focus too narrowly on cach small task).

Claim: repetitive practice
- clarifies correct discriminations and smooths performance
- *but* complex programming tasks are not merely scripts.

Claim: exploring a familiar application (the blackjack game)
- orients and motivates programmers by engaging prior knowledge
- *but* may encourage context-specific learning
- *but* people may spend too much time interacting with the application and not enough time learning about it.

Claim: error-specific explanatory material and recovery procedures
- assists people in making sense of unexpected problems
- sharpens concept of correct performance
- *but* people not experiencing these specific problems may become confused by the extra information.

Claim: decomposing target objectives into components enabling objectives and training each of these in turn
- allows complex target objectives to be systematically built up from parts
- *but* learners may become impatient and may reject activities that seem trivial or irrelevant
- *but* following steps may not facilitate retrieval and performance in real task settings.

Claim: making a pleasant, familiar experience contingent on a target performance
- reinforces the target performance
- *but* can undermine the intrinsic motivation for achievement.

Claim: working on a realistic task
- provides the learner with a framework for integrating and applying learning experiences
- *but* realistic tasks may be too difficult (instructional objectives may have to be inferred)
- *but* there may be too many kinds of task settings to support.

Claim: working on a familiar task
- orients and motivates learners by engaging prior knowledge
- *but* may encourage context-specific learning
- *but* may engage inappropriate prior knowledge.

Claim: incorporating planning and acting throughout the learning experience
- helps orient the learner to applying knowledge
- supports skill transfer
- *but* increases task complexity.

Claim: retrieval, elaboration, and inference making
- engages and sustains learners' attention
- makes skills more robust and accessible
- *but* learners might not have access to enough information to reason successfully
- *but* learners may be anxious about bearing such responsibilities.

Microworld claim: working in a simplified, familiar task environment (a microworld)
- motivates learning by doing
- provides a framework for analyzing and extending learning experiences.

Goal reification claim: reifying a learner's goals and plans
- promotes an abstract understanding of task structure, which leads to efficient action and broad transfer
- *but* the goal and plan language may be unfamiliar, abstract, and therefore difficult to comprehend.

Plan-based error messages claim: system-generated error messages couched in terms of goals and plans
- brings the appropriate planning abstractions to bear when they are needed
- spares the learner the burden of generating explicit goal and plan descriptions
- *but* learners may develop superficial understandings when errors are not made

- *but* goal-plan dialogues are restricted to errors and are not under learner control.

Reinstating goals claim: the coach's reinstating of goals for learners
- facilitates the resolution of problem solving impasses
- *but* this may rob learners of the opportunity of managing their own goals
- *but* the coach's intervention may be disruptive to ongoing problem solving and memory.

Confirmatory feedback claim: the coach's confirmation that learners are pursuing legitimate goals
- provides confidence and allows learners to focus attention on the chosen course of action
- *but* this may rob learners of the opportunity of evaluating their own goals.

System-generated goals claim: having the system generate goal structures throughout the course of problem solving
- promotes abstract understandings without requiring learners to generate solutions in an abstract language
- *but* recognizing goals may evoke poorer retention than generating goals
- *but* learners must draw correspondences between their own behavior and the display to get help.

C2.3. Learning Environment, Training

Claim: training on one's own
- eliminates the trainer role
- mitigates differences among students (self-confident students cannot monopolize learning interactions)
- allows training in a greater variety of work settings and schedules
- gives students more autonomy and responsibility for their own learning
- *but* makes it difficult to monitor progress or offer help
- *but* may diminish collaborative interactions among students.

Claim: providing a setting for training that is similar to the real work setting
- supports interaction between learners and their more experienced colleagues
- *but* could create confusion by blurring the distinction between training and working.

C2.4. Student Model Component, Procedural Training

Background tracking claim: tracking the learner's behavior automatically in a separate window
- provides a resource for learners to reinstate goals as they work

- minimizes the disruption of the learner's own activity
- *but* learners must manage their own help seeking.

Color-Coded telegraphic display claim: a color-coded telegraphic display of goals
- provides persistent feedback on the correctness of actions as well as access to further information
- *but* learners must learn the display's feature language and controls.

C2.5. Progress Assessment Component, Procedural Training

Fisheye view claim: dynamic fisheye views of the goal hierarchy
- reduces the overall complexity of the display
- focuses learner attention on the goal hierarchy pertinent to current behavior
- *but* it could conceal parts of the goal hierarchy that interest the learner
- *but* background control of display dynamics could distract, confuse, or intimidate the learner.

Radical shuffling claim: shuffling the goal list so that the current subgoal structure appears at the bottom of the display
- allows learners to easily find the analysis of the current goal
- *but* this changes the position of many goals in the tree and may disrupt understanding of the display.

Conservative shuffling claim: shuffling only the leaves of the tree, along with highlighting the current goal and expanding its subgoal structure
- allows learners to find the current goal and retain their grasp of previously posted goals
- *but* learners may become confused about whether the GoalPoster is a history list or a conceptual structure.

Claim: diagnosing and recovering from errors
- focuses and motivates learners
- helps sharpen a concept of correct performance
- *but* errors can be frustrating and disrupt task goals.

C3.   METADOMAIN: MANAGEMENT

C3.1.   Personnel Management Component

Browsing history claim: browsing a video database of statements, stories, and reflections of team members
- conveys–builds group vision

- accesses a variety of views
- provides direct and flexible access to views
- clarifies and enriches answers to queries by lots of collateral information
- *but* the query categories may not fit the user's goal
- *but* the amount of information to be browsed may overwhelm people.

Overview pitch claim: an overview pitch of project status and direction
- efficiently conveys and builds the group vision
- *but* creates normative averaging and power bias distortions.

Piecemeal understanding claim: pursuing questions of project vision, status, and direction through a series of interactions with colleagues
- accesses a variety of views
- *but* takes a lot of time and effort
- *but* can cause confusion and thrashing.

C4. GROUNDED DOMAIN: SPATIAL OBJECT SENSING OSM

System model claim

Artefact:	Shipboard Emergency Management System.
Description:	A model of the ship's status is displayed as a diagram showing compartments. The model displays normal operation of equipment and hazardous events in the location where they are detected.
Upsides:	Model helps user situation awareness of the current system state and makes the user aware of the context of a hazardous event.
Downsides:	Events may not be seen by the user if attention is not drawn to the model. Display of several hazard events at once may confuse the user.
Scenario:	The ship's captain is carrying out routine duties as well as monitoring the ship's state. A fire breaks out in number 3 hold and this is displayed on the system model. A warning is sounded to draw the captain's attention to the problem.

Event filters claim

Artefact:	Shipboard Emergency Management System: detector subsystem.
Description:	Hazardous events are detected by sensors. The system maintains a profile of events that are not considered dangerous, and these are recorded but not notified to the user. Events that pass through the filters are notified to the user without delay.
Upsides:	Filters remove unwanted low-level problems that could distract the users from more important tasks.
Downsides:	New but insignificant events might pass through the filter and confuse the user. Events that are screened out by the filter profile might become important if they occur in unusual circumstances.
Scenario:	Periodic changes of temperature and humidity occur in the ship's cargo, and these events are usually not important. Filters screen out

temperature changes within a preset range. A fire breaks out, which raises the temperature and triggers both this sensor and a smoke detector. Both events are signaled to the ship's captain as a fire hazard.

Event interpretation claim

Artefact:	Shipboard Emergency Management System: status display.
Description:	Hazardous events detected by the monitoring system are interpreted by the system according to the type of hazard detected. Actions to reduce or contain the hazard are suggested to the user.
Upsides:	Interpretation helps the user understand the nature of the hazard and take corrective action.
Downsides:	System's interpretation might mislead the user if it is not correct. Unexpected events may be misinterpreted.
Scenario:	Damage to a container during a storm causes spillage of caustic chemicals in number 3 hold. Sensors detect liquid in the hold and a change in the chemical composition of the air in the hold. The system interprets this hazard as a chemical spillage rather than a seawater-flooding danger in the hold.

Trace history claim

Artefact:	Shipboard Emergency Management: hazardous diagnosis subsystem.
Description:	When an object is associated with a hazardous condition, the system consults its database for any previous records of problems with the same object type or instance and displays previous records with corrective action taken (if recorded).
Upsides:	History helps user interpret the causes of the hazard and decide on corrective action.
Downsides:	User may jump to conclusion based on history of past accidents rather than reasoning how to deal with the current situation.
Scenario:	The ship's captain is carrying out routine duties as well as monitoring the ship's state. A fire breaks out in an auxiliary generator compartment. The system automatically traces the record of problems with the auxiliary generator and displays the history of dealing with previous fires: isolate circuit or use CO_2 extinguishers.

C5.   GENERALIZED TASK: INFORMATION RETRIEVAL

Preformed query claim

Artefact:	Preformed query library (INTUITIVE class) and user-interface menu selector.
Description:	A preformed query is attached to an icon or placed in a menu.
Upsides:	Provides rapid access to information; saves users effort in articulating queries.
Downsides:	Finding queries in a large library can be difficult. Queries inflexible. Cannot be adapted.

Scenario: The user interface presents a menu of queries that can be reused. The user selects a query that matches his or her need by selecting an icon or a menu option, and the system retrieves the information for presentation.

Visual conceptual maps claim

Artefact: Camerawise information display system.

Description: A graphical map displays a model of the database contents so the user can query by pointing to concept keywords on the map.

Upsides: Visualizing the database helps the user browse and explore the available information. Query by pointing to categories is simple.

Downsides: Finding specific items in large maps is difficult. Maps can become cluttered as databases scale up so wayfinding becomes difficult. Expressing complex queries by pointing is not possible.

Scenario: The user wishes to find information on camera aperture settings. The user scans the map to find the category camera settings and follows links to apertures. The user double clicks on this category node to retrieve information from the database.

Active thesaurus claim

Artefact: Multimedia Broker navigator.

Description: The system thesaurus displays terms describing the database contents in a hierarchy diagram. The user enters a term and this is used to query the thesaurus, which displays any areas containing the term. Any set of terms can be used to send queries to the thesaurus.

Upsides: Displaying areas of the thesaurus relevant to the user's current need helps the user to home in on the topics and keywords relevant to his or her search.

Downsides: The thesaurus may display too localized an area for general searches, and display of local areas may discourage browsing.

Scenario: The user wants to find information on company mergers in a database of newspaper articles from the Financial Times. The keyword "merger" is entered and the thesaurus displays subtrees of company information, and takeover stories.

Intelligent strategy planner claim

Artefact: Multimedia Broker search subsystem.

Description: The system gives the user advice on the search strategies to follow, based on a profile of the user's knowledge and a description of his or her information need. The system displays advice as heuristics for choice of keywords, forming and reforming queries, and evaluating retrieved documents for relevance.

Upsides: Search strategy advice helps novice users make more effective use of search engines.

Downsides: Novice users can find the advice hard to interpret; expert users find the advice annoying.

Scenario: The user has submitted a search that has retrieved a large number of results. The system asks the user to judge which results are relevant, if any. Once the user has marked a small number of the retrieved documents, the system advises, narrowing the current querying by adding more terms, selecting terms from the relevant documents, changing Boolean operators to constrain the query, and so on.

Feedback browser–presenter claim

Artefact: INTUITIVE browser tool.

Description: The system presents a summary of the retrieved result of a query, sorted in order of matching to the user's query if possible, or ranked according to user-defined criteria. The user may select any summary by double clicking it to view the whole document.

Upsides: Summarizing the results of a search helps the user to evaluate the relevance of the results.

Downsides: Large results sets can be difficult to browse. The ranking–sorting criteria may not be compatible with the user's view.

Scenario: The user has submitted a search that has retrieved a large number of results. The system displays the results in a ranked order list according to the type of document and the goodness of fit matching with keywords in the user's query.

Relevance feedback claim

Artefact: OKAPI information retrieval system (Robertson et al., 1997).

Description: The system evaluates the retrieved documents for relevance and then asks the user to mark keywords in the abstracts of documents selected by the user as relevant for his or her query. The system extracts these keywords and adds them to a subsequent query to retrieve similar documents.

Upsides: Search strategy helps users by extracting useful terms from appropriate documents and thereby making more effective use of search engines.

Downsides: Users may mark inappropriate terms or the terms chosen may not occur in other documents in the database.

Scenario: The user has submitted a search on company mergers in a newspaper article database, which has retrieved a large number of results. The system asks the user to judge which results are relevant. Once the user has marked a small number of the retrieved documents, the system requests the user to indicate relevant search terms in the selected abstracts. The user selects *takeovers* and *hostile bids*. The system adds these terms to the query and retrieves a smaller set of more relevant documents.

References

Ahlberg, C., & Shneiderman, B. (1994). Visual information seeking: tight coupling of dynamic query filters with starfield displays. In B. Adelson, S. Dumais, & J. Olson (Eds.), *Human Factors in Computing Systems: CHI 94 Conference Proceedings* (pp. 313–317). New York: ACM Press.

Ajzen, I., & Fishbein, M. (1980). *Understanding attitudes and predicting social behaviour*. Englewood Cliffs, NJ: Prentice-Hall.

Akin, O. (1986). *Psychology of architectural design*. London: Pion.

Alexander, C., Ishikawa, S., & Silverstein, M. (1977). *A pattern language*. Oxford: Oxford University Press.

Allen, J. F. (1987). *Natural language understanding*. Menlo Park, CA: Benjamin Cummings.

Alty, J. L. (1991). Multimedia: what is it and how do we exploit it? In D. Diaper & N. V. Hammond (Eds.), *People and Computers VI: Proceedings of the HCI'91 Conference* (pp. 31–41). Cambridge, MA: Cambridge University Press.

Anderson, J. R. (1985). *Cognitive psychology and its implications*. New York: Freeman.

Anderson, J. R. (1990). *The adaptive character of thought*. Hillsdale, NJ: Lawrence Erlbaum Associates.

Anderson, J. R., Corbett, A. T., Koedinger, K., & Pelletier, R. (1995). Cognitive tutors: lessons learned. *Journal of Learning Sciences, 4*, 167–207.

Andre, E., & Rist, T. (1993). The design of illustrated documents as a planning task. In M. T. Maybury (Ed.), *Intelligent multimedia interfaces* (pp. 94–116). Cambridge, MA: AAAI/MIT Press.

Anton, A. I., & Potts, C. (1998). The use of goals to surface requirements for evolving systems. In *Proceedings: 1998 International Conference on Software Engineering. Forging new links* (pp. 157–166). Los Alamitos, CA: IEEE Computer Society Press.

Arango, G., Schoen, F., & Pettengill, R. (1993). Design as evolution and reuse. In *Proceedings: 2nd International Workshop on Software Reusability (Advances in software reuse)* (pp. 9–18). Los Alamitos, CA: IEEE Computer Society Press.

Arens, Y., Hovy, E., & Vossers, M. (1993). On the knowledge underlying multimedia presentations. In M. T. Maybury (Ed.), *Intelligent multimedia interfaces* (pp. 280–306). Cambridge MA: AAAI/MIT Press.

Argyris, C. (1999). *On organizational learning* (2nd ed.). Oxford: Blackwell Business.

Back, T. (Ed.). (1997). *Handbook of evolutionary computation*. Oxford: Institute of Physics Publishing/OUP.

Bailey, R. W. (1982). *Human performance engineering: a guide for system designers*. Englewood Cliffs, NJ: Prentice-Hall.

Basili, V. R., & Rombach, H. D. (1988). The TAME project: towards improvement-orientated software environments. *IEEE Transactions on Software Engineering, 14*(6), 758–773.

Basili, V. R., & Weiss, D. M. (1984). A methodology for collecting valid software engineering data. *IEEE Transactions on Software Engineering, 10*(6), 728–738.

Batory, D. (1998). Domain analysis for GenVoca generators. In P. Devanbu, & J. Poulin (Eds.), *Proceedings: Fifth International Conference on Software Reuse* (pp. 350–351). Los Alamitos, CA: IEEE Computer Society Press.

Batory, D., Chen, G., Robertson, E., & Wang, T. (2000). Design wizards and visual programming environments: the GenVoca generators. *IEEE Transactions on Software Engineering, 26*(5), 441–452.

Beach, L. R., & Mitchell, T. R. (1978). A contingency model for the selection of decision strategies. *Academy of Management Review, 3*, 439–449.

Belkin, N. (1987). Information concepts for information science. *Journal of Documentation, 34*, 55–85.

Bellamy, R. K. E., & Carroll, J. M. (1990). Redesign by design. In D. Diaper, D. Gilmore, G. Cockton, & B. Shackel, (Eds.), *Proceedings: Third IFIP Conference on Human-Computer Interaction Interact 90* (pp. 199–205). Amsterdam: North-Holland.

Bellotti, V., Blandford, A., Duke, D., MacLean, A., May, J., & Nigay, L. (1996). Interpersonal access control in computer-mediated communications: a systematic analysis of the design space. *Human-Computer Interaction, 11*(4), 357–432.

Bellotti, V., Buckingham Shum, S., MacLean, A., & Hammond, N. (1995). Multidisciplinary modelling in HCI design: theory and practice. In I. R. Katz, R. Mack, L. Marks, M. B. Rosson, & J. Nielsen (Eds.), *Human Factors in Computing Systems: CHI 95 Conference Proceedings* (pp. 146–153). New York: ACM Press.

Bennett, K., Ramage, M., & Munro, M. (1999). A decision model for legacy systems. *IEE Proceedings: Software, 146*(3), 153–159.

Beyer, H., & Holtzblatt, K. (1998). *Contextual design: defining customer-centered systems.* San Francisco, CA: Morgan Kaufmann.

Biggerstaff, T. J., & Perlis, A. J. (1989). *Software reusability.* New York: Addison Wesley.

Borchers, J. (2000). *A pattern approach to interaction design.* Chichester: Wiley.

Borchers, J., & Muhlhauser, M. (1998). Design patterns for interactive musical systems. *IEEE Multimedia, 5*(3), 36–46.

Brereton, P., Budgen, D., Bennett, K., Munro, M., Layzell, P., Macaulay, L., Griffiths D., & Stannett, C. (1999). The future of software: defining the research agenda. *Communications of the ACM, 42*(12), 78–84.

Breuker, J., & Van der Velde, W. (1994). *CommonKADS Library for expertise modelling.* Amsterdam: IOS Press.

Browne, D. P., Totterdell, P., & Norman, M. A. (Eds.). (1990). *Adaptive user interfaces.* London: Academic.

Buckingham Shum, S. (1996). Analyzing the usability of a design rationale notation. In T. P. Moran & J. M. Carroll (Eds.), *Design rationale: concepts, techniques and use* (pp. 185–215). Mahwah, NJ: Lawrence Erlbaum Associates.

Cacioppo, J. T., Petty, R. E., & Kao, C. F. (1984). The efficient assessment of need for cognition. *Journal of Personality Assessment, 48*, 306–307.

Candy, L., & Edmonds, E. A. (2000). Creativity enhancement with emerging technologies. *Communications of the ACM, 43*(8), 62–65.

Card, S. K., Moran, T. P., & Newell, A. (1983). *The psychology of human computer interaction.* Hillsdale, NJ: Lawrence Erlbaum Associates.

Card, S. K., Robertson, G., & Mackinlay, J. D. (1991). The Information Visualizer: an information workspace. In S. P. Robertson, G. M. Olson, & J. S. Olson (Eds.), *Human Factors in Computing Systems: CHI 91 Conference Proceedings* (pp. 181–188). New York: ACM Press.

Carroll, J. M. (1990). *The Nurnberg Funnel: designing minimalist instruction for practical computer skill.* Cambridge, MA: MIT Press.

Carroll, J. M. (1995). *Scenario-based design: envisioning work and technology in system development.* New York: Wiley.

Carroll, J. M. (2000). *Making use: scenario-based design of human-computer interactions.* Cambridge, MA: MIT Press.

Carroll, J. M., & Campbell, R. L. (1989). Artifacts as psychological theories: the case of human-computer interaction. *Behaviour and Information Technology, 8*, 247–256.

Carroll, J. M., Kellogg, W. A., & Rosson, M. B. (1991). The task-artifact cycle. In J. M. Carroll (Ed.), *Designing interaction: psychology at the human-computer interface* (pp. 74–102). New York: Cambridge University Press.

Carroll, J. M., & Rosson, M. B. (1991). Deliberated evolution: stalking the view matcher in design space. *Human-Computer Interaction, 6*(3–4), 281–318.

Carroll, J. M., & Rosson, M. B. (1992). Getting around the task-artifact framework: how to make claims and design by scenario. *ACM Transactions on Information Systems, 10*(2), 181–212.

Carroll, J. M., & Rosson, M. B. (1995). Managing evaluation goals for training. *Communications of the ACM, 38*(7), 40–48.

Carroll, J. M., Singley, M. K., & Rosson, M. B. (1992). Integrating theory development with design evaluation. *Behaviour and Information Technology, 11*, 247–255.

Chandrasekaran, B., Keuneke, A., & Tanner, M. (1992). Explanation in knowledge systems: the roles of the task structures and domain functional models. In *Samos Workshop on Task Based Explanation*: *papers and abstracts* [unpaginated]. Athens: University of the Aegean.

Chen, P. (1976). The entity-relationship model: toward a unified view of data. *ACM Transactions on Database Systems, 1*(1), 9–36.

Cheng, P. W., & Holyoak, K. J. (1985). Pragmatic reasoning schemas. *Cognitive Psychology, 17*, 391–416.

Chi, E. H., Pirolli, P., & Pitkow, J. (2000). The scent of a site: a system for analyzing and predicting information scent, usage and usability of a web site. In T. Turner, G. Szwillus, M. Czerwinski, & F. Paterno (Eds.), *CHI 2000 Conference Proceedings: Conference an Human Factors in Computing Systems* (pp. 161–168). New York: ACM Press.

Chi, M. T. H., Glaser, R., & Rees, E. (1982). Expertise in problem solving. In R. Sternberg (Ed.), *Advances in the psychology of human intelligence* (pp. 7–75). Hillsdale, NJ: Lawrence Erlbaum Associates.

Clark, H. H. (1996). *Using language*. Cambridge: Cambridge University Press.

Coad, P., North, D., & Mayfield, M. (1995). *Object models: strategies, patterns and applications*. Englewood Cliffs, NJ: Prentice-Hall.

Coad, P., & Yourdon, E. E. (1991). *Object oriented analysis*. Englewood Cliffs, NJ: Yourdon Press.

Conklin, J., & Begeman, M. L. (1988). gIBIS: a hypertext tool for exploratory policy discussion. *ACM Transactions on Office Information Systems, 64*, 303–331.

Coplein, J. O. (1996). *Software patterns*. New York: SIGS Books.

Coplein, J. O. (1999). C^{++} idioms patterns. In N. Harrison, B. Foote, & H. Rohnert (Eds.), *Pattern languages of program design 4*. Reading, MA: Addison-Wesley.

Coutaz, J. (1994). System architecture modelling for user interfaces. In J. J. Marciniak (Ed.), *The encylopaedia of software engineering* (pp. 38–49). Chichester: Wiley.

Cowie, J., & Wilks, Y. (2000). Information extraction. In R. Dale, H. Moisl, & H. Summers (Eds.), *Handbook of natural language processing*. New York: Marcel Dekker.

Cox, R., McKendree, J., Tobin, R., Lee, J., & Mayes, T. (1999). Vicarious learning from dialogue and discourse. *Instructional Science, 27*, 431–458.

Czarnecki, K., & Eisenecker, U. W. (2000). *Generative programming: methods, tools and application*. Reading, MA: Addison-Wesley.

Daft, R. L., Lengel, R. H., & Trevino, L. K. (1987). Message equivocality, media selection, and manager performance: implications for information systems. *MIS Quarterly, 11*(3), 355–366.

Dardenne, A., Van Lamsweerde, A., & Fickas, S. (1993). Goal directed requirements acquisition. *Science of Computer Programming, 20*, 3–50.

Darken, R. P., & Sibert, J. L. (1996). Wayfinding strategies and behaviours in large virtual worlds. In M. J. Tauber, V. Bellotti, R. Jeffries, J. D. Mackinlay, & J. Nielsen (Eds.), *Human factors in Computing Systems: CHI 96 Conference Proceedings* (pp. 142–149). New York: ACM Press.

Davenport, T. (1993). *Process innovation: re-engineering work through information technology*. Boston, MA: Harvard Business School Press.

Davis, F. D. (1993). User acceptance of information technology: system characteristics, user perceptions and behavioral impacts. *International Journal of Man-Machine Studies, 38*, 475–487.

Davis, W. S. (1995). *Management, information and systems: an introduction to business information systems*. St. Paul, MN: West.

De Bono, E. (1991). *De Bono's thinking course*. London: BBC Books.

De Marco, T. (1978). *Structured analysis and systems specification*. Englewood Cliffs, NJ: Prentice-Hall.

Dix, A., & Mancini, R. (1998). Specifying history and backtracking mechanism. In P. Palanque & F. Paterno (Eds.), *Formal methods in human computer interaction* (pp. 1–23). London: Springer.

Djajadiningrat, J. P., Gaver, W. W., & Frens, J. W. (2000). Interaction relabelling and extreme characters: methods for exploring aesthetic interactions. In D. Boyarski & W. A. Kellogg (Eds.), *Conference Proceedings: DIS2000 Designing Interactive Systems: Processes, practices methods and techniques* (pp. 66–71). New York: ACM Press.

Downs, E., Clare, P., & Coe, I. (1992). *Structured systems analysis and design method: application and context* (2nd ed.). New York: Prentice-Hall.

Duke, D. J., & Harrison, M. D. (1994). Unifying views of interactors. In *Proceedings: Workshop on Advanced Visual Interfaces* (pp. 143–152). New York: ACM Press.

Earl, M., & Kahn, E. (1994). How new is business process redesign? *European Management Journal, 12*(1), 20–30.

EASYCOMP. (2001). *IST Project 1999–14191 EASYCOMP: Easy Composition in Future Generation Component Systems. Glossary* [online]. Available: www.easycomp.org Accessed 11 June 2001. Karlsruhe: Universitaet Karlsruhe.

Edwards, M. D. (1995). Hardware/software co-design: experiences with languages and architectures. In K. Buchenrieder & J. Rosenblit (Eds.), *CODESIGN computer-aided software/hardware engineering* (pp. 356–377). Los Alamitos, CA: IEEE Computer Society Press.

Elsom-Cook, M. (1988). Guided discovery tutoring and bounded user modeling. In J. A. Self (Ed.), *Artificial intelligence and human learning* (pp. 165–196). London: Chapman & Hall.

Elsom-Cook, M. (2000). *Principles of interactive multimedia*. London: McGraw-Hill.

Ezran, M., Morisio, M., & Tully, C. (1998). *Practical software reuse: the essential guide. European Systems & Software Initiative, Surprise Project*. Brussels: European Commission.

Falkenhainer, B., Forbus, K. D., & Gentner, D. (1989). The structure-mapping engine: algorithm and examples. *Artificial Intelligence, 41*, 1–63.

Fayad, M. E., & Johnson, R. E. (2000). *Domain-specific application frameworks: frameworks experience by industry*. New York: Wiley.

Feiner, S., & McKeown, K. R. (1990). Generating coordinated multimedia explanations. In *Proceedings: 6th IEEE Conference on Artificial Intelligence Applications* (pp. 290–296). Los Alamitos, CA: IEEE Computer Society Press.

Fenton, N. E. (1995). The role of measurement in software safety assessment. In *Proceedings: CSR/ENCRESS Conference, Bruges*. London: Centre for Software Reliability, City University.

Fenton, N. E., & Pfleeger, S. L. (1997). *Software metrics: a rigorous approach* (2nd ed.). London: International Thomson Computer Press.

Fickas, S., & Feather, M. S. (1995). Requirements monitoring in dynamic environments. In M. D. Harrison, & P. Zave (Eds.), *Proceedings: 1995 IEEE International Symposium on Requirements Engineering* (pp. 140–147). Los Alamitos, CA: IEEE Computer Society Press.

Fischer, G. (1996). Seeding, evolutionary growth and reseeding: constructing, capturing and evolving knowledge in domain-oriented design environments. In A. G. Sutcliffe, D. Benyon, & F. Van Assche (Eds.), *Domain knowledge for interactive system design; proceedings: TC8/WG8.2 Conference on Domain Knowledge in Interactive System Design, Switzerland* (pp. 1–16). London: Chapman & Hall.

Fischer, G., Girensohn, A., Nakakoji, K., & Redmiles, D. (1992). Supporting software designers with integrated domain-oriented design environments. *IEEE Transactions on Software Engineering, 18*(6), 511–522.

Fischer, G., Lindstaedt, S., Ostwald, J., Stolze, M., Sumner, T., & Zimmermann, B. (1995). From domain modeling to collaborative domain construction. In G. M. Olson, & S. Schuon (Eds.), *Conference proceedings: DIS '95 Symposium on Designing Interactive Systems: Processes, practices, methods and techniques* (pp. 75–85). New York: ACM Press.

Fischer, G., Nakakoji, K., Otswald, J., Stahl, G., & Summer, T. (1993). Embedding computer-based critics in the contexts of design. In S. Ashlund, K. Mullet, A. Henderson, E. Hollnagel, & T. White (Eds.). In *Human Factors in Computing Systems: INTERCHI 93 Conference Proceedings* (pp. 157–163). New York: ACM Press.

Fowler, M. (1997). *Analysis patterns: reusable object models*. Reading, MA: Addison-Wesley.

Franzke, M. (1995). Turning research into practice: characteristics of display based interaction. In I. R. Katz, R. Mack, L. Marks, M. B. Rosson, & J. Nielsen (Eds.), *Proceedings CHI'95: Human Factors in Computing Systems* (pp. 421–428). New York: ACM Press.

Freeman, P. A. (1987). A conceptual analysis of the Draco approach to constructing software systems. *IEEE Transactions on Software Engineering, 13*(7), 830–844.

Furnas, G. W. (1986). Generalized fisheye views. In M. Mantei, & P. Orbeton (Eds.), *Human Factors in Computing Systems: CHI 86 Conference Proceedings* (pp. 13–23). New York: ACM Press.

Galambos, J. A. (1986). Knowledge structures for common activities. In J. A. Galambos, R. P. Abelson, & J. B. Black (Eds.), *Knowledge structures*. Hillsdale, NJ: Lawrence Erlbaum Associates.

Gamma, E., Helm, R., Johnson, R., & Vlissides, J. (1995). *Design patterns: elements of reusable object-oriented software*. Reading, MA: Addison-Wesley.

Garmus, D., & Herron, D. (1996). *Measuring the software process*. Englewood Cliffs, NJ: Yourdon Press.

Gentner, D. (1983). Structure-mapping: a theoretical framework for analogy. *Cognitive Science, 7*, 155–170.

Gentner, D., & Stevens, A. L. (Eds.). (1983). *Mental models*. Hillsdale, NJ: Lawrence Erlbaum Associates.

Gigerenzer, G., & Goldstein, D. G. (1996). Reasoning the fast and frugal way: models of bounded rationality. *Psychological Review, 103*, 650–669.

Goguen, J. (1986). Reusing and interconnecting software components. *Computer, 19*, 16–28.

Gombrich, E. H. (1984). *The sense of order: a study in the psychology of the decorative arts*. Ithaca, NY: Cornell University Press.

Gould, J. D. (1987). How to design usable systems. In H.-J. Bullinger & B. Shackel (Eds.), *Proceedings: Second IFIP Conference on Human-Computer Interaction, INTERACT '87* (pp. xxxv–xxxix). Amsterdam: North-Holland.

Graham, I. (1996). Task scripts, use cases and scenarios in object oriented analysis. *Object-Oriented Systems, 3*, 123–142.

Greenspan, S., Borgida, A., & Mylopoulos, J. (1986). A requirements modelling language and its logic. *Information Systems, 11*(1), 9–23.

Grishman, R., & Kittredge, R. (Eds.). (1986). *Analysing language in restricted domains: sub-language description and processing*. Hillsdale, NJ: Lawrence Erlbaum Associates.

Griss, M. L., Favaro, J., & d'Alessandro, M. (1998). Integrating feature modeling with the RSEB. In P. Devanbu & J. Poulin (Eds.), *Proceedings: Fifth International Conference on Software Reuse* (pp. 76–85). Los Alamitos, CA: IEEE Computer Society Press.

Gruber, T. R. (1993a). *Towards principles for the design of ontologies used for knowledge sharing* (Knowledge Systems Laboratory Report KSL 93-04). Stanford, CA: Stanford University, Department of Computer Science.

Gruber, T. R. (1993b). A translation approach to portable ontology specifications. *Knowledge Acquisition, 5*, 199–220.

Guindon, R. (1990). Designing the design process: exploiting opportunistic thoughts. *Human-Computer Interaction, 5,* 305–344.

Guindon, R., & Curtis, B. (1988). Control of cognitive processes during software design: what tools are needed. In E. Soloway, D. Frye, & S. B. Sheppard (Eds.), *Human Factors in Computing Systems: CHI 88 Conference Proceedings* (pp. 263–269). New York: ACM Press.

Hammer, M. & Champy, J. (1993). *Re-engineering the corporation: a manifesto for business revolution.* London: Nicholas Brealy.

Harandi, M. T., & Lee, M. Y. (1991). Acquiring software design schemas: a machine learning perspective. In *Proceedings: 6th Conference on Knowledge Based Software Engineering* (pp. 239–250). Los Alamitos, CA: IEEE Computer Society Press.

Harris, Z. S. (1989). *The form of information in science: analysis of an immunology sublanguage.* Dordrecht: Kluwer Academic.

Harrison, N., Foote, B., & Rohnert, H. (1999). *Pattern languages of program design 4 (Software Pattern series).* Reading, MA: Addison-Wesley.

Harvard Business Review. (1998). *Harvard Business Review on knowledge management.* Cambridge, MA: Harvard Business School Press.

Hauser, J., & Clausing, D. (1988). The house of quality. *Harvard Business Review, 5,* 63–73.

Hayes-Roth, B., & Hayes-Roth, F. (1979). A cognitive model of planning. *Cognitive Science, 3,* 275–310.

Hix, D., Swan, J. E., Gabbard, J. L., McGee, M., Durbin, J., & King, T. (1999). User-centered design and evaluation of a real-time battlefield visualization virtual environment. In L. Rosenblum, P. Astheimer, & D. Teichmann (Eds.), *Proceedings: IEEE Virtual Reality '99* (pp. 96–103). Los Alamitos, CA: IEEE Computer Society Press.

Hoare, C. A. R. (1969). An axiomatic basis for computer programming. *Communications of the ACM, 12*(10), 576–583.

Hollnagel, E. (1998). *Cognitive Reliability and Error Analysis Method: CREAM.* Oxford: Elsevier.

Holyoak, K. J., & Thagard, P. (1989). Analogical mapping by constraint satisfaction. *Cognitive Science, 13,* 295–355.

Humphreys, K., Gaizauskas, R., Azzan, S., Huyck, C., Mitchell, B., Cunningham, H., & Wilks, Y. (1999). Description of the University of Sheffield LaSIE II system as used for MUC-7. In *Proceedings: 7th Message Understanding Conference.* San Francisco, CA: Morgan Kaufmann.

Ingwersen, P. (1996). Cognitive perspectives of information retrieval: interaction elements of a cognitive IR theory. *Journal of Documentation, 52*(1), 3–50.

ISO. (1997). *ISO 9241: Ergonomic requirements for office systems visual display terminals. Parts 10-16.* International Standards Organisation.

Jackson, M. (1983). *System development.* Englewood Cliffs, NJ: Prentice-Hall.

Jackson, M. (1995). *Software requirements and specifications: a lexicon of practice, principles and prejudices.* Wokingham: Addison-Wesley.

Jackson, M. (2001). *Problem frames: analysing and structuring software development problems.* Harlow: Pearson Education.

Jacobson, L. (1992). *Object-oriented software engineering: a user case-driven approach.* New York: ACM Press.

Jarke, M. (1992). *ConceptBase vn3.1 user manual.* Aachen, Germany: RWTH-Aachen.

Jarke, M., Bubenko, J., Rolland C., Sutcliffe, A. G., & Vassiliou, Y. (1993). Theories underlying requirements engineering: an overview of NATURE at genesis. In S. Fickas & A. C. W. Finkelstein (Eds.), *Proceedings: 1st International Symposium on Requirements Engineering* (pp. 19–31). Los Alamitos, CA: IEEE Computer Society Press.

John, B. E., & Kieras, R. E. (1995). The GOMS family of user interface analysis techniques: comparison and contrast. *ACM Transactions on Computer-Human Interaction, 3,* 320–351.

Johnson, P. (1992). *Human computer interaction: psychology, task analysis and software engineering.* London: McGraw-Hill.

Johnson, P., Johnson, H., Waddington, R., & Shouls, R. (1988). Task-related knowledge structures: analysis, modelling and application. In D. M. Jones & R. Winder (Eds.), *Proceedings: HCI'88* (pp. 35–61). Cambridge: Cambridge University Press.

Johnson-Laird, P. N. (1983). *Mental models: towards a cognitive science of language, inference and consciousness*. Cambridge: Cambridge University Press.

Jones, C. B. (1986). *Systematic software development using VDM*. London: Prentice-Hall.

Kahnemann, D., & Tversky, A. (1982). Intuitive prediction: biases and corrective procedures. In D. Kahnemann, P. Slovic, & A. Tversky (Eds.), *Judgement under uncertainty: heuristics and biases*. Cambridge: Cambridge University Press.

Keller, G., & Teufel, T. (1998). *SAP/R3 process oriented implementation*. Reading, MA: Addison-Wesley–Longman.

Kennedy-Carter. (2000). *Action specification language: executable UML* [online]. Available: http://www.kc.com/html/xuml.html Accessed November 2000.

Kiczales, G., des Rivieres, J., & Bobrow, D. (1991). *The art of the MetaObject protocol*. Cambridge, MA: MIT Press.

Kieras, D. E., & Polson, P. G. (1985). An approach to the formal analysis of user complexity. *International Journal of Man-Machine Studies, 22*, 365–394.

Kosslyn, S. M. (1980). *Image and mind*. Cambridge, MA: Harvard University Press.

Krasner, G. E., & Pope, S. T. (1988). A cookbook for using the model-view controller user interface paradigm in Smalltalk-80. *Journal of Object Oriented Programming, 1*(3).

Kuhlthau, C. (1991). Inside the search process: information seeking from the user's perspective. *Journal of the American Society for Information Science, 42*, 361–371.

Lakoff, G. (1987). *Women, fire and dangerous things: what categories reveal about the mind*. Chicago: University of Chicago Press.

Lam, W., McDermid, J. A., & Vickers, A. J. (1997). Ten steps towards systematic requirements reuse. In *Proceedings ISRE '97: 3rd IEEE International Symposium on Requirements Engineering* (pp. 6–15). Los Alamitos, CA: IEEE Computer Society Press.

Landauer, T. K. (1995). *The trouble with computers: usefulness, usability and productivity*. Cambridge, MA: MIT Press.

Landauer, T. K., & Dumais, S. T. (1997). A solution to Plato's problem: the latent semantic analysis theory of acquisition, induction and representation of knowledge. *Psychological Review, 104*, 211–240.

Laurillard, D. (1993). *Rethinking university teaching: a framework for the effective use of educational technology*. London: Routledge.

Lehman, M. M. (1990). Uncertainty in computer applications. *Communications of the ACM, 33*(5), 584–586.

Lenat, D. B. (1995). CYC: a large-scale investment in knowledge infrastructure. *Communications of the ACM, 38*(11), 33–38.

Lewis, B. (1993). Mind your language. *Electrical review, 226*(16), 24–26.

Lewis, M. L., & Anderson, J. R. (1985). Discrimination of operator schemata in problem-solving: learning from examples. *Cognitive Psychology, 17*, 26–65.

Liete, J. C., St Anna, M., & De Freitas, F. G. (1994). Draco-PUC: the technology assembly for domain oriented software development. In W. B. Frakes (Ed.), *Proceedings: Third International Conference on Software Reuse* (pp. 94–100). Los Alamitos, CA: IEEE Computer Society Press.

Loucopoulos, P., & Karakostas, V. (1995). *System requirements engineering*. London: McGraw-Hill.

MacLean, A., Young, R. M., Bellotti, V., & Moran, T. P. (1991). Questions, options and criteria: elements of design space analysis. *Human-Computer Interaction, 6*(3/4), 201–250.

Maiden, N. A. M. (1996). The transfer problem in analogical reuse. In I. Smith & B. Faltings (Eds.), *Proceedings: Advances in Case-Based Reasoning* (pp. 249–265). Berlin: Springer-Verlag.

Maiden, N. A. M., Mistry, P., & Sutcliffe, A. G. (1995). How people categorise requirements for reuse: a natural approach. In M. D. Harrison, & P. Zave (Eds.), *Proceedings: 1995 IEEE International*

Symposium on Requirements Engineering (pp. 148–155). Los Alamitos, CA: IEEE Computer Society Press.

Maiden, N. A. M., & Rugg, G. (1994). Knowledge acquisition techniques for requirements engineering. In *Proceedings: Workshop on Requirements Elicitation for System Specification.* Keele: University of Keele.

Maiden, N. A. M., & Rugg, G. (1996). ACRE: selecting methods for requirements acquisition. *Software Engineering Journal, 11*(3), 183–192.

Maiden, N. A. M., & Sutcliffe, A. G. (1992). Exploiting reusable specification through analogy. *Communications of the ACM, 35*(4), 55–64.

Maiden, N. A. M., & Sutcliffe, A. G. (1993). Requirements engineering by example: an empirical study. In S. Fickas, & A. C. W. Finkelstein (Eds.), *Proceedings: 1st International Symposium on Requirements Engineering* (pp. 104–112). Los Alamitos, CA: IEEE Computer Society Press.

Maiden, N. A. M., & Sutcliffe, A. G. (1994). Requirements critiquing using domain abstractions. In *Proceedings: IEEE International Conference on Requirements Engineering* (pp. 184–193). Los Alamitos, CA: IEEE Computer Society Press.

Maiden, N. A. M., & Sutcliffe, A. G. (1996). Analogical retrieval in reuse-oriented requirements engineering. *Software Engineering Journal, 11*(5), 281–292.

Malone, T. W., Yates, J., & Benjamin, R. I. (1987). Electronic markets and hierarchies. *Communications of the ACM, 30*(6), 484–497.

Mann, W. C., & Thompson, S. A. (1988). Rhetorical Structure Theory: toward a functional theory of text organisation. *Text, 8*(3), 243–281.

Marchionini, G. (1995). *Information seeking in electronic environments.* Cambridge: Cambridge University Press.

Maslow, A. H., Frager, R., McReynolds, C., Cox, R., & Fadiman, J. (1987). *Motivation and personality* (3rd ed.). New York: Addison-Wesley–Longman.

Matsumoto, Y. (1993). Experiences from software reuse in industrial process control applications. In *Proceedings: Advances in Software Reuse: selected papers from the Second International Workshop on Software Reusability* (pp. 186–195). Los Alamitos, CA: IEEE Computer Society Press.

Maybury, M. T. (1993). *Intelligent multimedia interfaces.* Cambridge, MA: AAAI/MIT Press.

McCabe, T. J. (1976). A complexity measure. *IEEE Transactions on Software Engineering, 2*(4), 308–320.

McMenamin, S. M., & Palmer, J. F. (1984). *Essential systems analysis.* Englewood Cliffs, NJ: Yourdon Press.

Messina, P., Culler, D., Pheiffer, W., Martin, W., Tinsley, O. J., & Smith, G. (1998). Architecture. *Communications of the ACM, 41*(11), 32–44.

Meyer, B. (1985). On formalism in specifications. *IEEE Software, 2*(1), 6–26.

Meyer, B. (1997). *Object oriented software construction.* Upper Saddle River, NJ: Prentice-Hall.

Moore, J. D., & Mittal, V. O. (1996). Dynamically generated follow-up questions. *Computer, 29*(7), 75–86.

Moore, J. D., & Swartout, W. R. (1990). Pointing: a way toward explanation dialogue. *AAAI-90 Proceedings: Eighth National Conference on Artificial Intelligence* (pp. 457–464). Cambridge, MA: MIT Press.

Moran, T. P., & Carroll, J. M. (1996). *Design rationale: concepts, methods and techniques.* Mahwah, NJ: Lawrence Erlbaum Associates.

Morel, M. J., & Faget, J. (1993). The REBOOT environment. In R. Prieto-Diaz, & W. B. Frakes (Eds.), In *Proceedings: Advances in Software Reuse: 1st International Workshop on Software Reusability* (pp. 80–89). Los Alamitos, CA: IEEE Computer Society Press.

M'Pherson, P. K. (1999). Adding value by integrating systems engineering and project management. In *Proceedings: IERE '99.* London: Institute of Electrical and Radio Engineers.

Mylopoulos, J., Borgida, A., Jarke, M., & Koubarakis, M. (1990). Telos: representing knowledge about information systems. *ACM Transactions on Office Information Systems, 8*(4), 325.

Neighbors, J. (1984). The Draco approach to constructing software from reusable components. *IEEE Transactions on Software Engineering, 10*(5), 564–574.

Neighbors, J. (1994). An assessment of reuse technology after ten years. In W. B. Frakes (Ed.), *Proceedings: 3rd International Conference on Software Reuse: Advances in Software Reusability* (pp. 6–13). Los Alamitos, CA: IEEE Computer Society Press.

Newell, A., & Simon, H. A. (1972). *Human problem solving.* Englewood Cliffs, NJ: Prentice-Hall.

Nigay, L., & Coutaz, J. (1995). A generic platform for addressing the multimodal challenge. In *Human Factors in Computing Systems: CHI 95 Conference Proceedings* (pp. 98–105). New York: ACM Press.

Norman, D. A. (1986). Cognitive engineering. In D. A. Norman & S. W. Draper (Eds.), *User-centred system design: new perspectives on human-computer interaction.* Hillsdale, NJ: Lawrence Erlbaum Associates.

Norman, D. A. (1988). *The psychology of everyday things.* New York: Basic Books.

Norman, D. A. (1999). *The invisible computer: why good products can fail, the personal computer is so complex, and information appliances are the solution.* Cambridge, MA: MIT Press.

Object Management Group. (2000). *CORBA: Common Object Request Broker Architecture* [online]. Available: http://www.omg.org Accessed August 2000.

Papert, S. (1980). *Mindstorms: children, computers, and powerful ideas.* New York: Basic Books.

Payne, J. W., Bettman, J. R., & Johnson, E. J. (1993). *The adaptive decision maker.* Cambridge: Cambridge University Press.

Pedagogical Patterns Project. (2000). *Success in teaching object technology* [online]. Available: http://www.oifia.info.unlt.eu.ar/ppp/ Accessed 2000.

Porter, M. E. (1980). *Competitive strategy.* New York: Free Press.

Potts, C., Takahashi, K., & Anton, A. I. (1994). Inquiry-based requirements analysis. *IEEE Software, 11*(2), 21–32.

Potts, C., Takahashi, K., Smith, J., & Ora, K. (1995). An evaluation of inquiry based requirements analysis for an Internet service. In M. D. Harrison & P. Zave (Eds.), *Proceedings: 1995 IEEE International Symposium on Requirements Engineering* (pp. 27–34). Los Alamitos, CA: IEEE Computer Society Press.

Prieto-Diaz, R. (1990). Domain analysis: an introduction. *Software Engineering Notes, 15*(2), 47–54.

Prieto-Diaz, R. (1991). Implementing faceted classification for software reuse. *Communications of the ACM, 34*(5), 88–97.

Quillian, M. R. (1966). *Semantic memory.* Cambridge, MA: Bolt, Beranak and Newman.

Rasmussen, J. (1986). *Information processing in human computer interaction: an approach to cognitive engineering.* Amsterdam: North-Holland.

Rational Corporation. (1999). *UML: Unified Modelling Language method* [online]. Available: ⟨http://www.rational.com⟩ Accessed 1999.

Reason, J. (1990). *Human error.* Cambridge: Cambridge University Press.

Reeves, B., & Nass, C. (1996). *The media equation: how people treat computers, television and new media like real people and places.* Stanford, CA/Cambridge: CLSI/Cambridge University Press.

Reubenstein, H. B., & Waters, R. C. (1989). The requirements apprentice: an initial scenario. In *Proceedings: 5th International Workshop on Software Specification and Design* (pp. 211–218). Los Alamitos, CA: IEEE Computer Society Press.

Riesbeck, C. K., & Schank, R. C. (1989). *Inside case-based reasoning.* Hillsdale, NJ: Lawrence Erlbaum Associates.

Rising, L. (Ed.). (1998). *The patterns handbook: techniques, strategies and applications.* Cambridge: Cambridge University Press.

Robertson, S. E., & Beaulieu, M. (1997). Research and evaluation in information retrieval. *Journal of Documentation, 53*(1), 51–57.

Robertson, S. E., Walker, S., & Beaulieu, M. (1997). Laboratory experiments with Okapi: participation in the TREC programme. *Journal of Documentation, 53*(1), 20–34.

Rodden, T. (1991). A survey of CSCW systems. *Interacting with Computers, 3*(3), 319–353.

Rosch, E. (1985). Prototype classification and logical classification: the two systems. In E. K. Scholnick (Ed.), *New trends in conceptual representation: challenges to Piaget's Theory.* Hillsdale, NJ: Lawrence Erlbaum Associates.

Rosch, E., Mervis, C. B., Gray, W., Johnson, D., & Boyes-Braem, P. (1976). Basic objects in natural categories. *Cognitive Psychology, 7*, 573–605.

Ross, D. T., & Schoman, K. E. (1977). Structured analysis for requirements definition. *IEEE Transactions on Software Engineering, 3*(1), 6–15.

Rosson, M. B., & Carroll, J. M. (1995). Narrowing the specification-implementation gap in scenario-based design. In J. M. Carroll (Ed.), *Scenario-based design: envisioning work and technology in system development* (pp. 247–278). New York: Wiley.

Rumelhart, D. E. (1975). Notes on a schema for stories. In D. G. Bobrow & A. M. Collins (Eds.), *Representation and understanding.* New York: Academic.

Rutledge, L., Hardman, L., & Van Ossenbruggen, J. (1999). The use of SMIL: multimedia research currently applied on a global scale. In *Proceedings: Multimedia Modeling 99* (pp. 1–17). Ottawa: World Scientific.

Sacks, H., Schegloff, E. A., & Jefferson, G. (1974). A simple systematics for the organization of turn-taking in conversation. *Language, 50*, 696–735.

Schank, R.C. (1982). *Dynamic memory: a theory of reminding and learning in computers and people.* Cambridge: Cambridge University Press.

Schon, D. (1983). *The reflective practitioner.* New York: Basic Books.

Searle, J. R. (1969). *Speech acts.* Cambridge: Cambridge University Press.

Shackel, B. (1986). Ergonomics in design for usability. In M. D. Harrison & A. F. Monk (Eds.), *People and computers: designing for usability: Proceedings: Second Conference of the BCS HCI Specialist Group* (pp. 44–64). Cambridge: Cambridge University Press.

Shaw, M. (1991). Heterogeneous design idioms for software architecture. In *Proceedings: 6th International Workshop on Software Specification and Design* (pp. 158–165). Los Alamitos, CA: IEEE Computer Society Press.

Shepard, R. N. (1967). Recognition memory for words, sentences and pictures. *Journal of Verbal Learning and Verbal Behaviour, 6*, 176–206.

Simon, H. A. (1973). The structure of ill-structured problems. *Artificial Intelligence, 4*, 181–201.

Singh, M. G., & Yang, J. B. (1994). An evidential reasoning approach for multiattribute decision making with uncertainty. *IEEE Transactions on Systems, Man and Cybernetics, 24*(1), 1–18.

Singh, M. G., & Zeng, X. J. (1996). Approximation properties of fuzzy systems generated by the min inference. *IEEE Transactions on Systems, Man and Cybernetics, 26*(1), 187–194.

Singley, M. K., & Carroll, J. M. (1996). Synthesis by analysis: five modes of reasoning that guide design. In T. P. Moran & J. M. Carroll (Eds.), *Design rationale: concepts, techniques, and use* (pp. 241–265). Mahwah, NJ: Lawrence Erlbaum Associates.

Smith, D. R. (1992). Track assignment in an airtraffic control system: a rational reconstruction of system design. In *Proceedings: KBSE 92, Knowledge Based Software Engineering* (pp. 60–68). Los Alamitos, CA: IEEE Computer Society Press.

Sommerville, I., & Kotonya, G. (1998). *Requirements engineering: processes and techniques.* Chichester: Wiley.

Sowa, J. F. (1984). *Conceptual structures: information processing in mind and machine.* Reading, MA: Addison-Wesley.

Sowa, J. F. (2000). *Knowledge representation: logical, philosophical and computational foundations.* Pacific Grove, CA: Brooks/Cole.

Spivey, J. M. (1989). *The Z notation.* Englewood Cliffs, NJ: Prentice-Hall.

Stenning, K., McKendree, J., Lee, J., Cox, R., Dineen, F., & Mayes, T. (2000). Vicarious learning from educational dialogue. In *Proceedings: Computer-Supported Cooperative Learning* (pp. 341–347). Stanford, CA: CSCL.

Sun Microsystems. (1999). *Java look and feel design guidelines*. Reading, MA: Addison-Wesley.

Sutcliffe, A. G. (1995). Requirements rationales: integrating approaches to requirements analysis. In G. M. Olson & S. Schuon (Eds.), *Designing Interactive Systems: DIS 95 Conference Proceedings* (pp. 33–42). New York: ACM Press.

Sutcliffe, A. G. (1996a). A conceptual framework for requirements engineering. *Requirements Engineering Journal, 1*(3), 170–189.

Sutcliffe, A. G. (1996b). Investigating the process of safety critical design. In J. Dobson (Ed.), *Proceedings: CSR Conference Human Factors in Safety Critical Systems*. London: The City University, Centre for Software Reliability.

Sutcliffe, A. G. (1996c). User-centred safety critical design. In J. Dobson (Ed.), *Proceedings: CSR Conference Human Factors in Safety Critical Systems*. London: The City University, Centre for Software Reliability.

Sutcliffe, A. G. (1997). A technique combination approach to requirements engineering. In *Proceedings: ISRE '97: 3rd IEEE International Symposium on Requirements Engineering* (pp. 65–74). Los Alamitos, CA: IEEE Computer Society Press.

Sutcliffe, A. G. (1998). Scenario-based requirements analysis. *Requirements Engineering Journal, 3*(1), 48–65.

Sutcliffe, A. G. (1999). Business modelling inter-process relationships. In D. Bustard (Ed.), *Proceedings: SEBPC Workshop on Systems Modelling for Business Process Improvement* (pp. 185–204). Coleraine: University of Ulster.

Sutcliffe, A. G. (2000a). Domain analysis for software reuse. *Journal of Systems and Software, 50*, 175–199.

Sutcliffe, A. G. (2000b). Requirements analysis for socio-technical system design. *Information Systems, 25*(3), 213–233.

Sutcliffe, A. G. (in press). *Multimedia and virtual reality: designing multisensory user interfaces*. Mahwah, NJ: Lawrence Erlbaum Associates.

Sutcliffe, A. G., Bennett, I., Doubleday, A., & Ryan, M. (1995). Designing query support for multiple databases. In K. Nordby, P. H. Helmersen, D. J. Gilmore, & S. A. Arnesen (Eds.), *Proceedings INTERACT-95: 5th International Conference on Human-Computer Interaction* (pp. 207–212). London: Chapman & Hall.

Sutcliffe, A. G., & Carroll, J. M. (1998). Generalizing claims and reuse of HCI knowledge. In H. Johnson, L. Nigay, & C. Roast (Eds.), *People and Computers XIII; Proceedings of the BCS-HCI 98 Conference* (pp. 159–176). Berlin: Springer-Verlag.

Sutcliffe, A. G., & Carroll, J. M. (1999). Designing claims for reuse in interactive systems design. *International Journal of Human-Computer Studies, 50*(3), 213–241.

Sutcliffe, A. G., & Dimitrova, M. T. (1999). Claims, patterns and multimedia. In A. Sasse & C. Johnson (Eds.), *Proceedings of INTERACT 99: Human Computer Interaction* (pp. 329–335). Amsterdam: IFIP/IOS Press.

Sutcliffe, A. G., & Ennis, M. (1998). Towards a cognitive theory of information retrieval. *Interacting with Computers, 10*, 321–351.

Sutcliffe, A. G., & Ennis, M. (2000). Designing intelligent assistance for end-user information retrieval. In C. Paris, N. Ozkan, S. Howard, & S. Lu (Eds.), *Proceedings OZCHI-2000* (pp. 202–210). Canberra: CSIRO/CHISIG.

Sutcliffe, A. G., Ennis, M., & Hu, J. (2000). Evaluating the effectiveness of visual user interfaces for information retrieval. *International Journal of Human-Computer Studies, 53*(5), 741–763.

Sutcliffe, A. G., Ennis, M., & Watkinson, S. J. (2000). Empirical studies of end-user information searching. *Journal of the American Society for Information Science, 51*(13), 1211–1231.

Sutcliffe, A. G., & Li, G. (2000). Connecting business modelling to requirements engineering. In P. Henderson (Ed.), *Software engineering for business process change: collected papers from the EPSRC Research Programme* (pp. 91–105). London: Springer.

Sutcliffe, A. G., & Maiden, N. A. M. (1990). How specification reuse can support requirements analysis. In P. Hall (Ed.), *Proceedings: Software Engineering '90* (pp. 489–509). Cambridge: Cambridge University Press.

Sutcliffe, A. G., & Maiden, N. A. M. (1991). *Transforming informal requirements: models for requirements elaboration and refinement* (internal document). London: The City University, Department of Business Computing.

Sutcliffe, A. G., & Maiden, N. A. M. (1992). Analysing the novice analyst: cognitive models in software engineering. *International Journal of Man-Machine Studies, 36*, 719–740.

Sutcliffe, A. G., & Maiden, N. A. M. (1993). Bridging the requirements gap: policies, goals and domains. In *Proceedings: 7th International Workshop of Software Specification and Design* (pp. 52–55). Los Alamitos, CA: IEEE Computer Society Press.

Sutcliffe, A. G., & Maiden, N. A. M. (1994). Domain modeling for reuse. In W. B. Frakes (Ed.), *Proceedings: 3rd International Conference on Software Reuse: Advances in Software Reusability* (pp. 169–177). Los Alamitos, CA: IEEE Computer Society Press.

Sutcliffe, A. G., & Maiden, N. A. M. (1998). The Domain Theory for requirements engineering. *IEEE Transactions on Software Engineering, 24*(3), 174–196.

Sutcliffe, A. G., Maiden, N. A. M., & Cooper, M. (1992). Information seeking and discourse structure in explanation. In *Samos Workshop on Task Based Explanation: papers and abstracts* [unpaginated]. Athens: University of the Aegean.

Sutcliffe, A. G., Maiden, N. A. M., Minocha, S., & Manuel, D. (1998). Supporting scenario-based requirements engineering. *IEEE Transactions on Software Engineering, 24*(12), 1072–1088.

Sutcliffe, A. G., & Patel, U. (1996). 3D or not 3D: is it nobler in the mind? In M. A. Sasse, R. J. Cunningham, & R. L. Winder (Eds.), *People and Computers XI. Proceedings: HCI-96* (pp. 79–94). London: Springer-Verlag.

Sutcliffe, A. G., & Ryan, M. (1998). Experience with SCRAM, a SCenario Requirements Analysis Method. In *Proceedings: IEEE International Symposium on Requirements Engineering* (pp. 164–171). Los Alamitos, CA: IEEE Computer Society Press.

Sutcliffe, A. G., Ryan, M., Hu, J., & Griffyth, J. (1998). Designing a multimedia application for the WWW: the Multimedia Broker experience. In C. Rolland, Y. Chen, & M. Q. Fang (Eds.), *Proceedings: IFIP WG 8.1 Working Conference Information Systems in the WWW Environment* (pp. 171–196). London: Chapman & Hall.

Tansley, D. S. W., & Hayball, C. C. (1993). *Knowledge-based systems: a KADS developer's handbook.* Hemel Hempstead: Prentice-Hall.

Taylor, C. N., Sutcliffe, A. G., Maiden, N. A. M., & Till, D. (1995). *Formal representations for domain knowledge* (Centre for HCI Design, School of Informatics Technical Report, 95/5). London: The City University.

Thimbleby, H. (1990). *User interface design.* Reading, MA: ACM Press/Addison-Wesley.

Tidwell, J. (2000). *Common Ground: a pattern language for human-computer interface design* [online]. Available: http://www.mit.edu/~jtidwell/common_ground_onefile.html Accessed 8 July 2000.

Toulmin, S. (1958). *The uses of argument.* Cambridge: Cambridge University Press.

Tracz, W. (1995). *Confessions of a used program salesman: institutionalizing software reuse.* Reading, MA: Addison-Wesley.

Uhl, J., & Schmid, H. A. (1990). *A systematic catalogue of reusable abstract data types.* Berlin: Springer.

Van Lamsweerde, A. (2000). Requirements engineering in the year 00: a research perspective. In *Proceedings: 22nd International Conference on Software Engineering* (pp. 5–19). New York: ACM Press.

Van Lamsweerde, A., & Letier, E. (2000). Handling obstacles in goal-oriented requirements engineering. *IEEE Transactions on Software Engineering, 26*(10), 978–1005.

Visser, W., & Hoc, J. M. (1990). Expert software design strategies. In J. M. Hoc, T. Green, R. Samurcay, & D. Gilmore (Eds.), *Psychology of programming.* London: Academic.

W3C. (2000). *World Wide Web Consortium: user interface domain, synchronised multimedia [SMIL]* [online]. Available: http://www. w3c.org/AudioVideo/ Accessed 1 November 2000.

Wehrend, R., & Lewis, C. (1990). A problem-oriented classification of visualization techniques. *Proceedings: First IEEE Conference on Visualization: Visualization 90* (pp. 139–143). Los Alamitos, CA: IEEE Computer Society Press.

Wenger, E. (1987). *Artificial intelligence and tutoring systems: computational approaches to the communication of knowledge*. Los Altos, CA: Morgan Kaufmann.

Wilenga, B., Van der Velde, W., Schreiber, G., & Akkermans, H. (1993). *Expertise model definition KADS* (Project Document No. KADS-II/M2/UvA). Amsterdam: University of Amsterdam.

Williamson, O. E. (1981). The economics of organisations: the transaction cost approach. *American Journal of Sociology, 87*(3), 548–577.

Williamson, O. E. (1992). Markets, hierarchies and the modern corporation: an unfolding perspective. *Journal of Economic Behaviour and Organisation, 17*(3), 335–352.

Winograd, T., & Flores, F. (1986). *Understanding computers and cognition: a new foundation for design*. Reading, MA: Addison-Wesley.

Wirfs-Brock, R., Wilkerson, B., & Wiener, L. (1990). *Designing object-oriented software*. Englewood Cliffs, NJ: Prentice-Hall.

Wright, P., Dearden, A., & Fields, B. (2000). Function allocation: a perspective from studies of work practice. *International Journal of Human-Computer Studies, 52*(2), 335–355.

Yourdon, E. E. (1989). *Modern structured analysis*. Englewood Cliffs, NJ: Prentice-Hall.

Yourdon, E. E., & Constantine, L. L. (1978). *Structured design*. New York: Yourdon Press.

Yu, E., Mylopoulos, J., & Lesperance, Y. (1996). AI models for business process reengineering. *IEEE Expert, August*, 16–23.

Zhou, M. X., & Feiner, S. K. (1998). Visual task characterization for automated visual discourse synthesis. In C.-M. Karat, A. Lund, J. Coutaz, & J. Karat (Eds.), *Human Factors in Computing Systems: CHI 98 Conference Proceedings* (pp. 392–399). New York: ACM Press.

Author Index

A

Ahlberg, C., 181
Ajzen, I., 256, 338
Akin, O., 78, 162
Akkermans, H., 43, 132
Alexander, C., 3, 38, 83, 237
Allen, J. F., 99
Alty, J. L., 76
Anderson, J. R., 8, 65, 88, 166, 179, 180
Andre, E., 159, 352
Anton, A. I., 98, 208
Arango, G., 2, 35, 97, 251
Arens, Y., 30
Argyris, C., 9, 166, 228
Azzan, S., 266

B

Back, T., 267
Bailey, R. W., 225
Basili, V. R., 76
Batory, D., 12, 16, 255
Beach, L. R., 338
Beaulieu, M., 337
Begeman, M. L., 9, 174
Belkin, N., 336
Bellamy, R. K. E., 176
Bellotti, V., 33, 174, 184, 223
Benjamin, R. I., 49
Bennett, I., 128, 243, 246
Bettman, J. R., 75, 338
Biggerstaff, T. J., 3
Blandford, A., 184
Bobrow, D., 262
Borchers, J., 241, 250
Borgida, A., 95, 114, 254
Boyes-Braem, P., 86, 88, 117

Breuker, J., 95
Browne, D. P., 53, 266
Bubenko, J., 20
Buckingham Shum, S., 12, 184

C

Cacioppo, J. T., 75
Campbell, R. L., 174
Candy, L., 162
Card, S. K., 94, 136, 183, 337
Carroll, J. M., 85, 137, 165, 174,
        175, 176, 177, 178, 181, 184,
        187, 189, 237, 239, 240, 242,
        245, 246, 337, 361
Champy, J., 43, 49
Chandrasekaran, B., 132
Chen, G., 12, 16
Chen, P., 89
Cheng, P. W., 88
Chi, E. H., 29
Chi, M. T. H., 88, 127
Clare, P., 2
Clark, H. H., 348
Clausing, D., 340
Coad, P., 28, 35
Coe, I., 2
Conklin, J., 9, 174
Constantine, L. L., 6, 44, 87, 200,
        201, 230
Cooper, M., 352
Coplien, J. O., 2, 3, 241, 250
Corbett, A. T., 166
Coutaz, J., 183
Cowie, J., 28, 266
Cox, R., 166, 253
Culler, D., 4
Cunningham, H., 266

Curtis, B., 70, 78, 88
Czarnecki, K., 262

D

d'Alessandro, M., 196
Daft, R. L., 257
Dardenne, A., 97, 129
Darken, R. P., 144
Davenport, T., 9, 43
Davis, F. D., 253, 256
Davis, W. S., 166
De Bono, E., 67
De Freitas, F. G., 254
De Marco, T., 2, 34, 44, 200
Dearden, A., 131
des Rivieres, J., 262
Dimitrova, M. T., 142, 161, 183, 246
Dineen, F., 166
Dix, A., 183
Djajadiningrat, J. P., 82
Doubleday, A., 128, 243, 246
Downs, E., 2
Duke, D., 183, 184
Dumais, S. T., 29, 74, 151, 241, 337
Durbin, J., 144

E

Earl, M., 43
EASYCOMP, 36
Edmonds, E. A., 162
Edwards, M. D., 255
Eisenecker, U. W., 262
Elsom-Cook, M., 165
Ennis, M., 144, 149, 151, 186, 247, 335
Ezran, M., 2

F

Fadiman, J., 253
Faget, J., 2
Falkenhainer, B., 115
Favaro, J., 196
Fayad, M. E., 43, 47, 145, 199, 251
Feather, M. S., 266
Feiner, S., 94, 136, 159, 342, 352
Fenton, N. E., 76, 340

Fickas, S., 97, 129, 266
Fields, B., 131
Fischer, G., 97, 116, 162, 180, 188
Fishbein, M., 256, 338
Flores, F., 142, 152, 346
Foote, B., 3, 47, 250
Forbus, K. D., 115
Fowler, M., 90
Frager, R., 253
Franzke, M., 180
Freeman, P. A., 254
Frens, J. W., 82
Furnas, G. W., 239

G

Gabbard, J. L., 144
Gaizauskas, R., 266
Galambos, J. A., 68
Gamma, E., 3, 15, 33, 38, 41, 43, 47, 58, 89, 90, 205, 250
Garmus, D., 44
Gaver, W. W., 82
Gentner, D., 65, 85, 86, 88, 115, 117
Gigerenzer, G., 340
Girensohn, A., 97
Glaser, R., 88, 127
Goguen, J., 35
Goldstein, D. G., 340
Gombrich, E. H., 83
Gould, J. D., 329
Graham, I., 68
Gray, W., 86, 88, 117
Greenspan, S., 254
Griffiths, D.
Griffyth, J., 128
Grishman, R., 254, 255
Griss, M. L., 196
Gruber, T. R., 251, 260
Guindon, R., 70, 78, 88

H

Hammer, M., 43, 49
Hammond, N., 184
Harandi, M. T., 88
Hardman, L., 5
Harris, Z. S., 255
Harrison, M. D., 183

Harrison, N., 3, 47, 250
Harvard Business Review, 189
Hauser, J., 340
Hayball, C. C., 251
Hayes-Roth, B., 78
Hayes-Roth, F., 78
Helm, R., 3, 15, 33, 38, 41, 43, 47,
    58, 89, 90, 205, 250
Herron, D., 44
Hix, D., 144
Hoare, C. A. R., 6
Hoc, J. M., 70, 162
Hollnagel, E., 109
Holyoak, K. J., 88, 92, 115
Hovy, E., 30
Hu, J., 128, 149
Humphreys, K., 266
Huyck, C., 266

I

Ingwersen, P., 245, 246
Ishikawa, S., 3, 38, 237
ISO, 235

J

Jackson, M., 17, 88, 90, 91, 93, 99
Jacobson, L., 93
Jarke, M., 20, 95, 114
Jefferson, G., 152, 346
John, B. E., 136
Johnson, D., 86, 88, 117
Johnson, E. J., 75, 338
Johnson, H., 88
Johnson, P., 87, 88, 132, 326
Johnson, R., 3, 15, 33, 38, 41,
    43, 47, 58, 89, 90, 145,
    199, 205, 250, 251
Johnson-Laird, P. N., 71–72, 77
Jones, C. B., 12

K

Kahn, E., 43
Kahnemann, D., 77, 339
Kao, C. F., 75
Karakostas, V., 11
Keller, G., 4, 33, 38, 41, 58, 166

Kellogg, W. A., 175
Kennedy-Carter, 255
Keuneke, A., 132
Kiczales, G., 262
Kieras, D. E., 136
Kieras, R. E., 136
King, T., 144
Kittredge, R., 254, 255
Koedinger, K., 166
Kosslyn, S. M., 329
Kotonya, G., 65, 201
Koubarakis, M., 95, 114
Krasner, G. E., 110
Kuhlthau, C., 335

L

Lakoff, G., 86
Lam, W., 203
Landauer, T. K., 29, 74, 151, 176, 241, 337
Laurillard, D., 165
Layzell, P.
Lee, J., 166
Lee, M. Y., 88
Lehman, M. M., 15
Lenat, D. B., 254
Lengel, R. H., 257
Lesperance, Y., 42
Letier, E., 38, 87, 201
Lewis, B., 166
Lewis, C., 94, 136
Lewis, M. L., 179, 180
Li, G., 167, 189
Liete, J. C., 254
Lindstaedt, S., 162
Loucopoulos, P., 11

M

M'Pherson, P. K., 340
Mackinlay, J. D., 183, 337
MacLean, A., 33, 174, 184, 223
Maiden, N. A. M., 12, 28, 33, 38,
    42, 65, 66, 70, 73, 75, 85, 92,
    95, 111, 112, 117, 122, 127,
    128, 153, 159, 197, 206, 208,
    222, 240, 324, 345, 352
Malone, T. W., 49
Mancini, R., 183

Mann, W. C., 30, 94, 158, 350
Manuel, D., 75
Marchionini, G., 144, 335
Martin, W., 4
Maslow, A. H., 253
Matsumoto, Y., 2
May, J., 184
Maybury, M. T., 142, 159, 342, 352
Mayes, T., 166
Mayfield, M., 28
McCabe, T. J., 44, 76
McDermid, J. A., 203
McGee, M., 144
McKendree, J., 166
McKeown, K. R., 342, 352
McMenamin, S. M., 93
McReynolds, C., 253
Mervis, C. B., 86, 88, 117
Messina, P., 4
Meyer, B., 6, 87, 97
Minocha, S., 75
Mistry, P., 85, 92, 117,
    127, 128, 324
Mitchell, B., 266
Mitchell, T. R., 338
Mittal, V. O., 342
Moore, J. D., 142, 342
Moran, T. P., 33, 94, 136,
    174, 223, 337
Morel, M. J., 2
Morisio, M., 2
Muhlhauser, M., 241, 250
Mylopoulos, J., 42, 95, 114, 254

N

Nakakoji, K., 97, 180, 188
Neighbors, J., 16, 254
Newell, A., 88, 94, 136
Nigay, L., 183, 184
Norman, D. A., 73, 106, 136, 137, 170,
    231, 232, 256
Norman, M. A., 53, 266
North, D., 28

O

Object Management Group, 4
Ora, K., 230

Ostwald, J., 162
Otswald, J., 180, 188

P

Palmer, J. F., 93
Papert, S., 74, 165
Patel, U., 186
Payne, J. W., 75, 338
Pedagogical Patterns Project, 250
Pelletier, R., 166
Perlis, A. J., 3
Pettengill, R., 2, 35, 251
Petty, R. E., 75
Pfleeger, S. L., 340
Pheiffer, W., 4
Pirolli, P., 29
Pitkow, J., 29
Polson, P. G., 136
Pope, S. T., 110
Porter, M. E., 166, 206
Potts, C., 98, 208, 230
Prieto-Diaz, R., 2, 29, 196, 199

Q

Quillian, M. R., 86

R

Rasmussen, J., 72, 144, 330
Rational Corporation, 22, 35, 208, 271
Reason, J., 69, 77, 339
Redmiles, D., 97
Rees, E., 88, 127
Reubenstein, H. B., 254
Riesbeck, C. K., 88
Rising, L., 3, 47, 250
Rist, T., 159, 352
Robertson, E., 12, 16
Robertson, G., 183, 337
Robertson, S. E., 337
Rodden, T., 192
Rohnert, H., 3, 47, 250
Rolland, C., 20
Rombach, H. D., 76
Rosch, E., 64, 86, 88, 117, 180
Ross, D. T., 34

Rosson, M. B., 175, 176
Rugg, G., 28, 65
Rumelhart, D. E., 86
Rutledge, L., 5
Ryan, M., 128, 243, 246

S

Sacks, H., 152, 346
Schank, R. C., 65, 87, 88, 181
Schegloff, E. A., 152, 346
Schmid, H. A., 2
Schoen, E., 2, 35, 251
Schoman, K. E., 34
Schon, D., 79, 162, 222, 243
Schreiber, G., 43, 132
Searle, J. R., 152, 349
Shackel, B., 76
Shaw, M., 88
Shepard, R. N., 68
Shneiderman, B., 181
Shouls, R., 88
Sibert, J. L., 144
Silverstein, M., 3, 38, 237
Simon, H. A., 69, 78, 88, 139
Singh, M. G., 76, 276
Singley, M. K., 176, 178, 187, 189, 237, 245
Smith, D. R., 89, 254
Smith, G., 4
Smith, J., 230
Sommerville, I., 65, 201
Sowa, J. F., 16, 30, 89, 97
Spivey, J. M., 12
St Anna, M., 254
Stahl, G., 180, 188
Stannett, C.
Stenning, K., 166
Stevens, A. L., 65
Stolze, M., 162
Summer, T., 180, 188
Sumner, T., 162
Sun Microsystems, 13
Sutcliffe, A. G., 12, 15, 20, 33,
    38, 42, 66, 70, 73, 75, 81, 85, 92, 95,
    111, 112, 117, 122, 127, 128, 131,
    142, 144, 149, 151, 153, 159, 161,
    167, 177, 180, 181, 183, 184, 186,
    189, 190, 197, 206, 208, 222, 225,
    234, 240, 243, 245, 246, 247, 324,
    335, 342, 345, 352

Swan, J. E., 144
Swartout, W. R., 142

T

Takahashi, K., 98, 208, 230
Tanner, M., 132
Tansley, D. S. W., 251
Taylor, C. N., 128
Teufel, T., 4, 33, 38, 41, 58, 166
Thagard, P., 92, 115
Thimbleby, H., 235
Thompson, S. A., 30, 94, 158,
    350
Tidwell, J., 250
Till, D., 128
Tinsley, O. J., 4
Tobin, R., 166
Totterdell, P., 53, 266
Toulmin, S., 174
Tracz, W., 1, 2, 3, 28, 251
Trevino, L. K., 257
Tully, C., 2
Tversky, A., 77, 339

U

Uhl, J., 2

V

Van der Velde, W., 43, 95, 132
Van Lamsweerde, A., 38, 87, 97, 129,
    201
Van Ossenbruggen, J., 5
Vassiliou, Y., 20
Vickers, A. J., 203
Visser, W., 70, 162
Vlissides, J., 3, 15, 33, 38, 41, 43, 47, 58,
    89, 90, 205, 250
Vossers, M., 30

W

W3C, 5
Waddington, R., 88
Walker, S., 337

Wang, T., 12, 16
Waters, R. C., 254
Watkinson, S. J., 151, 247
Wehrend, R., 94, 136
Weiss, D. M., 76
Wenger, E., 165
Wiener, L., 3, 93, 100
Wilenga, B., 43, 132
Wilkerson, B., 3, 93, 100
Wilks, Y., 28, 266
Williamson, O. E., 167, 191
Winograd, T., 142, 152, 346
Wirfs-Brock, R., 3, 93, 100
Wright, P., 131

Y

Yang, J. B., 76, 276
Yates, J., 49
Young, R. M., 33, 174, 223
Yourdon, E. E., 6, 35, 44, 87, 200, 201, 230
Yu, E., 42

Z

Zeng, X. J., 276
Zhou, M. X., 94, 136, 159
Zimmermann, B., 162

Subject Index

A

Abstraction
  analogical memory, 66
  definition, 36, 38
  design for reuse, 200
  Domain Theory, 89
  enterprise resource plans (ERP),
      40–41, 43
  hardware, 7
  identification of, 207–217
  in knowledge-level reuse, 205
  information models, 22
  knowledge management reuse, 43–44
  layers of reuse, 37–38
  Object System Models (OSM), 40, 42–43
  of data, 202–203
  overview, 38, 59
  patterns, 41, 43
  problems of, 7, 38
  procedural, 203–205
  reasoning, 71
  semantic networks, 63
  stability, 40
  trade-off formula, 39
  user models, 23
  versus granularity, 36–37
  wisdom, 9
Abstraction context, 37, 38
Acceptability, 46, 47–49
Accounting Object Transfer class, 103, 127,
      276–278
Across-domain reuse, 13
Action family, 136, 137–139, 142,
      307–309
Actions, 132
Active Sensing class, 109, 298
Actual utility, 257–258
Adaptability, 6

Adaptation, 52–54, 253–254
Advisor for Intelligent Reuse toolset, 112–124
Agent Behavior Sensing class, 108, 297
Agent Control class, 109–110, 298–300
Agents, 96
Alexandrine patterns, 3
Analogical memory, 65–68
Analysis–Modeling task, 144, 146, 318–321
Application generation, 15–17, 255, 263–264
Application program interfaces (API), 12,
      13, 35
Architecture frameworks, *see* Framework
      architectures
Argumentation knowledge, 9
Argumentation schema, 158–161, 350–358
Argumentation theory, 174
Arguments, 9
Artefacts, *see* Claims
Aspect-oriented languages, 262, 263
Assemble task, 308–309
Associate task, 140, 147, 148, 149, 311

B

Beliefs, 67
Biddable domains, 91
BIM Prolog, 114, 115
Black-box design by configuration, 50
Black-box reuse, 35–36, 51, 54–55
Brand identity, 257

C

CAL, *see* Computer-aided learning (CAL)
      architectures
Cardinality relations, 100
Case-based reasoning, 71

Categorical memory, 64–65
Categorization class, 304
Category-sorted reports, 303
Causal domains, 91
Causal explanation schema, 160–161, 355–356
Causal reasoning, 71
Chunks, 8, 60–61
Claims
  business knowledge, representing, 189–193
  classification of, 180–183, 237–239
  design by reuse, 221
  design metadomain, 359–361
  documentation, 179–181
  education metadomain, 361–367
  framework for reuse, 181–184
  generalization, 235–236, 239
  Information Retrieval task, 370–372
  levels of, 189–193
  link to theory, 180–181
  linking to domain models, 184–189
  management domain, 367–368
  overview, 175
  retrieval, 240–241
  schema, 177–179
  searches for, 240–241
  Spatial Object Sensing OSM, 368–369
  types, 180
  validity of, 176
Claims maps, 237–240
Claims reuse, *see also* Knowledge reuse;
    Reuse
  case study, 243–247
  claim retrieval, 240–241
  claims networks, 237–240
  factoring contributions, 231–232
  factoring issues, 230–231
  factoring process, 228–235
  knowledge transfer, 241–243
  linking claims to domain models, 236–237
  methods, 228–230
  process, 240–243
Clarification pattern, 346, 347
Classes, *see also* Object System Model (OSM)
  Accounting Object Transfer class, 103, 127,
    276–278
  Active Sensing class, 109, 298
  Agent Behavior Sensing class, 108, 297
  Agent Control class, 109–110, 298–300
  Categorization class, 304
  Conceptual Object Allocation class, 285
  Conceptual Object Construction class, 294

definition, 68
Deterministic Agent Control class, 300
Financial Object Allocation class, 277, 285
Message Transfer class, 107, 290–292
Object Allocation class, 104–105, 283–584
Object Composition class, 105, 286–287,
    288, 293
Object Construction class, 106, 292–293, 301
Object Containment class, 102, 118, 122, 273
Object Decomposition class, 105–106,
    287–289
Object Hiring class, 103–104, 122, 279–281
Object Inventory class, 102–103, 118, 122,
    274–276
Object Logistics class, 106–107, 289–290
Object Property Sensing class, 108, 297–298
Object Returning class, 103, 122, 278–279
Object Sensing class, 107–108, 294–296
Object Servicing–Repair class, 104, 281–283
Object Simulation class, 110–111, 300–302,
    301
Object System Model (OSM), 102–111
Passive Sensing class, 109, 298
patterns movement, 3
Physical Object Allocation class, 284–285
Physical Object Construction class, 293–294
Physical Object Transfer class, 290
Probabilistic Agent Control class, 300
Progress Tracking class, 304
Spatial Object Sensing class, 108, 295, 297
Classification
  categorical memory, 65
  component libraries, 29
  Conceptual Structures Theory, 30–31
  controlled vocabulary, 29
  definition, 10
  Dewey Decimal Classification (DDC), 28, 29
  genres, 237–239
  hierarchical, 29
  hypertext map, 29–30
  of claims, 180–183, 237–239
  ontologies, 30
  problems with, 31
  reasoning, 71
  Rhetorical Structure Thoery, 30
  search alternative, 29
  Universal Decimal Classification (UDC), 28,
    29
Classification explanation schema, 160
Classification pattern, 353
Classify task, 140, 148, 310–311

Cognitive psychology
  decision making, 75–77
  learning, 68–69
  memory, 60–68, 72–75
  problem solving, 69–75
Cohesion analysis, 200–201
Cohesive models, 87–88
Command dialogue, 154–155
Command pattern, 349–350
Communicate task, 141–142, 147, 313
Communication family, 141–143, 313
Compare task, 141, 312
Comparison pattern, 356
Component engineering paradigm, 258–262,
    264, 265
Component libraries, *see* Libraries, component
Component-based engineering, 4–5, 6, 264–268
Composition explanation schema, 160
Composition pattern, 354
Computer-aided learning (CAL) architectures,
    165
Computer-aided software engineering (CASE)
    tools, 28
Conceptual Object Allocation class, 285
Conceptual Object Construction class, 294
Conceptual objects, 99
Conceptual Structures Theory, 30–31
Configuration, 54–55
Connection problem frames, 19
Constrained Command pattern, 350, 351
Constructivist learning theories, 74
Control constructs, 132
Controlled vocabulary, 28, 29, 81
Conversational learning, 166
Coordination tools, 168
Copyright, 28
Coupling, 44–45, 201–202

D

Data, 8
Data abstraction, 202–203
DDC, *see* Dewey Decimal Classification
    (DDC)
Decide task, 141, 312
Decision making, 75–77, 145, 337–340
Declarative knowledge, 65
Declarative memory, 8, 67
Deductive reasoning, 71
Description, formal, 10

Decision support subsystem, 124–125
Design
  aim of, 252
  as metadomain, 162–163, 359–361
  by adaptation and parameterization, 50
  creative, 82–83
  definition, 10
  models of, 78–79
  new approaches to, 252–255
  overview, 162
  user behavior, 252–254
  versus reuse, 78
Design by reuse
  abstraction identification, 207–217
  case study, 213–217, 218–219, 223–225
  claims, 221
  definition, 80
  design knowledge transfer, 219–225
  design rationale, 221–222, 223, 225
  generic process, 197, 198, 199
  generic system models, 217–219
  overview, 207
Design for reuse, 80, 196–197, 198,
    199–205
Design knowledge, 219–225
Design process, 78–79
Design rationale, 173–174, 221–222, 223, 225
Design-based reuse, 10, 11
Designers, 26–27, 53
Deterministic Agent Control class, 300
Dewey Decimal Classification (DDC), 28, 29
Diagnosis task, 144, 146, 330–333
Dialogue acts, 152
Dialogue controller, 117
Dialogue models, 152–161
Difference reports, 303
Disassemble task, 309
Discourse acts, 152–153
Documentation, 26, 28, 57, 62, 179–181
Domain events, 99
Domain models, 184–189, 236–237
Domain Theory
  abstraction, 89
  components, 92
  design by reuse, 207–213, 217–218,
    219–222
  design by reuse case studies, 213–217,
    218–219, 223–225
  design for reuse, 199–205
  formalization of, 128–129
  framework, 88–95

Domain Theory (*cont.*)
  generic tasks, 94–95
  goals, 91
  governing principles, 91
  granularity, 89
  grounded domains, 92–93
  INTUITIVE Project, 124–127
  knowledge types, 95–100
  object-oriented patterns, 90
  problem frames, 91–92
  problem models, 88
  tenets of, 89
  validation studies, 127–128
Domain-oriented languages, 263–264

E

Education metadomain, 163–166, 361–367
Education-support architectures, 165
Embedded models, 17–20, 21–22, 23, 44–45,
  260, 267
Empirically grounded claims, 180
End-user programming, 264–268
Enterprise resource plans (ERP), 4, 5, 40–41,
  43, 44, 47, 55
Episodic memory, 63–64
ERP, *see* enterprise resource plans (ERP)
Errors in problem solving, 77
Evaluate task, 139, 147, 148, 149, 308
Events, 99–100
Evolutionary reuse, 13
Examples, 68
Experimentally derived claims, 180
Experts, 79–80
Explain task, 142, 313–314
Explanation and Advising task, 145, 146,
  340–343
Explanation schema, 159–161
Exploration-Sensing family, 142–143, 314–315
Exponential effects, 77
External memory, 62

F

Factoring process for claims reuse, 228–235
Factual domain knowledge, 67
Fast-path decisions, 75
Financial Object Allocation class, 277, 285
Flexibility, 14–15, 45

Forecasting task, 145, 146, 344–345
Formal Command pattern, 349
Four worlds model, 20–22
Fourth-generation language, 16–17
Framework architectures, 46–47, 51
Functional cohesion, 200–201

G

General-purpose learning machines,
  266–267
Generalization, 7, 38, 71, 235–236, 239
Generalized tasks
  Analysis-Modeling task, 144–146, 318–321
  application example, 149–152
  definition, 134
  Diagnosis task, 144–146, 330–333
  examples, 147–149
  Explanation-Advising task, 144–146,
    340–343
  Forecasting task, 145, 146, 344–345
  Information Acquisition task, 144, 146,
    316–318
  Information Retrieval task, 144, 146,
    149–152, 333–337, 370–372
  Judgement-Decison Making task, 144, 146,
    337–340
  KADS, 147
  Matching task, 145, 146, 343–344
  Navigation task, 144, 146, 328–330
  overview, 94–95, 143, 315–316
  Planning-Scheduling task, 144, 146,
    326–327
  Progress Tracking task, 144, 146,
    325–326
  Validation-Testing task, 144, 146,
    321–325
Generative approach, 16
Generative architectures, 195
Generic dialogues, 152–161, 345–358
Generic system model, 126–127
Generic tasks
  Action Family, 136, 137–139
  Action family, 307–309
  Communication family, 141–143, 313
  definition, 134
  examples, 147–149
  Exploring-Sensing Family, 142–143,
    314–315
  families of, 136–143, 307–315

Information Processing family, 139–141, 309–312
organization, 132–134
overview, 94–95, 99, 132, 134, 136
taxonomies, 136
Genres, 237
Glass-box reuse, 35
Goal-oriented models, 87–88
Goals, 90–91, 98–99, 132, 133, 161, 201
Granularity, 6–7, 36–37, 44–45, 46–47
Grounded domains, 92–93, 368–369,
    see also Object System Model (OSM)
Grounded theory, 180

H

Hardware, 7
Heuristics, 10
Hierarchical classification, 29
Horizontal-market products, 14
Hypertext map, 29–30

I

Identify task, 311–312
Indexes, 10, 12, 26, 28, 29, 57, 81
Indicative requirements, 17
Informal Command pattern, 349–350
Information, 8
Information Acquisition task, 144, 146, 316–318
Information models, 22–23
Information Processing family, 139–141, 309–312
Information retrieval subsystem, 125
Information Retrieval task, 144, 146, 149–152, 333–337, 370–372
Information System Model (ISM), 93, 111, 302–305
Information systems architecture, 167
Inspiration, 69–70
Interaction schema, 155–158, 345–350
Interactive simulations, 75–76
Interfaces, 35, 54, 217, 218, 247, see also
    Application program interfaces (API)
International Standards Organization (ISO), 3
Interpret task, 139, 148, 149, 308
INTUITIVE Project, 124–127, 243–247
Issue-based information systems (IBIS), 174, 175

J

Judgment–Decision making task, 145, 146, 337–340

K

KADS generalized tasks, 147
KAOS specification language, 129
Key objects, 96
Knowledge, 8–10, 65, 67, 81, 219–225
Knowledge acquisition, 25, 57, 80
Knowledge documenter, 227–228
Knowledge harvester, 227
Knowledge management resuse, 10–12, 13, 36, 43–44, 57
Knowledge manager, 228
Knowledge reuse, 2, 7–10, 49, 69, 205–207, 205–207, see also Claims reuse

L

Languages, 67, 254–255, 262–264
Latent Semantic Indexing (LSI) algorithm, 241
Learning, 68–69, 73–75, 166
Learning machines, 266–267
Lexical domains, 91
Libraries, component, 2, 26, 28–31, 45–46, 73–75, 267–268
Locate task, 143, 314–315
Long-term memory, 61–62, 63–68

M

Management information systems architecture, 167
Management metadomain, 166–168, 169, 367–368
Marketing software, 256–258
Matching task, 145, 146, 343–344
Means ends analysis, 71
Measures, 76
Media Communication Theory, 257
Memory activation, 69
Memory, human, 7–10, 61–62, 63–68, 72–75, 77, 87
Mental models, 71–72
Message Transfer class, 107, 290–292

Metadomains
  claims, 188–189, 359–372
  design, 162–163, 359–361
  education, 163–166, 361–367
  management, 166–168, 169, 367–368
  overview, 93–94, 161
  research, 168–170
  training, 163–166
Metrics, 76
Middleware market, 4
Model task, 139–140, 309–310
Model View Controller abstraction, 110
Modular decomposition, 203
Monitor task, 143, 314
Motivation, 253
Motivation pattern, 357

N

Natural categories theory, 86
Natural-language statements, 67
Natural-language understanding system,
    254–255
Navigation task, 144, 146, 328–330
Negotiate Position pattern, 350

O

Object Allocation class, 104–105, 283–584
Object Composition class, 105, 286–287, 288,
    293
Object Construction class, 106, 292–293, 301
Object Containment class, 102, 118, 122, 273
Object Decomposition class, 105–106, 287–289
Object Hiring class, 103–104, 122, 202, 279–281
Object Hiring Model, 42
Object Inventory class, 102–103, 118, 122,
    274–276
Object Logistics class, 106–107, 289–290
Object properties, 99
Object Property Sensing class, 108, 297–298
Object Returning class, 103, 122, 278–279
Object Sensing class, 107–108, 294–296
Object Servicing–Repair class, 104, 281–283
Object Simulation class, 110–111, 300–302, 301
Object System Model (OSM), *see also* Classes;
    Grounded domains
  abstraction, 40, 42–43, 207–217
  case study, 213–217, 218–219, 223–225

costs, 56
coupling, 202
decision support subsystem, 124–125
design knowledge transfer, 219–225
generic system model, 126–127,
    217–219
granularity, 47
grounded domains, 93
hierarchy of, 101
information retrieval subsystem, 125
interfaces, 217, 218
INTUITIVE Project, 124–127
knowledge types, 95–100
reuse overview, 111
reuse toolset 112–124
validation studies, 127–128
Object-oriented development, 35
Object-oriented methods, 68
Object-oriented patterns, 15–16, 41–42, 44, 47,
    90, *see also* Patterns
Objects, 68, 96, 97, 99, 132, 201
Ontologies, 30
Operationally grounded claims, 180
Opportunistic resue, 1
Optative requirements, 18
Orient task, 143, 315
OSM, *see* Object System Model (OSM)

P

Parameterization, 6, 203
Passive Sensing class, 109, 298
Pattern language, 3
Pattern recognizers, 25
Patterns, *see also* Object-oriented patterns
  abstraction, 41, 43
  Alexandrine, 3
  causal explanation pattern, 355–356
  Clarification pattern, 346, 347
  Classification pattern, 353
  Command patterns, 349–350
  Comparison pattern, 356
  Composition pattern, 354
  costs, 56
  Motivation pattern, 357
  Negotiate Position pattern, 350
  overview, 250–251
  Persuasion pattern, 357
  Propose Action pattern, 348
  Propose Idea pattern, 348–349

Questioning pattern, 346
Sequence Tracing pattern, 356–357
task-based explanation pattern, 354–355
Patterns movement, 3
People models, 23
Perceived utility, 257–258
Persuasion pattern, 357
Physical Object Allocation class, 284–285
Physical Object Construction class, 293–294
Physical Object Transfer class, 290
Physical world models, 20–22
Plan task, 138–139, 307–308
Planning–Scheduling task, 144, 146, 326–327
Postconditions, 132
Preconditions, 132
Primary states, 98, 100
Primitive tasks, see Generic tasks
Probabilistic Agent Control class, 300
Problem decomposition, 71
Problem frames, 18–19, 91–92
Problem models, 88
Problem solving, 69–75, 77, 79–80
Procedural abstraction, 203–205
Procedural memory, 65
Procedures, 10, 68
Process-generation approach, 16
Product reuse, 12
Progress Tracking class, 304
Progress Tracking task, 144, 146, 325–326
Proof of concept claims, 180
Propose Action pattern, 348
Propose Idea pattern, 348–349
Purchasing decisions, 256–258

Q

Questioning pattern, 346

R

Reasoning, 70–75
Recall, 61, 77
Recognition, 61
Record task, 313
Reference architectures, 46
Relabeling, 82
Relationships, 100
Reports, 303
Reputation, 258

Requirements capturer, 116
Requirements critic, 116
Requirements explainer, 116–117
Requirements Monitoring, 266
Research, 168–170
Retrieval
classification, 29–30
design reuse, 12
for problem solving, 70
human memory, 61, 69
implications of cognitive psychology, 73–75
in task model, 81
knowledge-management systems, 10
of claims, 240–241
Retrieval assistant, 228
Reuse, see also specific reuse types
across-domain reuse, 13
approaches to, 15–17
barriers to success, 26–28
by application generation, 255
component engineering paradigm, 258–262, 264, 265
cost–benefit analysis, 50–57
generic process, 196–199
history, 1, 2–3, 250–251
impact of, 2
implications of cognitive psychology, 73–75
implications of human memory, 73–75
layers of, 14–16, 37–38
limitations for software reuse, 4
models, 17–25
motivations for, 4–5
paradigms for, 34–36
problems with, 5–7
process of, 25–26, 27
trade-offs, 50–57
Reuse support tools, 112–124
Rewards, 27
Rhetorical Structure Theory (RST), 30, 158–159, 350, 352
Role-playing, 82
Rote learning, 69
Rule-based matcher, 115–116
Rules, 10, 11–12, 65, 72–73, 204

S

Scale relations, 100
Scenarios, 68
Scope, 45–46

Script–memory theories, 87
Search task, 143, 314
Searches, 29, 57, 240–241
Secondary states, 98, 100
Select task, 311
Semantic networks, 10, 63
Sequence Tracing pattern, 356–357
Skill-based reuse, 73
Slow-path decisions, 75
Software
    application generation architectures, 263–264
    as service, 252–255
    aspect-oriented languages, 262, 263
    component engineering paradigm, 258–262,
        264, 265
    cost factors, 256, 257
    end-user programming, 264–268
    evolution of, 267
    future directions of, 249–250
    marketing of, 256–258
    models of, 23–24
    new approaches to design, 252–255
    purchasing decisions, 256–258
    real-world connection, 17–20
    reuse limitations, 4
    subject-oriented languages, 262–263
    user behavior, 252–254
    user effort, 252–253
Sort task, 140–141, 149, 310
Spatial Object Sensing class, 108, 295, 297
Stability, 40
Standards, 3–4, 5, 12, 13, 28–29, 251
State transitions, 97–98
States, 98, 132
Stative conditions, 100
Strategies, 67, 70–72
Structural approach, 16
Structure matcher, 115
Structure objects, 97
Structure-matching theory, 86–87
Sublanguages, 255, 264, 266

T

Task knowledge schema, 132
Task model of reuse, 80–82

Task-artefact theory, 175, 176
Task-based explanation schema, 160, 354–355
Task-support facilities, 150
Tasks, 132, see also Generalized tasks; Generic
    tasks
Taxonomic knowledge, 10
Taxonomies, 10–11, 136
Technology acceptance models, 256
Template architectures, 46–47
Temporal relations, 100
Temporal reuse, 13
Test task, 312–313
Theory prediction, 180
Thesauri, 28
Time events, 99
Time-ordered reports, 303
Tool support, 28
Tools, 28, 112–124, 168
Training, 163–166
Transform task, 309
Trend reports, 303
True reuse, 1
Tutorial architectures, 164–165

U

Universal Decimal Classification (UDC),
    28, 29
User behavior, 25, 73, 252–254, 253–254
User models, 23
Users, 252–253, 264–268
Utility, 257–258

V

Validation–Testing task, 144, 146, 321–325
Vertical-market products, 14

W

White-box reuse, 35, 55–57
Wisdom, 9
Working memory, 60–61, 77
Workpieces problem frames, 18–19